Decoding Boundaries in Contemporary Japan

This book sheds light on the changing nature of contemporary Japan by decoding a range of political, economic and social boundaries. With a focus on the period following the inauguration of Prime Minister Koizumi Junichirō, the book grows out of a recognition that, with the Koizumi administration playing a more proactive role internationally and moving ahead with deregulation and the 'structural reform' of the economy domestically, a range of boundaries have been challenged and re-inscribed. Here 'boundaries' refers to the ways in which contemporary Japan is shaped as a separate entity by the inscription and re-inscription of political, economic and social space creating insiders and outsiders, both internationally and domestically. The central argument of the book is that, in order to achieve the twin goals of greater international proactivity and domestic reform, the government and other actors supporting Koizumi's new direction for Japan needed to take action in order to destabilize and reformulate a range of extant boundaries. While boundaries often remain invisible, the aim of this book is to promote an understanding of their significance by uncovering their pivotal role.

Decoding Boundaries in Contemporary Japan brings together contributions from leading and emerging scholars from the UK, Japan and the United States. It will appeal to scholars and students of Japan as well as social scientists with an interest in borders and boundaries, and political scientists interested in Asia.

Glenn D. Hook is Professor of Japanese Politics and International Relations, and Director of the Graduate School of East Asian Studies at the University of Sheffield, UK. He is concurrently the Director of the National Institute of Japanese Studies (NIJS), an international centre of excellence with the University of Leeds funded by the British authorities. His research interests are in Japanese politics, international relations and security, particularly in relation to East Asia. His recent work includes *Japanese Responses to Globalization* (co-editor, Palgrave, 2006); *Japan's International Relations: Politics, economics and security*, third edition (co-author, Routledge, 2011); and *Contested Governance in Japan: sites and issues* (editor, Routledge, 2005).

Sheffield Centre for Japanese Studies/ Routledge Series

Series Editor: Glenn D. Hook

Professor of Japanese Studies, University of Sheffield

This series, published by Routledge in association with the Centre for Japanese Studies at the University of Sheffield, both makes available original research on a wide range of subjects dealing with Japan and provides introductory overviews of key topics in Japanese Studies.

Contents

List of illustrations

Figures

Tables

List of contributors

Lindsay BLACK is Lecturer in the International Relations of East Asia at the Department of Japanese Languages and Cultures, Leiden University, the Netherlands. His research interests comprise International Relations theory and East Asian regionalism, contemporary maritime affairs in East/Southeast Asia, and Japan's international relations. He is presently revising for publication his dissertation, *All at sea? Japan's response to the contemporary maritime security threats posed by infidels, pirates and barbarians*, which adopts an English School theoretical framework to examine Japan's response to maritime security threats posed by actors considered to be outside or hostile to the international society. In addition, he is working on an edited manuscript entitled 'Sovereignty and Humanitarian Intervention in the International Society of East Asia: historical legacies and new dynamics', and a co-authored project entitled 'East Asian Approaches to Human Security: the concept and practice of human security in Japan and China's international relations'.

Hugo DOBSON is Professor of Japan's International Relations in the School of East Asian Studies and the National Institute for Japanese Studies at the University of Sheffield, UK. His research interests are in Japan's international relations, the G8, G20 and global governance, and the role of images in international relations. He is the co-author of *Japan's International Relations: politics, economics and security* (Routledge, 2011, third edition); co-editor of *Britain and Japan in the Contemporary World: responses to common issues* (RoutledgeCurzon, 2003) and *Global Governance and Japan: the institutional architecture* (RoutledgeCurzon, 2007); and is the author of *Japan and United Nations Peacekeeping: new pressures, new responses* (RoutledgeCurzon, 2003), *Japan and G7/8, 1975 to 2002* (RoutledgeCurzon, 2004) and *The Group of 7/8* (Routledge, 2007).

Roger GOODMAN is Nissan Professor of Modern Japanese Studies, and Professorial Fellow at St Antony's College and currently Head of the Social Sciences Division at the University of Oxford. He is the author of *Japan's International Youth: the emergence of a new class of schoolchildren* (Oxford University Press, 1990; published in Japanese as *Kikokushijo*, Iwanami Shoten, 1993), and *Children of the Japanese State: the changing role of child protection* *institutions in contemporary Japan* (Oxford University Press, 2000; published in Japanese as *Nihon no jidōyōgo: jidōyōgogaku e no shōtai*, Akashi Shoten, 2006). He is the editor or co-editor of and author in: *Ideology and Practice in Modern Japan* (1992, Routledge); *Case Studies on Human Rights in Japan* (Japan Library, 1996); *The East Asian Welfare Model: welfare Orientalism and the state* (Routledge, 1998); *Family and Social Policy in Japan* (Cambridge University Press, 2002); *Can the Japanese Change their Education System?* (Symposium Books, 2002); *Global Japan: the experience of Japan's new immigrant and overseas communities* (RoutledgeCurzon, 2003); *The 'Big Bang' in Japanese Higher Education: the 2004 reforms and the dynamics of change* (Transpacific, 2005); and *Ageing in Asia: Asia's position in the new global demography* (Routledge, 2007), among other titles.

HASEGAWA Harukiyo is Professor of Human Resource Management in the Doshisha Business School, Kyoto, and an Honorary Fellow of the White Rose East Asia Centre. His research interests are in Japanese business, globalization and human resource management. His publications include *The Steel Industry in Japan: a comparison with Britain* (Routledge, March 1996); *Japanese Business Management: restructuring for low growth and globalization* (co-editor and contributor, Routledge,1997); *The Political Economy of Japanese Globalisation* (co-editor and contributor, Routledge, 2001); *Japanese Responses to Globalization* (co-editor and contributor, Palgrave, 2006); *New Horizons in Asian Business and Management* (co-editor and contributor, Palgrave Macmillan, 2007) and *Asian Business and Management: theory, practice, and perspectives* (co-editor, Palgrave Macmillan, 2009).

Glenn D. HOOK is the Toshiba International Foundation Anniversary Research Professor of Japanese Politics and International Relations in the School of East Asian Studies, University of Sheffield, and Director of the National Institute of Japanese Studies, UK. His research interests are in Japanese politics, international relations and security, particularly in relation to East Asia. His recent work includes *Ending the Postwar in Japan: structure, actors, norms and challenges* (co-editor, Routledge, 2010); *Japan's International Relations: politics, economics and security* (co-author, Routledge, 2005, second edition); and *Contested Governance in Japan: sites and issues* (editor, RoutledgeCurzon, 2005).

MUTO Hiromi is Professor of Public Administration, Hosei University. His research interests are in administration of public works, the tendering system and procedure, the civil service system, *amakudari*, privatization or marketization of public services, congestion charges, and road administration. His recent work includes *Jichitai no Nyūsatsu Kaikaku* (Imajin Shuppan, 2006); *Jichitai Gyōsei no Shijōka* (editor, Kōjin-sha, 2006); *Jichitai Keiei Kaikaku* (editor, Gyosei, 2004), *Nyūsatsu Kaikaku* (Iwanami Shoten, 2003), and *Bunken Shakai to Kyōdō* (editor, Gyosei, 2001). His latest work is *Dōro Gyōsei* (Tokyo University Press, 2008).

SHINODA Tomohito is Professor of International Relations at the International University of Japan, located in Niigata, Japan. His research covers Japan's domestic politics, decision making in foreign policy and U.S.–Japan relations. His publications include *Koizumi Diplomacy: Japan's kantei approach in foreign and defense affairs* (University of Washington Press, 2007); 'Becoming more realistic in the post-cold war: Japan's changing media and public opinion on national security', *Japanese Journal of Political Science*, 8, 2, 2007; 'Japan's top-down policy process to dispatch the SDF to Iraq', *Japanese Journal of Political Science*, 7, 1, 2006; and 'Japan's Cabinet Secretariat and its emergence as core executive', *Asian Survey*, 45, 5, 2005.

Key-young SON is Visiting Associate Professor of International Politics at Tohoku University, Japan. His research interests include Asian and international politics and political economy. His latest book is *South Korean Engagement Policies and North Korea: identities, norms and the sunshine policy* (Routledge, 2006). His latest articles are 'From a fault line to a catalyst: an emerging Korean confederation and the contour of a Northeast Asian security community', *Policy Forum*, Korea Economic Institute, Washington D.C., October 15, 2008; and 'Entrenching "identity norms" of tolerance and engagement: lessons from rapprochement between North and South Korea', *Review of International Studies*, 33, 3, 2007.

Patricia G. STEINHOFF is Professor of Sociology at the University of Hawai'i at Manoa. Her research interests include social movements, conflict, and the Japanese left. She recently edited the third edition of the *Directory of Japan Specialists and Japanese Studies Institutions in the United States and Canada* (3 vols, University of Hawai'i Press for the Japan Foundation, 2006) and the companion volume of survey analysis, *Japanese Studies in the United States and Canada: continuities and opportunities* (University of Hawai'i Press for the Japan Foundation, 2007) for which she also wrote the US chapters. Her most recent academic publications include 'Radical outcasts versus three kinds of police: constructing limits in Japanese anti-emperor protest', *Qualitative Sociology*, 29, 3, 2006; and (co-authored with Gilda Zwerman) 'When activists ask for trouble: state-dissident interactions and the New Left cycle of resistance in the United States and Japan', in Christian Davenport, Hank Johnston, and Carol Mueller, eds, *Repression and Mobilization* (University of Minnesota Press, 2005) and 'Kidnapped Japanese in North Korea: the New Left connection', *Journal of Japanese Studies* 30, 1, 2004. She co-edited *Doing Fieldwork in Japan* (University of Hawai'i Press, 2003) with Theodore Bestor and Vickey Lyon Bestor. She is also the author of *Shi e no Ideology: Nihon sekigunha* (Iwanami Bunko Modern Classics Series, Iwanami Publishing Company, 2003), which is a republication of *Nihon Sekigunha: sono shakaigakuteki Monogatari* (Kawade Shobo Shinsha, 1991).

Shogo SUZUKI is Lecturer in Politics, University of Manchester. His research interests include international relations theory with reference to East Asia,

Chinese foreign policy, and Sino-Japanese relations. His recent publications, which have been published in the *European Journal of International Relations, The Pacific Review*, and *Asian Perspective*, have covered issues on contemporary Sino-Japanese identity politics and China and Japan's encounter with the European international order in the nineteenth century. His latest book is entitled *Civilisation and Empire: China and Japan's encounter with the European International society* (Routledge, 2008).

UCHIYAMA Yū is Associate Professor of Political Science at the University of Tokyo. His research interests are in Japanese politics and comparative politics of advanced democracies. His work includes *Koizumi Seiken* (Chūō Kōron Shinsha, 2007); and *Gendai Nihon no Kokka to Shijo* (University of Tokyo Press, 1998). He has just published *Koizumi and Japanese Politics: reform strategies and leadership style* (Routledge, 2010). He is now editing a book on the roles of expertise in policy-making in advanced democracies.

Peter VON STADEN is Lecturer in International Business at the Bristol Business School, the University of the West of England and Visiting Fellow at the Centre for East Asian Studies, the University of Bristol. His research interests are in the relationship between business and government in modern Japan and institutional adaptivity. His latest book, *Business-Government Relations in Prewar Japan* (Routledge, 2007), considers their 'partner-competitor' relationship seen through the amalgamation of the iron and steel industry (1916–34). Current research examines the role played by rigidity in mental models and institutions in the approach of business and government to crises in Japan's postwar political economy.

Preface and acknowledgements

The current volume, *Decoding Boundaries in Contemporary Japan: the Koizumi administration and beyond*, grew out of papers first presented at an international workshop held at Wortley Hall near Sheffield and at a plenary session held at the University of Sheffield, 14–15 March 2008. The participants came together in the recognition that, following the establishment of the Prime Minister Koizumi Junichirō administration (2001–06), political, economic and social boundaries had been shifting in Japan as the administration sought to establish a more proactive international role for the nation and to move ahead with deregulation and the 'structural reform' of the domestic political economy. Here 'boundaries' refers to the ways in which contemporary Japan is shaped as a separate entity by the inscription and reinscription of political, economic and social space in a way to create insiders and outsiders, both internationally and domestically. The twin challenges of forging a more proactive role for Japan and reforming the economy have remained beyond the Koizumi years. New governments have consolidated, revised and rejected the policies implemented under Koizumi, but the key role his administration played in setting the agenda for twenty-first century Japan has remained as a legacy for future administrations.

This book would not have been possible without the cooperation and support of a number of people, starting with Takeda Hiroko, who contributed enormously to the intellectual content of the project. I owe a deep debt of gratitude to the participants in the workshop and plenary, especially the presenters, who in the intervening period have revised their papers in response to the comments made by the discussants, the anonymous referees and myself. Thanks are very much due to the referees: I am always grateful to the generosity of anonymous colleagues who spare their time to comment on the work of others, and the referees for this volume are no exception. I am pleased to say the book has been improved immensely as a result of their constructive input. Finally, I am grateful to Michelle Johnson for her help in editing the chapters and the Toshiba International Foundation, Chubu Electric Power Company and the funders of the White Rose East Asia Centre (the Economic and Social Research Council, Arts and Humanities Research Council and Higher Education Funding Council for England) for financial support in hosting the above event and in producing this volume.

GDH
March 2010

A note on the text

Following Japanese convention, the family name precedes the given name unless the author of a source publishes in English and does so using the reverse order. Long vowels are indicated by a macron, except in the case of common place and other names, such as Tokyo.

Introduction

Why boundaries?

Glenn D. Hook

The purpose of this book is to illuminate the changing nature of contemporary Japan by decoding a range of political, economic and social boundaries, with a focus on the period following the inauguration of Prime Minister Koizumi Junichirō's administration (2001–06), the longest serving Liberal Democratic Party (LDP) administration since that of Prime Minister Satō Eisaku (1964–72). A rapid turnover of LDP prime ministers came in Koizumi's wake – Abe Shinzō (2006–07), Fukuda Yasuo (2007–08) and Asō Tarō (2008–09) – none of whom faced the electorate, and then followed the defeat of Asō and the election of Hatoyama Yukio's Democratic Party of Japan (DPJ) in the landslide general election victory of August 2009. Nevertheless, the transformations set in motion through Koizumi's promotion of a more proactive role for Japan internationally, and the implementation of deregulation and 'structural reforms' domestically, helped to set the agenda for future administrations. True, each LDP administration offered a somewhat different emphasis, with prime ministers Fukuda and Asō in particular less supportive of the domestic reform agenda championed by Koizumi, but a greater international role for Japan and a restructuring of the domestic political economy and more widely society have remained as core issues for future governments. With the election of the DPJ, moreover, a call for new social benefits, such as an election pledge for child allowances, and a greater focus on playing an international role in East Asia, as illustrated by Hatoyama's announcement of promoting an East Asian Community, point to the changes the DPJ government is seeking to put in place. Nevertheless, the new government is similarly faced with the need to deal with the legacy of structural reform as well as the country's international role. Internationally, indeed, the new prime minister's call for equal partnership with the United States and the outstanding issue of transferring the Marine Corps Airbase Futenma from Ginowan to Henoko, Nago, has taken on an increasing salience, especially in the wake of the January 2010 election of a new Nago mayor opposed to the relocation of the base to the city. These processes of change have been facilitated by the negotiation of the dissolution, shift and reinscription of a range of political, economic and social boundaries at the heart of contemporary Japan. The consequence has been the creation of newly inscribed boundaries enabling the embrace of new actors as well as the shrinking of boundaries to exclude others. Understanding the transitional nature of boundaries serves to deepen our knowledge of contemporary Japan, as by exposing the way boundaries function, their implications become much clearer.

Here boundaries serve as a heuristic device to shed light on the transformations now taking place in political, economic and social space in contemporary Japan, whether engendered endogenously or exogenously. The central argument of the book is that, in order to achieve the twin goals of greater international proactivity and domestic reform, the government and other actors supporting the new direction for Japan pushed forward by the Koizumi administration needed to take action in order to destabilize and reformulate a range of extant boundaries. This task was achieved by deploying material as well as normative resources, including the production of new discourses about the way these resources should be deployed. While boundaries often remain invisible, the aim of this book is to promote an understanding of their significance by uncovering their pivotal role in contemporary Japan.

This chapter provides a backdrop for the following chapters, which are organized in terms of a number of key levels on which boundaries function. They examine the implications of the shift in boundaries on the international, national and local, as well as societal levels. As a whole, the book aims to demonstrate how, in the wake of the Koizumi administration, the meaning and implication of boundaries on each of these levels became contested, leading to their blurring, crossing and reinscription in the course of contesting the future orientation of Japan. The chapter is divided into three sections. Section 1 examines the meaning of boundaries generically. The next section proceeds to a general discussion of the way boundaries have shifted in the wake of the Koizumi administration. The final section concludes the chapter by introducing the structure of the book.

1. The meaning of boundaries

It is clear from the extant research that, whether physical or metaphysical, boundaries serve most fundamentally to distinguish between insiders and outsiders. A large body of research on boundaries from the anthropological or sociological perspective has focused on the way symbolic and social boundaries distinguish between and among insiders and outsiders as groups of people, with ethnic boundaries being of particular concern (Lamont and Molnár 2002; Wimmer 2008). But boundaries function much more widely. For what is inside or outside differs: not just people, but states, businesses and other actors seek to inscribe, embed, maintain and shift boundaries in the process of making distinctions between insiders and outsiders. So political and economic, not just social, actors invest considerable resources into challenging and affirming boundaries, although many of us take them for granted as they appear natural and uncontested. Nevertheless, changes in power constellations within and between political, economic and social agents can lead to their contestation and exposure as the product of a particular way of viewing the world. Certain boundaries are temporary, others more permanent, but the potential for them to shift remains.

In one respect, physical boundaries can provide the basis for the borders separating sovereign territorial states, as with the role of rivers or other geographical features as the basis for territorial boundaries employed in dividing contiguous states. Here legal, formalistic, territorial boundaries, that is, borders, give a sense of durability to the state. But the boundaries separating states are not simply legal borders, but political, economic and social boundaries, too. At the international level, states may be insiders or outsiders of international organizations, whether global or regional, as illustrated by the continuing contestation over membership of the United Nations for Taiwan following the take up of the security council seat by the People's Republic of China in 1972, or membership for states viewed as inside or outside of a particular regional grouping, as seen in the debate over India's membership of the East Asian Summit. But the way boundaries are drawn internationally is not simply in terms of membership of formal institutions or organizations. As we will see later in the discussion of the branding of 'rogue states', states can be viewed as being outside of the boundaries of international society, not accepted as a member, despite their sovereign territorial credentials. At the same time, the borders of a state blur the complex web of inter-human relations that are intertwined across these formal divisions between members of one political community and another. In this case, some form of boundary crossing takes place (Tilly 2005: 182), thereby challenging the legal basis of the insider–outsider distinction the state purports. This calls for us to transcend epistemologies centred solely on the state, taking account of cross-border processes. For certain boundaries are porous and can be blurred through complex human interaction linking people on one side of the border to those on the other.

In another respect, social and symbolic boundaries, rather than legal borders, separate ethnic groups. Here value is imputed to the distinction between insiders and outsiders in order to divide groups and establish a common understanding of the location and meaning of ethnic boundaries (Wimmer 2008). As boundaries serve to distinguish between those on the inside and those on the outside, categories arise out of boundaries, and vice versa (Tilly 2005). But different ethnic groups may belong to the same or different categories of people within states, as illustrated by citizenship. For instance, citizens belonging to one ethnic group may be enfranchised and enjoy the right to vote in one polity, whether at the local, national or international level, but not in another, where their status is not citizen but alien: here the category of citizenship trumps ethnicity. As Day and Shaw have outlined (2002), those opposed to alien suffrage support a formal understanding of the boundaries and membership of the state, with doubts expressed about the extent of an alien's commitment to it. Yet the flow of members of different ethnic groups across the borders separating states means that the social and symbolic boundaries dividing the nation and the state increasingly cut across the boundaries of the nation. Certainly, the nation and the state are different (Wilson and Donnan 1998), but a state can respond to the challenge to the nation posed by the flow of aliens across state borders by seeking to embrace new members of the community in the nation. In this way, cross-border migration poses a challenge to at least three important boundaries: the territorial boundary of the state, the political boundary of citizenship, and the social and symbolic boundary at the heart of the national community (Bauböck 1998).

In this way, boundaries function to establish differences between insiders and outsiders, whether in terms of states, ethnic groups or other groupings. But the distinctions inscribed by boundaries can be found much more broadly, as the following chapters on Japan make clear. The next section sets the context for those chapters by highlighting how the move to the Koizumi administration brought to the forefront a number of political, economic and social boundaries.

2. The Koizumi administration and beyond

The focus on the Koizumi administration (2001–06) and beyond stems from a concern with the implication for the stability and shift of a range of political, economic and social boundaries in the face of the call made by the administration to play a greater international role and implement domestic reforms. The background to Koizumi's rise to power was a rapid turnover of prime ministers – 10 in the preceding 12 years – and a groping by previous leaders towards a response to globalization and the neo-liberal agenda. Of course, previous LDP administrations had prioritized some of the same or similar goals to Koizumi, but the prime minister and his administration disseminated particularly powerful discourses in support of Japan's international proactivity based on closer cooperation with the United States as well as deregulation and domestic reforms based on neoliberalism. Thus, the calls Koizumi made to carry out reform 'without sanctuary' led to increased clarity, intensification and consolidation of the direction of change domestically. Internationally, the focus was on closer cooperation with the United States, with much less concern about the deterioration of relations with China and South Korea due to the prime minister's visit to Yasukuni shrine and the glossing of Japanese war-time aggression in school textbooks. While Koizumi adopted a populist strategy and presidential style of leadership to promote his agenda and stay in power for over five years, the three LDP prime ministers to immediately follow him were only able to stay in power one year or less, all becoming prime minister without facing an election. The Opposition increasingly gained in confidence and power after Koizumi stepped down, especially following the defeat of Prime Minister Abe's administration in the 2007 Upper House election. This enabled the opposition parties to use their majority to delay or even put a stop to government legislation. With the election of the DPJ in the general election of July 2009, the end of 54 years of near continuous LDP rule came to an end. From then on the DPJ has been faced with the task of formulating and implementing policy, not just challenging it.

International boundaries

At the international level, the Koizumi and following LDP administrations sought to move away from the identity of Japan as a 'peace state,' carving out a greater role for the nation as an international ally of the United States, as seen in the prime minister's support of the wars in Afghanistan and Iraq. Japan's peace identity is rooted in Article 9 of the constitution, which remains as a constraint on how military resources are deployed by the Japanese government. The coexistence of Article 9 and the Self-Defence Forces (SDF), along with the United States–Japan security treaty, meant the Koizumi administration needed to launch a range of political challenges to the existing boundaries of constitutional interpretation in order to be able to deploy the SDF in new international roles. This was carried out in the context of Koizumi's support for the 'war on terror' following the 11 September 2001 attacks on the United States. Here the prime minister offered his immediate support to the administration of President George W. Bush. In light of the boundary-inscribing remark by the president that, 'You're either with us or against us in the fight against terror,' Koizumi had clearly demonstrated he was with the United States. In order to play an international role in the unfolding 'war on terror,' the government quickly passed the Anti-terrorism Special Measures Law in November 2001, suggesting the importance of stretching the legal boundaries governing the SDF's activities. The law provided a new legal basis for the Japanese military to conduct overseas activities, enabling the Maritime SDF (MSDF) to start operations in refuelling, interdiction and logistical support for US naval and other warships in the Indian Ocean involved in the war in Afghanistan. Given opposition to the new law both inside and outside of the Diet, a sunset clause was appended. As a result, the LDP needed to extend the law three times, in 2003, 2005 and 2006, before the Upper House refused to support a further extension following the LDP's loss of its majority in the July 2007 election. This led to a three-month hiatus in the military operations carried out but, in January 2008, the Fukuda administration managed to renew them for another year on extension of the Diet session. The mission would have ended altogether, except for the Lower House overturning the Upper House vote. Meanwhile, Japan hosted the Afghan reconstruction conference in January 2002 and has been involved in the country's reconstruction through close cooperation with agencies of the United Nations. These efforts have had a main focus on education, health, and other civilian-focussed activities as well as finance for the resettlement of Afghan refugees and internally displaced persons in Kandahar and elsewhere. Following the election of Hamid Karzai in 2004, the Japan International Cooperation Agency (JICA) began to promote rural development, such as improving rice cultivation; providing for basic human needs; training approximately 10,000 teachers and the rebuilding of schools; as well as urban development, as illustrated by the completion of the Kabul Airport Terminal in 2008. Although Japan's main focus in Afghanistan thus has been on reconstruction, more traditional security issues, such as the demobilizing and disarming of troops, have been on the agenda, too (JCA n.d.).

As far as Iraq is concerned, the government in July 2003 passed another controversial, time-limited law in order to support the US war in Iraq, the Iraq Special Measures Law, enabling the government to despatch the SDF to Iraq in 2004. This deployment was a major reinscription of the boundaries on deployment of Japanese troops overseas. Although the government did not despatch soldiers for combat, it broke precedence by sending 600 ground troops to Samawah, southern Iraq during a war situation, without the sanction of the United Nations. This was the first time for an LDP-government to send the SDF to a country at war.

The troops, who suffered no casualties, were involved in reconstruction efforts from March 2004 until July 2006 following an extension of their deployment by the Koizumi government. The main tasks completed were the reconstruction of public facilities, like schools, water purification, and so on (McCormack 2004). At the same time, the Air Self-Defence Forces (ASDF) airlifted humanitarian and reconstruction supplies into Iraq for the ground troops. After their withdrawal in July 2006, the ASDF continued to use Kuwait as a base to supply the multinational forces in Iraq, airlifting materials and transporting mainly US troops between Kuwait and Iraq. In all, Japanese forces were involved in reconstruction work and troop transportation activities for a total of five years, with the last soldiers returning home from Kuwait in February 2009.

In this way, the boundaries on the deployment of the SDF were shifted, with ground troops for the first time despatched to an active war zone, albeit not for fighting, and the MSDF and ASDF despatched in order to provide logistical support for war. The involvement of Japanese troops in these forms of cooperation suggests how, even in the 'post-9/11 world', the LDP government remained constrained in the use of the full power resources of the state, with no troops taking part in the fighting. Nevertheless, this more proactive role should still be regarded as a watershed in the history of the SDF. Putting boots in the desert demonstrated Japan was playing a quite different role to the first Gulf War of 1990–91, when the security boundary was restricted to sending minesweepers after the end of the conflict. Thus, unlike other US allies such as the United Kingdom and South Korea, the Koizumi and following LDP administrations have not sent combat troops to fight overseas, and have thus not expanded the boundaries of the constitution to the extent of the use of coercive force. In this sense, the call made by the US for Japan to play a military role in Iraq was not answered with combat soldiers, as is well illustrated by the role of Australian and UK soldiers in protecting the SDF, even though Samawah was a relatively safe and not densely populated part of the country.

Reflecting the new government's shift of political boundaries after taking office, the DPJ put an end to the refuelling mission in January 2010 on expiry of the law's period in force. This change illustrates how the DPJ is implementing policies more in tune with the ideas of the former party leader, now Secretary General, Ozawa Ichiro, who has called for the SDF not to be involved in 'coalitions of the willing' without the backing of the United Nations, and to play more of an international role as a 'normal state' (Ozawa 1994). Under the new DPJ government, instead of supplying fuel, the government has offered financial assistance of $5 billion over five years to Afghanistan for civilian projects such as job retraining and the development of the country's infrastructure. At the same time, though, in line with the LDP's longstanding policy of gaining a permanent seat on the United Nations Security Council (UNSC) (Drifte 1999), which Koizumi hoped would be realized during his premiership, the new DPJ government is similarly attempting to make the transition from outsider to insider in the UNSC, albeit without success. The new government's position was clearly stated at the UN in September 2009, when Prime Minister Hatoyama confirmed his government would continue to pursue a permanent seat on the UNSC (Hatoyama 2009). At the regional level, the tension between an Asia Pacific and an East Asia boundary to the region in carving out a more proactive role for Japan has led to varying attempts to ensure a place for Japan in regional groupings. Differently bounded meetings take place, as with the Asia Pacific Economic Cooperation forum (21 participants), Association of Southeast Asian Nations (ASEAN) Regional Forum (27 participants), ASEAN (10 participants) Plus Three (China, Japan and South Korea) and the East Asia summit (16 participants), with Japan playing a role in each. With the advent of the Hatoyama government, the contested nature of the boundaries of the region have been highlighted even further, as the prime minister has put forward the idea of creating an East Asian Community, but without stipulating clearly the membership of this community and the relationship his concept shares with the existing regional groupings (*New York Times*, 26 August 2009). Finally, in addition to these international boundaries, the boundary between the peaceful and coercive use of instruments of national power in playing a role internationally remains of central concern, with the move from the LDP to the DPJ suggesting that, at least at the start of its term in office, the new government is not only questioning the use of the SDF in support of US strategy, as illustrated by the end of fuel supplies in support of the war in Afghanistan, but is also questioning the nature of the alliance, as seen by the controversy over the relocation of the Futenma base in Okinawa and the call for a more 'equal' relationship.

Domestic boundaries

Domestically, the Koizumi administration aimed at consolidating a neoliberal approach to questions of political economy through reform and deregulation. This brought about a shift in the boundaries between the state, market and society, with the market being given greater priority as a way to try to revive the economy. Three elements are central to the deregulation and structural reforms introduced by Koizumi: reform of the postal services and quangos such as the Japan Highway Public Corporation; decentralization of power to local authorities, with reduction of central government subsidy and increase in local tax-raising powers; and deregulation in such areas as education, employment, medical care, and so on (Teranishi 2009 6–7; also see, Sakai 2006: 2). While the early efforts at reform were not necessarily successful (George Mulgan 2002), and not all reforms have been implemented or implemented fully, the Koizumi administration continued to forge ahead with tackling the government debt, the privatization of the postal services and highways, 'pork barrel' public works projects, welfare reform, and so on. Clearly, many of the changes introduced by Koizumi reflected the appraisal of markets as being more efficient than central government and the need to control spending. The administration's implementation of budget caps played a particularly important role in reducing the public works and welfare budgets under future administrations, as the caps created an automatic constraint on spending. While the neoliberal approach was perceived as a way to revitalize the economy, one of the outcomes of the type of deregulation and structural reforms carried out by the Koizumi government was a change in employment patterns, bringing about a weakening of job security for many and a resulting increase in the number of irregular and part-time workers. This went hand-in-hand with a widening of the disparity between the rich and poor (Miura 2005).

Of the LDP prime ministers to follow Koizumi, Abe stands out as the prime minister who called for the implementation of a right-of-centre agenda, including constitutional revision (see Mito 2008, for details). Indeed, unlike with preceding prime ministers, who had been vocal about constitutional change before taking up high office, Abe became the first prime minister to call for revision during his own term in office (Watanabe 2007: 9). While his administration proved unsuccessful in the attempt to shift the boundaries of the constitution, it did succeed in pushing ahead with a revision of the Fundamental Law on Education. The new legislation, which was passed in December 2006, shifts the boundaries in favour of 'patriotism' and 'tradition' in school education. Neither of the two following LDP prime ministers sought to put revision of the constitution at the top of their political agenda. However, in line with the need to gain popular approval for constitutional revision, the procedures to hold a national referendum in order to be able to revise the constitution were established in May 2007 under Prime Minister Abe, with the new law scheduled to come into force in May 2010. This legislation has laid the groundwork for any future prime minister to move forward with revision, although the election of the DPJ government has put the issue of constitutional revision on hold.

The new Hatoyama administration came to power on the basis of a party manifesto trumpeting a new politics, aimed at moving the focus of policy 'from concrete to people.' The goal is to cut bureaucratic waste and direct savings to causes such as child allowances, free high school tuition, toll-free expressways, tax reduction for small- and medium-sized enterprises, and so on. These measures are part of a strategy to revitalize local communities and promote a people-centred, low-carbon economy with less disparity between the rich and the poor, as illustrated by the elderly and children living in poverty along with the large numbers of unemployed and laid-off workers. It remains to be seen how many of the domestic goals the DPJ have announced will be realized, but the first few months in office suggest the boundaries between new and old policies will continue to be contested. The following chapters will hopefully provide at least some insights into the role boundaries have played during the Koizumi administration and beyond.

3. Structure of the book

The book has been structured in a way to move the level of analysis of boundaries from the international to the societal level. The first four chapters deal with boundaries on the international level, starting with Hugo Dobson's 'Diplomacy on the boundaries: the G8, international society and Japan's instrumentalization of liminality', which examines the role of Japan in one of the main sites of global governance, the G8. The chapter demonstrates how Japanese policy makers have played an important role in the G8 by inscribing boundaries in a way to broaden the group's agenda and by working to increase as well as to limit the membership of the group. One of the novel features of Dobson's chapter is his use of 'liminality' to illuminate the way the Japanese government has developed policies to deal with particular states in international society. It has sought in some cases to maintain the boundary of membership while pressing for the boundary to be expanded in others. The picture this chapter paints is of a Japan willing and able to play a role in global governance through the G8.

The next chapter by Shogo Suzuki, 'The strange masochism of the Japanese right: redrawing moral boundaries in Sino-Japanese relations', is a critical analysis of the right-wing in Japan and the attempt a phalanx of actors on the political right is making to redraw the moral boundaries of Sino-Japanese relations through the use of a range of media, including comic books and cartoons. One of the main purposes behind the right's focus on moral boundaries is to burnish Japan's identity as an honourable and respected member of international society, not one tainted by the legacy of history: war responsibility, aggression and 'comfort women' are outside the boundary of Japanese identity for the right. This approach goes hand-in-hand with its depiction of an immoral and unethical China that uses the 'history card' to exploit the relationship with Japan and bolster nationalism at home. But what is needed, the author argues, are not the moral boundaries drawn by the right but moral boundaries drawn in a way to enable reconciliation and a mutually accepted understanding of history between the two nations.

The third chapter moves on to analyse another key bilateral relationship in East Asia, that with North Korea. Key-young Son's 'Japan's responses to actors outside the boundaries of international society: "rogue states" and North Korea's nuclear threats', discusses Japan's relationship with a state the government views as outside of the boundaries of international society. The chapter starts from the position that, as seen in a range of cases, as indeed with China, the boundaries of international society are malleable and 'insiders' and 'outsiders' can change. The author elucidates the nature of the responses made by Japanese policy makers to the perceived North Korean nuclear threat through a careful examination of relations between the two sides in the wake of Prime Minister Koizumi's visit to North Korea in 2002. With Kim Jong-il's admission to the prime minister of the abduction of Japanese nationals, however, the potential for the North to become a member of international society was abandoned by Japan in favour of keeping it as an outsider, where it still remains today.

Chapter four, 'Navigating the boundaries of the interstate society: Japan's response to piracy in Southeast Asia' by Lindsay Black, is the last chapter dealing with boundaries on the international level. The focus here is similarly on 'outsiders', in this case the pirates in the seas of Southeast Asia. The chapter traces how both Japanese seafarers and trade face an increasing risk of piratical attack in traversing in particular the narrow waters of the Malacca Straights, one of the world's most important shipping lanes and a vital conduit for oil bound from the Middle East to Japan. In response to this risk, the government has promoted regional collaboration against pirates, hosting conferences and launching operations to combat pirates and piratical acts. The author argues that Japanese policy makers have been skilful in building cooperation with other regional actors, steering a course that takes into account the boundaries of both sovereignty and international law. The end result demonstrates how the Japanese government has been playing a proactive role in dealing with non-traditional forms of security.

The following three chapters move on to address both national and local political boundaries. Chapter five, 'Stronger political leadership and the shift in policy-making boundaries in Japan' by Shinoda Tomohito, deals with the change in boundaries following the launch of the Koizumi administration. The author here points to a dramatic change in the way policy has been made, with a much greater emphasis on top-down decision making and a 'presidential' style of leadership rather than a policy-making process dominated by the bureaucracy. Despite resistance, the administration successfully forged ahead with 'structural reform' at home, as illustrated by the privatization of the postal services as well as with a more proactive foreign policy abroad, as illustrated by the despatch of the SDF to Iraq. The success Koizumi achieved was facilitated by the change in policy-making boundaries set in place through earlier institutional reforms by Prime Minister Hashimoto Ryūtarō. As seen later, however, not all prime ministers have been willing or able to take advantage of these boundary changes, especially given the lack of a government majority in the upper house of the Diet and the later victory of the DPJ.

The sixth chapter by Uchiyama Yū, 'Leadership strategies: (re)drawing boundaries among and within parties in Japan', examines how national leaders are able to bolster their leadership positions by exploiting the potential to establish boundaries in society, as in the case of Prime Minister Koizumi's strategy. The chapter demonstrates how, in order to push through domestic reforms, the prime minister used the 'friend' and 'enemy' distinction successfully in order to paint the internal opponents of his reform plans as the enemy standing against the public good. By focusing on how Koizumi and later prime ministers have inscribed boundaries both among and within Japanese political parties, the author is able to shed a penetrating light on the different leadership styles of Japanese prime ministers and elucidate how four main ways of drawing and redrawing boundaries have been deployed: by placing weight on the boundary between government and opposition, building consensus among political parties, encouraging splits in the party, or promoting splits in other parties.

Chapter seven turns to the local political level: Muto Hiromi's chapter, 'The problem of boundaries for Japan's local authorities: mergers, public services and the growing disparity in Japanese society', discusses the national government's changes and attempted changes to local boundaries in Japan with a focus on the 'Heisei reforms'. It details how the legal boundaries between and among different levels of sub-national political authorities in Japan have been transformed, with a particular emphasis on the recent 'Heisei' merger of municipalities in the historical context of earlier reforms. In addressing the issue of municipal mergers, the chapter demonstrates how two important issues related to boundaries have emerged, the first in terms of the transformation in the legal boundary between the public and private, and the second in terms of the metaphysical boundary between the citizen and the local authorities. The author shows clearly how the change in the boundaries between the public and the private provision of public services has created a range of problems and how local citizens are largely bereft of any sense of shared identity with the new bodies created out of the mergers.

In the following four chapters, we examine a number of key boundaries at the societal level, starting with Peter Von Staden's 'Boundaries in Japan's business and government relationship: regression, change and façades', which starts us out by addressing the transition in boundaries between business and government. One of the key arguments developed in this chapter is that, in order to understand the changes in these boundaries, both the shape and direction of the Japanese political-cal economy needs to be taken into account at the macro level of structure and the micro level of individual behaviour. While the extent of change may be debated, the author comes down clearly on the side of those who see a fundamental trans-formation of the 'developmental state' of earlier years. Instead of the 'iron triangle' of the governing party, bureaucracy and big business, a much more pluralistic and complex relationship has emerged in Japan, where especially big business enjoys a high degree of independence from the government. The chapter demonstrates in detail how a plurality of voices has now come to be heard from the business world, which often differ based on the size, industrial sector and other factors affecting business interests.

Then, in chapter nine, Hasegawa Harukiyo's 'Adjusting the boundaries between Keidanren and labour unions in Japan: a critical reappraisal of globalization and democracy', examines the boundaries between business and labour and how these have shifted in the context of globalization. The chapter traces some of the major transitions in these boundaries during the past two decades and shows how capital has expanded at the cost of labour. While both capital and labour have support at the political party level, the two are mismatched in terms of access to the corridors of power: capital is represented by the powerful business association, Keidanren, which has strong and close ties with the LDP, whereas labour is represented by unions and the opposition parties. With less than a fifth of the workforce now unionized and an increasing number of both men and especially women employed as irregular workers, labour is far weaker than business politically. Given the lack of a strong countervailing voice, the author is concerned about the health of Japanese democracy. What is needed, he argues, is for the workers to become more fully aware of their poor working conditions as a crucial step on the road to build-ing a stronger democracy in Japan.

Chapter ten by Patricia Steinhoff is entitled 'Shifting boundaries in Japan's crim-inal justice system'. It demonstrates through extensive empirical data how legal boundaries are maintained, challenged and shifted in the process of the dynamic relationship between and among international standards, the state, particularly political and bureaucratic actors, and civil society. The author presents two case studies in order to elucidate how these three interact. The first case, which focuses on the trial of the Japanese Red Army leader, Shigenobu Fusako, highlights the expansion of the boundaries of the criminal justice system beyond the shores of Japan. This offers a fascinating insight into the complex way the criminal justice system and the New Left have interacted over the years. The murder of a mother and her daughter in Hikari City by a minor is the second case taken up. Here the author details how the call by the family of the victims for retributive justice played a key role in the court's decision to shift the boundaries of the justice system. This led to the imposition of the death penalty on a minor.

The final chapter, 'The rapid redrawing of boundaries in Japanese higher education' by Roger Goodman, investigates how the boundaries in higher education have been changing in contemporary Japan. The author shows how the drive at the national level to encourage Japanese universities to become more competitive has led to a major shake-up in the ivory tower. Crucial here has been the change in the boundaries of the legal basis of national universities: further to new legislation, Japan's higher education institutions have been made into independent entities with a greater responsibility for their own financial well being. At the same time, the decrease in the population of 18-year-old students means universities have to become more adaptive. The chapter outlines in rich detail how the system is becoming much more complex in the process, with increasing numbers of casualized academics, a higher number of newly appointed posts with PhDs minted overseas, more foreigners employed at both research-intensive and service universities, and a greater offering of courses taught in English. Despite such changes, the author argues that the boundaries between the good and the not-so-good universities remain intact, as illustrated by the concentration of competitive funding in the elite institutions and the gradual institutionalization of the gap between research-intensive and service universities.

In this way, the chapters to follow focus on a range of contemporary phenomena in Japan, with our contributors able to shed new light on the way boundaries at both the international and domestic levels serve political, economic and societal purposes.

References

Bauböck, Rainer (1998) 'The crossing and blurring of boundaries in international migration: challenges for social and political theory', in Rainer Bauböck and John Rundell (eds) *Blurred Boundaries: migration, ethnicity, citizenship*, Brookfield, CT: Ashgate, pp. 17–52.
Day, Stephen and Shaw, Jo (2002) 'European Union electoral rights and the political participation of migrants in host polities', *International Journal of Population Geography*, 8: 183–99.
Drifte, Reinhard (1999) *Japan's Quest for a Permanent Security Council Seat. A matter of pride or justice?* London: Macmillan.
George Mulgan, Aurelia (2002) *Japan's Failed Revolution: Koizumi and the politics of economic reform*, Canberra: Asia Pacific Press.
Hatoyama, Yukio (2009) Address by H.E. Dr Yukio Hatoyama, Prime Minister of Japan, at the sixty-fourth session of the General Assembly of the United Nations, 24 September. Online. Available: http://www.kantei.go.jp/foreign/hatoyama/statement/200909/ehat_0924c_e.html (accessed 4 February 2010).
JCA (n.d.) Disarmament, Demobilization and Reintegration in Afghanistan. Online.

Available: www.jca.apc.org/~jann/Documents/DDR.pdf (accessed 10 February 2010).

Lamont, Michèle and Molnár, Virág (2002) 'The study of boundaries in the social sciences', *Annual Review of Sociology*, 28: 167–95.

McCormack, Gavan (2004) 'Remilitarizing Japan', *New Left Review*, 29: 29–45.

Mito, Takamichi (2008) 'Japan's Constitutional revision debate under prime minister Abe Shinzō and its implications for Japan's foreign policy', *Japanese Studies,* 28, 1: 59–71.

Miura, Atsushi (2005) *Karyū Shakai: Arata na kaisō shūdan no shutsugen*, Tokyo: Kōbunsha.

Ozawa, Ichiro (1994) *Blueprint for a New Japan: the rethinking of a nation*, New York: Kodansha America.

Sakai, Yoshihiro (2006) 'Japan's Economy in the Post-Koizumi Era', *Japan Chair Platform.* Online. Available: http://csis.org/files/media/csis/pubs/060426_jcp.pdf (accessed 15 January 2010).

Teranishi, Juro (2009) 'Neo-liberalism and market-disciplining policy in Koizumi reform: were we really development-oriented?' Online. Available: http://www2.ier.hit-u.ac. jp/~nisizawa/teranishi.pdf (accessed 4 February 2010).

Tilly, Charles (2005) *Identities, Boundaries, and Social Ties*, Boulder, Colorado: Paradigm.

Watanabe, Osamu (2007) *Abe Seikenron: shinjiyūshugi kara shinhoshushugi e*, Tokyo: Junpōsha.

Wilson, Thomas M. and Donnan, Hastings (1998) 'Nation, state and identity at international borders', in Thomas M. Wilson and Hastings Donnan (eds) *Border Identities: nation and state at international frontiers*, Cambridge: Cambridge University Press, pp. 1–30.

Wimmer, Andreas (2008) 'The making and unmaking of ethnic boundaries: a multilevel process theory', *American Journal of Sociology*, 113, 4: 970–10.

1 Diplomacy on the boundaries

The G8, international society and Japan's instrumentalization of liminality

Hugo Dobson

The objective of this edited volume is to explore how the normative, theoretical and physical boundaries of the Japanese state, and in particular its behaviour, have been negotiated, inscribed and reinscribed as a result of changes in international and domestic structures. Within this broader project, this chapter is concerned with the international level where this has been most obvious in attempts to become a 'normal state', implying a greater contribution to international society. The debate on Japan's contribution to international society has traditionally been portrayed as a tension between financial contributions and a human contribution, the most high-profile example of this debate being the controversy surrounding Japan's 'tardy' response to the 1991 Gulf War, which a decade later continued to inform Japan's contribution to the US-led 'war on terror'. However, faced by this stark bipolar choice, Japan's contribution to international society and the delineation of its boundaries through agenda-setting, the extension of membership and the exclusion of outlying states have tended to be overlooked.

This chapter highlights the Japanese government's participation in one of the central fora of global governance and international society – the Group of 8 (G8) summit. Admittedly, in recent years there has been a rapid expansion in the number of 'Gs' that threaten to eclipse the G8, the most notable of which was the upgrading of the Group of 20 (G20) meeting of finance ministers to the leaders' level for the first time at Washington in November 2008 in response to the US mortgage-triggered global financial crisis. However, the post-crisis settlement of this 'Gaggle of Gs' (Culpeper 2003) has yet to be negotiated and remains inchoate, thus providing this chapter with the opportunity to look back upon previous attempts to expand and reorganize the G8, 'one of the central institutions of our age' (Hajnal and Kirton 2000: 5). On the one hand, it examines how the Japanese government has sought to redefine, renegotiate and/or limit the boundaries of international society through attempts to control the membership of this forum.[1] On the other hand, it also explores the question of how the Japanese government has responded and reacted to the inclusion and exclusion of a number of countries in this forum specifically, and in some cases international society at large, namely Australia, Indonesia, Russia, China and North Korea.

To this end, the chapter employs the concept of liminality in order to capture the strategy employed by the Japanese government in handling certain states and their position towards international society. Liminality comes from the Latin *limen* meaning threshold and describes a transitional temporal/physical space between one state and another, examples of which might include birth, puberty, graduation, marriage and/or death (Van Gennep 1960). In the words of Victor Turner:

> The attributes of liminality or of liminal personae ('threshold people') are necessarily ambiguous, since this condition and these persons elude or slip through the network of classifications that normally locate states and positions in cultural space. Liminal entities are neither here nor there; they are betwixt and between the positions assigned and arrayed by law, custom, convention, and ceremonial. . . . Thus liminality is frequently likened to death, to being in the womb, to invisibility, to darkness, to bisexuality, to the wilderness, and to an eclipse of the sun or moon.
>
> (1995: 95)

In other words, this chapter is exploring the murky, ambiguous areas on the boundaries of both the G8 and international society, the no man's land that is neither completely accepted as part of international society but equally cannot be captured by the term 'rogue states' outside the society's boundaries (see Chapter 3).

The application of the concept of liminality to the study of International Relations (IR) is so far embryonic at best (for a rare example, see Den Boer 2003). What is more, the application of liminality to the study of Japan has largely been confined to the fields of literature, religion and anthropology, although one attempt to apply the concept to the study of Japanese domestic politics exists (Kishima 1991). In the related field of Japan's foreign relations, the extant literature is bereft of attempts to import and apply this potentially illuminating concept. For example, liminality might afford the opportunity to overcome the dead-end discourse on reactivity versus proactivism in Japanese foreign policy that has dominated debates on the subject for some decades now, producing plenty of heat but not much light (Calder 1988, 2003; Yasutomo 1995). As liminal spaces are also regarded as spaces of opportunity, the Japanese government's instrumentalization of liminality could provide a bridge between these two characterizations of Japan's role in the world. Thus, this chapter demonstrates how the Japanese government has sought both to obfuscate and reinforce the boundaries of international society in order to take advantage of theoretical, physical and diplomatic liminal spaces in pursuit of its national interests through the G8. This chapter proceeds by first establishing the definition and boundaries of international society and thereafter its relationship to the G8. It then turns to explore five examples of Japanese diplomacy on the boundaries of the G8: the cases of Australia, Indonesia, China, Russia and North Korea.

1. International society and its boundaries

It is liberal/idealist IR theory that is most strongly predicated on the 'myth' that international society exists (Weber 2001: 35–57), and more specifically, international society is a concept most closely associated with the English School of IR. Despite significant differences among thinkers in the English School tradition, the central assertion is that in the absence of a Leviathan, state behaviour is not necessarily and solely motivated by realist interpretations of power politics and can in fact be influenced by shared moral and legal norms and values. In other words, international society provides a way out of the impasse between realists and liberals. International society, as opposed to the international system, has been defined by Hedley Bull in the following oft-quoted sentence:

> A *society of states* (or international society) exists when a group of states, conscious of certain common interests and common values, form a society in the sense that they conceive themselves to be bound by a common set of rules in their relations with one another, and share in the working of common institutions.
>
> (Bull 2002: 13)

Although debates have taken place as to the necessity of a common culture before a society of states could emerge (Dunne 1998: 124–29), and it is questionable as to whether this is an argument for the existence of international society as a fact of international relations, or a normative statement, Bull's words can be read as 'a more or less optimal solution to the problem of how to accommodate a plurality of cultural values within a well-ordered international system', rather than 'a mid-point along the path to a universal community of humankind' (Dunne 1998: 11). Putting debates between realists and liberals and among those in the English School to one side, what is important for this chapter's discussion is the word 'common' and the extent to which commonality can be agreed upon among states in the values, norms, principles, rules and institutions (defined broadly to include practices such as war and diplomacy in addition to international organizations and fora) by which they provide governance and delineate the boundaries of acceptable and unacceptable behaviour in international society.

Moreover, it is also necessary to delineate how far the boundaries of international society (or more accurately interstate society) extend. In other words, this is a question of *membership*. International society is traditionally regarded by members of the English School as having steadily expanded outward from Europe to embrace decolonized states; states that do not share Euro-centric commonalities are regarded as existing outside of the perimeters of international society. Yet the extent of solidarity and the commonalities among this society of states are not static, fluctuate across time and are constantly (re)negotiated, allowing or preventing collective action as a result. Traditionally, state sovereignty and non-intervention have provided the common values shared by the society of international states. However, in the post-Cold War and post 9/11 periods, these values have come under attack as new emerging commonalities – such as the proactive promotion of democracy and preventive action – have competed for acceptance within international society. The following section explores the role that the G8, as one of the central mechanisms of global governance, has played in establishing these boundaries of international society.

2. The G8 and the boundaries of international society

At its first meeting in the château of Rambouillet in November 1975, the G6 (minus Canada and, more importantly for this discussion, Russia) stated their commonalities that, in the absence of any explicit membership criteria, have served as the defining commonalities among the participants in this forum. Article 2 of the Rambouillet Declaration stated that:

> We came together because of shared beliefs and shared responsibilities. We are each responsible for the government of an open, democratic society, dedicated to individual liberty and social advancement. Our success will strengthen, indeed is essential to, democratic societies everywhere. We are each responsible for assuring the prosperity of a major industrial economy. The growth and stability of our economies will help the entire industrial world and developing countries to prosper.
>
> (G6 1975)

The keywords here are: (1) responsibility; (2) democracy; (3) prosperity; and (4) stability. Faith in liberal democracy and its promotion across the globe is the chief commonality that defines the membership of this select group, but in addition, the G8 is also assuming a burden to provide the public goods and leadership required to ensure the future and peaceful development of the entire world. If democracy and prosperity are secured at home within the G6 countries, it was believed that this would contribute to democratic development and economic prosperity across the globe.

In this light, Articles 3, 10 and 12 proceeded to reach out to countries not directly included in this group of modern-day great powers:

> To assure in a world of growing interdependence the success of the objectives set out in this declaration, we intend to play our own full part and strengthen our efforts for closer international cooperation and constructive dialogue among all countries, transcending differences in stages of economic development, degrees of resource endowment and political and social systems.
>
> We look to an orderly and fruitful increase in our economic relations with socialist countries as an important element in progress in détente, and in world economic growth.
>
> A cooperative relationship and improved understanding between the developing nations and the industrial world is fundamental to the prosperity of each. Sustained growth in our economies is necessary to growth in developing countries; and their growth contributes significantly to health in our own economies.
>
> (G6 1975)

This could be regarded as a forerunner to the policy of outreach that significantly altered the nature and future of G8 summitry in the first decade of the twenty-first century by bringing non-G8 countries into an extended dialogue and questioning the boundaries of membership. Thus, it could be argued that the Japanese government's attempts (explored later on) to embrace Australia, Indonesia and China are true to the 'spirit of Rambouillet', and its stance towards Russia and North Korea is not.

Yet, despite this initial spirit of outreach, the G8 has concomitantly over the four decades of summitry defined and *reinforced* the boundaries of international society. On the one hand, by maintaining largely its original membership, it has reinforced its self-proclaimed position as a concert of great powers: a clear boundary at the heart of international society. On the other hand, in its statements and declarations, it has sought to reach out beyond this initial boundary to the far reaches of international society and attempt to define its membership.

Further explication is necessary at this point. Although the language of summit documentation very rarely (if at all) refers to 'international society', the 'international community' it has cited in an iterative fashion over the four decades of G8 summitry is coterminous with English School definitions of international society and will therefore be used interchangeably in this chapter. The term 'international community' first appeared in 1980 in three political declarations resulting from the Venice Summit of that year urging a common approach to the problem of refugees, the Soviet invasion of Afghanistan and hijacking. Thereafter, numerous references to the international community can be found in summit documentation that concentrate on specific issues, namely terrorism, aid and climate change. For example, in the case of terrorism, the first attempt to connect the international community and terrorism was the Declaration on International Terrorism made at the 1984 London Summit. It stated that:

> The Heads of State and Government recognized that this is a problem which affects all civilized States. They resolved to promote action through competent international organizations and among the international community as a whole to prevent and punish terrorist acts.

> (G7 1984a)

Two years later, the Statement on International Terrorism issued at the 1986 Tokyo Summit reinforced this approach 'Recognizing that the continuing fight against terrorism is a task which the international community as a whole has to undertake, we pledge ourselves to make maximum efforts to fight against that scourge' (G7 1986).

In the case of aid, the Economic Declaration at the 1984 London Summit was the first to highlight the role of the international community:

> We are greatly concerned about the acute problems of poverty and drought in parts of Africa. We attach major importance to the special action program

for Africa which is being prepared by the World Bank and should provide renewed impetus to the joint efforts of the international community to help.

(G7 1984b)

Finally, the 1989 Paris Summit Economic Declaration was the first statement to highlight another issue of concern to the international community that would come to appear more centrally on the G7/8's agenda in future years, climate change 'We believe that the conclusion of a framework or umbrella convention on climate change to set out general principles or guidelines is urgently required to mobilize and rationalize the efforts made by the international community' (G7 1989a).

However, putting issue-based statements to one side, other declarations made by the G8 have had the effect of delineating the membership and boundaries of international society. Broadly speaking, the G8 has regarded membership of the United Nations (UN) to be the guiding criterion for membership, as seen in numerous statements including the Political Declaration issued at the 1991 London Summit:

The international community faces enormous challenges. But there is also reason for hope. We must reinforce the multilateral approach to the solution of common problems and work to strengthen the international system of which the UN, based on its Charter, remains so central a part. We call on the leaders of other nations to join us in that cause.

(G7 1991a)

However, specific countries have been cast out of international society regardless of their membership of the UN. For example, the Political Declaration issued at the 1988 Toronto Summit included the following statement suggesting strongly that the Soviet Union was not part of international society until it had completely withdrawn its troops from Afghanistan (G7 1988). Similarly, the G7 stated in the 1991 London Summit Economic Declaration that 'The safety situation in Central and Eastern Europe and the Soviet Union deserves particular attention. This is an urgent problem and we call upon the international community to develop an effective means of coordinating its response' (G7 1991b).

Russia's exclusion from the international community was even more explicitly addressed in the Chairman's Statement at that year's summit 'We flag the prospect of a transformed Soviet Union wholeheartedly rejoining the international community, about which we shall hear President Gorbachev's views tomorrow' (G7 1991c).

This process of realizing this prospect of Russia's return to international society was highlighted in the 1993 Tokyo Summit Political Declaration 'We also look to Russia to promote its diplomacy based on the principle of law and justice and to continue to play constructive and responsible roles in the international community' (G7 1993).

And again, in the 1994 Naples Summit's Chairman's Political Statement:

The meeting has also given us the opportunity for an exchange of views on the reform process in Russia, a historic task that President Yeltsin and the Russian government continue to bring forward with the confirmed support of the international community.

(G7 1994)

In the case of China, the 1989 Paris Summit's Declaration on China similarly suggested that China was not considered part of international society:

We call on the Government of the People's Republic of China to do what is necessary to restore confidence in Hong Kong. We recognize that the continuing support of the international community will be an important element in the maintenance of confidence in Hong Kong.

(G7 1989b)

In the case of Iraq, in the aftermath of the 1991 Gulf War, the London Summit Economic Declaration of that year stated that 'Together the international community has overcome a major threat to world peace in the Gulf. But new challenges and new opportunities confront us' (G7 1991b).

The Political Declaration at the same summit stated that:

We note that the urgent and overwhelming nature of the humanitarian problem in Iraq caused by violent oppression by the Government required exceptional action by the international community. . . . The international community cannot stand idly by in cases where widespread human suffering from famine, war, oppression, refugee flows, disease or flood reaches urgent and overwhelming proportions.

(G7 1991a)

The 2001 Genoa Summit's Conclusions of Foreign Ministers again placed Iraq outside of the international community 'The resumption of co-operation with the UN is a necessary step to the suspension and eventual lifting of the sanctions and will allow for a reintegration of Iraq into the international community' (G8 2001a).

Thus, both in word and deed, the G8 has adjudicated on the commonalities and membership of a constantly changing international society as the English School of IR understands it, or the international community as the G8 has referred to it, suggesting the intricate link between boundaries and membership.

3. Japan's instrumentalization of liminality

So, as an original member of this mechanism of global governance, the focus now shifts to the role played by the Japanese government in negotiating, inscribing and reinscribing the boundaries of international society through the G8. As will be demonstrated later in five cases, the concept of liminality captures the strategy adopted by the Japanese government in a way that brings the link between membership and boundaries into relief.

Australia and Indonesia

In the case of the G8's interaction with two accepted members of international society – Australia and Indonesia – the Japanese government has demonstrated an innovative approach largely independent of the majority of its fellow summiteers that has sought to engage these non-G8 countries within the deliberations at the centre of international society by creating a liminal space.

As regards Australia, its membership of the summit had been discussed prior to the first G6 summit in 1975 but ultimately no invitation was extended. However, this did not deter the Japanese government from pursuing a strategy of attempting to include Australia in the summit process. Upon the conclusion of the 1985 Bonn Summit, for example, Prime Minister Nakasone Yasuhiro extended an invitation to the other summit leaders to Tokyo the following year and highlighted Australia's possible participation in order 'to mark the advent of the Pacific Age' (*The Japan Times*, 5 May 1985). Similarly, Prime Minister Miyazawa Kiichi's sherpa at the third Tokyo Summit in 1993, Matsuura Kōichirō, was eager to include Australia as part of Japan's role as the representative of the Asia-Pacific region at the summit (Gyōten *et al.* 1993: 39). It took until the 2008 Hokkaidō-Tōyako Summit for the Japanese government to be successful in realizing this goal by inviting Australian Prime Minister Kevin Rudd to participate in the meeting of the leaders of major economies and the outreach working lunch on the final day of the summit.

Faced by the failure of these attempts prior to 2008, the Japanese government adopted a strategy of bringing Australia into a liminal space on the boundary between international society and the G8 by engaging with the Australian government through pre- and post-summit dialogues. For example, before the 1979 Tokyo Summit, the first G7 summit to be held in Asia, Prime Minister Ōhira Masayoshi declared his intention to visit Australia after the summit in order to report its outcomes (*The Japan Times*, 19 June 1979). Similar initiatives were evident ahead of the 1981 Ottawa Summit, when Foreign Minister Sonoda Sunao met with the Australian foreign minister in New York before his arrival in Ottawa (*The Japan Times*, 16 July 1981). Finally, before the 1982 Versailles Summit, Prime Minister Suzuki Zenkō welcomed Australian Prime Minister Malcolm Fraser to Tokyo in May to discuss the recovery of the world economy with the upcoming G7 summit in mind (*Asahi Shimbun*, 22 May 1982).

In the case of Indonesia, the Japanese government similarly sought to embrace it within the summit process through a strategy of liminality. For example, Ōhira met with Indonesian President Suharto before the first 1979 Tokyo Summit to discuss issues of regional concern at the upcoming summit (*The Japan Times*, 8 June 1979). Four years later, in preparation for the 1983 Williamsburg Summit, Nakasone promised Suharto in a telephone conversation that he would communicate Association of Southeast Asian Nations (ASEAN) views to the summit (*The Japan Times*, 15 May 1983). Finally, before the 1991 London Summit, Foreign

Minister Nakayama Tarō met with Suharto and discussed a range of Asian perspectives on summit issues, particularly on aid and trade (*Mainichi Shimbun*, 15
June 1991).

However, the 1993 Tokyo Summit represented the most active attempt on the
part of the Japanese government to instrumentalize a strategy of liminality and
create a diplomatic (and physical) space on the edges of the summit to include
non-summit members. To some extent, this presaged the policy of 'outreach' that
became a characteristic of the G8 in the first decade of the twenty-first century.
For Suharto's part, he wanted the opportunity to speak to the summit leaders in
his capacity as chairman of the Non-Aligned Movement (NAM) and threatened to
visit Tokyo during the summit even if uninvited (*The Japan Times*, 7 April 1993).
On the Japanese side, the Ministry of Foreign Affairs (MOFA) was sensitive to the
opinions of fellow summiteers who opposed Suharto's attendance and was seeking
to placate and accommodate the Indonesian president. Thus, it eventually arranged
an unofficial meeting between Suharto and interested leaders on the edges of the
summit (*The Japan Times*, 1 May 1993; *Mainichi Shimbun*, 27 May 1993; *The
Japan Times*, 17 June 1993).

The Tokyo Summit took place from 7 to 9 July and overlapped with Suharto's
visit from 4 to 7 July. During this time, he conducted meetings with Miyazawa to
discuss the issues of East Asian interest that Japan would promote to the summit
leaders as host and representative of the region, and with US President Bill Clinton
on the morning before the summit officially began to communicate NAM's views
and discuss trade, human rights and East Timor. The liminal and seemingly con-
tradictory position of Suharto at the summit was captured in the media observation
that he was 'the summit's most prominent uninvited guest' (*Far Eastern Economic
Review*, 15 July 1993: 78). Once again, it was not until the 2008 Hokkaidō-Tōyako
Summit that the Japanese government successfully invited Indonesian President
Susilo Bambang Yudhoyono to participate officially alongside Australia in the
meeting of the leaders of major economies and the outreach working lunch on the
final day of the G8 summit.

The liminal space in question in the cases of Australia and Indonesia exists on
the boundary between international society and the G8 as a self-appointed *direc-
toire* of that society (see Figure 1.1). Either through pre- and post-summit briefings
or unilateral and consensual invitations, the Japanese government has sought to
blur the distinction between the two sides of this boundary. To a great extent the
Japanese government has been more innovative than its other summit partners
in these efforts and its motivation can be found in the government and people's
overall attitude to the G8 summit process: a desire to secure and reinforce its self-
appointed position as the sole representative of the Asian region (*Ajia no daihyō*).
Throughout the four decades of summitry at the highest level, Japanese prime
ministers and MOFA officials repeatedly have been eager to shift the attention of
the Western members away from Europe and North America towards economic,
political and security issues in Asia. Promoting liminal spaces in the membership of the G8 has supported the realization of this goal as well as the shifting of
boundaries.

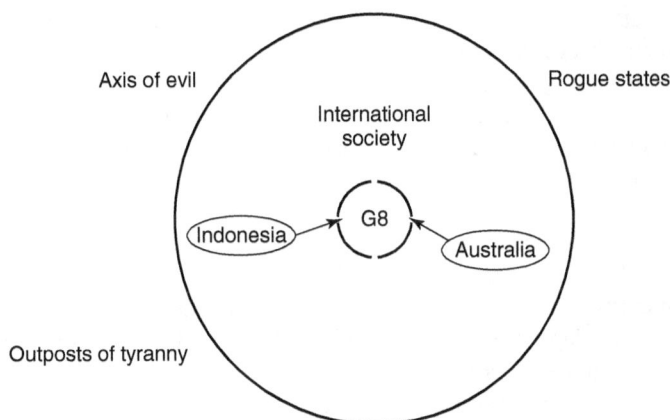

Figure 1.1 The case of Australia and Indonesia

China

Recent discussions of G8 expansion have focused upon China as the most likely future member of any expanded forum. The interest appears to be mutual and despite a tradition of opposition to the G8 summit process, the Chinese government has over recent years exhibited a growing interest in the institutions and mechanisms of global governance generally, and membership of the G8 specifically. As Professor Jia Qingguo of Beijing University has explained, 'China is a more and more active member of the international community – and the G8 stands for prestige' (*The Japan Times*, 31 May 2003). To this end, Chinese President Hu Jintao accepted the French government's invitation and participated at the 2003 Evian Summit for the first time as part of an enlarged dialogue meeting and since then has participated in each of the subsequent six summits. At first glance, it appears that the G8 is instrumentalizing a strategy of liminality as part of its policy of outreach similar to that utilized by Japan *vis-à-vis* Australia and Indonesia, which seeks to blur the distinction between international society and the G8's central position within that society.

However, despite recent developments, the G8's relationship with China has a longer history characterized by efforts to exclude it both from international society and the summit process, as demonstrated in the summit documentation outlined in Section 2 earlier. What is more, Japan's position has shifted from one of divergence from its G8 partners in its past attempts to use liminality to include China within international society to resisting its complete integration within the G8 in the face of its fellow summiteers' creation of liminal spaces to accommodate China.

China first became the focus of the G7's attention with the Tiananmen Square massacre of 1989. In reaction, the Western summit members denounced the Chinese government's behaviour as outside the realms of what is acceptable in international society and used the G7 to introduce sanctions; the French hosts of the 1989 Paris Summit were particularly eager to place human rights at the centre of the summit's agenda upon the bicentennial of the French Revolution. In contrast, the Japanese government sought to appeal to the other summiteers to soften and eventually lift these sanctions by operating a strategy of liminality along the boundary between membership of and exclusion from international society. Prior to the summit, Prime Minister Uno Sōsuke conducted the customary meetings with former prime ministers and summit participants and was urged to resist G7 attempts to isolate China and introduce sanctions (*Asahi Shimbun*, 10 July 1989 evening edition; *Mainichi Shimbun*, 11 July 1989).

The interests and motivations shaping Japan's rejection of sanctions included a desire to protect Japanese business interests in China and a fear that isolation rather than engagement might provoke a backlash from the Chinese (Takagi 1995: 102–05). Pre-summit preparations continued along a similar line when MOFA Minister Mitsuzuka Hiroshi met with US President George H. W. Bush a month before the summit and stated that 'to ensure peace and stability in Asia, sanctions that further isolated China should not be imposed' (*The Japan Times*, 29 June 1989). Ten days before the summit, Mitsuzuka announced that the Japanese government would oppose any singling-out of China for criticism at Paris (*The Japan Times*, 5 July 1989).

However, the extent to which the Japanese government was isolated from its summit partners on this issue was reflected not only in the French desire to include a strong statement on Tiananmen Square but also in US Secretary of State James Baker's call for a united front on the issue of human rights' abuses in China (*The Japan Times*, 5 July 1989). Whereas Japan was attempting to create a liminal space on the boundary between inclusion in and exclusion from international society, its G7 summit partners failed to distinguish liminal opportunities and instead perceived clearly distinguished boundaries. Ultimately, the Japanese government was in the short term and for the most part unsuccessful and the G7 issued a political declaration on the second day of the summit that condemned 'the violent repression in China in defiance of human rights' and agreed that 'the examination of new loans by the World Bank be postponed'. However, the declaration's call for 'the Chinese authorities to create conditions which will avoid their isolation and provide for a return to cooperation based upon the resumption of movement towards political and economic reform, and openness' can be seen as recognition of Japan's concerns and evidence of its attempts to keep China engaged (G7 1989b; Takagi 1995: 104–05). After the summit, the Japanese government maintained its engagement with China by instructing MOFA officials to brief their Chinese counterparts about summit discussions (*The Japan Times*, 18 July 1989).

The policy of creating a liminal space on the edge of international society was continued the following year at the 1990 Houston Summit. The political declaration entitled 'Securing Democracy' stated that the G7:

> acknowledge some of the recent developments in China, but believe that the prospects for closer cooperation will be enhanced by renewed political and economic reform, particularly in the field of human rights. We agree to

maintain the measures put into place at last year's Summit, as modified over the course of this year. We will keep them under review for future adjustments to respond to further positive developments in China. For example, in addition to existing lending to meet basic human needs, we will explore whether there are other World Bank loans that would contribute to reform of the Chinese economy, especially loans that would address environmental concerns.

(G7 1990)

Finally, in August 1991, Prime Minister Kaifu Toshiki was the first G7 leader to visit post-Tiananmen China where he announced the full resumption of Japanese yen loans (Takagi 1995: 107).

Thus, as regards the G7's first substantial engagement with China, the Japanese government was able to blur the distinct boundary between exclusion from and inclusion in international society, which its summit partners were attempting to uphold, and keep China within the boundaries of international society by modifying the statements of the 1989 Paris Summit and acting independently of the G7.

Thereafter, China's relations with the G8 entered a new stage at the beginning of the twenty-first century when attention shifted to Chinese representation at the summit. Thus, the boundary had shifted from the outer limits of international society to the division between international society and the G8 and, as mentioned earlier, the G8's approach has been one of outreach that seeks to create liminal spaces at the edge of the summit for China (and other touted members) to participate. Although the Japanese government enacted a similar policy as seen in Prime Minister Obuchi Keizō's unsuccessful pre-outreach attempt to invite China to the 2000 Okinawa Summit as an observer (which was met with little interest) and Prime Minister Fukuda Yasuo's successful inclusion of China on the final day of the 2008 Hokkaidō-Tōyako Summit as part of an outreach meeting with the Group of 5 (Brazil, China, India, Mexico and South Africa), there are clear boundaries to the Japanese government's enthusiasm for China's full participation in the future. The Japanese government supports Chinese participation as long as it is limited to the enlarged dialogue meeting and the G8 + G5 Heiligendamm Process started in 2007, where the boundaries of the G8 are not compromised and China enters a demarked liminal space. As regards full membership of an expanded forum, in contrast to the support expressed by G8 countries such as Germany and the UK, the Japanese government has been more reticent, believing that China does not necessarily share the same core values common to the summit countries that serve as informal membership criteria, as highlighted earlier in Section 2. Moreover and possibly as important from the Japanese government's perspective, it finds its role as Asia's sole representative at the summit under threat. In this light, it becomes clear why it has instrumentalized the strategy of liminality at the boundary between acceptance into and rejection from international society, but not at the boundary between acceptance into and rejection from the G8 (see Figure 1.2). Whatever the post-crisis settlement of the Gs may be, conflict could emerge with other summit countries that are promoting a policy of outreach closer to the model instrumentalized by Japan *vis-à-vis* Australia and Indonesia (see Figure 1.1).

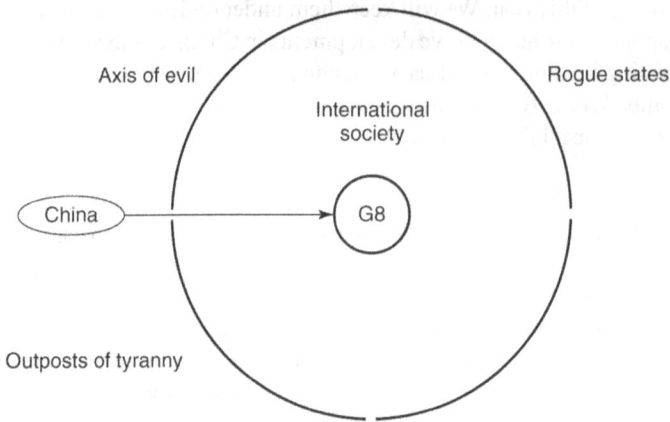

Figure 1.2 The case of China

The Soviet Union/Russia

As discussed earlier, the G7 used its statements and communiqués to cast the Soviet Union outside the boundary of international society. The Soviet Union returned the compliment by traditionally regarding the G7 summits throughout the Cold War as self-appointed and elitist, unrepresentative and largely ceremonial. However, towards the end of the 1980s and during the 1990s as the Cold War structures of bipolarity collapsed, the G7/8 provided one of the chief mechanisms by which the former Soviet Union's transition to capitalism and democracy and acceptance into international society were managed. From the 1989 Paris Summit onwards, where a first attempt was made to invite President Mikhail Gorbachev to attend the meeting in response to his 'letter of surrender' tendered to the G7 leaders and the G24 was created to funnel assistance to Eastern Europe, the G7 addressed in iterative fashion, the issue of providing assistance to the Soviet Union/Russia. What is more, in addition to the assistance provided, it was the inclusion of Russia within the boundaries of the G8 that functioned as an important vehicle for bringing the former Communist superpower into the fold of international society broadly and one of its central mechanisms of global governance specifically.

The incremental trajectory of Russia's inclusion with an expanded G8 was as follows: at the 1989 Paris Summit the French hosts tried but failed to invite Gorbachev; the 1991 London Summit saw Gorbachev participate as an invited guest; at the 1994 Naples Summit, Yeltsin was invited as a 'participant'; the two-day 1996 Nuclear Safety and Security Summit was held in Moscow (providing the first opportunity for Prime Minister Hashimoto Ryūtarō to meet Yeltsin); Yeltsin was invited to attend political discussions at the 1997 Denver Summit, which was known as the Summit of the Eight but not the G8. It was the following year at the

Birmingham Summit that the term 'G8' was used for the first time; Russia's complete integration into the G8 was confirmed at the 2002 Kananaskis Summit when the decision was made that Russia would host the 2006 summit in St Petersburg. Throughout this 17-year process, Russia's main objective was to win acceptance into international society and gain the status associated with membership of this club of modern-day great powers. However, in the run-up to Russia's first summit in 2006 and especially after the 2008 Hokkaidō-Tōyako Summit, Russia's failure to comply with its G8 pledges, its lurch towards authoritarianism under President Vladimir Putin, and its intervention in Georgia during the summer of 2008 under President Dmitry Medvedev led to calls from the US and Europe for Russia's G8 membership to be withdrawn (Jordan 2008).

Within this arc of diplomatic activity, the Japanese government and its people's sentiment was one of resisting the momentum towards Russia's inclusion within both international society and the boundaries of the summit club. On the one hand, as regards the concrete issue of extending assistance to the Soviet Union as the Cold War ended, in contrast to many of its summit partners, especially France and West Germany, the Japanese government opposed providing any concrete assistance while its relations with the Soviet Union continued largely to be shaped, as today, by the Soviet (now Russian) occupation of the Northern Territories. At the time that the G7 was seeking to agree on an aid package for the Soviet Union, Nakayama expressed stubborn opposition until the territorial dispute had been resolved and went further by asking whether this was an effective means of promoting democracy (*Asahi Shimbun*, 5 July 1990); he went as far as comparing it to throwing money into a ditch (*Yomiuri Shimbun*, 22 July 1990).

On the other hand, as discussion shifted during the 1990s from assisting the Soviet Union to embracing Russia within an expanded G8, it was the Japanese government's staunch opposition to Russia's membership that dragged the process out and ensured that the 1997 Denver Summit would be dubbed the 'Summit of the Eight', rather than the G8. Moreover, at the 1998 Birmingham Summit, Hashimoto had to fight to protect Japan's right to host the 2000 summit against Yeltsin's attempts to upset the agreed order and stake Russia's claim as host in that year. The Japanese government's overall strategy of stalling entry was based largely on maintaining and reinforcing the boundaries of international society, the G8's central position within that society and the informal criteria based on shared norms and values that bind it together. In recent years, the proverbial chickens have come home to roost with calls in the US and Europe for the reconsideration of Russia's membership of the G8, as mentioned earlier. This is easier said than done as the G8 has no declared procedure or precedence for disbarring a member. The Japanese government could be forgiven for taking a self-righteous attitude towards its summit partners, as it was always openly wary as regards the integration of the Soviet Union originally and Russia later, suggesting the political value of instrumentalizing liminal space.

In contrast to the case studies of Australia, Indonesia and China, a strategy of liminality, or muddying the space between the two states of exclusion from and membership of the international community or the G8, was never instrumental-

Figure 1.3 The case of Russia

ized. Considering the Japanese government failed completely in its attempts to resist the other G8 countries' desire to integrate the former Soviet Union into international society and Russia into the G8 (see Figure 1.3), the effectiveness of such an alternative approach of keeping Russia in a state of limbo on one of the two boundaries is worthy of speculation. Having invited Russia into the G8, it is now unclear as to how it could be uninvited. A strategy of retaining Russia in a liminal space in relation to the G8 might have made the task easier and concomitantly maintained the integrity of the summit's shared norms in the face of calls for further expansion.

North Korea

In the case of the G8's handling of North Korea and its nuclear programme, the Japanese government has once again eschewed a strategy of liminality in favour of a position that reinforces the boundaries of international society and excludes outsiders (see Figure 1.4). However, unlike that displayed towards Russia, this intransigence has resonated with most other summiteers and can be seen in the language used in summit documentation. It portrays North Korea as a 'rogue state' beyond the boundaries of international society. For example, the 1994 Naples Summit's Chairman's Political Statement emphasized North Korea's position outside of international society:

> Following the death of Kim Il Sung, we must continue to seek a solution to the problem created by North Korea's decision to withdraw from the International Atomic Energy Agency [IAEA]. We urge the DPRK to continue to engage the Republic of Korea [ROK] and the international community, including a

continuation of the talks with the US and going forward with the scheduled summit with the ROK.

(G7 1994)

The Conclusions of G8 Foreign Ministers who met at Miyazaki in the run-up to the 2000 Okinawa Summit similarly placed North Korea outside of the international community:

We reaffirm our support for the ROK's policy of engagement. We welcome the recent steps taken by North Korea toward dialogue with the international community. In this context, we look forward to a constructive response to international concerns over security, non-proliferation, humanitarian and human rights issues.

(G8 2000)

The 2001 Genoa Summit's Statement on Regional Issues struck a more conciliatory tone but still placed North Korea at the margins of the international community:

We expect the DPRK to implement its announced moratorium on missile launches and a constructive response to international concerns over security, non-proliferation, humanitarian and human rights issues that is essential to the reduction of tensions in the region and to further integration of the DPRK into the international community.

(G8 2001b)

However, the meeting of the G8 Foreign Ministers in Paris in 2003 reinforced the threat posed by North Korea to the international community: 'The North Korean

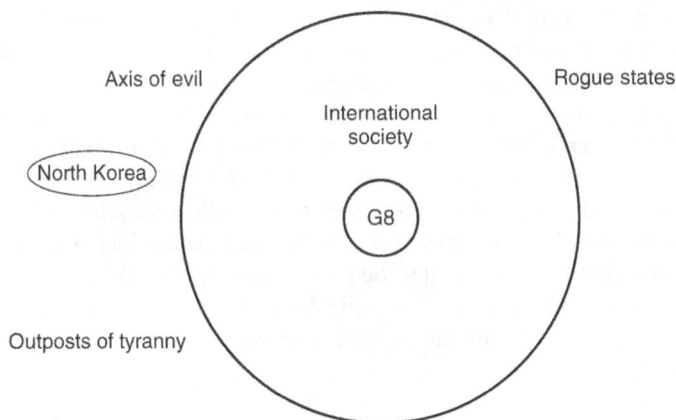

Figure 1.4 The case of North Korea

nuclear issue constitutes a threat to international peace and stability. North Korea's compliance with its non-proliferation commitments is a matter of concern for the entire international community' (G8 2003).

Similar statements were included in the Chair's Summaries issued at the 2005 Gleneagles Summit and the 2007 Heiligendamm Summit respectively:

> On North Korea, we support the Six Party Talks and urged North Korea to return promptly to them. We call on North Korea to abandon its nuclear weapons-related programmes. Action is also long overdue for North Korea to respond to the international community's concern over its human rights record and the abductions issue.
>
> (G8 2005)

> We also urge North Korea to respond to other security and humanitarian concerns of the international community, including the early resolution of the issue of abductions.
>
> (G8 2007)

Prime Minister Koizumi Junichirō reinforced this positioning of North Korea beyond the boundaries of international society when he explained that, with regard to the issue of the kidnappings of Japanese citizens by North Korean government agents throughout the 1970s and 1980s (*racchi jiken*):

> [s]ome of the [G8] leaders expressed that they really found it very difficult to understand the abductions. I also find it very difficult to understand the abductions. Why did they have to kidnap Japanese nationals? I certainly understand the pains and the grief of the parents who had their children abducted. It is utterly inhuman.
>
> (MOFA 2003)

As explored elsewhere (Dobson 2004), one of the Japanese government's goals in promoting a tough line was to attempt to link the abduction issue to the G8's treatment of North Korea's nuclear development programme in order to secure international support; in other words, it was attempting to multilateralize a bilateral issue. This could be seen in the final declaration of the G8 Foreign Ministers' meeting held prior to the 2003 Evian Summit: 'They [G8 Foreign Ministers] supported the efforts made by the different parties to seek a comprehensive solution by peaceful means to the North Korean nuclear issue and to other matters including unresolved humanitarian problems such as the abduction issue' (G8 2003).

This issue appeared explicitly in some form of G8 documentation at the following five summits up until the Statement on Political Issues issued at the 2008 Hokkaidō-Tōyako Summit:

> We express our continuous support for the Six-Party process towards the verifiable denuclearization of the Korean Peninsula and the eventual

normalization of relations between the relevant Six-Party members through the full implementation of the Joint Statement of 19 September 2005, including the resolution of the outstanding issues of concern such as the abduction issue.

In contrast to the isolation that the Japanese government encountered as a result of its independent hard-line policy towards Russia's engagement with the G7, the G8 was willing to speak with one voice on this issue. However, some of Japan's summit partners, most notably the US, moved away from reinforcing boundaries and have instead dangled carrots by removing North Korea from its list of terrorist-sponsoring states in October 2008, thereby creating opportunities for engagement and the redrawing of boundaries in international society.

Conclusion

This chapter introduces the concept of liminality into the study of Japan's international relations in the specific context of the membership of international society and the G8 forum that occupies a central position therein. What immediately comes into relief is a clear dichotomy in the application of this strategy. On the one hand, liminality appears to have provided the opportunity for inclusion, as seen in the cases of Australia and Indonesia's participation in the G8 or China's membership of international society. On the other hand, however, it does not appear to have functioned as a mechanism for exclusion. Rather, when attempting to exclude a country from international society or the G8, the maintenance of strict boundaries has tended to prevail. For the most part, the latter has proved to be an unsuccessful strategy for the Japanese government. It failed in its attempts to exclude Russia along these lines and was faced by an overwhelming majority among its summit partners in favour of opening up spaces to embrace Russia within an expanded G8. Nevertheless, in the case of handling North Korea as an issue, the consensual nature of the G8 was again important and facilitated the Japanese government's successful promotion of its national bilateral interests in a multilateral forum and the maintenance of North Korea's pariah status outside the boundaries of international society. In short, although they may be transformed by liminality, the nature, membership and other characteristics of institutions still matter.

Within this necessarily limited exploration, a number of potentially illuminating areas for future research can be identified. The Japanese government's strategy of liminality clearly predates the G8's policy of outreach that has tried over recent years to imbue the forum with greater legitimacy. Thus, the Japanese government deservedly can claim to be an innovative summiteer. At the same time, this strategy serves the promotion of its national interests and position as Asia's representative within the summit process. Ultimately, this approach could be seen as particularly suited to Japan, with its preference for a 'quietly proactive diplomacy' that stresses informality, multiple levels of activity and long-term policymaking (Hook *et al.* 2005: 444–48). Moreover, if we think of liminality in relation to Mikhail Bakhtin's concept of the *carnivalesque*, it similarly creates a time and space in which usually unacceptable behavior becomes acceptable. Thus, the instrumentalization of liminality creates the opportunity for the Japanese government to behave in a more proactive manner beyond the boundary of what would normally be regarded as acceptable. If liminality can be regarded as a particularly appropriate concept for making sense of Japan's international relations in this case, its application in other areas of Japan's diplomatic activity, and especially in other multilateral fora, may yield equally useful analyses.

Note

1 For the sake of clarity, G6 will be used to refer to the first summit meeting of the leaders of France, Italy, Japan, the US, the UK and West Germany held at Rambouillet in 1975; G7 will be used to refer to the period from 1976 to 1997 when Canada joined the original six; and G8 will be used more generally and also to refer to the specific period since Russia officially became the eighth member at the 1998 Birmingham Summit.

References

Bull, Hedley (2002) *The Anarchical Society: a study of order in world politics*, Basingstoke: Palgrave.

Calder, Kent E. (1988) 'Japanese economic foreign policy formation: explaining the reactive state', *World Politics*, 40, 4: 517–41.

—— (2003) 'Japan as a post-reactive state', *Orbis*, 47, 4: 605–16.

Culpeper, Roy (2003) 'Systemic Reform at a Standstill: a flock of "Gs" in search of global financial stability'. Online. Available: https://tspace.library.utoronto.ca/retrieve/1095 (accessed 11 December 2009).

Den Boer, Andrea (2003) *Beyond Politics: Emmanuel Levinas' biblical humanism*, unpublished thesis, Kent University.

Dobson, Hugo (2004) 'Japan and the G8 Evian Summit: bilateralism, East Asianism and multilateralization', *G8 Governance*, 9: 1–17. Online. Available: http://www.g7.utoronto.ca/governance/dobson_g8g.pdf (accessed 14 January 2008).

Dunne, Tim (1998) *Inventing International Society: a history of the English School*, Basingstoke: Palgrave.

G6 (1975) *Declaration of Rambouillet*, 17 November. Online. Available: http://www.g8.utoronto.ca/summit/1975rambouillet/communique.html (accessed 19 February 2008).

G7 (1984a) *Declaration on International Terrorism*, 9 June. Online. Available: http://www.g8.utoronto.ca/summit/1984london/terrorism.html (accessed 4 March 2008).

—— (1984b) *The London Economic Declaration*, 9 June. Online. Available: http://www.g8.utoronto.ca/summit/1984london/communique.html (accessed 4 March 2008).

—— (1986) *Statement on International Terrorism*, 5 May. Online. Available: http://www.g8.utoronto.ca/summit/1986tokyo/terrorism.html (accessed 4 March 2008).

—— (1988) *Political Declaration: Securing Democracy*, 20 June. Online. Available: http://www.g8.utoronto.ca/summit/1988toronto/political.html (accessed 4 March 2008).

—— (1989a) *Economic Declaration*, 16 July. Online. Available: http://www.g8.utoronto.ca/summit/1989paris/communique/environment.html (accessed 4 March 2008).

—— (1989b) *Declaration on China*, 15 July. Online. Available: http://www.g8.utoronto.ca/summit/1989paris/china.html (accessed 4 March 2008).

—— (1990) *Political Declaration: securing democracy*, 10 July. Online. Available: http://www.g8.utoronto.ca/summit/1990houston/political.html (accessed 4 March 2008).

—— (1991a) *Political Declaration: strengthening the international order*, 16 July. Online. Available: http://www.g8.utoronto.ca/summit/1991london/political.html (accessed 4 March 2008).

—— (1991b) *Economic Declaration: building world partnership*, 17 July. Online. Available: http://www.g8.utoronto.ca/summit/1991london/communique/index.html (accessed 4 March 2008).

—— (1991c) *Chairman's Statement*, 16 July. Online. Available: http://www.g8.utoronto. ca/summit/1991london/chairman.html (accessed 4 March 2008).

—— (1993) *Political Declaration: striving for a more secure and humane world*, 8 July. Online. Available: http://www.g8.utoronto.ca/summit/1993tokyo/political.html (accessed 4 March 2008).

—— (1994) *Chairman's Statement*, 10 July. Online. Available: http://www.g8.utoronto.ca/summit/1994naples/chairman.html (accessed 4 March 2008).

G8 (2000) *Conclusions of the Meeting of the G8 Foreign Ministers' Meeting* [sic], 13 July. Online. Available: http://www.g8.utoronto.ca/foreign/fm000713.htm (accessed 4 March 2008).

—— (2001a) *Conclusions of the Meeting of the G8 Foreign Ministers' Meeting* [sic], 18–19 July. Online. Available: http://www.g8.utoronto.ca/foreign/fm091901_conclusion.html (accessed 4 March 2008).

—— (2001b) *G8 Statement on Regional Issues*, 21 July. Online. Available: http://www. g8.utoronto.ca/summit/2001genoa/regionalissues.html (accessed 4 March 2008).

—— (2003) *Summary of the G8 Presidency: G8 foreign ministers meeting in Paris*, 22–23 May. Online. Available: http://www.g8.utoronto.ca/foreign/fm230503.htm (accessed 5 February 2008).

—— (2005) *Chair's Summary*, 8 July, Online. Available: http://www.g8.utoronto.ca/summit/2005gleneagles/summary.html (accessed 4 March 2008).

—— (2007) *Chair's Summary*, 8 June. Online. Available: http://www.g8.utoronto.ca/summit/2007heiligendamm/g8–2007-summary.html (accessed 4 March 2008).

Gyōten, Toyō, Nukazawa, Kazuo, Matsuura, Kōichirō and Mine, Yoshiki (1993) 'Zadankai: Nihon wa Ajia Taiheiyō no daihyō toshite no kōdō o', *Gaikō Fōramu*, 56, March: 22–39.

Hajnal, Peter I. and Kirton, John (2000) 'The evolving role and agenda of the G7/G8: a North American perspective', *NIRA Review*, 7, 2: 5–10.

Hook, Glenn D., Gilson, Julie, Hughes, Christopher W., and Dobson, Hugo (2005) *Japan's International Relations: politics, economics and security*, London: Routledge.

Jordan, Pamela (2008) 'Expel Russia from the G8?' *Open Democracy*, 15 August. Online. Available: http://www.opendemocracy.net/russia/article/should-russia-be-expelled-from-G8 (accessed 4 September 2008).

Kishima, Takako (1991) *Political Life in Japan: democracy in a reversible world*, Princeton: Princeton University Press.

MOFA (2003) *Press Conference*, 3 June. Online. Available: http://www.mofa.go.jp/policy/economy/summit/2003/press.html (accessed 5 February 2008).

Takagi, Seiichiro (1995) 'Human rights in Japanese foreign policy: Japan's policy towards China after Tiananmen', in James T. H. Tang (ed.) *Human Rights and International Relations in the Asia-Pacific Region*, London and New York: Pinter, pp. 97–111.

Turner, Victor W. (1995) *The Ritual Process: structure and anti-structure*, New York: Aldine de Gruyter.

Van Gennep, Arnold (1960) *The Rites of Passage*, Chicago: The University of Chicago Press.

Weber, Cynthia (2001) *International Relations Theory: a critical introduction*, Routledge: London.

Yasutomo, Dennis T. (1995) *The New Multilateralism in Japan's Foreign Policy*, New York: St Martin's Press.

2 The strange masochism of the Japanese right

Redrawing moral boundaries in Sino-Japanese relations

Shogo Suzuki

As the Chinese New Year approached in 2007, another food scare involving Chinese products flared up in Japan. The culprit this time was Chinese dumplings (*gyōza* or *jiaozi*), often eaten during Chinese New Year celebrations. The incident itself can be described as a minor diplomatic irritant, and it appears that both sides dealt with the matter in a routine manner through diplomatic channels. Chinese Foreign Ministry Official He Yafei expressed his regret and told Japanese Foreign Minister Kōmura Masahiko that the Chinese authorities had stopped exporting the dumplings and were investigating the matter (Asahi.com 2008a). In light of this issue, the two governments also agreed to speed up the ratification of a treaty designed to further Sino-Japanese cooperation on criminal investigations.

The Japanese right, however, appears to have interpreted this incident in a rather different light. 'The Japanese government and media who grovel to the Chinese Communist Party (CCP), as well as companies who are only interested in profits', the Ishin Seitō Shinpū (Restoration Party – New Wind) website roared, 'are responsible for hiding the Chinese food product terrorism incident and threatening the lives and security of the Japanese' (Ishin Seitō Shinpū 2008). The party's Tokyo representative Suzuki Nobuyuki also lamented that the greedy (*haikin shugi*) Japanese firms were seemingly indifferent to this incident, and wrote in his blog:

> These people are not Chinese and neither are they CCP cadres. Can they really be engaged in commerce at the expense of their country? CCP cadres apparently save money and invest overseas. They care about themselves rather than their country, and they don't respect or trust their country. *But we Japanese are different. We used to be different.*[1]
>
> (Suzuki 2008, emphasis added)

While not necessarily using similar inflammatory language, the *Sankei Shimbun* correspondent Komori Yoshihisa voices his scepticism of joint efforts by China and Japan to tackle the problem. According to Komori, Japan needs to think about itself first and ensure that contaminated Chinese goods do not enter Japanese borders. He argues further than Sino-Japanese cooperation is not feasible because of the fundamental *difference* between China and Japan. Komori argues: 'the emergence of poisonous goods in China is not a special case limited to one factory or area. It is a phenomenon involving the political and economic system, and social values of the *entire* country' (Komori 2008).

These responses are somewhat curious, to say the least. While it is true that Beijing often lacks the capacity to enforce central government food standards regulations, it is not as if the authorities do not care or are unaware of these problems. Furthermore, this food scare issue is qualitatively different from territorial disputes, which can and often have taken on a zero-sum nature. It is neither in China nor Japan's interest to lose valuable trade, and this gives ample scope for Sino-Japanese cooperation. The fact that both governments have successfully managed the food scare issue and agreed to cooperate further confirms this point (Asahi.com 2008b). The idiosyncratic responses of the Japanese right, however, seem to almost negate the possibility of cooperation. Constructivist scholarship of International Relations has argued that social actors' interests are determined by their identities (Wendt 1999). By actively *differentiating* between China and Japan's identities and drawing strict boundaries between the two states, the Japanese right's point of view minimizes the possibility of bilateral cooperation.

But why would the Japanese right feel the need to differentiate Japan from China when cooperation is in this particular case clearly in the interests of both sides? The central argument of this chapter draws on English School debates of 'legitimate membership' of international society (Gong 1984; Suzuki 2005; Clark 2005), and suggests that this phenomenon is part of an attempt by the Japanese right to inscribe boundaries between Japan and China in order to shore up Japan's identity as a 'righteous, honourable' state. Japan's image has recently taken a battering as a result of former Prime Minister Koizumi Junichirō's controversial visits to Yasukuni Shrine (for more on the shrine, see Breen 2008), which brought the thorny issue of Japanese war responsibility into sharper international focus. In the post-Cold War international society which is argued to be characterized by an increasing concern for liberal democratic governance and respect for human rights – including human rights abuses which took place in the past, as seen by an increase in state apologies issued by former colonial powers for their historical crimes – such developments were damaging for Japan's claims to legitimate membership of this social group (Clark 2005: 159–61; Gibney and Roxstrom 2001). In order to contest this, the Japanese right has sought to redraw the *moral boundaries* between Japan and its loudest critic, China. By doing so, such individuals have sought to bring *China's* legitimacy as a member of international society into question. This is done in various ways: one way is to engage in a Japanese form of 'Orientalism', which portrays China as 'irrational' or 'childlike', and thereby unfit for membership of 'civilized' international society. Another way is to contrast Japan's democratic system of governance with the authoritarian Chinese regime, taking advantage of the aforementioned 'humanitarian turn' in international society, and placing China 'beyond the pale'. Whichever strategy is employed, the goal is the same: by portraying China as an 'unethical' state that unfairly and hypocritically vilifies Japan by playing the 'history card', the Japanese right aims to shore up

Japan's identity as an 'ethical' state and restore its claims to 'legitimate' membership within the society of states.

A blanket term such as the 'Japanese right' should be used with some caution. In using this term, this chapter includes individuals who appear to hold one or more of the following three viewpoints, which will be expanded upon as follows: First, there are individuals within the Japanese right who can be characterized by their revisionist tendencies towards the 'Tokyo War Crimes Tribunal History', which depicted Japan as an aggressor in the Asia-Pacific War. A second trait is a general dissatisfaction with Japan's 'weak diplomacy'. However, the Japanese right is different from what Hughes calls the 'normalisers' who call for Japan to be a more 'proactive military power' (Hughes 2004: 49) but do not see the post-war settlement in an entirely negative light. The Japanese right often does share the belief with 'normalisers' that Japan should shake off the post-1945 normative restrictions that have prevented Japan from playing a prominent role in security matters. The right's stance, however, tends to be closer to the Japanese 'Gaullist' position, which adopts a dim view of post-World War II Japan as unnecessarily subservient to foreign interests – usually those of the United States (US), China, or Korea – and unable to 'function as a truly independent sovereign state' (Hughes 2004: 51).

Finally, there is a strong sense of dislike towards the People's Republic of China (PRC). This characteristic is the most common unifier for individuals of the Japanese right as defined in this chapter, even though some of them may not be historical revisionists. At one level, there is a genuine sense of anger towards the highly xenophobic form of anti-Japanese demonstrations in China. As we seek to demonstrate below, many members of the Japanese right believe that Beijing's loud protests about Japan's attitude towards its war responsibility stem from domestic political needs. The result is a growing sense of irritation and exasperation that Chinese demands are never going to stop interfering in Japan's internal affairs. Agawa Hiroyuki, a writer well known for his works which portray a positive image of the Japanese Imperial Navy, writes that there is a 'Sino-centric mindset, unchanged for 1,800 years, deep down in the Chinese psyche . . . Even if the Yasukuni or textbook problems quieten down, they will soon find new issues and order us about again and again' (Agawa 2001: 78).

The chapter proceeds as follows. First, it examines the Japanese right's attempts to contest the negative images of Japan prompted by Koizumi's Yasukuni visits, the comfort women issue and Japan's war responsibility. The second section explores how the Japanese right has redrawn moral boundaries between Japan and China, and how this is intended to restore Japan's moral standing in the international community. Japan's atrocities towards Asian peoples have become increasingly acknowledged in both domestic society and the international community in recent years, despite the Japanese right's attempts to deny or trivialize them. This poses a severe threat to the Japanese right's attempts to restore national pride and international respect for its country. In order to contest what it considers as Asian attempts to stigmatize Japan, the right has sought to portray Japan as a morally upright state which is undeserving of such negative treatment. This process of national identity formation, however, requires an 'Other' which is used to high-light the identity of the 'Self' by emphasizing *difference*. Accordingly, the Japa-nese right has chosen to depict the PRC as an unethical, uncivilized state which is involved in a conspiracy to denounce and relentlessly 'bully' Japan. However, in order to highlight a 'victimizing' China, the Japanese right has had to construct an identity of a 'victimized' Japan. This ironically necessitates the maintenance of a 'weak' Japan, for which the Japanese right has constantly criticized the Japanese left.

1. War responsibility and Japanese identity

The Japanese right's most recent attempts to redraw the moral boundaries between China and Japan can be interpreted largely as a response to the increasing criti-cism Japan has received for the manner in which it has faced up to its imperialist history. While the Japanese right is by no means monolithic, the reactions of key members of the right to issues of Japan's imperialist history illuminate a number of traits commonly shared among members of this group.

First, calls for Japan to face its imperialist past are disputed by the Japanese right as a reproduction of the historical narrative created by the Tokyo War Crimes Tribunal (known as *Tokyo Saiban Shi Kan* in Japanese), which, the group argues, unfairly painted a malevolent picture of Japan and Japanese imperialism. While some do not necessarily endorse the more revisionist view that the Asia-Pacific War was aimed at liberating the Asian states from European colonialism, most do view the judgement of the Tribunal as hypocritical, as it derided Japanese aggres-sion in the region while absolving European/American colonialist powers (Yoshida 2005: 12–16). This breeds the perception that the Japanese have been brainwashed into accepting a negative image of their country. As Sakurai Yoshiko states:

> American values which condemned Japan were instilled into small children and youth, who did not know the process by which Japan entered the war. If only the war-time generation had told them about this, we could have pre-vented this 'brainwashing'. It makes me cross to think about it.
>
> (Sakurai 2002: 57)

As the most vociferous critics of Japanese 'historical amnesia' tend to be China and Korea, this sentiment becomes particularly acute whenever Tokyo is perceived to be engaging in 'kowtow diplomacy' (*dogeza gaikō*), primarily by accommodating China and Korea's concerns.

Second, the Japanese right believes that the acceptance of the 'Tokyo War Crimes Tribunal narrative' and Japan's wrongdoing during the Asia-Pacific War exerts a powerful and perverse influence over the Japanese nation. The Japanese right claims that this particular interpretation of history has the effect of making Japanese citizens 'hate' their country. This results in an education which teaches younger generations to feel '. . . "ashamed to be born Japanese", "a sense of dis-like for a country whose forefathers [lit. grandfathers] were murderers" . . . and instil a feeling that "I am part of an inferior race and the descendant of criminals"' (Atarashii Kyōkasho o Tsukuru Kai [a]), thus besmirching the memories of the Japanese war dead. The views of a Japanese international lawyer who supported the Tokyo War Crimes Tribunal and depicted the Asia-Pacific War as a 'war of extreme aggression' are thus depicted as 'filthy, rotten hatred and disdain . . . towards the Japanese people . . . which makes one feel ill' (Tanizawa 2005: 167). The Japanese Society for History Textbook Reform has responded in similar fashion to recent government moves to provide a clearer depiction of the role played by the Japanese military in forcing civilian mass suicides in Okinawa:

> The approval of writing about military-forced [mass suicides] . . . is a path towards allowing for anti-military and anti-Japanese ideology. Moreover, this harms the honour of those who died in the suicides, their relatives, the ex-military personnel, the populace of Okinawa prefecture and the Japanese people and state.
>
> (Atarashii Kyōkasho o Tsukuru Kai 2008: 2)

To make matters worse, such views are seen to breed a treacherous group of Japanese who act in a servile way towards the Chinese and Koreans. These anti-Japanese Japanese (*han nichi teki nipponjin*) side with Beijing and Seoul and pressure Tokyo to capitulate to Chinese and Korean demands. This effectively emasculates the Japanese state, as it renders Japan unable to stand up to such blatant acts of interference in Japan's 'domestic affairs'. It also magnifies Japan's poor international image and prevents it from playing a political role in the international community that is commensurate with its economic power. In the eyes of the Japanese right, then, such 'traitors' are 'masochistic'. By calling for the maintenance of the pacifist Constitution and its Article 9 and supporting China and Korea in political disputes, the *han nichi techi nipponjin* are bent on perpetuating a weak, feeble Japan with little political and military power in the international community. Although not in the specific context of Sino-Japanese or Sino-Korean relations, Hayashi Fusao demonstrates this point when he cites Muramatsu Takeshi's reportage of masculine, fiercely patriotic American soldiers in Vietnam, and juxtaposes this with the unpatriotic (and presumably feminine) Japanese citizenry (Hayashi 2006: 15–16), unable and unwilling to stand up for Japan's vital interests.

In this context, China's decrying of Japan's 'historical amnesia' constitutes a grave challenge to the Japanese right's ongoing attempts to construct a 'strong', 'internationally respected' identity for the Japanese state. The first challenge is that Chinese (and indeed other Asian states' and people's) criticisms of Japanese war crimes make it difficult for the Japanese right to relativize Japan's imperialism and reduce its moral responsibility. This is because China, alongside Korea and Taiwan, was primarily a *victim* of Japanese aggression. Japan's other main adversary of World War II, the US, can be interpreted as both a 'victim' of Japan and (more importantly) an 'aggressor' against Japan because of its fire-bombing of Japanese cities or the dropping of the atomic bombs in Hiroshima and Nagasaki. As such, the US–Japan war does not completely challenge the Japanese right's attempts to enhance Japan's international standing: Japan's unsavoury wartime atrocities can be relativized alongside American war-time atrocities or their 'criminal' post-war 'brainwashing' of the Japanese people, and any American criticism of Japanese war crimes can be dismissed as 'hypocritical'. Such arguments, however, are difficult to pull off against China (and indeed other Asian victims of Japanese aggression). While the US and China can both (as we will see in the case of China later on) be seen as 'victimizers' who try to keep Japan in a lowly international position, the Japanese right cannot easily label the Chinese as 'victimizing' Japan as they can with the US when it comes to moral conduct during World War II. The Asian states and peoples who bore the brunt of some of the most horrific Japanese atrocities during the Asia-Pacific War did not have the military power to inflict damage on Japanese lives to the same extent as the US did.

This puts the Japanese right on the defensive. Chinese (and other Asian states') charges of Japan's aggression cannot be dismissed easily, and threatens the right's attempts to construct a 'righteous' Japanese state which can hold its head high and be accorded the international respect it deserves. Conservative writer Kamisaka Fuyuko's interview with Katō Kōichi, the Liberal Democratic Party (LDP) Diet member who has called for the construction of an alternative war memorial to Yasukuni Shrine, provides a typical example of this point:

> Katō: Electioneering for the past 30 years has given me the opportunity to ask octogenarians about what happened in the past. When I ask them, 'Is it true that the Japanese military did cruel things to the Chinese?', most reply 'Yes, it's true'.
> Kamisaka: Wars do make people go crazy, don't they. . . . When the Japanese were leaving Manchuria, many of them were treated very cruelly by the Chinese as well. What the Soviets did in Siberia [to Japanese Prisoners of War] and America's dropping of the atomic bomb was pretty cruel too.
> (Kamisaka and Katō 2006: 139)

Here, Kamisaka employs a typical strategy of juxtaposing Chinese, American, and Soviet atrocities alongside Japanese ones, and attempts to demonstrate that Japan was not the only aggressor.[2] It is interesting to note, however, that when it comes to the subject of China, Kamisaka is forced to concede that the Japanese *did* commit atrocities. Even though she attempts to absolve Japanese soldiers from their responsibilities in atrocities by claiming they had gone 'crazy', she is unable to accuse Japan's Asian victims of hypocrisy, and this has the effect of undermining her attempts to downplay Japan's ethical responsibility for its war crimes.

The second challenge for the Japanese right is that the Asian protests appear – at least in its eyes – to have had the effect of further entrenching the 'masochistic' or 'un-patriotic' view of Japan and its history among the populace. There are a number of facets to this. First, criticisms of Japan's 'historical amnesia' have highlighted Japanese aggression in Asia and actually diluted the notion that Japan was a 'victim' of the war.[3] The history controversy surrounding Koizumi's visits to the Yasukuni Shrine also prompted intense domestic debates on Japan's war responsibility. One of the results of this was a report on Japan's war responsibility published by the *Yomiuri Shimbun* (Tennichi 2007: 45). The report's conclusions tend to focus on how political and military leaders were responsible for caus- ing suffering among the Japanese people, and Japan's *international* responsibili- ties arguably fade into the background. However, it is important to note that the *Yomiuri* findings portrayed the Asia-Pacific War as motivated by Japan's quest for resources, rather than the liberation of colonized Asian peoples, as some seg- ments in the Japanese right argue. The report also implicates a wider segment of Japanese society for the responsibility of carrying out the war. By widening the number of Japanese 'victimizers' beyond the narrow confines of the Japanese militarists, *Yomiuri* reminds their 'many readers of their ongoing relationship to the past' (Morris-Suzuki 2007: 188).

Furthermore – the limitations of the *Yomiuri* project notwithstanding – the number of Japanese who consider Japan to be a 'victimizer' towards Asian states and peoples is also rising. Yoshida notes that 'since the 1980s there has been a sharp rise in the number of people admitting to the aggressive nature of the [Asia- Pacific War]' (Yoshida 2005: 243), even though an NHK poll conducted in 1982, 1987 and 1994 showed that 30–40 per cent of respondents still considered such wars 'inevitable' for a resource-poor country like Japan to survive (Yoshida 2005: 244–46).[4] A *Yomiuri* poll conducted in October 2005 also indicated that 34.2 per cent of respondents considered both wars with China and the US as 'wars of aggression' (*shinryaku sensō*), while a further 33.9 per cent considered the Sino- Japanese War as a 'war of aggression'. This means that as far as the Sino-Japanese War of 1931–45 is concerned, 68.1 per cent believed that Japan was the aggres- sor. Furthermore, 47 per cent were of the opinion that the Japanese needed to feel a continued sense of responsibility towards the damages inflicted on Asia (as opposed to 44.8 per cent who felt that this was no longer necessary) (*Yomiuri Shimbun Sensō Sekinin Kenshō Iinkai* 2006: 212, 215). Most significant is that this poll was conducted in the context of increased anti-Chinese sentiment (*kenchū kanjō*) (Cabinet Office of the Japanese Government 2007),[5] and a growing sense of exasperation that Japan had apologized enough times to China.

Such awareness has arguably begun to be reflected in Japanese history text- books as well. While detailed depictions of the Nanjing Massacre or the Comfort Women issue have declined since 1997, Alexander Bukh argues that textbooks in use since 2002 have moved beyond exclusively focussing on Japanese 'vic- timhood'. Instead, the textbooks 'continue to note the forced labour of Koreans and Chinese . . . thus creating a sense of commonality and solidarity between the Japanese people and the Chinese and Koreans' (Bukh 2007: 697). Japan's colo- nization is depicted as 'imperialist', much to the chagrin of the Japanese right, which has again sought to counter this by claiming that Japan's colonization of Korea was 'carried out legally, according to international law', making it quali- tatively different from European imperialism, which took others' land by force (Atarashii Kyōkasho o Tsukurukai [b]).[6] Furthermore, while there is less written on the Nanjing Massacre, Bukh points out that 'the majority of textbooks have come to include a photograph that depicts rallies in Japan celebrating the fall of

Nanjing', which 'can be seen as an attempt, however vague, to encourage Japanese students to think about the general population's complicity' in the Sino-Japanese war (Bukh 2007: 699).

In addition, the politicization of the history issue has split public opinion with regard to how history should be remembered, and this – in the eyes of the Japanese right – constitutes the second facet of the entrenchment of 'masochistic' views of Japan and its history in Japanese society. Despite the weariness towards repeated Chinese and Korean protests, the Japanese populace is also aware that the perceived insensitivity towards Asian suffering has damaged Japan's international image, and needs to be taken into account accordingly (Okamoto and Tanaka 2005: 33–41). A *Yomiuri* poll of October 2005 showed 51.2 per cent were in favour of Prime Minister Koizumi Junichirō's visits to Yasukuni Shrine, while 42.7 per cent were opposed. However, when Chinese and Korean criticisms were taken into account, a total of 50.6 per cent were in favour of either removing the tablets of the Class A war criminals from Yasukuni Shrine or constructing a new memorial for the war dead, as opposed to 41.5 per cent who were in favour of continuing the use of the Shrine (*Yomiuri Shimbun Sensō Sekinin Kenshō Iinkai* 2006: 208). Concern for improved neighbourly relations has also resulted in Prime Ministers Abe Shinzō and Fukuda Yasuo eschewing visits to Yasukuni Shrine.

This, of course, is unacceptable to the Japanese right. In its eyes, Chinese and Korean criticisms of how Japan remembers its war amount to blatant political 'interference'. Domestic calls to take international criticism into account provide ample evidence that Japan continues to engage in weak, 'kowtow diplomacy', and remain in the 'masochistic' post-war mindset which has prevented it from assuming a more assertive role in the international community. Referring to Japanese weakness in dealing with Chinese criticism of history textbooks, Ishihara Shintarō claims: 'Japan should refute what should be refuted. It is because we haven't done this that Japan is *not taken seriously in the international community*' (Ishihara 2005: 98, emphasis added).

Furthermore, pressure groups such as the Japan Association of War-bereaved Families (*Nihon Izokukai*), make it their agenda to interpret the acts of the war dead as 'patriotic acts', as part of their campaign to improve the state's treatment of the war-bereaved families. This process, however, rests on the belief that '[i]t's not fair to criticize [Japanese colonialism] as aggressive by today's standards' (Kamisaka and Katō 2006: 141), which leaves 'no space for critical evaluations of cooperation in the war effort, because all military involvement was deemed "good" or at least non-negotiable' (Seraphim 2006: 83). The questioning of the legitimacy of Yasukuni Shrine as a war memorial, however, has the effect of questioning the morality of the war dead. As post-war Japan owes its existence to the 'sacred' sacrifices of the war dead, domestic refusal to commemorate them is equivalent to denying Japan's 'glorious' national identity, while international criticism also amounts to foreign encroachment of Japanese identity (see Figure 2.1). As Komori notes, with reference to Chinese demands to remove the tablets of Class A war criminals from Yasukuni Shrine, 'Japan cannot gain China's satisfaction unless it stops being Japan' (Komori 2005: 163).

Figure 2.1 'We Japanese are having our identity invaded'

Source: 'We Japanese are having our identity invaded', from Kobayashi Yoshinori, *Yasukuni Ron* (Tokyo: Gentōsha, 2005: 179). Note the Chinese, Korean, and American flags in the background, which leaves the readers with little doubt of who the 'invaders' are.

Worse still for the Japanese right, domestic congruence with such foreign voices is tantamount to a blind reproduction of foreign attempts to construct a dishonour-able identity of Japan as an 'aggressor' or 'imperialist state' which inflicted harm and suffering on Asian states and peoples. Recognition of this identity means that Japan's subservient, lowly international role becomes something to be accepted as atonement for its past. This also means that the Japanese people continue to be ashamed of their country. Their 'lack of patriotism' means that they do not resist grave foreign interference, particularly over how Japan should remember its impe-rialist history. For the Japanese right, what Hayashi called the 'crazy' situation which occurred almost 40 years ago, where the Japanese populace had 'become strangely feminized (*hen ni joseika*) and lost its manliness (*otoko rashisa, otoko kusasa*)', unable to love and too cowardly to sacrifice individual lives for the country (Hayashi 2006: 16), continues to this very day (see Figure 2.2).

2. Redrawing moral boundaries, protecting Japanese identity

So how has the Japanese right responded to China's latest challenge to the right's attempts to construct a 'righteous', 'strong' Japan which is respected by both its citizens and the international community? It appears that the main strategy to date has been to emphasize the immorality of China and its criticisms, and contrast this to a 'moral' Japan which is undeserving of this treatment. The Japanese right

Figure 2.2 'Traitorous' Jiang Zemin

Source: This clip is a typical example of how the Japanese right regard any domestic debates which seek to accommodate international criticism – particularly that emanating from China, as the caricature of Jiang Zemin shows – as 'traitorous'. The liberal *Asahi Shimbun* and *Mainichi Shimbun* come under particular criticism. The clip reads (from right to left): 'Just look at how many traitorous journalists, intellectuals, civic groups, and politicians have taken the side of the enemy. . . .!'; 'Why don't we create a new national [war dead] cemetery so Master China won't get angry?'; 'Why not remove the memorial tablets of the Class A war criminals?'; 'Even LDP politicians, frightened [of China], make such utterances'. From Kobayashi Yoshinori, *Yasukuni Ron* (Tokyo: Gentōsha, 2005: 179).

claims that 'whatever facet of Chinese criticisms you look at, Japan gets criticized as an extremely unethical state' (*dōgisei no kiwamete usui kuni*) (Komori 2005: 160). In order to combat this, the Japanese right has engaged in the redrawing of Sino-Japanese moral boundaries, emphasizing the 'morality' and 'goodness' of the Japanese state. This can be understood both as 'cultural nationalism with a moral core' or as a process of 'constructing national community as a moral phenomenon' (Todd *et al.* 2006: 378). Crucial to this movement is the positing of an 'unethical China' which serves to dilute memories of Japan's unsavoury past and bring the morality of the Japanese state into sharper focus. This is part and parcel of the process of identity-formation, in which a contrasting 'Other' is posited in order to shore up the identity of the 'Self'.

It should be acknowledged that the process of 'Othering' does not necessarily entail the delineation of the 'Self' from *negative* 'Others', as some scholars have argued (Mercer 1995). Several works have convincingly demonstrated the existence of multiple, overlapping 'Selves' in any given society, and the existence of 'positive Others' also demonstrates that these identities need not be constructed by positing a 'negative Other' (Neumann and Welsh 1991; Neumann 1996; Gries 2005).

Furthermore, it is important to note that these boundaries are not always sharply delineated according to national boundaries. As noted briefly earlier, the Japanese left, which is generally sympathetic with Asian criticisms of Japan's 'historical amnesia', is frequently placed *outside* the Japanese moral boundaries as perceived by the Japanese right. The Japanese left is typically depicted as 'anti-Japanese' or as being comprised of individuals with 'an irresponsible existence *lacking nationality and agency'* who place themselves on the side of the *Chinese* boundaries (Takahashi 2005: 186, emphasis added). By doing so, the Japanese right also achieves the aim of 'purifying the Japanese nation from dual others – non-Japanese and "anti-Japan Japanese"' (Takahashi 2005: 136). Such political aims by the Japanese right were visible in the furore surrounding the Japan Institution of International Affairs (JIIA)' suspension of the 'JIIA Commentary' website and electronic newsletter. 'JIIA Commentary' had published an article by Tamamoto Masaru (who was also the editor of the website) which argued that the nationalist hawks were attempting to forward a revisionist view of Japan's history of aggression in Asia because 'they wish[ed] to revive the connection between sovereign statehood and the right to belligerency' (2005/06: 60). The article came under heavy attack by Komori Yoshihisa (cited in McNeill 2006a), who claimed that the 'essays unilaterally condemned the thinking of the government and ruling camp . . . as dangerous, and categorized the attacks on Japan by China and other countries as proper'. He took particular offence to Tamamoto's use of the term the 'cult of Yasukuni', stating that it was a 'derogatory term used to mean a fanatical religious group such as the Aum Shinrikyo believers in Japan' and that the article was ultimately 'anti-Japan', as it used 'sensational, emotional and insulting words of the kind frequently used generally by the Western left or by China to bash Japan'. Komori then went on to assert that an institution such as the JIIA, which received governmental subsidies and came under the Ministry of Foreign Affairs' jurisdiction, should not be sending out 'anti-Japan' messages and undermining the national interest. The website was quickly closed, and Tamamoto's essay taken offline.[7] Komori somewhat disingenuously stated 'I don't support suppressing personal views. . . . I didn't advocate closure or suspension. I don't have a personal vendetta against the writer of the JIIA articles. He is free to write somewhere else' (cited in McNeill 2006a), displaying an almost blithe ignorance of the influence and consequences of his own writings. The JIIA also stated that no pressure had been applied to the organization to suspend the 'JIIA Commentary'; but it did create the perception that the Japanese right had successfully 'purified' an anti-Japan element that had dishonoured the nation (Clemons 2006; McNeill 2006b).

China as an alien entity

In spite of the existence of these 'anti-Japanese' domestic 'Others', the Japanese right's attempts to recover an 'honourable' Japanese identity in the face of Chinese criticisms of the history issue seem to have entailed the construction of a highly negative Chinese 'Other'. One way of doing this is to paint various aspects of China, Chinese society and the Chinese nation as fundamentally 'immoral' and 'different' from Japan. Some individuals engage in a Japanese 'Orientalist' discourse which was frequently used in the late-nineteenth century to emphasize Japan's identity as a member of the 'civilized' European international society (Gong 1984; Suzuki 2005). Tanizawa portrays China (and Korea) as uniquely 'childlike' because they are unable to deal with bilateral issues with Japan 'rationally' through diplomatic channels, unlike the rest of the 'mature' nations (which, from this perspective, naturally includes Japan) (Tanizawa 2005: 359).[8] In a depiction which has some parallels with European depictions of non-European peoples in the late-nineteenth century, Tanizawa Eiichi claims that China's irrational responses to Sino-Japanese bilateral issues gives ample proof that the PRC has 'not attained full maturity to becoming a modern state' (2005: 359). In a similar vein, Taiwanese-born scholar Kō Bunyū (Huang Wenxiong) asserts that the 'level of public morality among the Chinese populace is really low' (Kō 2005: 14). One manifestation of this 'low morality' is 'selfishness' (*jikochū*). This essentialized characterization provides the explanation for Chinese demands towards Japan, which are dictated *entirely* by the former's myopic needs. 'Because the Japanese are a nation who care so much about others (*omoiyari no aru minzoku*)', Kō claims, 'they always try to please others, to the point of even ingratiating themselves with others' (2001: 272). Again, we see a stark contrasting of a fundamentally 'good' Japanese nation with a negative, 'selfish' Chinese nation which seemingly has no qualms about unfairly taking advantage of Japan.

Others utilize the 'humanitarian turn' that post-Cold War international society has taken by highlighting China's authoritarian (and therefore fundamentally 'uncivilized') form of governance. This, of course, has the effect of placing the PRC outside the boundaries of international society, while simultaneously rehabilitating Japanese 'legitimate' membership that had been placed under doubt because of Chinese criticisms of Japan's lack of atonement for its historical wrongs. Nakanishi Terumasa, for instance, claims that China is 'an extreme class society', where the rulers make use of ethics in order to rule, while the ruled 'don't believe in any ethics whatsoever, and live in the world of pragmatism' (Nakanishi 2001: 190). Moreover, as their behaviour towards Taiwan and their domestic governance shows, they are irrational and corrupt; given this view, it is no small wonder that Nakanishi concludes thus: 'Japan and China are *too different* to have face-to-face relations, as the "Sino-Japanese friendship arguments" suggest' (2001: 194, emphasis added).

In line with this focus on moral boundaries, Komori Yoshihisa contrasts China and Japan's political institutions. He argues that Japan, as a democracy, is a country of high moral standing, and this of course differentiates the Japanese state from the PRC and its inherently unethical autocratic system of governance. 'Unlike China's one-party dictatorship', Komori continues, 'Japan, as one of the most democratic countries in the world, fully guarantees the rights of free speech and assembly' (2005: 161). Even China's recent economic developments are interpreted as an outcome of immoral behaviour. In a discussion about China's growing economic clout, Fukada Yūsuke downplays his fellow discussant's claim that Chinese factory workers' skills have improved greatly. Implying that the Chinese have utilized their growing skills to make fake products, Fukada argues: 'Saying that the Chinese are good at making fakes is pretty much the same as them being good at pick pocketing' (Fukada and Kusano 2001: 199). He then adds that it was the *Japanese* investors or directors who went to great lengths to 'teach all there is to know' (*tetori ashitori de oshieta*) to the Chinese regarding how to improve the quality of Chinese-made goods (Fukada and Kusano 2001: 199), thus juxtaposing a 'kindly' Japan with an immoral China who often uses Japanese-taught skills to make fake products, 'robbing' Japanese firms. In Fudaka's eyes, China is '. . . what America calls a "rogue state"' (*narazumono kokka*) (Fukada and Kusano 2001: 201).

The cartoonist Kobayashi Yoshinori also claims that the Chinese attack Yasukuni Shrine because of their *fundamentally different* way of remembering the dead. In his view, the Japanese treat all their dead as gods, and this means that even those who commit some wrong during their lifetimes are treated with respect. The Chinese, in contrast, continue to punish their enemies even after their deaths. Their attitude towards the dead is 'absolute intolerance' (*zettai fukanyō*) (Kobayashi 2005: 42). Kobayashi claims that the Chinese 'kill their sworn enemies and eat their flesh and organs; they whip the bodies of the dead; grind their [enemies'] bones to a powder and drink them; and refuse to forgive their enemies' descendants' (Kobayashi 2005: 42; cf Kō 2001: 272). This point is made by juxtaposing two contrasting images. An illustration depicts Japanese society living harmoniously with its dead. This is immediately followed by a grotesque illustration of the Chinese denigrating their dead (see Figure 2.3), giving the impression of a

Figure 2.3 Contrastive societies, Japan and China

Source: The frame on the right depicts a tranquil society, and states: 'We Japanese coexist with God and exist in the same space with the spirits of the dead'. In sharp contrast, the illustration in the middle claims that traditionally the Chinese have been highly intolerant of their enemies, even when they are dead. The left frame depicts the grotesque way in which the Chinese are alleged to treat their dead. It reads: The Chinese 'kill their sworn enemies and eat their flesh and organs; they whip the bodies of the dead; grind their [enemies'] bones to a powder and drink them; and refuse to forgive their enemies' descendants'. Source: Kobayashi Yoshinori, *Yasukuni Ron* (Tokyo: Gentōsha, 2005: 42).

highly cruel, uncivilized Chinese culture. It is not difficult to see how such images can cement the view that any form of Sino-Japanese cooperation is impossible, when the images contrast and differentiate the countries so starkly. The two states' identities appear to have no overlap at all, so it seems, therefore, that there is very little hope for any common interests to emerge. Such images send the message that, even if Japan were to compromise with China, the 'immoral Chinese' would selfishly try and maximize their own interests, while the 'moral Japanese' would lose out; thus, it is simply not worth the effort.

History as a tool: positing an anti-Japanese conspiracy

A second and most popular way the Japanese right constructs a highly negative, immoral Chinese 'Other' and redraws moral boundaries is by depicting PRC criticisms of Japan's history and its 'historical amnesia' as a part of a cynical move by the Chinese government to whip up patriotic sentiment to bolster its legitimacy. In recent years, various scholars and pundits have argued that Beijing's protests about how Japan interprets history often coincide with the regime's need to whip up nationalist sentiment and fulfil certain domestic political goals (Tanaka 1983; Whiting 1995: 295–316; Rose 1998; Zhao 1998: 287–302; Downs and Saunders 1998/99: 114–46; He 2007: 43–74). Since the Reform and Opening period, the CCP regime has been relying increasingly on nationalism to replace (the effectively bankrupt) communist ideology as its basis for legitimacy. As part of this drive, there have been concerted 'patriotic campaigns' designed to bolster citizens' loyalty towards the regime by reminding them of the CCP's role in throwing off foreign oppression and modernizing China. Japan, as one of the key aggressors of China and the largest foreign threat the Chinese communists faced, naturally plays an extremely prominent role in this process.

While this argument may not be inaccurate, it is important to note that it is based on a number of problematic assumptions. First, by seeing history as a 'tool' used by the political elite, it is assumed that leaders are (somewhat mysteriously) detached from historical memories and can cynically manipulate them. Second, and crucially, this interpretation ignores the fact that for the Chinese government to utilize anti-Japanese sentiment for political needs, there needs to be a *receptive audience* in the first place for such rhetorical political action to succeed. As a result, the Chinese citizens end up being depicted as mindless puppets who can be brainwashed and manipulated at will by the 'puppet masters' in Beijing (Gries 2004; Suzuki 2007: 27–28).

The Japanese right, however, have eagerly embraced this argument. Kobayashi's cartoon epitomizes this view. He depicts the Chinese as empty vassals who are to be filled in with pernicious anti-Japanese emotion by a decidedly sinister-looking Jiang Zemin (see Figure 2.4). Similarly, in a discussion with Chinese scholars Liu Jiangyong and Bu Ping about the Yasukuni Shrine controversy, Takubo Tadae and Sakurai Yoshiko note their suspicion that the 'history issue' is nothing but a political card played by Beijing (Sakurai *et al.* 2005: 102–3). Nakanishi also claims that 'China packages the Senkaku, Taiwan, United Nations, and the East

The strange masochism of the Japanese right 49

日本が何回謝ろうとODAで6兆円出そうとかかわりなく

中国政府は一般国民に日本への怒りと憎しみを保たせるため次々造り

「抗日記念館」やら「抗日記念公園」を

ありとあらゆる手段を使って

「日本鬼子(リーベンクィツ)」「日冦(日本の賊とも)」の残虐を強調し

一般国民を洗脳していく

300000人

Figure 2.4 China responds to Japanese apologies

Source: (From right to left) 'No matter how many times Japan apologizes, or gives out JPY6 trillion (*roku chō*) in Official Development Assistance, the Chinese government builds "anti-Japan [War] Memorial Museums" or "anti-Japan [War] Memorial Parks in order to maintain Chinese citizens' anger and hatred towards Japan; it uses all methods to emphasize the cruelty of the "Japanese Devils" or "Japanese Bandits", and brainwash the Chinese people'. Kobayashi Yoshinori, *Yasukuni Ron* (Tokyo: Gentōsha, 2005: 44).

China Sea gas field issues together and uses the "history card" to demand concessions from Japan' (2005: 115).[9] Furthermore,

> ... it is worth noting that the stone-throwing and slogan-chanting demonstrators are grinning ... I have long been wondering what this grin means, but now I have really realized: it is because there is a 'choreographer' behind the scenes allowing the demonstrators to legitimately engage in wanton acts of destruction. However, since all of these demonstrations are *entirely staged* [and not genuine], they feel a slight pang of their consciences. It is this sense of guilt that results in their grinning.
>
> (Nakanishi 2005: 119, emphasis added)

The crucial reason why these arguments have been so popular among the Japanese right is because they are extremely effective in exonerating the Japanese from their own war responsibilities. By claiming that 'history issues' are nothing but a political tool, the Japanese right can conveniently ignore and trivialize the fact that the Chinese government can only use the 'historical card' because memories and experiences of Japanese brutalities are still held by many Chinese people regardless of CCP manipulation. Rather than Japanese imperialism or Japanese 'historical amnesia' being the cause of anti-Japanese sentiment, the *Chinese government* becomes the primary culprit for deteriorating Sino-Japanese relations. Furthermore, for its cynical interference in Japanese domestic affairs – be it Koizumi's visits to Yasukuni Shrine or Japanese history textbooks – it is in fact *China* who ought to be apologizing to Japan, not the other way round. As Kō argues: 'For the Chinese government's frequent interference in internal affairs under the name of peace and friendship . . . the Japanese government should demand that China apologize' (2005: 216).

It is worth noting that such arguments by the Japanese right have uncomfortable similarities with Holocaust denials. If one argues that Chinese criticisms of Japan's dark history are a product of cynical ulterior motives, this easily leads to arguments that anti-Japanese sentiments are a product of a conspiracy. In similar fashion to Holocaust deniers who claim the existence of a Zionist conspiracy behind anti-Nazi discourse, Takahashi Tetsuya argues, such claims by the Japanese right also:

> . . . rest on the assumption of a universal 'conspiracy' behind such 'fabrications' . . . the main culprits of this 'conspiracy' are 'foreign states which hate Japan for its prosperity' such as Russia, America and other Western powers, China and Korea . . . as well as 'anti-Japan Japanese citizens' and the 'anti-Japan Japanese media'.
>
> (2005: 132–33)

The Japanese right, however, seems disturbingly oblivious to this. In her debate with Liu and Bu, Sakurai states that the Western journalist whose reports form the basis of China's claim that 300,000 perished in the Nanjing massacre was on the payroll of the Chinese Nationalist Party (KMT). Furthermore, she argues that the gruesome photos of the vivisections carried out by the notorious Unit 731 'is a photo of a Japanese victim butchered by the KMT in the 1928 Jinan incident' (Sakurai *et al.* 2005: 109). Similarly, Komori reports that anti-Japan Chinese-American lobby groups played a huge role behind the US House of Representatives' passing of Resolution 121, which called on Japan to make a formal apology to comfort women. 'These Chinese lobby groups', Komori continues, 'don't criticize Japan because it has done or said anything new. Their objective is to continuously bash Japan for these kinds of [historical] issues. Mike Honda is nothing but a "means" to this end' (2007). Komori claims that his own agenda for writing this is the need for objective reporting. However, given that he does not mention Japan's moral responsibilities in the same report (it should be noted, however, that Komori does not deny the existence of comfort women), his writings again serve to highlight the unjustness of Resolution 121, treating this as nothing but an expression of a Chinese conspiracy. Given this, Komori's reporting reads more like a nationalistic knee-jerk reaction to 'anti-Japanese' sentiments and Chinese interference in domestic affairs, rather than 'objective' reporting.

3. Perpetuating 'masochism': the Japan that is bullied

As we have seen, the Japanese right's attempts to contest Chinese criticisms of Japan's historical past rely heavily on redrawing Sino-Japanese moral boundaries and depicting a highly unethical China. This serves a number of purposes for the Japanese right. First, by highlighting the immorality of the Chinese people, Chinese culture and Chinese political institutions, Japan's own negative image is relativized. Second, and perhaps more importantly, by depicting both governmental and popular Chinese anger towards Japan's 'historical amnesia' as disingenuous, the Japanese right can then argue that Japan is *wholly undeserving* of such attacks by the Chinese. In a typical statement of this kind, Komori again complains that China's criticisms of Japan 'totally ignore Japan's morality' (2005: 161). Furthermore, in Komori's mind, Beijing's 'unethical' autocratic system of governance and/or aggressive foreign policy behaviour means that 'it is China that is the state which lacks morality in the most universal sense, and it has no right whatsoever to denounce Japan based on the past, while ignoring Japan's present' (Komori 2005: 161–62).

The biggest irony here is that this argument – that Japan is being unjustly criticized, is the 'victim' of a sinister anti-Japanese international conspiracy led by China – necessitates the positing of a 'bullied' Japan. This is not to say that the Japanese right want Tokyo to wallow in this weak status. The Japanese right has often decried the Japanese left for blaming Japan for all the wrongdoings during World War II. The right charges that this 'masochistic' attitude fails to remove the negative image given to Japan unjustly in the Tokyo War Crimes Tribunal, and the resulting international and domestic distrust of the Japanese state makes Japan 'weak', incapable of resisting Chinese and Korean interference and unable to take on a larger political/military role commensurate with its economic power (Nakanishi 2001: 189).

However, in order to avoid China's stigmatization of the Japanese state, the Asia-Pacific War, and the Japanese war dead, the Japanese right has had to claim that it is in fact Japan who is the injured party. In his cartoon *Yasukuni Ron*, Kobayashi does precisely this. While he remains critical of Japanese politician's cowardice in the face of Beijing and Seoul's 'interference' in Japan's domestic affairs, at the same time he portrays both states in almost sinister, demonic terms. The Chinese and Koreans are depicted as shadowy figures with sinister grins on their faces, while at the same time Koizumi appears as both a cowardly and bullied individual, head bowed in shame and humiliation at this 'unjust' treatment (see Figure 2.5). In the face of strong evidence of Japanese war crimes in Asia, this seems to be the only feasible way in which the Japanese right can make any of its arguments carry moral weight. It is this redrawing of the moral boundaries of Sino-Japanese relations which has resulted in a strange masochism within the Japanese right. Japan is seen – and *needs* to be seen – as a victim of a domestic and international anti-Japan conspiracy, being constantly bullied by an arrogant, wicked China bent on unfairly vilifying Japan for its own selfish domestic needs. The Japanese right's need to create a 'sadistic' Chinese 'Other' has necessitated the positing of a weak, cowardly and masochistic Japanese 'Self'. If the Japanese

Figure 2.5 Japan's 'unjust humiliation'

Source: While Koizumi Junichirō is described as cowardly, we may also note that Koizumi is also portrayed as being humiliated and bullied by the Chinese. The demonic depictions of China and Korea also serve to highlight Japan's 'unjust humiliation', which is designed to reduce the moral authority of Chinese and Korean protests over Japanese war responsibility. Source: Kobayashi Yoshinori, *Yasukuni Ron* (Tokyo: Gentōsha, 2005: 28).

left is guilty of maintaining the 'weakness' of Japan by kowtowing to Chinese and Korean demands and diminishing Japan's international prestige, the Japanese right has proved itself to be just as 'guilty' of reifying a 'weak' Japan, albeit for different purposes.

Conclusion

Recent controversies over the 'history issue' in Sino-Japanese relations can be interpreted as part of a quest for identity. It seems that both China and Japan serve as indispensable 'Others' for both Japanese (right-wing) nationalists and Chinese nationalists in the attempt to redraw moral boundaries. The Japanese right appears to be outraged and fearful that Japan may be ostracized because of its perceived 'historical amnesia'. While Chinese criticisms may be brushed off as politically motivated, when this condemnation spreads outside of Asia – as can be seen by the passing of US House Resolution 121 in July 2007 and the widespread public-ity received by Iris Chang's book *The Rape of Nanking* (1997) – this causes acute anxiety among the Japanese right. Their fears have arguably been heightened by the fact that all Japanese prime ministers since Koizumi have refused to visit Yasukuni Shrine, which effectively means (in the eyes of the right) succumbing to the unjust demands of China. Worse still, in December 2009 the emperor broke with protocol to meet with Chinese vice president Xi Jinping at the request of the newly elected Democratic Party of Japan government, furthering suspicion that the 'moral' Japan is being unnecessarily obsequious to the Chinese government. In order to re-establish Japan as a state worthy of respect within the boundaries of the international community, the right has 'Othered' China as immoral. This particular characterization of China is intended to be juxtaposed against the morally upright Japanese 'Self', which is simultaneously beyond and undeserving of such international shame.

Interestingly, we see a similar pattern taking place in China, where Japan serves as an important, bullying 'Other'. In the post-Cold War international community where legitimate membership is increasingly being defined in terms of 'democratic governance' and respect for human rights, China has frequently been seen as an 'Other' by the West. This has resulted in a series of 'humiliations' for the PRC, such as regular criticisms over its human rights record, its failure to host the 2000 Olympics or the protest against the 2008 Olympic torch procession. Furthermore, because of this negative image, even China's rise is greeted with suspicion and alarm. Consequently, many Chinese feel – much to their frustration and anxiety – that China remains outside the boundaries of and has yet to be accepted by the (Western-dominated) international community. In order to re-establish China as a 'moral actor', Chinese nationalists and the political elite have 'Othered' Japan as a victimizer of China. This emphasis on a 'bullying' Japan helps shore up the PRC's identity as a 'humiliated, victimized state' which deserves respect and should not be ostracized by other states (Shih 1995: 539–63; Gries 2004; Suzuki 2007).

This mutual 'negative Othering' may not bode well for future Sino-Japanese relations. At present, it appears that neither state is a 'revisionist state' which seeks to upset the balance of power within Northeast Asia (Van Ness 2002). However, the identity crises which both states face appear to have resulted in a quest for what Mitzen calls 'ontological security', which 'refers to the need to experience oneself as a whole, continuous person in time . . . in order to realize a sense of agency' (Mitzen 2006: 342). The problem is that both Chinese and Japanese (right-wing) nationalist quests for a stable, 'honourable' identity in the international community seems to entail the 'Othering' of each other in a negative fashion: as Mitzen states, this is a classic case where 'conflict persists and comes to fulfill identity needs', and 'breaking free can generate ontological *in*security' (Mitzen 2006: 343).

Conventional studies of security in the Asia-Pacific seem to be poorly equipped to deal with this phenomenon. Christensen, for instance, has acknowledged that historical animosity between China and Japan plays a crucial part in the emergence of security dilemmas between the two states. His policy recommendations, however, are for the US to play a balancing role, containing China, while simultaneously making sure that Japan stays within the US–Japan security alliance, so that it will not seek to expand its military capabilities (Christensen 1999: 49–80). These arguments do have their merits, but they are 'stopgap measures': they cannot in any way alter the manner in which the two states seek 'ontological security' by persisting in positing a negative 'Other'. Furthermore, while the Japanese right's antagonism towards the PRC could potentially bring Japan more closely to Washington geopolitically, this can lead to even greater Japanese security dependence on the US – this is something the Japanese right have long wanted to avoid in the first place.[10] While the US may be more palatable to them than the PRC, the Japanese right is unlikely to accept a subordinate position *vis-à-vis* the Americans for the sake of confronting China.

This, however, does not mean that Sino-Japanese relations are doomed to remain mired in hostility. As pointed out earlier, while the role of an 'Other' is crucial in identity formation, this 'Other' need not be a hostile one. Furthermore, there are multiple forms of 'identities' within Chinese and Japanese societies which are actively beginning to contest the way in which Chinese and Japanese identities have to be defined through acrimonious images of each other (Ma 2002: 41–47; Le 2004). The existence of peace movements in Japan has long been highlighted, but it is also worth examining the increasing amount of critical discourse on 'narrow', jingoistic nationalism within China. There have also been attempts to come to a shared understanding of history between the two states (as well as Korea) ('Dongya Sanguo de Jinxiandaishi' Gongtong Bianxie Weiyuanhui 2005), which may play a role in halting the construction of 'hostile Others' through history education – an issue which has continued to dog Sino-Japanese relations. Encouragingly, such initiatives have now been taken up at the official level. Following Prime Minister Abe Shinzō's visit to China, the two states agreed to appoint research teams to engage in joint history research. Although both sides may not be able to agree to a singular historical narrative, it is hoped that the process would help ameliorate the vicious cycle of constructing hostile 'Others' in national identity formation and the inscription of moral boundaries. Future scholarship could enrich the study of Asian security by examining and highlighting potential pathways in which mutually hostile images of China, Japan, and Korea can be removed. This chapter only identifies some of the factors which cause this undesirable phenomenon. However, perhaps the time is now ripe for us to look beyond causality and examine pathways towards a genuinely peaceful East Asia, where the 'Other' can be transformed from a 'bullying Other' into a 'desirable Other'. The way moral boundaries are drawn will be crucial in this process.

Notes

1 Note that Suzuki Nobuyuki uses the term shina jin for 'Chinese' (widely considered derogatory), rather than the more neutral Chūgoku jin.
2 It is worth noting that in the context of China, Kamisaka's argument ignores the existence of Japanese war orphans who were adopted and brought up by Chinese parents, which may challenge or relativize her point about Chinese cruelty towards Japanese refugees.
3 Franziska Seraphim (2006: 261–63) notes that globalization and the democratization of states such as Taiwan and South Korea were crucial causal factors in Asian victims speaking out against Japanese war crimes.

4 Yoshida points out that this sentiment hinders any attempts to think seriously about Japan's war responsibility, as it only encourages some form of apology for the 'outcome' of a particular act, the morality of which is not seriously questioned.

5 The Japanese Cabinet Office's survey conducted in October 2007 reveals that 63.5 per cent of respondents reported 'unfriendly feelings' (shitashimi o kanjinai) vis-à-vis China. Of Japan's immediate neighbours, only Russia had a worse image, with 81.6 per cent reporting 'unfriendly feelings'.

6 This argument is made in response to the textbook published by the Teikoku Shoin publishers.

7 Tamamoto's essay was subsequently reproduced in the World Policy Journal, which is cited here. In a personal communication with the author, Tamamoto has confirmed that the contents of this article are identical with that which appeared in 'JIIA Commentary'.

8 It is interesting to note that some conservative scholars who may not necessarily fit into the 'Japanese right' as defined in this chapter, are making similar points. The historian Hata Ikuhiko, referring to the recent campaigns to improve the etiquette of Beijing citizens in preparation for the Olympics, notes that the Chinese are like 'primary school students; frankly speaking, that's the level they're at, so there really isn't any need to pay much attention [to their complaints about Japanese textbooks]'. See Hata Ikuhiko and Shunji Taoka (2005: 87). It is interesting to note how the US occupiers used images of gender and immaturity in referring to the Japanese, which demonstrates that 'Orientalism', whether it be by Westerners or Japanese, is often used as a powerful discourse to depict a negative 'Other'. See Shibusawa (2006).

9 This article was published shortly after the April 2005 anti-Japanese demonstrations, so in this context, the 'UN issue' presumably means Japan's candidacy for a permanent membership of the United Nations Security Council, which the Chinese opposed.

10 For this point, I am indebted to the anonymous referees of this chapter.

References

Agawa, Hiroyuki (2001) 'Genkō ni omou', *Bungei Shunjū*, 79, 11: 77–78.

Asahi.com (2008a) 'Nitchū Sōsa Kyōryoku o Honkakuka: Jōyaku Shōnin Isogu: Gyōza Jiken'. Online. Available: http://www.asahi.com/international/update/0131/TKY200801310245.html (accessed 8 February 2008).

—— (2008b) ' "Saihatsu Bōshi e Kyōryoku": Reitō Gyōza Jiken de Nitchū Zaimushō – Gyōza Yakubutsu Konnyū'. Online. Available: http://www.asahi.com/special/080130/TKY200802100082.html (accessed 10 February 2008).

Atarashii Kyōkasho o Tsukuru Kai (a) 'Tondemo Kyōkasho'. Online. Available: http://www.tsukurukai.com/02_about_us/02_maso_01.html (accessed 8 February 2008).

—— (b) 'Tondemo Kyōkasho: Teikoku Shoin'. Online. Available: www.tsukurukai.com/02_about_us/2_maso/maso01_file/teikoku170.html (accessed 8 February 2008).

—— (2008) *Tsukuru Kai Fax Tsūshin*, 224, 1 February: 1–2.

Breen, John (ed.) (2008) *Yasukuni, the War Dead and the Struggle for Japan's Past*, London: Hurst and Columbia University Press.

Bukh, Alexander (2007) 'Japan's history textbooks debate: national identity in narratives of victimhood and victimization', *Asian Survey*, 47, 5: 683–704.

Cabinet Office of the Government of Japan (2007) 'Gaikō ni kansuru Yoron Chōsa'. Online. Available: http://www8.cao.go.jp/survey/h19/h19-gaiko/2–1.html (accessed 16 February 2008).

Chang, Iris (1997) *The Rape of Nanking: the forgotten holocaust of World War II*, London: Penguin.

Christensen, Thomas J. (1999) 'China, the US-Japan alliance, and the security dilemma', *International Security*, 23, 4: 49–80.

Clark, Ian (2005) *Legitimacy in International Society*, Oxford: Oxford University Press.

Clemons, Steven (2006) 'The rise of Japan's thought police', *The Washington Post*, 27 August 2006. Online. Available: http://www.washingtonpost.com/wp-dyn/content/article/2006/08/25/AR2006082501176_pf.html (accessed 11 November 2009).

'Dongya Sanguo de Jinxiandaishi' Gongtong Bianxie Weiyuanhui (2005) *Dongya Sanguo de Jinxiandaishi*, Beijing: Shehui Kexue Wenxian Chubanshe.

Downs, Erica Strecker and Saunders, Philip C. (1998/99) 'Legitimacy and the limits of nationalism: China and the Diaoyu islands', *International Security*, 23, 3: 114–46.

Fukada, Yūsuke and Kusano, Atsushi (2001) 'Shinshutsu Nippon kigyō wa mata nakasareru', *Bungei Shunjū*, 79, 11: 195–202.

Gibney, Mark and Roxstrom, Erik (2001) 'The status of state apologies', *Human Rights Quarterly*, 23, 4: 911–39.

Gong, Gerrit W. (1984) *The Standard of 'Civilization' in International Society*, Oxford: Clarendon Press.

Gries, Peter Hays (2004) *China's New Nationalism: pride, politics, and diplomacy*, Berkeley: University of California Press.

—— (2005) 'Social psychology and the identity-conflict debate: is a "China threat" inevitable?' *European Journal of International Relations*, 11, 2: 235–65.

Hata, Ikuhiko and Taoka, Shunji (2005) 'Chūgoku no gōman, Nippon no meisō', *Gendai*, 39, 8: 80–88.

Hayashi, Fusao (2006) *Daitōa Sensō Kōtei Ron*, Tokyo: Natsume Shobō.

He, Yinan (2007) 'Remembering and forgetting the war: elite mythmaking, mass reaction, and Sino-Japanese relations, 1950–2006', *History and Memory*, 19, 2: 43–74.

Hughes, Christopher W. (2004) 'Japan's Re-emergence as a "Normal" Military Power?' *Adelphi Paper*, 368–69, London: International Institute for Strategic Studies.

Ishihara, Shintarō (2005) 'Pekin Orinpikku o danko boikotto seyo', *Bungei Shunjū*, 83, 8: 94–103.

Ishin Seitō Shinpū (2008) 'Seimei: Chūgoku san Shokuhin Higai ni kanshite Seifu to Masumedia ni Tsuyoku Kōgi suru'. Online. Available: http://sokuho.sblo.jp/article/10323470.html (accessed 8 February 2008).

Kamisaka, Fuyuko and Katō, Kōichi (2006) 'Chūgoku to Yasukuni dotchi ga okashii', *Bungei Shunjū*, 84, 11: 130–42.

Kō, Bunyū (2001) 'Chūgoku ga kirawareru nanatsu no riyū', *Bungei Shunjū*, 79, 11: 270–76.

—— (2005) *Han Nichi Kyōiku o Aoru Chūgoku no Taizai*, Tokyo: Nihon Bungeisha.

Kobayashi, Yoshinori (2005) *Yasukuni Ron*, Tokyo: Gentōsha.

Komori, Yoshihisa (2005) 'Ko Kintō "Yasukuni hinan" wa sekai no hijōshiki', *Bungei Shunjū*, 83, 11: 154–63.

—— (2007) 'Ianfu Ketsugian no Suishin no Shuyaku wa Yahari Chūgoku Kei Dantai Datta'. Online. Available: http://komoriy.iza.ne.jp/blog/month/200706/1/ (accessed 28 February 2008).

—— (2008) 'Chūgokusei Gyōza ni Taisuru *Asahi Shimbun* no Kimyō na Shasetsu: Nihon to Iu "Kuni" no Gainen ga Okirai?' Online. Available: http://komoriy.iza.ne.jp/blog/entry/471282/ (accessed 9 February 2008).

Le, Shan (ed.) (2004) *Qianliu: Dui Xiaai Minzu Zhuyi de Pipan yu Fansi*, Shanghai: Huadong Shifan Daxue Chubanshe.

Ma, Licheng (2002) 'Duiri Guanxi Xin Siwei: Zhongri Minjian Zhi You', *Zhanlüe Yu Guanli*, 6: 41–47.

McNeill, David (2006a) 'The struggle for the Japanese soul: Komori Yoshihisa, *Sankei Shimbun*, and the JIIA controversy', *Japan Focus*, 5 September 2006. Online. Available: http://www.japanfocus.org/-David-McNeill/2212 (accessed 19 December 2009).

—— (2006b) 'Softly, softly: Did the Japan Institute of International Affairs buckle under right-wing pressure? No says Ambassador Satoh Yukio. Yes, say his critics', *Japan Focus*. Online. Available: http://www.japanfocus.org/-David_McNeill-/2466 (accessed 19 December 2009).

Mercer, Jonathan (1995) 'Anarchy and identity', *International Organization*, 49, 2: 229–52.

Mitzen, Jennifer (2006) 'Ontological security in world politics: state identity and the security dilemma', *European Journal of International Relations*, 12, 3: 341–70.

Morris-Suzuki, Tessa (2007) 'Who is responsible? The *Yomiuri* project and the legacy of the Asia-Pacific war in Japan', *Asian Perspective*, 31, 1: 177–91.

Nakanishi, Terumasa (2001) 'Ogoreru "Chūka teikoku" hisashikarazu', *Bungei Shunjū*, 79, 11: 188–94.

—— (2005) 'Nippon kigyō yo, "Kōga no noroi" kara sameyo', *Bungei Shunjū*, 83, 8: 114–24.

Neumann, Iver B. and Welsh, Jennifer M. (1991) 'The Other in European self-definition: an addendum to the literature on international society', *Review of International Studies*, 17, 4: 327–48.

Neumann, Iver B. (1996) 'Self and Other in international relations', *European Journal of International Relations*, 2, 2: 139–74.

Okamoto, Yukio and Tanaka, Akihiko (2005) 'Ko Kintō seiken o yurugasu "aikoku" bōsō to sekai no shisen', *Chūō Kōron*, June: 33–41.

Rose, Caroline (1998) *Interpreting History in Sino-Japanese Relations: a case study in political decision making*, London: Routledge.

Sakurai, Yoshiko (2002) *GHQ Sakusei no Jōhō Sōsasho: 'Shinsōbako' no Jubaku o Toku*, Tokyo: Shōgakukan.

Sakurai, Yoshiko, Takubo, Tadae, Liu, Jiangyong and Bu, Ping (2005), 'Yasukuni sanpai no nani ga warui to iu no da', *Bungei Shunjū*, 83, 11: 94–111.

Seraphim, Franziska (2006) *War Memory and Social Politics in Japan, 1945–2005*, Cambridge, MA: Harvard University Press.

Shibusawa, Naoko (2006) *America's Geisha Ally: reimagining the Japanese enemy*, Cambridge, MA: Harvard University Press.

Shih, Chih-yu (1995) 'Defining Japan: the nationalist assumption in China's foreign policy', *International Journal*, 50: 539–63.

Suzuki, Nobuyuki (2008) 'Taiwan chizu hyōki to shokuhin tero wa dōkon!' Online. Available: http://blogs.yahoo.co.jp/ishinsya/28913619.html (accessed 8 February 2008).

Suzuki, Shogo (2005) 'Japan's socialization into Janus-faced European international society', *European Journal of International Relations*, 11, 1: 137–64.

—— (2007) 'The importance of 'Othering' in China's national identity: Sino-Japanese relations as a stage of identity conflicts', *The Pacific Review*, 20, 1: 23–47.

Tanaka, Akihiko (1983) '"Kyōkasho Mondai" o meguru Chūgoku no seisaku kettei', in Okabe Tatsumi (ed.), *Chūgoku Gaikō: seisaku kettei no kōzō*, Tokyo: Nihon Kokusai Mondai Kenkyūjo.

Takahashi, Tetsuya (2005) *Sengo Sekinin Ron*, Tokyo: Kōdansha.

Tamamoto, Masaru (2005/06) 'How Japan imagines China and sees itself', *World Policy Journal*, 22, 4: 55–62.

Tanizawa, Eiichi (2005) *Jigyaku Shikan mō Yametai! Hannichi Teki Nihonjin e no Kokuhatsujō*, Tokyo: Wakku Shuppan.

Tennichi, Takahiko (2007) 'The *Yomiuri* project and its results', *Asian Perspective*, 31, 1: 43–60.

Todd, Jennifer, Muldoon, Orla, Trew, Karen, Cañás Bottos, Lorenzo, Rougier, Nathalie and McLaughlin, Katrina (2006) 'The moral boundaries of the nation: he constitution of national identity in the southeastern border counties of Ireland', *Ethnopolitics*, 5, 4: 365–82.

Van Ness, Peter (2002) 'Hegemony, not anarchy: why China and Japan are not balancing US unipolar power', *International Relations of the Asia-Pacific*, 2, 1: 131–50.

Wendt, Alexander (1999) *Social Theory of International Relations*, Cambridge: Cambridge University Press.

Whiting, Allen S. (1995) 'Chinese nationalism and foreign policy after Deng', *China Quarterly*, 142: 295–316.

Yomiuri Shimbun Sensō Sekinin Kenshō Iinkai (2006) *Kenshō: sensō sekinin*, Tokyo: Chūō Kōronsha.

Yoshida, Yutaka (2005) *Nihonjin no Sensō Kan,* Tokyo: Iwanami Shoten.

Zhao, Suisheng (1998) 'A state-led nationalism: the patriotic education campaign in post-Tiananmen China', *Communist and Post-Communist Studies*, 31, 3: 287–302.

3 Japan's responses to actors outside the boundaries of international society

'Rogue states' and North Korea's nuclear threats

Key-young Son

> If only it were all so simple! If only there were evil people somewhere, insidiously committing evil deeds, and it were necessary only to separate them from the rest of us and destroy them. But the line dividing good and evil cuts through the heart of every human being.
>
> Alexander Solzhenitsyn (quoted in Cumings 2004: 1)

The expression 'rogue states' is opaque in terms of its usage. Despite the fact that it has been used to name a band of states violating international norms, norms are violated not just among the failed or marginalized states in the international system, but among the great powers that 'do not regard themselves as bound by international norms' (Chomsky 2000: 1). The United States and like-minded states have often categorized North Korea, Iraq, Iran, Syria and Cuba, among others, as 'rogue states' for violating a multitude of international norms (Litwak 2000). By deploying such a derogatory term, these states aimed to draw a dividing line between a group of 'rogue states' and the rest of the world. This particular demarcation of a boundary is based on the belief that there exists a society of states which are largely bound together by shared norms, rules and institutions, while a gang of 'rogue states' exists outside the boundaries of this society.

Japan is known for sharing the norms, rules, institutions and, most importantly, a common identity with the Western and pro-Western states in the world. Since the late nineteenth century, in fact, Japan attempted to reconstruct its identity, aspiring to join the ranks of Western states rather than remaining merely one of the East Asian states (Gong 1984). In the wake of defeat in World War II, Japan remained closely aligned with the United States. Trapped by the external pressure emanating from the Cold War and the internal gridlock resulting from the tension between pacifist and conservative forces, the Japanese state appeared largely 'ambiguous' and 'reactive' in terms of its security orientations in spite of its dramatic rise as an economic superpower. Known as a 'peace state', 'reluctant ally' or 'cheque-book' diplomat (Funabashi 1991), Japan was not in a position to actively identify the sources of threats and develop a comprehensive security framework of its own during the Cold War years. As the stronger partner of the bilateral alliance, the

United States devised grand Cold War strategies and exercised political and military influence over Japan's policy-making processes. Japan's domestic political landscape remained stalemated, creating the foundation for the prolongation of its status as an accidental 'peace state'. Even though it belonged to the capitalist bloc, however, the Japanese state had been reluctant to draw a clear boundary between international society, to which it belonged, and those outside it. Most of all, Japan found it hard to shift its identity from a 'peace state' to a regional or global politico-military player during the Cold War, in spite of the presence of rightist forces seeking to radically reshape the state's security identity.

The end of the Cold War, however, provided Japan with an opportunity to review its traditional security identity and sharpen its strategic calculations regarding its place in the world. At the turn of the twenty-first century, Japan proceeded further to introduce independent strategic thinking in framing its security identity within the context of the traditional military alliance with the United States. This new process has accelerated since 1998, when North Korea test-launched a multistage missile over the Japanese archipelago and detonated a nuclear device in 2006, threatening directly Japan's national security. These hard security issues have been further complicated by issues related to human security, such as the abduction of Japanese nationals by North Korean agents in the 1970s and 1980s (McCormack 2005). Responding to these external threats and rising domestic antagonism against North Korea, Prime Minister Koizumi Junichirō and his successors from the Liberal Democratic Party (LDP) attempted to radically reform Japan's security identity by pinpointing North Korea as the main source of insecurity and seeking an expanded military role in its alliance relationship with the United States. All these developments led the Japanese state to push North Korea outside the boundaries of international society and freeze all forms of assistance, including humanitarian aid, effective December 2004, when it determined that human remains repatriated to Japan from North Korea were not those of abducted Japanese citizens.

This chapter aims to enhance our understanding of regional and international politics in East Asia by shedding light on how Japan sought to demarcate its boundaries of association. In particular, it is argued that, in the first decade of the twenty-first century, the Japanese state attempted to draw clear boundaries of association: strengthening its alliance with the United States, on the one hand, and seeking to minimize contacts with 'rogue states', such as North Korea, on the other. This chapter builds on the concept of 'international society', proposed by the English School, as a prism through which to examine the debate on whether international society exists as a subset of the international system and, if so, how to draw a dividing line between the members and non-members of this society (Bull 2002; Buzan 1993, 2004; Bellamy 2004; Saunders 2006; Linklater and Suganami 2006).

In addition, this chapter takes the position that the boundaries crisscrossing the international system, which includes all states interacting strategically in relation to one another, are fluid and both scholars and practitioners find it difficult to decide whether a specific state should be part of international society or left outside it (Bull 2002: 15). There should be no monolithic understanding of this delinea-tion, since strategic interactions could happen from time to time to readjust the boundaries, just as in the case when Prime Minister Koizumi visited North Korea twice, in September 2002 and May 2004, as part of his efforts to normalize diplo-matic relations. In this way, we cannot say that Koizumi and his LDP successors took a dogmatic position in terms of drawing a clear boundary of association, but still it is argued that the concept of a boundary is particularly useful in illustrating the way in which the successive administrations attempted to distance Japan from what it identified as a 'rogue state' and enmesh itself more deeply with the US-led security alliance. It is still too early to predict how Prime Minister Hatoyama Yukio of the Democratic Party of Japan, who took office in September 2009, will redraw the boundaries of association. At the outset, Hatoyama declared repeatedly his intention of improving relations with countries with different value systems, such as China and North Korea, as part of his long-term goal of establishing an East Asian community. Hatoyama's anti-LDP diplomacy will be a good test case of how rigid the boundaries of association established by the previous LDP administrations have become. Deeply immersed in the reshaping of Japan's alliance relations with the United States and many pending domestic issues, however, Hatoyama had not followed up on his agenda of launching 'fraternal diplomacy' *vis-à-vis* North Korea by the end of the year.

Although it is difficult to define in one word Japan's security identity in the early twenty-first century, chiefly because the nation's identity remains in flux, one thing clear to international society is the fact that Japan attempted to crimi-nalize and ostracize North Korea rather than engage it. Locating 'Sameness' or 'Otherness' in relation to the significant Others around the Self is one of the quintessential processes of setting the boundaries of association and forming identity (Neumann 1996). Japan has shown signs of emerging as a proactive regional player capable of taking joint military actions, if necessary, against a common enemy, which its alliance with the United States was originally meant to fight.

Thus, the aim of this chapter more specifically is to illustrate how Japan has redrawn the boundaries of association after the end of the Cold War, and how it has treated North Korea as one of the 'rogue states'. To explain this process, we first elaborate on the notion of boundaries between international society and states outside it by using the theoretical orientation of the English School. Second, we illustrate how Japan has worked on redefining its security identity by drawing the boundaries of association. Third, the chapter offers a detailed account of how Japan has responded to North Korea's nuclear threats since 2002, when the second nuclear crisis gripped the attention of international society. Finally, we conclude with the argument that the drawing of the boundaries of association is not just the business of great powers capable of exercising structural influences in any given international society, but also that of small and medium powers finding themselves in the different stages of identity politics *vis-à-vis* their neighbours. In short, this chapter aims to explain why Japan's relationship with North Korea constitutes a case in which an individual state's identity politics became increasingly salient in drawing the boundaries of association, thus limiting the influences of power and shared ideas and institutions within international society.

1. Boundaries of international society

One of the English School's contributions to international relations theory is its development of the concept of 'international society'. In contrast to the realist idea of an international system, which reflects a worldview in which egoistic states operate in a way similar to billiard balls, the English School envisioned the possibility and materialization of international society. As an example, Wight argues that city states in ancient Greece and their neighbouring powers, such as Persia and Carthage, formed an international system (Wight 1977). Excluding these two non-Greek powers, the Greek city states formed an international society, as they shared common rules, interests and institutions under the pan-Hellenic order. The Greek city states were also held together by a common culture and identity, effectively forming a world society (Wight 1977).

International society, though existing in a more civilized form than the international system, however, is not a group of enlightened states. The main institutions of international society, according to Bull, are diplomacy, war, balance of power, great power management and international law (Bull 2002). Because of these factors, the member states of international society enjoy a certain degree of autonomy and stability, while a war is waged to keep international society intact. For instance, Buzan highlights the institution of sovereignty as a bedrock in preventing the elimination of a state from international society (Buzan 1993: 347), as noted:

> By these criteria the defining boundary between international system and society is when units not only recognize each other as being the same type of entity but also are prepared to accord each other equal legal status on that basis.
>
> (Buzan 1993: 345)

In sum, the criteria in differentiating international society from an international system seems to be: (1) whether the states share common rules and institutions (Bull and Watson 1984: 1); (2) whether they have common interests and thus impose restraints on each other in the use of force (Bull 2002: 4); (3) whether they have a common identity and culture (Buzan 1993: 335–36); and (4) whether they share common norms (Litwak 2000).

Therefore, 'rogue states', which are supposed to share no common norms, rules, institutions, interests, or identities with the members of international society, could be regarded as existing outside the boundaries of the society (Black 2006). The term 'rogue states' does not have any standing in international law, but is still crucial in directing the policies of the states belonging to international society (Litwak 2000). Often, the term brackets a group of states violating international norms, practices and laws by developing weapons of mass destruction, engaging in terrorism and failing to meet human rights standards in domestic governance (George 1993). In particular, the term 'rogue states' was the invention of the United States which, as the sole post-Cold War superpower, attempted to propagate its ideas across the world as a 'norm entrepreneur' (Finnemore and Sikkink 1998). North Korea was labelled as one of the 'rogue states' for violating such international norms as nuclear non-proliferation and human rights. North Korea, which joined the Nuclear Non-Proliferation Treaty (NPT) in 1985 under the pressure of the Soviet Union, left the NPT soon after the start of the second nuclear crisis in 2002. According to the 'Country Reports on Human Rights Practices' published by the US Department of State in 2008, North Korea was listed as one of the serious violators of human rights for continuing to 'control almost all aspects of citizens' lives, denying freedom of speech, press, assembly, and association, and restricting freedom of movement and workers' rights' (US Department of State 2008).

In spite of the presumed co-existence of international society and a group of 'rogue states' outside of it, not all the members of international society are necessarily expected to act in unison in their relation to a 'rogue state'. The members of the European Union have been particularly critical of the way the United States branded some states as 'rogues' and took coercive actions against them unilaterally (Saunders 2006). The US's use of the term 'rogue states' did not enjoy global recognition, precisely because it lacked transparency and rationality in terms of the choice of some states as 'rogues' out of a multiple of candidates. The United States has been arbitrary in determining which states are 'rogues', even though some candidate states were involved in almost the same efforts to develop nuclear weapons: North Korea is a 'rogue', while Pakistan is an ally with the status of 'a major non-NATO ally' (*New York Times*, 19 March 2004). Despite North Korea's development of nuclear weapons, Chinese leaders do not treat North Korea as a 'rogue state'. Indeed, Chinese officials and scholars have expressed sympathies with North Korea, often portraying it as struggling to survive with limited resources in a hostile international environment created by capitalist states encircling it (Zhang and Brown 2000).

Tension and sporadic norm violation arising from the discrepancies in state preferences and the identity politics of individual states within international society may pose challenges to the survival of any given international society. Nevertheless, this chapter argues that the existence of international society is possible not simply because of the existence of material and ideational power, exercised by great powers as 'norm entrepreneurs' in the process of setting the criteria for membership, or collective ideas and institutions, shared and embedded among the member states. The survival of international society is possible partly because of the oversight and tolerance of individual states' sporadic violations of shared ideas and norms, as long as these violations do not put the survival of international society *per se* at stake, which will be illustrated in connection with Japan's relations with North Korea in the following sections. Therefore, a sense of common identity, reinforced by shared ideas and constitutive norms, could work as a 'shock absorber' to maintain the integrity of international society in the event of sporadic violations of common norms and rules by individual states.

2. Japan's boundaries of international society

This section aims to illustrate how Japan draws and adjusts the boundaries of its association. Japan, which belonged to the US-led capitalist bloc during the Cold War, became a key member of an ever-expanding international society bound together by such ideas, norms and institutions as democracy, market economy and the World Trade Organization (WTO). Therefore, it is safe to argue that Japan and North Korea have no history of association as members of the same international society. Since the birth of the Democratic People's Republic of Korea, the official name of North Korea, as a communist state in 1948 under the stewardship of the Soviet Union, Japan has remained one of the frontline states in containing communism. However, did Japan adopt the common patterns of behaviour in its relations with those outside its own international society?

In spite of the US's blanket sanctions against North Korea following the 1950–53 Korean War, Japan had not been deterred by the dominant two-world vision of the Cold War, characterized by an intense ideological rivalry and all-out competition between the capitalist and communist blocs. For instance, Japan sought to maximize its security through non-military means, living up to its mantle of 'a peace state'. Distancing itself from the political and ideological confrontations at the global level, Japan had devised its policies towards the communist bloc, including North Korea, under the principle of *seikei bunri*, or separating politics from economics (Fouse 2006: 136). North Korea, which prioritized cut-throat competition with South Korea, had also taken pragmatic steps and attempted to maximize its national interests through the improvement of economic and cultural ties with Japan (Roy 1988). Therefore, annual two-way trade between Japan and North Korea had steadily grown to the USD500 million mark in 1980 and then maintained that level until 1997 in spite of some temporal fluctuations (Mimura 2005). However, North Korea's economic hardship from the late 1990s and Japan's trade sanctions, imposed since North Korea's multi-stage missile test in 1998, brought bilateral trade down to USD252 million in 2004. Overall, the different political ideologies between the two states did not hamper bilateral exchange, because both states had prioritized economic growth over political considerations (Shin 1981). Partly because of the strong presence of the leftist forces in Japan, such as the Japan Socialist Party (JSP) as the number one opposition party during the Cold War, North Korea, which had been a proactive member of the communist bloc and the non-aligned movement, was rather viewed as a standard bearer of the Korean nation, while South Korea was widely seen as a puppet of the United States under the virtual occupation of the US military (Kurata 2000).

When the communist bloc was torn apart with the collapse of the Soviet Union at the end of the 1980s, North Korea refused to join the global capitalist structure and sought its own way of survival. North Korea's penchant to develop nuclear weapons and its anti-American stance were enough to make it into one of the 'rogue states' for the United States, seeking to prevent the spread of weapons of mass destruction in a fluid post-Cold War security environment. During and immediately after the Cold War, Japan, enmeshed in its alliance with the United

States and concerned about the potential emerging rivalry with China, had failed initially to set out a grand strategy in relation to the Korean Peninsula. With the governing political elite complacent about Japan's association with North Korea, academics did not pay much attention to Japan's North Korea policy, except for a handful of Korea experts producing a series of monographs and articles (Cha 2000: 249). Up until the mid-1990s, it could be argued that Japan did not possess clear strategic security goals in dealing with North Korea. Some scholars viewed Japan as seeking to prop up North Korea as part of the *status quo* policy aiming to maintain the Korean divide (Cha 1999: 12). Just as European states felt uneasy with German unification, Japan has been concerned with the emergence of a unified Korea. In particular, from the perspective of geopolitics, the Korean Peninsula has often been called the 'dagger pointed at the heart' of Japan. Accordingly, South Korea, a staunch anti-communist state during the Cold War, had been highly critical of Japan's 'equidistance policy' as a sinister plot to perpetuate the Korean divide (Curtis 1993). Japan's policy might have come from a more practical necessity, since its assistance to North Korea could be interpreted as a proactive effort to prevent the collapse of the regime and the influx of large-scale refugees rather than a grand scheme to keep the Korean Peninsula divided (Hughes 1999: 170).

With Japan's security identity remaining fluid in relation to North Korea, Japan was able to maintain a relatively good working relationship with North Korea during the Cold War. In this security environment, pro-Pyongyang ethnic Koreans in Japan were not subject to crackdowns by the Japanese authorities in spite of their close ties with the Pyongyang regime and involvement in various illegal and unlawful practices. Accordingly, while diplomatic pressure was exerted by South Korea, the Japanese government did not take harsh actions against the pro-North Korea organizations in Japan, which had often played a crucial role in helping North Korean spies infiltrate into South Korea in the 1960s and 1970s (Cha 2000: 258). The end of the Cold War also paved the way for the opening of political negotiations to improve bilateral relations. In 1990, Kanemaru Shin of the LDP and Tanabe Makoto of the JSP made a visit to Pyongyang, carrying a personal letter from Prime Minister Takeshita Noboru. The visit produced what is called a three-party declaration (LDP, JSP and the Workers' Party of North Korea), which called for diplomatic normalization between the two countries. In January 1991, diplomatic negotiations on normalization opened and continued until May 1992, before breaking down because of differences over the modalities of colonial compensation and diplomatic pressures from the United States and South Korea.

Since the late 1990s, however, Japan started a process of sharpening its security identity and, in particular, the Koizumi administration (2001–06) masterminded Japan's emergence as a proactive player in international and regional security. Once Japan recognized the need for the presence of enemies in order to redraw its security identity, it followed the pattern of what the United States did during the Cold War to inflate the threats from the Soviet Union and step up military preparedness in consideration of the worst-case scenarios (Campbell 1998). North Korea, which has repeatedly threatened Japan with both words and actions, was an easy target of manipulation. Though implicit as an official doctrine,

Japan's *boundary politics*, at the turn of the twenty-first century, clearly aimed to highlight North Korea's 'Otherness' and minimize all forms of association with the state, which engaged in a series of 'rogue' behaviours: the pursuit of nuclear and missile programmes, the dispatch of spy ships and the abduction of Japanese nationals.

Under the Koizumi administration, there were a number of exceptional moments in Japan–North Korea relations, just like the US Cold War politics was not marked by the consistent implementation of containment strategies, but checkered with moments of rapprochement, called détente. Like the conservative Nixon–Kissinger team had enjoyed a certain leeway in interacting with the communist bloc, the conservative Koizumi administration succeeded in realizing the prime minister's visits to North Korea in 2002 and 2004. Initially, Koizumi's diplomacy aiming to normalize diplomatic relations with North Korea, the last country to do so except for Taiwan, received a positive response domestically (McCormack and Wada 2005; Wada 2009). When Koizumi's achievements were subject to close scrutiny by the media and the public, however, the questions of the allegedly dead abductees rose prominently rather than the successful return of five abductees. North Korean chairman Kim Jong-Il's apology for the abduction and the incursion of 'spy ships' into Japanese waters backfired and contributed to consolidating North Korea's image as a terrorist state. The Japanese political landscape, characterized by the rise of the right wing and the decline of the left, and the public space, abuzz with the ideals of human security, pressed the administration in an unprecedented manner to drop Japan's traditional complacency in diplomacy and sharpen up the boundaries of association.

The process of criminalizing and ostracizing North Korea from international society was relatively smooth because of North Korea's violation of various international norms and the George W. Bush administration's support of Japan's rise as a regional security partner ready to take joint actions against North Korea. Domestically, the Japanese mass media, especially TV news shows, made sensational reports on the abduction issue, portraying North Korea as a terrorist state. When it determined that the level of media coverage was not high enough, the Abe Shinzō administration instructed Nippon Broadcasting Corporation (NHK) to increase its coverage of the abduction issue (Wada 2009).

In fact, to a large degree, foreign policy is a boundary-drawing political act involving the construction and demarcation of the Self and the Other (Campbell 1998: 62). According to the Copenhagen School of security studies, a state's identity is the effect of reiterated, successful foreign policy behaviour. Wæver explains the process in which a certain problem is elevated to the level of an existential threat through an act of speech which clearly distinguishes the Self from the relevant Others (Wæver 1996). The articulation of a long list of threats from North Korea, such as nuclear weapons, missiles and terrorist acts, often repeated and exaggerated by politicians and journalists, could create a perception that Japan urgently needs to take security measures or face destruction. By identifying the existential threats emanating from the Other, the Japanese state comes to terms with 'who we are'.

However, this new phase of Japan's identity dynamic *vis-à-vis* North Korea started to show signs of excessive rigidity to the extent that it would demand that North Korea be left outside the boundaries of international society until it liquidates all forms of 'rogue' behaviour of the past. If the United States had prioritized an irreversible denuclearization of North Korea, Japan called for the liquidation of other 'rogue' behaviour in addition to denuclearization, such as the return of all Japanese nationals kidnapped by North Korean agents in the 1970s and 1980s and the punishment of those responsible for these criminal acts. When North Korea refused to take conciliatory steps in connection with the abduction issue, Japan became the only state among the member states of the six-party talks to boycott energy assistance to the North. Japan refused to accept the shared idea among the participants of the six-party talks – the United States, China, Russia and South Korea – that it was time to remove North Korea from the US State Department's list of state sponsors of terrorism and offer energy assistance in return for denuclearization (*Washington Post*, 20 March 2007). Japan's obsession with North Korea's 'rogue' behaviour and conviction that it cannot coexist peacefully with a 'rogue state' led to Japan's distrust of international institutions, in this case the six-party nuclear talks, and a refusal to bind itself to an international agreement, which will be illustrated in detail in the next section.

In sum, the boundaries of international society are malleable, since its member states enjoy some leeway in deciding their boundaries of association, which are often products of domestic politics depending on, among others, norms, interests, pre-established identities or the result of some speech acts contributing to the formation of a new identity. Such identity politics could offer some insight in analyzing the way in which the Japanese state came to befriend an enemy state during the Cold War and then deny any forms of association with a 'rogue state' after the end of the Cold War.

3. Japan's responses to North Korea's nuclear threats

North Korea's die-hard penchant for the development of nuclear weapons has been arguably one of the most important security issues affecting Northeast Asia since the end of the Cold War. As the world's second largest economic superpower, Japan has been expected to play a crucial role in devising and implementing international efforts to coax the state to give up its 'rogue' behaviour and join the ranks of international society. Nevertheless, Japan was not a proactive player in regional security arrangements when North Korea touched off the first nuclear crisis by declaring that it was leaving the NPT in 1993. Short of any sizable political and diplomatic leverage over North Korea, Japan had to play an indirect diplomatic role mainly through policy coordination with the United States and South Korea, called the Trilateral Coordination and Oversight Group. Rather than raising its own voice, Japan waited on the sidelines for the United States to handle the case directly with North Korea. When the United States struck a nuclear deal with North Korea in October 1994 under the name of the Agreed Framework, Japan had no option but to join the Korean Peninsula Energy Development Organization

(KEDO) as a founding member along with South Korea and promise a financial contribution reaching up to USD1 billion.

South Korea, especially the Kim Young-sam administration, had been against any independent Japanese attempts to enter into direct negotiations with North Korea or escalate tension unilaterally. When North Korea's famine reached crisis level in 1995 after devastating floods, for instance, Japan offered 300,000 tons of rice to the North. Since the amount dwarfed South Korea's assistance of 150,000 tons, President Kim assailed Japan for attempting to block inter-Korean rapprochement. Japan's policy with North Korea was viewed largely as drifting partly because of pressure from the United States and South Korea and partly because of its lack of grand strategies (Hughes 1999: 171). Even though it took swift action against North Korea's test of a multi-stage Taepodong missile, which flew over the Japanese archipelago in 1998, by cutting contributions to an international reactor project in North Korea and cancelling flights, Prime Minister Obuchi Keizō's action was rather seen as proportionate to the level of the shock the Japanese public experienced. Japan could not be freed from its Cold War inertia in security affairs, even though it was slowly moving to strengthen its alliance with the United States and formulate legal and administrative frameworks in the event of contingencies in East Asia (Ducke 2002: 144).

In October 2002, North Korea made it clear in its diplomatic contact with the United States that it would maintain the right to nuclear deterrence, a statement interpreted by the United States and the members of international society as evidence of its operation of clandestine nuclear programmes and a flagrant violation of the international norm of non-proliferation. The incident came shortly after Prime Minister Koizumi visited Pyongyang for the first-ever summit meeting with North Korean leader Kim Jong-il on 17 September 2002. North Korea's admission to the existence of nuclear programmes was a clear violation of the Pyongyang Declaration signed by Koizumi and Kim. According to the declaration, 'Both sides confirmed that, for an overall resolution of the nuclear issues on the Korean Peninsula, they would comply with all related international agreements'. By 'all related international agreements', the two states referred to the 'Agreed Framework', signed in Geneva between the United States and North Korea in 1994, which produced a deal enabling North Korea to give up its nuclear programmes in return for the construction of light-water reactors, economic assistance and diplomatic recognition. Since the US's disclosure of North Korea's position on nuclear issues came right after Koizumi's celebrated first visit to Pyongyang, it was speculated that the United States might have attempted to derail the process of rapprochement between North Korea and Japan (Cumings 2003).

In fact, Prime Minister Koizumi's visit to North Korea in 2002, which led to North Korean leader Kim's admission to the abduction of Japanese nationals, became a monumental event from the perspective of Japan's drawing of boundaries within international society and outside it. Despite Kim's admission to the abduction of Japanese nationals and his offering of an apology, Koizumi faced increasing pressure from Japan's civil society to take stern measures against North Korea to shed light on the remaining mysteries of these incidents and secure the custody of any additional survivors. Admitting it had kidnapped 13 Japanese nationals, North Korea returned 5 survivors, while claiming that the 8 others were all dead. Initially, Koizumi mobilized various policy options on hand to resolve the abduction issue. On the bilateral level, the prime minister revisited Pyongyang in 2004 to seek a comprehensive deal on the issues of bilateral concerns, including the abduction issue and diplomatic normalization. Even though North Korea took additional conciliatory actions by sending to Japan the families of the abductees, as well as the remains of the dead, Japanese public opinion turned extremely negative about any future dealings with North Korea. Following Koizumi's first visit to North Korea in 2002, the *Yomiuri Shimbun* (20 September 2002) published an opinion poll showing that 91 per cent of respondents believed that the issue of abduction should be fully addressed before Japan normalizes relations with North Korea. After the second visit in 2004, opinion polls by major newspapers reported that a majority of Japanese (56 per cent in the *Yomiuri Shimbun*, 61 per cent in the *Asahi Shimbun* and 72 per cent in the *Mainichi Shimbun*) were against the food and medicine aid Koizumi offered to North Korea (*Kyodo News*, 25 May 2005).

With the Koizumi and Abe administrations convinced that it was almost impossible to secure a complete account of the abductions from North Korea to meet the high expectations from Japan's civil society, they moved to suspend the existing channels of communication and transportation, as well as humanitarian aid to North Korea. Despite some concessions to the Japanese government in a response to Koizumi's unusual diplomatic efforts, however, North Korea also stuck to the original position that it had done everything it could in terms of the abduction issue, while its nuclear programmes were to be resolved only through bilateral talks between Pyongyang and Washington.

Japan's boundary politics were not just the product of North Korea's violation of international norms, but the fruit of Japanese society's identification of North Korea as a state which does not share any common norms, rules or institutions with Japan. If North Korea's development of nuclear weapons and missiles provoked Japan's ruling elite, its abduction of Japanese nationals directly led the public to perceive North Korea as one of the criminal states posing a threat to the safety of individual citizens, and hence a 'rogue'. Nevertheless, Japan's boundary politics appeared 'abnormal' to other states, because it prioritized the resolution of the abduction issue over the nuclear issue within the framework of the six-party talks. From the perspective of human security, North Korea has claimed that the Koizumi, Abe Shinzō and Fukuda Yasuo administrations have ignored such issues as the litigations of Asian victims of Japan's colonial rule, which involved making women into 'wartime sexual slaves' and men into forced labourers, while devoting themselves to resolving the issue of the kidnapping of Japanese nationals (*KCNA*, 31 January 2008). The former, which affected millions of Asians, took place about 60 years ago in a state-level operation of imperial Japan, while the latter occurred about 30 years ago in isolated cases in which less than 20 Japanese nationals were kidnapped by North Korean agents for espionage purposes.

The interplay of the second nuclear crisis and Japan's changing perception of security made the Koizumi and Abe administrations recalibrate the identity of

Japan as a proactive player in regional security. In the aftermath of North Korea's departure from the NPT in January 2003, the hawkish members of the Koizumi and Abe administrations, along with some local autonomous bodies, devised new ideas and policies on how to clearly demarcate the boundaries of association by seeking to isolate North Korea from international society. In February 2004, the Japanese Diet, primarily targeting North Korea, revised the Foreign Exchange and Foreign Trade Laws, which opened the way for the government to take actions to control remittances and trade. In June 2004, another law was enacted to facilitate the ban on the entry of specified ships from a specific state. In November 2004, Prime Minister Koizumi approved the proposal to implement five-stage economic sanctions on North Korea, authored by the Countermeasures Headquarters for the North Korea Abduction Issue of the ruling Liberal Democratic Party: (1) freezing or postponement of humanitarian assistance; (2) tighter supervision or embargo on remittances and capital transactions; (3) partial suspension of trade; (4) a ban on some North Korean ships entering Japanese ports and total suspension of trade; and (5) a total ban on North Korean ships (*Kyodo News*, 5 November 2004).

In sum, Japan has adopted a series of actions against North Korea on multiple levels: (1) the international level, such as pressing the United States to keep North Korea on the list of states sponsoring terrorism; (2) the bilateral level, such as suspending government-level assistance to North Korea, including humanitarian aid, as well as cutting the flow of human and material traffic; and (3) the domestic level, such as depriving pro-North Korean organizations in Japan of any privileges they had enjoyed in the past. These actions, comprising Japan's diplomatic, financial and social policies, created serious repercussions in Japan's international relations and domestic society.

First, Japan linked a breakthrough in the six-party nuclear talks, which called for the removal of North Korea from the US list of state sponsors of terrorism, to the successful resolution of the abduction issue. North Korea, which had been subject to comprehensive US sanctions since the Korean War, was added to the terrorism list after its bombing of a South Korean airliner in 1987. Even though North Korea condemned all forms of terrorism and took other actions in a desperate effort to secure a US decision to remove it from the list, the United States dragged its feet, citing, for example, North Korea's accommodation of Japanese Red Army terrorists. Those on the list face a series of sanctions under different US laws, such as a ban on dual-use items under the Export Administration Act of 1979; a ban on US foreign assistance including the Export-Import Bank credits and guarantees under the Foreign Assistance Act of 1961; and ineligibility for the Generalized System of Preferences under the Trade Act of 1974. Therefore, keeping North Korea on the list serves as one of the best ways of isolating the state from international society.

However, the second stage of the six-party agreement, reached on 3 October 2007, called on North Korea to declare and disable all of its existing nuclear facilities, while the other participating states were to provide it with 950,000 tons of fuel. In addition, the United States was to remove North Korea from the list of states sponsoring terrorism (*New York Times*, 4 October 2007). In the first part of the deal, North Korea had suspended its nuclear activities by shutting down a reactor in Yongbyon. With North Korea sabotaging the resolution of the abduction issue, the Japanese representatives to the six-party talks attempted to prevent or at least slow down the process of reaching an agreement on nuclear issues alone. According to the website of the Ministry of Foreign Affairs (MOFA), Foreign Minister Komura Masahiko said in a press briefing on 14 December 2007, 'it is of utmost importance that we advance the issue of denuclearization in a manner that is well-balanced with advancing Japan–North Korea relations' (MOFA 2007a). The biggest obstacle in advancing bilateral relations was obviously the abduction of Japanese nationals.

In the last year of his four-year second term, however, President George W. Bush's administration moved swiftly to remove North Korea from the terrorism list in accordance with the progress of the six-party talks as part of the administration's efforts to secure a major foreign policy achievement before the end of its tenure. Perplexed by the US's shift of attitude towards North Korea, Japan made all-out efforts to persuade President Bush and the US Congress to keep the 'rogue' on the list, until North Korea took positive actions for the resolution of the abduction issue. The Japanese administration made a similar request to the other participating states of the six-party talks, such as China and South Korea (*Washington Post*, 17 May 2008). Japan kept this position up until the United States and North Korea cleared all hurdles for a breakthrough in the second stage of the nuclear deal, making US representative Christopher Hill request a special bilateral meeting with North Korean chief negotiator Kim Kye-kwan to discuss the abduction issue (*Yonhap News*, 25 May 2008). However, President Bush moved to drop North Korea from the terrorism list and lift some trade sanctions against the wishes of Japan (*Washington Post*, 27 June 2008). Japan had to satisfy itself only with North Korea's promise to reopen the investigation into the abduction issue (*Asahi Shimbun*, 14 June 2008).

Japan also refused to join international efforts to provide energy assistance to North Korea in return for disabling its nuclear facilities, perplexing the other participants of the six-party talks. According to the joint statement, issued on 13 February 2007, following the six-party talks, the five participating states promised to provide 'economic, energy and humanitarian assistance up to the equivalent of one million tons of heavy fuel oil (HFO)' to North Korea, upon its 'complete declaration of all nuclear programs and disablement of all existing nuclear facilities, including graphite-moderated reactors and reprocessing plant' (*International Herald Tribune*, 13 February 2007). In an unusually strong diplomatic initiative, however, Japan made it clear that it had no intention of joining the efforts to offer energy assistance. In a press briefing on 3 October 2007, Foreign Minister Komura said that, as long as there is no change of North Korea's policy on the abduction issue, 'There will be no change in Japan's policies' (MOFA 2007b). North Korea reacted hysterically to Japan's adherence to the abduction issue, calling it an attempt to sabotage the six-party talks and even questioning Japan's qualifications as a member of the nuclear talks (*KCNA*, 10 March 2007).

Second, Koizumi and his successors took actions against North Korea in the direction of banning the bilateral flow of humans and goods. In the wake of the second nuclear crisis which started in January 2003, then Chief Cabinet Secretary Abe Shinzō made public the idea of searching North Korean vessels visiting Japan, such as the 9,672-ton North Korean ferry *Man Gyong Bong-92*, which was in service between Niigata and Wonsan to transport ethnic Koreans visiting their relatives in North Korea (*Asahi Shimbun*, 13 May 2003). Abe also revealed his intention to strengthen the supervision of financial institutions run by pro-North Korean organizations. The ferry and these financial organizations had been under suspicion of being the channels for illegal remittances to North Korea. Out of USD120 million sent from Japan to North Korea in the years 2000–02, according to the estimates of the Japanese Ministry of Finance, USD107 million was transferred by North Korean boats, while only USD13 million was transmitted through banks (*Yomiuri Online*, 28 June 2003). In addition, a North Korean defector testified to the US Senate committee that the *Man Gyong Bong-92*, built in 1992 with funds from the pro-Pyongyang General Association of Korean Residents in Japan, was the main means of transporting 90 per cent of the state's missile parts (*BBC News*, 9 June 2003). When there was no sanction in place, the ferry made about 20 to 30 trips a year between Japan and North Korea. When the Japanese authorities planned to launch a large-scale inspection by mobilizing about 1,900 police and customs officers, the North Korean ferry cancelled its scheduled arrival in Niigata on 9 June 2003. North Korea's official Korean Central News Agency (KCNA) quoted a Foreign Ministry spokesman as denouncing Japan for actively participating in the US efforts to 'establish an institution' to inspect North Korean ships and aircraft (*New York Times*, 8 June 2003).

The way the North Korean news organizations portrayed Japan's action to strengthen the inspection of North Korean vessels is illustrative of this chapter's discussion of the drawing of the boundaries of international society. The KCNA described the action as 'part of the Bush administration's foolish and shameful moves to ostracize the DPRK politically and morally on the international arena and isolate and stifle it by terming it a "rogue state"' (*New York Times*, 10 June 2003). This statement means that North Korea had obviously interpreted Japan's sanctions as an attempt to isolate North Korea from international society as part of its boundary politics. These sanctions, a sign of Japan's assertive diplomacy, contributed to Koizumi's popularity with an NHK survey reporting that 59 per cent of voters supported the prime minister in June 2003, up 5 percentage points from another survey from the previous month.

Until 2002, Japan was North Korea's second-largest trading partner, only after China, partly owing to the presence of the pro-Pyongyang Korean community in Japan. However, Japan's economic sanctions contributed to curbing bilateral trade with North Korea significantly from 2003. The volumes of Japan's exports to and imports from North Korea, which reached USD132.25 million and USD235.27 million respectively in 2002, decreased to USD90.34 million and USD172.3 million in 2003 and USD88.54 million and USD164.04 million in 2004 (Mimura 2005). In this way, Japan's strengthened actions to control bilateral exchange with

North Korea after the second nuclear crisis and the controversy over the abduction of Japanese nationals were very effective in curbing bilateral trade, even though the impact could be reduced over time, in case North Korea found substitute trading partners possibly from China and South Korea.

Japan has strengthened sanctions against North Korea especially in the wake of the 'abduction fiasco'. As part of the summit agreement between Koizumi and Kim in May 2004, Japan pledged 250,000 tons of food to North Korea. But only 80,000 of the pledged amount was actually delivered in 2004, because Japan suspended humanitarian aid to North Korea following a controversy over the true identity of the supposed remains of Yokota Megumi, one of the abductees who allegedly perished, which North Korea had returned to Japan. According to Japan's DNA tests, the bones were not the remains of Megumi, but a mixture of those from unrelated persons. But the DNA tests which prompted Japan to take stern actions against North Korea were dismissed as scientifically unreliable in an article by David Cyranoski in the 3 February 2005 issue of the international journal *Nature* (Cyranoski 2005; also see McCormack 2005). Nevertheless, Japan has stuck to the position that it would not lift sanctions until North Korea offered substantial evidence as to the whereabouts of the abductees.

Beyond a ban on humanitarian aid, Japan started to take full-scale economic sanctions against the North from 2006. When North Korea tested seven missiles, including a long-range Taepodong-2 (4,000–6,000 kilometres), on 5 July 2006, Japan became the first state to unilaterally impose a package of nine-point sanctions against it, including a ban on the entry of North Korean officials, chartered flights and ferry services, such as the *Man Gyong Bong-92* (*Asahi Shimbun*, 6 July 2006). After North Korea's nuclear test on 9 October 2006, Japan expanded the scope of the ban on all types of North Korean-registered ships, while prohibiting all imports from North Korea, barring North Korean visitors and banning Japanese exports of 24 items, including luxury food items. Prime Minister Fukuda, who followed his predecessors' policy of isolating North Korea, said in an interview with the *Washington Post*, 'The nuclear issue, the missile issue that imposes a threat to Japan and the abduction issue would come as a set of three – called a trilogy . . . Lacking any one of the three would not solve the matter' (17 May 2008).

Third, the worsening relationship between the two states has affected negatively the status of the pro-North Korean community in Japan. As the legacy of Japan's colonial rule, especially its mobilization of labourers and military draftees during the 1939–45 period of World War II, the number of Korean residents in Japan reached 2.3 million soon after the war. Even though a majority returned to their homelands, more than 600,000 to date remain and have become one of the largest minority communities in Japan. Those Koreans, called *zainichi* (literally, staying in Japan), were originally deprived of their Japanese passports when the San Francisco Peace Treaty took effect in 1952. The 'statelessness' of this community was partially resolved when Japan signed a treaty of diplomatic normalization with South Korea in 1965, allowing them to acquire South Korean nationality (Chee 1983). However, Japan did not establish diplomatic relations with North Korea and 25 per cent of Koreans residing permanently in Japan are regarded as members of the pro-Pyongyang General Association of Korean Residents in Japan, better known as Chongryon or Chosen Soren. Given the fact that Japan does not have diplomatic relations with North Korea, the Chongryon headquarters, located in Chiyoda Ward, Tokyo, played a role as North Korea's de facto embassy to the extent that it could issue North Korean passports. Despite political and social discrimination in Japanese society, these Koreans, holding the status of special permanent residents, had decided to lead a life in Japan carrying North Korean passports as a symbol of their allegiance to the Pyongyang regime. Often, this allegiance is expressed in the form of regular remittances to their family members and relatives in North Korea via various legal and illegal means. Even though it considered adopting policies to cut this flow of money into North Korea right after the first nuclear crisis in 1993, the Japanese government did not take actions for fear of negative repercussions from North Korea and the pro-North Korean community in Japan (Ducke 2002: 148).

However, once the boundaries of international society were sharpened amid the interplay of Japan's shifting security identity and North Korea's provocative actions, the pro-Pyongyang Koreans faced a series of crackdowns by Japan's law enforcement authorities in connection with their illegal and unlawful activities. First, local governments started imposing taxes on the properties of the Chongryon headquarters and provincial branch offices from 2003. They had been exempt from property taxes since 1972, when progressive Tokyo Governor Minobe Ryōkichi recognized them as an equivalent of North Korea's diplomatic missions. In a tacit recognition of its role, the headquarters enjoyed unofficial diplomatic immunity from taxation, as well as a certain level of extraterritoriality. In July 2003, however, the Tokyo metropolitan government decided to impose JPY46 million (USD400,000) in property tax on the properties operated by Chongryon, reversing the 1972 decision. The decision was initiated by Tokyo Governor Ishihara Shintarō, one of the best-known right-wing politicians, who had often expressed his displeasure with the Korean residents in Japan. Chongryon declined to pay, which led to the seizure of three Chongryon properties.

The Chongryon headquarters became the target of hate crimes, especially in the wake of North Korean leader Kim's admissions regarding the abduction of Japanese nationals in 2002. As a resolute step, which could deal a serious blow to the operation of Chongryon, the Japanese government-backed Resolution and Collection Corporation sued Chongryon for payment of JPY62.7 billion in loans that it had borrowed from the failed pro-Pyongyang Chogin credit unions (*Asahi Shimbun*, 30 June 2007). In a desperate effort to rescue the headquarters from being auctioned off, Chongryon had been looking for a buyer that would allow it to stay put after its sale. Chongryon's weakened position produced a high-profile fraud case which involved a group of Japanese traders, including Ogata Shigetake, 73, a former director-general of the Public Security Intelligence Agency, which is actually in charge of monitoring Chongryon's activities. Ogata and other accomplices were arrested for this fraud in which they attempted to take over Chongryon's properties without paying the promised money (*Asahi Shimbun*, 29 June 2007). Contemplating the case, however, North Korea refrained from bringing

Japan's action against the Chongryon headquarters to the negotiating table of the six-party talks. A North Korean Foreign Ministry spokesman described the actions by the Resolution and Collection Corporation as 'an act of flagrant violation of our republic's sovereignty' (*Yonhap News*, 1 July 2007). Despite its displeasure with Japan's action, North Korea attempted to salvage a deal on the nuclear issues by preventing other issues from hampering the progress of the six-party talks.

As evidence of the shift of Japan's security identity, Japanese officials started to discuss the possibility of a pre-emptive strike against military targets in North Korea, identified as one of the 'rogue states'. Soon after North Korea test-fired the long-range Taepodong-2 on 5 July 2006, Japan's Foreign Minister, Asō Tarō, said on NHK on 9 July, 'if a missile, armed with a nuclear bomb, was heading towards Japan, we cannot sit idle' (*Asahi Shimbun*, 10 July 2006). The other senior officials of the Koizumi administration, including Defence Agency chief Nukaga Fukushirō, raised the possibility of acquiring intercontinental ballistic missiles and long-range strategic bombers capable of pre-emptive strikes. North Korea's nuclear test exacerbated a sense of insecurity among the Japanese public, given that the state has already deployed the medium-range Rodong missiles which put Japan within their range. With only a narrow strip of water dividing the two states, the level of insecurity has been qualitatively different from that experienced by most Americans, who remain outside of the range of North Korea's most sophisticated missiles. In his meeting with South Korean Prime Minister Koh Kun, Japan's Defence Agency Chief, Ishiba Shigeru, said, 'North Korea's Rodong missiles cannot reach the United States. They will not use them against South Koreans, since they belong to the same nation. Therefore, we have the fear that they will aim at Japan' (*Yonhap News*, 29 March 2003). The *Yomiuri Shimbun* (17 October 2006) reported that 81 per cent of those polled felt severe threats from North Korea. The *Asahi Shimbun* (11 October 2006) also said in a survey that 62 per cent of the respondents were 'strongly threatened' by the nuclear test. Supported by the rising fear on the public level, the Japanese state endeavoured to draw clear boundaries of association, thus pushing a 'rogue' state like North Korea outside of international society.

Conclusion

This chapter aimed to offer an analysis of Japan's evolving relationship with North Korea from the perspectives of how the boundaries of international society are negotiated and how North Korea was pushed outside the Japanese version of international society. As part of its efforts to become a proactive player in regional security at the turn of the twenty-first century, Japan has strengthened its alliance with the United States at the cost of its relations with North Korea. In this process, Japan has not only suspended humanitarian and economic assistance to North Korea, but antagonized pro-North Korean residents in Japan. With the Japanese authorities' crackdown on their illegal and unlawful activities strengthened, this community has faced the peril of survival in Japan's increasingly hostile environment. Overall, Japan's new sense of the boundaries of international society, a product of the state's reiterated foreign and domestic policy actions, offers a clear yardstick in judging what is tolerable or not in terms of the actions of North Korea and the pro-North Korean community in Japan. Nevertheless, the boundaries of international society, as mentioned earlier, are malleable and subject to bargaining. When the United States and South Korea make some progress in bilateral or multilateral negotiations with North Korea, Japan is likely to face increasing international and domestic pressure to re-engage with North Korea and rethink the boundaries of its association.

This chapter used the English School's idea of international society to illustrate Japan's boundary politics *vis-à-vis* North Korea. Great powers play the role of 'norm entrepreneurs' in drawing the boundaries of association and setting the membership criteria of international society, as the United States did as a hegemonic power during and after the Cold War. Although Japan belonged to the US-led capitalist bloc during the Cold War, it also enjoyed some leeway in setting its own boundaries of association by keeping relatively close economic ties with North Korea. When the United States shifted its policies towards North Korea to resolve outstanding nuclear issues in 2007, which could be seen as an initial US effort to redraw the boundaries of association and accept North Korea as a member of international society, Japan refused to follow suit, citing North Korea's 'rogue' behaviour. In sum, this chapter illustrated that the business of drawing the boundaries of association is not just that of great powers, but that of individual states. Japan's boundary-setting behaviour creates a case in which the idea of international society has only limited effect on the choice of individual states. The chapter shows that Japan's boundaries of association were rather the product of its identity politics: during the Cold War, Japan kept good working relations with North Korea as a 'peace state', while the post-Cold War era led Japan to sharpen its security identity as a regional military power, thus identifying North Korea as a threat. Overall, we have highlighted the malleable boundaries of international society, largely affected by the preferences and identity dynamics of individual states in spite of the material power of hegemonic states and the shared ideas and institutions in any given international society. Although there exists a society of nation states, the boundaries of association are fluid and malleable, testifying to the unswerving importance of domestic identity politics and state preferences in deciding which states are inside or outside of international society.

References

Bellamy, Alex (ed.) (2004) *International Society and its Critics*, Oxford: Oxford University Press.

Black, Lindsay (2006) 'All at Sea? Japan's Response to the Contemporary Maritime Security Threats Posed by Infidels, Pirates and Barbarians', unpublished thesis, University of Sheffield.

Bull, Hedley (2002) *The Anarchical Society: a study of order in world politics*, New York: Palgrave.

Bull, Hedley and Watson, Adam (eds) (1984) *The Expansion of International Society*, Oxford: Oxford University Press.

Buzan, Barry (1993) 'From international system to international society: structural realism and regime theory meet the English School', *International Organization*, 47, 3: 327–52.

—— (2004) *From International to World Society? English School theory and social structure of globalization*, Cambridge: Cambridge University Press.

Campbell, David (1998) *Writing Security: United States foreign policy and the politics of identity*, Minneapolis: University of Minnesota Press.

Cha, Victor (1999) *Alignment Despite Antagonism: The United States-Korea-Japan security triangle*, Stanford: Stanford University Press.

—— (2000) 'Japan's grand strategy on the Korean peninsula: optimistic realism', *Japanese Journal of Political Science*, 1, 2: 249–74.

Chee, Choung-Il (1983) 'Japan's post-war mass denationalization of the Korean minority in international law', *Korea and World Affairs*, 7, 1: 81–113.

Chomsky, Noam (2000) *Rogue States: the rule of force in world affairs*, London: Pluto Press.

Cumings, Bruce (2003) 'Wrong Again', London Review of Books. Online. Available: http://www.lrb.co.uk/v25/n23/cumi01_.html (accessed 20 May 2008).

—— (2004) 'Decoupled from history: North Korea in the "axis of evil"', in Andre Schiffrin (ed.) *Inventing the Axis of Evil*, New York: The New Press.

Curtis, Gerald (ed.) (1993) *Japan's Foreign Relations after the Cold War*, New York: M.E. Sharpe.

Cyranoski, David (2005) 'DNA is burning issue as Japan and Korea clash over kidnaps', *Nature,* 443, 445 (3 February 2005). Online. Available: http://www.nature.com/nature/journal/v433/n7025/full/433445a.html (accessed 2 February 2009).

Ducke, Isa (2002) *Status Power: Japanese foreign policy making toward Korea*, New York: Routledge.

Finnemore, Martha and Sikkink, Kathryn (1998) 'International norm dynamics and political change', *International Organization*, 52, 4: 887–918.

Fouse, David (2006) 'Japan's post-cold war North Korea policy: hedging toward autonomy?' in Yoichiro Sato and Satu Limaye (eds) *Japan in a Dynamic Asia*, Oxford: Lexington Books.

Funabashi, Yoichi (1991) 'Japan and the new world order', *Foreign Affairs,* 70, 58–74.

George, Alexander (1993) *Bridging the Gap: theory & practice in foreign policy*, Washington: United States Institute of Peace.

Gong, Gerrit (1984) *The Standard of 'Civilisation' in International Society*, Oxford: Clarendon Press.

Hughes, Christopher (1999) *Japan's Economic Power and Security: Japan and North Korea*, London: Routledge.

Kurata, Hideya (2000) 'Dialogue and Deterrence: The 1970s as Prototype', Paper presented at a conference entitled 'North Korea policy after the Perry report: a trilateral (Japan, the Republic of Korea, and the United States) workshop', on 3–4 March 2000. Online. Available: http://fellowships.ssrc.org/abe/conferences_and_other_program_events/Kurata_Dialogue_and_Deterrence.pdf (accessed 20 June 2008).

Linklater, Andrew and Suganami, Hidemi (2006) *The English School of International Relations: a contemporary reassessment*, Cambridge: Cambridge University Press.

Litwak, Robert (2000) *Rogue States and US Foreign Policy: containment after the cold war*, Washington DC: Woodrow Wilson Center Press.

McCormack, Gavan (2005) 'Disputed bones: Japan, North Korea and the "nature" controversy', *Japan Focus*, 18 April. Online. Available: http://www.japanfocus.org/-Gavan-McCormack/1949 (accessed 24 October 2009).

McCormack, Gavan and Wada, Haruki (2005) 'The Strange Record of 15 Years of Japan–North Korea Negotiations', *Japan Focus*. Available: http://www.japanfocus.org/-Gavan-McCormack/1894 (accessed 24 October 2009).

Mimura, Mitsuhiro (2005) *An Analysis of the Economic Effects of Japan's Economic Sanctions against North Korea*, Seoul: Korea Institute for International Economic Policy.

MOFA (2007a) 'Press conference by Minister for Foreign Affairs Masahiko Koumura'. Online. Available: http://www.mofa.go.jp/announce/fm_press/2007/12/1214.html (accessed 24 June 2008).

—— (2007b) 'Press conference by Minister for Foreign Affairs Masahiko Koumura'. Online. Available: http://www.mofa.go.jp/announce/fm_press/2007/10/1003–2.html (accessed 24 June 2008).

Neumann, Iver (1996) 'Self and Other in international relations', *European Journal of International Relations*, 2, 2: 139–74.

Roy, Denny (1988) 'North Korea's relations with Japan: the legacy of war', *Asian Survey*, 28, 12: 1280–93.

Saunders, Elizabeth (2006) 'Setting boundaries: can international society exclude "rogue states"?' *International Studies Review*, 8, 1: 23–53.

Shin, Jung Hyun (1981) *Japanese-North Korean Relations: linkage politics in the regional system of East Asia*, Seoul: Kyunghee University Press.

US Department of State (2008) 'Country reports on human rights practices'. Online. Available: http://www.state.gov/g/drl/rls/hrrpt/2007/100464.htm (accessed 26 August 2008).

Wada, Haruki (2009) 'Japan–North Korea relations – a serious stalemate', *Japan Focus*. Online. Available: http://www.japanfocus.org/-Wada-Haruki/3176 (assessed 12 November 2009).

Wæver, Ole (1996) 'European security identities', *Journal of Common Market Studies*, 34, 1: 103–32.

Wight, Martin (1977) *Systems of States*, Leicester: Leicester University Press.

Zhang, Xizhen and Brown, Eugene (2000) 'Policies toward North Korea: a time for new thinking', *Journal of Contemporary China*, 9, 25: 535–45.

4 Navigating the boundaries of the interstate society

Japan's response to piracy in Southeast Asia

Lindsay Black

An hour after leaving the port of Kuala Tangjong, Indonesia, on 22 October 1998, pirates clambered aboard and hijacked the *Alondra Rainbow*, a Japanese merchant vessel transporting aluminium ingots to the port of Miike, Fukuoka Prefecture. The pirates kidnapped the crew of the *Alondra Rainbow*, consisting of the Japanese Captain, Ikeno Kō, and Chief Engineer, Ogawa Kenzō and 15 Filipino seamen, and, 7 days later, set them adrift on a life raft in the Bay of Bengal. The pirate gang renamed the *Alondra Rainbow* to disguise its identity and, under the new name of the *Mega Rama*, transferred half of the cargo to another ship, before heading to Fujairah in the United Arab Emirates. The Japanese owners of the vessel contacted the Japanese Ministry of Transport (MOT, now the Ministry of Land, Infrastructure and Transport – MLIT) which dispatched a Japan Coast Guard (JCG) vessel to search for the missing merchant ship and crew. On 16 November, an Indian naval vessel, the *INS Prahar*, after a day-long chase, captured the *Mega Rama* in the Indian Ocean (*The Hindu*, 21 November 1999: 1; *New Straits Times*, 29 November 1999: 29; Hino 2000: 104–05; Takai 2002: 6–7; Mukundan 2002: 62–63; Terashima 2001: 38). An Indian court later sentenced the pirates to seven years of hard labour (Yamada 2003: 136). The previous year there had been a similar attack on the *Tenyu*, a Japanese owned and Korean manned vessel, but since the *Alondra Rainbow* incident involved the presence of a Japanese Captain and Chief Engineer on board, this case received far greater media coverage in Japan, and compelled the Japanese government to act (Terashima 2001: 38–39).

The piratical attack on the *Alondra Rainbow* occurred as piracy was rising in the Southeast Asian region (see Figure 4.1). From 1993 to 2000, when piracy figures peaked, acts of piracy in Southeast Asia increased from 16 attacks per year to 242 attacks per year (ICC-IMB Piracy Report 2002: 5), the majority of which occurred in Indonesian waters (Nippon Foundation 2005). The *Alondra Rainbow* incident coupled with the surge in piratical acts in this region highlighted the threat to both Japanese crews and trade navigating the narrow Malacca Straits, through which 80 per cent of Japan's oil imports pass (Yamada 2003: 143–44). Were the Malacca Straits to become blocked as a result of an act of piracy, this would threaten not only Japanese lives, but also the health of the Japanese economy, as ships would be rerouted around southern Sumatra to the tune of between USD200,000 and USD300,000 per ship (Graham 2006: 25–31). The location of piratical attacks in

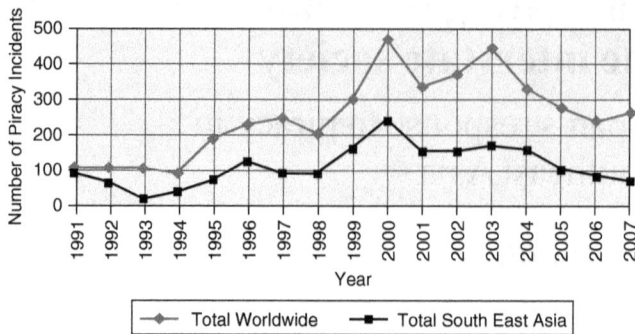

Figure 4.1 Total numbers of piracy incidents worldwide 1991–2007

Source: International Maritime Bureau Piracy Report 2005, 2006, 2007.

Southeast Asia, coupled with the international nature of contemporary maritime shipping, to which the multinational identities of the owners, flag, crew, pirates, merchandise, black markets, and maritime authorities are testament, underscored the need for international cooperation to combat piracy in Southeast Asia (Takai 2002: 7; Mukundan interview by author, 22 April 2003).

Japan's response to maritime piracy in Southeast Asia had to directly confront and overcome the international legal boundaries of sovereignty and non-intervention, as well as the definition of piracy in international law, that inhibit regional cooperation on this transborder security issue. In addition, Japan's anti-piracy response has had to confront historical and normative boundaries that undermine Japan's ability to play a security role in the East Asian region. Finally, the Japanese government has endeavoured to tackle the power political boundaries that inhibit the extent to which Southeast Asian states can respond to the problem of piracy. To accomplish this, the Japanese government initiated a series of regional anti-piracy conferences that led to the emergence of a regional network of maritime safety and security experts and organizations, headed by officials from Japan's Ministry of Foreign Affairs (MOFA) and the JCG (Mukundan interview by author, 22 April 2003). By implementing operational and legal measures, this regional network has succeeded in reducing piratical attacks in the Southeast Asian region; though its work is ongoing, it has already begun to remap the boundaries of maritime order in the East Asian interstate society (Mukundan 2002: 62; Yong Tiam Kui *New Straits Times*, 17 August 2003: 4; ICC-CCS 2006).

This chapter charts the course of Japan's response to piracy in Southeast Asia by first situating contemporary acts of maritime piracy within the broad theoretical debates on regionalism and the English School conception of the interstate society.[1] The English School can provide a rich conceptual framework that takes into account both the history and the expansion of regionalist projects which are transforming the boundaries of East Asia. At the same time, regional approaches can also inform the English School by accentuating the disjuncture between the institutions that regulate the global interstate society and the way in which states within a region tackle regional issues, highlighted in this case, by the surge of piracy in Southeast Asia around the turn of the twenty-first century (see Figure 4.1). Anti-piracy strategies have been inhibited by specific boundaries, including the inadequacies of international law, as well as the principles of non-intervention and a respect for sovereignty in Southeast Asia, encapsulated in the 'ASEAN way' (Acharya 2001: 47–72). Japan's proactive response to maritime piracy in Southeast Asia has circumvented these boundaries in a relatively short period, generating the potential for further regional maritime cooperation among newly established Coast Guard authorities. The empirical evidence indicates not only that the boundaries of the global interstate society are malleable and subject to the reinterpretations of state representatives at the regional level, but also that the development of regional interstate societies can reveal deficiencies in the interstate institutions to be rectified at the global level.

1. International society: theoretical boundaries

A combination of interrelated globalizing forces, including transborder production networks, rapid transfers of capital in international financial markets, state-of-the-art military technology and ecological change, have weakened the capacity of states to exercise their authority over their own sovereign borders (Beeson 2007: 1–25; Scholte 2000). In East Asia, these forces have generated the impetus for regional cooperation and integration to mitigate the impact of and to take advantage of the opportunities provided by globalization (Kim 2003: 3–18; Pempel 2005: 3–6, 10). States are also contesting where and how the boundaries of regional cooperation in East Asia are being drawn, engendering competition between Japan, China and the US for regional leadership (Katzenstein 2006: 32; Gilson 2007). None of the dominant international relations theories has provided an adequate account of this combination of regional dynamics and global pressures (Rozman 2004: 6–17; Hurrell 1995: 71–73; Ravenhill 2002: 169–79), highlighting the need for alternative theoretical frameworks that comprehend the distinct history, societies, diversity and international political economy of the East Asian region (Kang 2003).

The socially constructed nature of regionalism requires a theoretical framework that incorporates the notion of societal evolution. A theory which adopts a tiered approach can demonstrate how a group of states might begin to perceive their interests as being better met through collaboration at the regional level, then explain how this collaboration becomes institutionalized and evolves over time to become a more cohesive entity incorporating a sense of regional awareness and identity (Hurrell 1995: 71–73). This process can be understood both from a historical perspective that captures change within state structures and between interstate relations over the course of centuries (Buzan and Little 2000; Diamond 2005), as well as from the perspective of states addressing contemporary regional problems (Tsunekawa 2005). This chapter seeks to adopt a tiered approach, considering both the above perspectives, in order to elucidate how Japan's response to maritime piracy in Southeast Asia has wider implications for regionalist projects in East Asia.

The English School has received inadequate attention as a theory able to explain the rise of regional projects in East Asia, despite all the elements of Hurrell's tiered approach being present within the English School's conceptualization of the international, or, more recently, interstate society. Since Buzan's call to reconvene the English School, the School's theorists have drawn on the work of constructivist scholars to compare pluralist and solidarist interstate societies.[2] Interstate societies can become more pluralist or solidarist depending on the interaction between member states. For example, an interstate society can become more solidarist, the more it develops its rules and institutions (Buzan 2004: 139–60; Alagappa 2002: 41–52). Buzan's work, in particular, has highlighted both the need to further conceptualize interstate societies at the regional, rather than the global level (Buzan 2004: 205–27; Buzan and Wæver 2003). Hence, English School scholars regard regionalism as an interstate process to agree, create, and institutionalize the boundaries of acceptable conduct between states in a politically determined region.

It is beneficial to conceive of interstate societies at the regional level where the interaction capacity is higher between neighbouring states. The interaction capacity of an interstate society refers to the aggregation of technical capacity and resources, as well as commonly held norms that regulate the behaviour of actors and institutions. The greater the interaction capacity between states in an interstate society, the greater the possibilities are for enhanced social cohesion, technological standardization and progress (Buzan *et al.* 1993: 69–73; Buzan and Little 2000: 79–83). This is particularly relevant in the case of combating piracy in Southeast Asia, and the concept of interaction capacity highlights the technological developments and enhanced contact and cooperation between regional maritime authorities resulting from the anti-piracy conferences the Japanese government has hosted. On the other hand, pirates have also benefited from the proliferation of technology, such as global positioning systems (GPS), as well as the rise in maritime trade within and transported through the East Asian region, which presents maritime marauders with a greater number and a wider range of targets.[3] Regional interstate societies are also better able to address issues that are more regional or subregional than national or global in scope, such as the transboundary problem of air pollution or 'haze' in Southeast Asia, the drugs trade and human trafficking, financial measures to regulate cross border capital movements, and regional trade agreements (Campbell 2005: 220–24; Elliott 2004: 184–85; Weatherbee 2005: 272–74; Tsunekawa 2005). Though prevalent globally, piracy is also an issue that can be better addressed at the regional level, owing to the transborder nature of contemporary piracy, as well as regional differences between the types of piratical attacks and the capacity of states to combat the problem.

The concept of a regional interstate society adopts Bull and Watson's definition of an international society in which 'states . . . have established by dialogue and consent common rules and institutions for the conduct of their relations, and recognise their common interest in maintaining these arrangements' (Bull and Watson 1984: 1). The key distinction is only between the adoption of a regional as opposed to a global level of analysis, which is justified by the emergence of regional issues and higher interaction capacity within a region, both of which are connected with the phenomenon of globalization. The common rules and institutions of an interstate society therefore determine the agreed boundaries for interstate action within a given region. According to Bull, the primary goal of the interstate society is to maintain order between states, meaning that states uphold a mutual respect for each other's sovereign territory and rights, determine international laws and act through diplomatic means to regulate interstate behaviour, maintain a balance of power between member states, yet also are prepared to engage in war should a state or non-state actor threaten to disrupt the order or existence of the interstate society. While it is for all states to act in accordance with the common rules and institutions of the interstate society, the Great Powers play a central role in identifying and determining the response to the actors who have, through their conduct, abrogated the rules and institutions of the interstate society. This response may range from public condemnation and political persuasion, to economic sanctions, to military coercion and may necessitate an adjustment of the rules and institutions of the interstate society (Bull 2002: 16–19, 111–12, 122–30, 134–36, 156–66, 180–83, 194–201). In short, member states of an interstate society determine the boundaries of appropriate behaviour and agree to conduct their relations within these boundaries in order to make the relations between the member states more predictable and secure.

These boundaries can be usefully categorized into three different types that correspond to Hurrell's division of Bull's international society into the combination of power political order, international legal order, and shared values. Power political institutions include the balance of power, the role of the Great Powers, Great Power management and the institution of war. International legal order refers to how states perceive sovereignty, international law, international organizations, agreed rules, norms and conventions. Finally, there is a conception of social order that highlights the patterns and norms of interaction between member states. For example, social order in a more solidarist interstate society would refer to the values member states hold in common and the sense of belonging to a particular society that assists communication between members, and enhances feelings of obligations between members (Hurrell 2002: 18–22). The socio-historical interactions between states in a regional interstate society, as well as with states from beyond the region, influence how states construct these shared values or normative boundaries. These power political, legal and normative boundaries intersect and overlap, as Great Powers impose new international laws or alternative normative understandings of intervention limit how Great Powers act in the interstate society (see Finnemore 2003, for example). Nonetheless, for the purposes of analysis and clarity, it is useful to distinguish between these boundaries in order to comprehend how these boundaries have shaped Japan's response to maritime piracy in Southeast Asia.

2. Power political boundaries

Japan's response to piracy in Southeast Asia corresponds to the notion of power politics, particularly Great Power management: while Southeast Asian states have been inhibited from tackling piracy due to a lack of financial and operational capabilities, the Japanese government has offered to provide financial and operational support. The surge in maritime piracy in Southeast Asia is attributed to Southeast Asian states lacking the finances to pay for patrols of their extensive coast lines and, in particular, the Malacca Straits (Pugh 1993: 9; Vagg 1995: 66–67; Menefee 1996: 131; Chalk 1998: 91–92; Renwick and Abbott 1999: 190–91). This lack of finances inhibited the long-term institutionalization of coordinated anti-piracy patrols between Malaysia, Indonesia and Singapore that began in the early 1990s (Nakamura 2001: 18; Takai 2002: 16–18; Emmers 2004: 47–48). The Asian Financial Crisis in 1997 further undermined attempts to address maritime piracy, as littoral governments channelled capital into rebuilding their economies, rather than into funding their already insubstantial maritime authorities. This weakened the ability of Southeast Asian states to respond to piracy or even to pay their maritime police or naval officials. As a result of receiving inadequate wages, the maritime authorities themselves, particularly in Indonesia, either engaged in or, in return for payoffs, turned a blind eye to piratical acts in their jurisdictions (Takai 2002: 14–15; Tagliacozzo 2001: 265; Vagg 1995: 68–69; Sullivan *Houston Chronicle*, 13 May 2001: 31). The most notable example of official perpetration of piracy occurred on 17 March 2004, when the Indonesian naval vessel, the *KAL Youtefa, KAL-I-502* attacked a commercial Malaysian vessel, the *Yayasan Tujuh*, off Jayapura, Irian Jaya, Indonesia (ICC-IMB Piracy Report third quarter 2004: 29).

The Asian Financial Crisis also increased poverty, leading Southeast Asian people to seek alternative and sometimes criminal means of subsistence, including piracy (Vagg 1995: 65–66; Renwick and Abbott 1999: 192; Frécon 2002: 63, 65–66; Liss 2003: 57–59, 60–62; Young and Valencia 2003: 269; Honna 2006: 52–53).[4] Transnational crime groups recruited desperate migrants to coastal areas and benefited from technological advances and the availability of modern weaponry, including Global Positioning Devices, transistor radios, machine guns and outboard motors, to coordinate attacks against ships (Pugh 1993: 7; Frécon 2002: 53–54, 78–80; Honna 2006: 53). Worsening financial conditions in Southeast Asia created a vicious cycle exacerbating acts of maritime violence that required Great Power management.

As the pre-eminent Great Power in the East Asian region, the United States has played a key role in maintaining stability and providing public goods, such as the freedom of navigation through the region's sea lanes. Southeast Asian governments accepted the stabilizing security role of the United States, both during and after the Cold War, as these governments have focused on domestic security and economic development rather than regional security, in order to tackle separatist threats within their states (Bellamy 2004: 161–64). For example, ASEAN states, viewing the US military as a check against China's military rise and as a provider of key public goods in the East Asian region, responded negatively to Chinese calls for Asian unity in demanding that the US military withdraw from East Asia at the end of the Cold War (Shambaugh 2004/5: 70). Nevertheless, though Southeast Asian states recognize the benefits of US security commitments to the East Asian region, they do not automatically acquiesce in US security proposals. In April 2004, both Malaysia and Indonesia opposed a plan by Admiral Thomas Fargo, then Commander of US Forces in the Pacific, to establish a Regional Maritime Security Initiative (RMSI) to combat rising piracy and counter potential acts of maritime terrorism in the Malacca Straits, citing that such an initiative would infringe upon their sovereign rights and that the presence of US marines in the Malacca Straits would encourage rather than deter terrorism (*Maritime Industry Research Centre*, 2004: 57; *Business Times*, 22 June 2004; Tōi 2006: 127). The example of the RMSI demonstrates that there are limits to what East Asian states will accept in terms of intervention into their sovereign affairs. This chapter argues that Japan, as a powerful political and economic power in the East Asian interstate society, has been successful in tackling piracy precisely because it has manoeuvred within the boundaries of international law and regional norms.

3. Legal boundaries

The United Nations Convention on the Law of the Seas (UNCLOS), signed in 1982 and ratified in 1994 defines acts of piracy as occurring only on the high seas, outside the sovereign jurisdiction of states, and only for private, and not political, ends (Oceans and the Law of the Sea 1982; Barrios 2005). While contemporary piracy manifests itself differently both between and within regions and states, a common feature of piracy is that few piratical acts occur on the high seas. Even when pirates attack a ship in a foreign jurisdiction or on the high seas, the pirates take advantage of territorial boundaries, by retreating to their native waters, safe in the knowledge that foreign maritime authorities cannot pursue criminals across sovereign maritime boundaries (Mo 2002: 347; Pugh 1993: 7; Frécon 2002: 53–54, 78–80). The principal reason inhibiting 'hot pursuit' is that a number of state signatories to UNCLOS were reluctant to relinquish any control over their sovereign jurisdiction. As the promulgation of any international law is necessarily a compromise between the representatives of signatory states to that law, so the extent to which Article 101 in UNCLOS can successfully confront the problem of contemporary maritime piracy is limited. States in the interstate society will invariably seek to protect their own sovereign interests and promote a policy of non-intervention in their state's domestic affairs (Linklater 1996: 104–9; Little 2003: 453; Cutler 1991: 55–57). While Article 101 demonstrates the solidarity among states in the interstate society, as these member states have convened to enact a law to combat a global ill, by omitting acts perpetrated by politically motivated violent actors or incidents occurring within a state's territorial waters, so Article 101 also shows that individual state interests determine the boundaries of the interstate response to piracy (Bull 2002: 259, 264; Konaka 2006: 40–43).

Additional international regulations regarding maritime safety, such as the International Ship and Port Security (ISPS) and the 1988 Convention for the Suppression of Unlawful Acts against the Safety of Maritime Navigation (SUA), do address certain deficiencies of UNCLOS. The ISPS Code, which came into effect on 1 July 2004, requires commercial maritime vessels to create ship security plans and designate crew members to oversee the security of the vessel, thereby enhancing a crew's capacity to detect threats to their ship (Weeks 2003: 18; Song 2003: 464–66; *Ninushi to Yuso*, 2004: 15–16). Similarly, Japan has encouraged Southeast Asian states to ratify SUA (MLIT 2003), a maritime security convention which, though principally aimed at combating terrorism, is broad enough to cover all acts of maritime violence and robbery that threaten the navigational safety of a vessel (Menefee 1996: 9; Menefee 1997: 38–42; Beckman 2002: 329–30). There is therefore a certain degree of overlap between Japan's response to piracy and measures Japan has adopted to confront maritime terrorism in the aftermath of 11 September, as improving ship security against the piracy threat automatically bolsters security *vis-à-vis* the maritime terrorist threat, though crucially, these efforts may not tackle the underlying motivations that differentiate piracy and terrorism.

Nonetheless, as most Southeast Asian states have not endorsed the SUA treaty, and as the ISPS Code focuses primarily upon ship security rather than on maritime policing, so the deficiencies of the UNCLOS definition of piracy remain. Alternatives to the UNCLOS definition can be found in both the International Maritime Bureau (IMB) and International Maritime Organization's (IMO) definitions of piracy.[5] The IMB's definition encompasses all acts of maritime violence or depredation committed against a ship wherever the ship is attacked. Any act meeting this definition is recorded by the IMB's Piracy Reporting Centre in Kuala Lumpur. The IMO definition distinguishes between piracy on the high seas according to the UNCLOS definition, and armed robbery against ships that occur within a state's sovereign waters. Southeast Asian states, particularly Indonesia and Malaysia, oppose the adoption of the IMB definition because it makes no distinction between the high seas and a state's territorial waters (Renwick and Abbott 1999: 192, 196; Honna 2006: 53). Furthermore, by including all acts of violence and depredation, the piracy figures recorded by the Piracy Reporting Centre include acts of petty theft in port, as well as seajackings of the *Alondra Rainbow* mould. The maritime authorities of Southeast Asia assert that the IMB's approach blends all types of piracy together, exaggerating the problem of piracy, so that the privately funded IMB can demonstrate its relevance and continue to operate through private donations (Murphy 2007: 23; Eklöf 2006: 93–94, 97). Though the IMO's definition has gradually been accepted by most states in the Southeast Asian region over the course of Japan-sponsored anti-piracy conventions and Japan's anti-piracy efforts, Southeast Asian states' values and experience as an interstate society also create normative boundaries that inhibit interstate cooperation to address piratical violence in Southeast Asia.

4. Normative boundaries

The East Asian interstate society can be categorized as a pluralist, rather than a solidarist, interstate society (Buzan 2004: 238; Bellamy 2004: 169–71). As Malaysia and Indonesia's opposition to the IMB definition of piracy and to the RMSI demonstrates, relations between member states are predicated on a respect for sovereign boundaries and non-interference in other states' internal affairs. As a result of these normative boundaries, East Asian states have not sought to substantially institutionalize the myriad of regional organizations, such as the ASEAN Regional Forum (ARF) or the Asia Pacific Economic Cooperation (APEC) forum, that have proliferated since the end of the Cold War, because of the rules and norms by which these organizations function. ASEAN-centred diplomacy is oriented around the consensus-building approach and the norm of non-interference embodied in the 'ASEAN way', delaying the institutionalization of verbal commitments between members (Weatherbee 2005: 121). As a result, despite both the ARF and APEC possessing a security remit, neither organization has played a significant role in combating piracy in Southeast Asia.

ASEAN states' experiences of colonialism and imperialism have also led them to oppose intrusions into their sovereign affairs. Southeast Asian leaders regularly employed pirates as a means to secure the boundaries of their rule in the pre-colonial interstate society of Southeast Asia. Perceiving piracy as a threat to their empires, the British and Dutch authorities signed the Anglo-Dutch Treaty of 1824 and initiated anti-piracy patrols which had eradicated piracy in Southeast Asia by the 1870s. However, this anti-piracy campaign also served to impose the values, laws, rules, and norms of the European interstate society upon Southeast Asian states and strengthened European trade at the expense of merchants from the Southeast Asian region, thereby consolidating colonial rule over Southeast Asian states (Andaya and Andaya 1982: 130–33; Eklöf 2006: 11–13). As European powers began to dominate and transform the Southeast Asian interstate society, so engaging in piracy became a way of resisting colonial rule in addition to being a violent means of obtaining money and goods (Hyslop 1989: 12; Yamada 2003: 162–63). The past suppression of piracy in the Malacca Straits, by the British and Dutch navies, partly explains Malaysia and Indonesia's reluctance to allow international anti-piracy patrols in their sovereign waters today, as it was precisely by such means that Southeast Asian states were subjugated in the nineteenth century.

In addition to the ways in which the identity of a state *vis-à-vis* the interstate society influences how the state acts, it also matters whether Great Powers have imposed the rules and institutions of an interstate society upon weaker states, and whether these weaker states then accept these rules and institutions. While Bull and Watson's definition of an international society stressed mutual acceptance of that society, Buzan has incorporated Wendt's notion of mode/depth socialization to broaden the English School's conception of how a state might belong to an interstate society. Echoing Wendt, Buzan argues that states may be coerced by a Great Power into joining an interstate society, as with the case of an empire.

Alternatively, states may calculate independently of external powers that it is in their best collective interests to be a part of an interstate society, as is the case in a pluralist interstate society. Finally, states may come to believe in the fundamental tenets of an interstate society, as occurs in a solidarist interstate society. The more an actor, whether a state or a non-state actor, believes that the rules and institutions of the interstate society of which it is a member are legitimate, the smaller the chance that an actor will violate the rules or rebel against the interstate society. Hence, a solidarist society is the most stable form of interstate society (Buzan 2004: 102–08, 143–46, 208–09, 211) in which member states are the least likely to engage in outlawed behaviour.

As the example of the Anglo-Dutch Treaty of 1824 indicates, Great Powers act as norm entrepreneurs in determining outlaws of the interstate society (Finnemore and Sikkink 1998; Saunders 2006: 25, 35, 37–38). Defining outlaws enables these Great Powers to revise the existing regulations of the interstate society and establish new rules and create institutions to combat outlawed behaviour (Buzan and Little 2000: 66, 136, 177, 200, 204, 400).[6] When Great Powers transform the boundaries of the interstate society through coercion, subjugated states erect normative boundaries, such as sovereignty and non-intervention, to resist the further development of rules and institutions in a given interstate society. The rules and institutions that designate outlaw categories and actions, as well as the response of members of an interstate society to acts committed by outlaws can thereby enable analysts to chart the boundaries and measure the acceptance of the boundaries of the interstate society. Japan's response to maritime piracy in Southeast Asia serves as an example of how the power political, legal and normative boundaries inhibiting maritime security action against these outlaws have been engaged and in some ways overcome. That Japan should have led the response to maritime piracy in Southeast Asia is important considering Japan's imperial history in the region and the constraints that determine the boundaries of Japan's security role in the world.

5. Japan's proactive response to maritime piracy in Southeast Asia

Japan has been regarded in the international relations literature as somewhat of an anomaly; 'an economic giant, but a political pygmy' (Miyashita 2003: 180). Japan emerged at the end of the Cold War with the second largest military budget in the world, despite maintaining that budget at under 1 per cent of its GDP throughout the Cold War. Yet, in the first crisis of the post-Cold War period, the 1990–91 Gulf War, the Japanese government did not dispatch its Self-Defence Forces (SDF) to the Middle East until after the hostilities had ended, despite pressure from the interstate society (Hughes 2004: 41–42). One must therefore examine the boundaries inhibiting Japan playing a greater security role in global affairs.

Explanations of Japan's limited security role are often explained by pacifist norms rooted in Article 9 of the Japanese Constitution that prohibits Japan from possessing a military force (Hook 1996: 1–10).[7] While the post-Cold War era has seen a dramatic transformation of Japan's military forces, the SDF still remains constrained in the types of security role it is permitted to perform and the areas to which it can be deployed. The constraints on Japan's military deployment abroad are external as well as internal, with the Koreas and China all voicing opposition to or concern about the development of the SDF because of Japanese aggression and expansionism during and prior to World War II (Samuels 2007: 65–67, 109–32; Green 2001: 193–94, 202–03; Hughes 2004: 21–24, 41–42). Though Southeast Asian states have largely forgiven Japan's imperial past (Singh 2002; Smith 2006: 179–82), many of these states are reluctant to have any foreign military operate in their sovereign territory, as could be observed in Malaysia and Indonesia's rejection of Admiral Fargo's RMSI proposal.

In a July 2002 interview, Nawano Yoshihiko, the director of the JCG, noted that the JCG rather than the Maritime Self-Defence Force (MSDF) is dispatched on anti-piracy missions abroad because China and Southeast Asian states are sensitive to missions undertaken by Japanese military forces. Nawano states:

> In order to avoid friction [with China and Southeast Asian states] it is a maritime police force like ours that has to respond. The JCG responds in the same way to incidents surrounding the Senkaku Islands. Even though the purpose of the MSDF is to preserve the integrity of all of Japan's territory, it is the JCG that puts to sea.
>
> (Quoted in Tazaki 2002: 49)

Unrestricted by the Japanese Constitution and distinct from Japan's imperial history, the Japan Coast Guard circumvents the boundaries that have traditionally inhibited Japan's security role (Samuels 2007/8: 110–11).[8] In the case of maritime piracy in Southeast Asia, this has enabled experts from the JCG to challenge the power political, legal, and normative boundaries inhibiting an anti-piracy response.

An alternative explanation for Japan's limited security role is captured in Kent Calder's notion of a 'reactive state' (1988; 2003). According to Calder, parochial political interests and bureaucratic in-fighting within Japan's policy-making system requires US pressure in order for the Japanese government to formulate proactive policies. The actions and discourse of Hatoyama Yukio's Democratic Party of Japan (DPJ) administration, which, since assuming office in September 2009, has clearly intended to wrestle policy-making power away from the bureaucracy in order to execute more proactive foreign policies supports Calder's argument. Nonetheless, Calder's argument that Japan has not pursued proactive foreign policies to safeguard the 'stability of the global economic community' (2003, 605), contrasts with the evidence presented in this chapter concerning Japan's response to maritime piracy in Southeast Asia. Instead of a 'reactive state', this chapter prefers to categorize Japan as an 'adaptive state' attuned to changes in its international environment and particularly focused on building regional cooperation in East Asia that extends beyond Japan's bilateral ties to the US (Berger 2007).

6. Navigating subregional boundaries

Japan has confronted a series of power political, legal, and normative bounda-ries within the context of the interstate subregional society of Southeast Asia in responding to piracy (Yamada 2006b: 26, 28). Navigating these boundaries has meant the sustained focus of Japanese policy makers on this issue in holding anti-piracy conferences, enacting anti-piracy exercises, conducting training programs and helping Southeast Asian states build their own coast guard authorities based on the Japan Coast Guard model. Throughout these efforts, the Japan Coast Guard has remained central to the fight against piracy in Southeast Asia since the attack on the *Alondra Rainbow* in 1998.

Conferences

At the ASEAN Post-Ministerial Conference in the Philippines in November 1999, Prime Minister Obuchi Keizō responded to the *Alondra Rainbow* incident by announcing his intention to hold the first regional anti-piracy conference in Tokyo. The conference, entitled the 'Regional Conference on Combating Piracy and Armed Robbery against Ships', went ahead in April 2000 and included mari-time officials, and shipping associations of the 10 ASEAN countries, as well as India, Sri Lanka, Bangladesh, South Korea, China, Hong Kong and Japan, as well as delegates from the IMO. The conference generated three documents that high-lighted the need to tackle piracy within the territorial waters of Southeast Asian states, develop the capabilities of Southeast Asian maritime authorities (primarily through the Japanese government providing financial aid and training), and pro-mote international cooperation to combat piracy. These three documents were the 'Tokyo Appeal', the 'Asia Anti-Piracy Challenge 2000' statement and the 'Model Action Plan' (*Asahi Shimbun*, 28 April 2000: 3; Kaijō Hōanchō Kokusaijika 2002: 145; MOFA 2005; MLIT 2000a; MLIT 2000b; Japan Shipping Association [JSA] 2000).

While these three documents did not detail concrete measures and duties to tackle acts of piracy and armed robbery at sea in Southeast Asia, the conference did assemble maritime experts in the region together to discuss ways of tackling piracy and generated ongoing dialogue and cooperation (Terashima 2001: 39; Mukundan interview by author, 22 April 2003). This network of maritime experts further developed the initial framework to combat piracy at the 'Asia Cooperation Conference on Combating Piracy and Armed Robbery' congregated on 4 and 5 October 2001 (MOFA 2005). Though the 2001 Conference failed to outline spe-cific anti-piracy measures, such as coordinated anti-piracy patrols, thereby high-lighting the extent to which Southeast Asian states were concerned about foreign intervention in their sovereign waters (*Mainichi Shimbun*, 5 October 2001: 5), delegates did agree to the creation of a Maritime Policy Bureau's Expert Meeting to Tackle Piracy.[9] This Expert Meeting, comprising maritime officials from across East Asia and led by section chiefs and department heads from Japan's Ministry of Foreign Affairs (MOFA) and the Japan Coast Guard, created the framework for an Information Sharing Centre (ISC) to disseminate data on piracy to the relevant state authorities in the East Asian region (Yamada 2006a: 9–10; MOFA 2003). On 11 November 2004, 16 Asian states signed the Regional Cooperation Agreement on Combating Piracy and Armed Robbery against Ships in Asia (ReCAAP) agreeing to establish the ISC in Singapore (*BBC Monitoring Asia Pacific*, 11 November 2004: 1; MOFA 2005).

As well as being the first regional institution to combat piracy in East Asia, the ISC also overcame the definitional problem of Article 101 in UNCLOS by adopting the IMO definition of armed robbery against ships which encourages states to respond to acts of violence and depredation in their waters (Umezawa 2003). Furthermore, though 'hot pursuit' of pirates across maritime boundaries is not permitted in Southeast Asia, the ISC can notify the relevant maritime authorities to continue a chase conducted by a neighbouring maritime organization when the pursuit crosses the state's sovereign maritime boundary. The ISC can also handle confidential juridical cases between East Asian states through the Centre's network of regional maritime officials (Umezawa interview by author, 2 April 2004). Finally, the ISC produces up-to-date statistics on piracy in the East Asian region (Kuribayashi 2003: 39; Umezawa interview by author, 2 April 2004).

Though the ISC has overcome many of the legal boundaries and Southeast Asian concerns about sovereignty, critics charge that it may replicate the work of the IMB's Piracy Reporting Centre in Kuala Lumpur (Mukundan interview by author, 22 April 2003) and will prove unpopular among commercial vessels that will prefer to contact the Piracy Reporting Centre, because of its institutional history, combined with its status as a non-government, and therefore neutral, organization (Yamada interview by author, 10 November 2004). Furthermore, despite the inauguration of the ISC on 29 November 2006, both Malaysia and Indonesia have refrained from becoming contracting members of the Centre (ReCAAP ISC 2008), stating that piracy in their sovereign waters is a crime that falls under their own national laws and that information exchanges with other countries would infringe upon their sovereignty (Yamada 2006a: 10–11; Murphy 2007: 24; Yamada 2007: 12–13). The absence of two of the key Southeast Asian states that have witnessed the largest number of piracy cases in their waters further underlines the difficulty for Japan in overcoming the issue of non-intervention that forms the primary boundary of the Southeast Asian subregional interstate society.

Exercises and training

In terms of exercises and training, the Japan Coast Guard Academy in Hiroshima began to enrol foreign exchange students after the 'Regional Conference on Combating Piracy' in April 2000 (*Asahi Shimbun*, 29 April 2000: 38; Nakamura 2006: 22–23). Exchange students at the JCG Academy follow a six-year program, which includes a year of intensive Japanese language training, designed to improve the students' knowledge and capacity to respond to the issue of piracy in Southeast Asia. The JCG has also organized Maritime Crime Seminars to bolster the capacities of regional maritime authorities to combat piracy (Kaijō Hōanchō Kokusaijika

2002: 145; Kaijō Hōan Daigaku – Kokusai kōryū kikakushitsu 2006: 38–41). The Nippon Foundation has also promoted the training of officers from Southeast Asian maritime authorities, by providing Sasakawa scholarships to attend the World Maritime University in Sweden, the International Maritime Law Institute in Malta, the Seafarers International Research Centre of Cardiff University and at the Division for Ocean Affairs and the Law of the Sea of the UN Office of Legal Affairs (Nippon Foundation 2004).

The Japanese government dispatched Japan's first anti-piracy mission, comprising members of MOFA, Ministry of Transport (MOT) and the Maritime Safety Agency (MSA), to survey the problem of piracy in Southeast Asia from 19 to 26 September 2000. The survey group also laid the groundwork for Japan Coast Guard vessels to be dispatched to the Southeast Asian region on anti-piracy exercises, the exchange of JCG personnel, education, technical assistance, and maritime security seminars. In November 2000, a JCG vessel was dispatched to Malaysia and India to conduct an anti-piracy exercise (Kaijō Hōanchō Kokusaijika 2002: 145; MOFA 2005). This anti-piracy exercise has been followed by frequent visits and exercises by the JCG to Southeast Asia. Though the role of the JCG has been limited to anti-piracy drills because of the importance of non-intervention and sovereignty norms in Southeast Asia, the JCG's participation in these exercises has enhanced the capabilities of Southeast Asian maritime authorities (Umezawa interview by author, 2 April 2004; Kuribayashi 2003: 39). The efforts of the Japan Coast Guard are welcomed in Southeast Asia as the Japan Coast Guard is second only to the US Coast Guard in terms of equipment, ships, training and capabilities. Unlike the US Coast Guard, the JCG is a police organization and does not perform a military function. This enables the JCG to build networks with similar organizations in the region more freely than a military force could (Ogawa 2002: 136–37, 161–66; Yamada 2006b: 28). Engaging in anti-piracy exercises with the JCG or receiving training from the JCG has had a significant impact upon overcoming the operational boundaries that have limited the anti-piracy responses of Southeast Asian maritime authorities.

Proliferation of coast guard organizations and Japanese Official Development Assistance (ODA)

As one of the most advanced Coast Guard forces in the world, the JCG also provides a model for Southeast Asian states to imitate. The JCG has therefore played a fundamental role in the creation of Coast Guard authorities throughout Southeast Asia. In November 2001, the Japan International Cooperation Agency (JICA) helped fund the Indonesian Maritime Safety Information System (MSIS). This system enables the maritime strategy headquarters in Jakarta to coordinate anti-piracy activities with Indonesian maritime security offices in Belawan, Domai and Tanju Uban, as well as to maintain cooperation with international maritime agencies and foreign governments (Takai 2002: 19). The JCG has aided the Philippines' Coast Guard since 2002 and helped to set up the Malaysian Maritime Enforcement Agency (MMEA) in 2004 (Bradford 2004: 500; Terashima interview by author, 22 July 2004). In December 2005, Indonesia's President Susilo Bambang Yudhoyono ordered the establishment of an Indonesian Coast Guard for which JICA provided funding (Habara 2008: 53; Honna 2006: 52–53; Nakamura 2006: 25; Yamada 2007: 13–14).

The Japanese government has also provided funding for three anti-piracy patrol vessels to the Indonesian government. These vessels were delivered in the wake of the piratical attack on the Japanese owned vessel, the *Idaten*, in March 2005, in which the Japanese Captain and Chief Engineer, as well as a Filipino crew member, were taken hostage and ransomed. This ODA, at a cost of JPY700 million per ship, broke Japan's Arms Export Ban, as the bullet-proofing on the ships' windshields constitutes a military vessel (Honna 2006: 52–53). The three boats are manned by the Indonesian Marine Police and patrol near Riau, North Sumatra and Jakarta (MOFA 2006). The Philippine Coast Guard also received three patrol boats from the Japanese government in 2006 (Samuels 2007/08: 103). Such aid can significantly bolster Indonesia and the Philippine's anti-piracy response in piracy prone areas, helping Indonesian and Filipino maritime authorities overcome the operational boundaries that inhibit maritime security action.

Conclusion

Power political, legal and normative boundaries determine the extent to which states can combat piracy in the interstate society of East Asia. Nonetheless, as these boundaries are socially constructed, interstate interaction can reformulate the contours of these boundaries to enable cooperation in the fight against piracy. Japan has worked proactively to eradicate piracy in Southeast Asia within the confines of the boundaries of the interstate society of East Asia. The Japanese government has also sought to reshape those same boundaries through aid, exercises and training to tackle power political boundaries, institutionalizing the ISC to address the legal boundaries hindering hot pursuit, and through regional conventions and the establishment of Coast Guard authorities throughout the region to foster regional cooperation to challenge normative boundaries.

By leading regional anti-piracy efforts, Japan has forged a new security role for itself in the region through the dispatch of the JCG. The JCG has improved the capabilities of regional maritime organizations, where its military counterpart, the MSDF, because of historical and constitutional factors, could not. More than this, though, the JCG has provided the model for an expanding group of coast guard organizations that form a regional framework comprised of maritime experts (Tōi 2006: 128). These experts, through regional maritime security efforts, have the potential to further remap the boundaries that define behaviour within the interstate society of East Asia.

Japan's response to piracy in Southeast Asian waters is also a model for the Japanese government and other members of the interstate society to replicate across the globe. In March 2009, the Japanese government passed an anti-piracy law permitting the dispatch of both the MSDF and JCG to the Gulf of Aden to protect international shipping from a rise in Somali piracy. While the dispatch of the MSDF indicates a break with the Japanese government's reliance on the JCG to respond to piracy, in reality only the JCG personnel on board the MSDF vessels can actually board suspect ships and arrest pirates. According to Japan's new anti-piracy law, the MSDF were only dispatched to the Gulf of Aden because the JCG does not have sufficient vessels and personnel of its own to conduct patrols and escorts at such a distance from the Japanese mainland (Yamada interview by author 6 August 2009). In addition, the Japanese government is focussed on building the capacities of East African and Middle Eastern coastal authorities. For example, the Djibouti Code of Conduct, signed in January 2009 and designed to tackle Somali piracy, cites ReCAAP as its inspiration and calls for the creation of Information Sharing Centres in the East Africa region (IMO 2009: 3, 7). Hence, Japan's response to Southeast Asian piracy has significant ramifications for combating maritime piracy in other regional interstate societies.

Transforming the boundaries of the interstate society of East Asia is a contentious process. The anti-piracy efforts of the Japanese government and the JCG have not yet overcome the core normative boundaries of non-intervention and a respect for state sovereignty in the Southeast Asian interstate society. These enduring norms of sovereignty and non-intervention are rooted in Southeast Asia's history of suffering under Western and Japanese colonial and imperial regimes, coupled with the need for contemporary Southeast Asian governments to consolidate their rule by focusing on internal security threats. A comparison of Southeast Asian piracy in the contemporary and colonial eras reveals that with Great Power support, or at least extensive security forces, piracy can be eradicated. The important difference between these two time periods is how states define themselves or are defined by others in the interstate society to which they belong. Coercive means of governing maritime territory in the colonial era have pushed East Asian states, today, to resist Great Power intrusions into their internal affairs, as Malaysia and Indonesia's response to the RMSI proposal demonstrated. Boundaries have a history that is perceived according to whether a boundary was created through belief, calculation or by coercion.

Proponents of the English School are concerned with how the boundaries of appropriate behaviour by state and non-state actors, defined in terms of power political, legal and normative factors, in interstate societies have been conceived, obeyed, abused and reformulated to transform order within interstate societies. The boundaries of the East Asian interstate society have long been defined in terms of the imperialist interstate societies into which it was subsumed or in opposition to these imperialist interstate societies. While this shared history can promote regionalist projects that bind the interstate society closer together, shared histories can also serve to divide the region as past animosities are rekindled in the present (Beeson 2007: 62–63). An alternative path is for an interstate society to find a common cause in combating a threat posed by a type of actor all members perceive of as an outlaw of their society, as has occurred in the case of piracy in Southeast Asia (Honna 2006: 52–53). Doing so establishes a stronger and more solidarist interstate society based on belief, rather than calculation or coercion. For English School proponents, states redefining the boundaries and transforming regional interstate societies in response to outlawed behaviour provide new and fruitful avenues for research.

Notes

1 Hereafter, to maintain consistency and avoid confusion, all references will be to the interstate rather than the international society. Though prior to Buzan (2004) no proponent of the English School referred to the interstate society, it is clear from the early work of the English School that its advocates were primarily interested in a society formed by states, as Bull and Watson's definition of an international society attests (1984: 1).
2 In Buzan's work, there are six types of interstate society. These societies are drawn along a spectrum of pluralist to solidarist interstate societies. The social interstate societies are located at the far pluralist end, while confederative societies are located at the far solidarist end. For the sake of simplicity and coherence, this chapter will focus only on the pluralist/solidarist dichotomy. The only exception to this, is the discussion of East Asian colonial history in which European and American imperial societies were imposed upon East Asian states. On Buzan's spectrum of interstate societies, these imperial societies would be termed power political interstate societies (Buzan 2004: 158–60).
3 The East Asian interstate society comprises both Northeast Asia and Southeast Asia. The boundaries of this interstate society can be conceived of in terms of the ASEAN Plus Three (APT). Taiwan and North Korea are omitted from this definition as Taiwan is not recognized as an independent sovereign state by the interstate society and North Korea has not 'established by common dialogue and consent [the] common rules and institutions' of the interstate society of East Asia and does not 'recognize their . . . interest in maintaining these arrangements' (Bull and Watson 1984: 1).
4 Stephan Eklöf disagrees with the conclusion that the Asian Financial Crisis caused instances of piracy to rise in Southeast Asia, noting that the rise in piracy figures occurred after the end of 1998 (see Figure 4.1), over a year after the end of the financial crisis. Eklöf does, however, acknowledge that the Asian Financial Crisis did have an impact upon the abilities of Southeast Asian states to adequately finance their maritime police organizations. Moreover, instances of piracy undertaken by poor migrants to coastal areas are likely to have been petty thefts, as these groups are unlikely to have possessed the means to carry out more ambitious acts. As Eklöf notes, acts of petty theft are often not reported and therefore not recorded on the IMB's piracy figures (Eklöf 2006: 102–03, 137–38).
5 The IMB is the maritime crime investigation section of the International Chamber of Commerce, whereas the IMO is attached to the United Nations, establishing and monitoring compliance of international maritime regulations. The exact wording of the IMB's definition of piracy is, 'an act of boarding or attempting to board any ship with the apparent intent to commit theft or any other crime and with the apparent intent or capability to use force in the furtherance of that act'. According to the IMO, the armed robbery against ships

> means any unlawful act of violence or detention or any act of depredation, or threat thereof, other than an act of 'piracy', directed against a ship or against persons or property on board such ship, within a state's jurisdiction over such offences.
> (both definitions are cited in the ICC-IMB Piracy Report 2002: 3)

6 The position of proxenoi, an antecedent to the contemporary ambassador, in the interstate society of Greek city-states, evolved in part in response to piratical attacks in the Mediterranean that threatened interstate trade (Buzan and Little 2000: 210). Of course, members of a power political interstate society may sponsor and legitimize piratical acts, as occurred in the designation of privateers during the Golden Age of piracy in the

Caribbean (Yamada 2007: 2–4). It was only with the emergence of a more solidarist interstate society that the Grotian principle of mare liberum (freedom of the seas) deemed pirates as hostes humani generis (enemies of mankind) (Herrmann 2002: 444).

7 The norm of pacifism can be defined as 'a powerful constraint on the government's use of military force as a legitimate instrument of state policy' (Hook et al. 2001: 74).

8 There is a great deal of confusion surrounding the role and mission of the JCG. Samuels has suggested that 'the nascent transformation of the JCG into a *de facto fourth branch of the Japanese military* may be the most significant and least heralded Japanese military development since the end of the Cold War' (Samuels 2007/8: 95, emphasis added) and that the JCG is a *quasi-military unit* because some of its members train with US special forces (Samuels 2007/8: 92). Later in the same article, Samuels states that the advantage of the JCG over the MSDF is that it can perform roles that the MSDF, because of Japan's imperial history and the MSDF's status as a navy, cannot. The JCG is able to perform these roles, including participation in anti-piracy exercises, 'because of its *nonmilitary character*' (Samuels 2007/8: 110, emphasis added). The JCG is not a military force, but a maritime police and rescue force tasked with securing Japanese sovereign waters from violations of Japanese and international law and protecting life and property at sea (Henmi 2006: 10–16, 87–89; Ogawa 2002: 106–15, 165–66).

9 The Japan Foundation continues to pay for yearly anti-piracy meetings in Tokyo between the directors of national maritime organizations from across the region (Yamada 2006b: 28).

References

Acharya, Amitav (2001) Constructing a Security Community in Southeast Asia: ASEAN and the problem of regional order (Politics in Asia), London and New York: Routledge.

Alagappa, Muthiah (ed.) (2002) *Asian Security Order: instrumental and normative features*, Stanford: Stanford University Press.

Andaya, Barbara Watson and Andaya, Leonard Y. (1982) *A History of Malaysia*, Basingstoke: Macmillan.

Barrios, Erik (2005) 'Casting a wider net: addressing the maritime piracy problem in Southeast Asia', *Boston College International and Comparative Law Review*, 28, 1: 149–64. Online. Available: http://www.bc.edu/schools/law/lawreviews/meta-elements/journals/bciclr/28_1/03_FMS.htm (accessed 24 October 2005).

Beckman, Robert (2002) 'Combatting piracy and armed robbery against ships in Southeast Asia: the way forward', *Ocean Development and International Law*, 33, 3–4: 317–42.

Beeson, Mark (2007) *Regionalism and Globalization in East Asia: politics, security and economic*, Basingstoke and New York: Palgrave Macmillan.

Bellamy, Alex J. (2004) 'The pursuit of security in Southeast Asia: beyond realism', in Mark Beeson (ed.) *Contemporary Southeast Asia – regional dynamics, national differences*, Basingstoke and New York: Palgrave Macmillan, pp. 156–77.

Berger, Thomas (2007) 'The pragmatic liberalism of an adaptive state', in Thomas Berger, Mike Mochizuki, and Jitsuo Tsuchiyama (eds) *Japan in International Politics – the foreign policies of an adaptive state*, Boulder, Colorado: Lynne Rienner, pp. 259–300.

Bradford, John F. (2004) 'Japanese anti-piracy initiatives in Southeast Asia: policy formulation and the coastal state responses', *Contemporary Southeast Asia*, 26, 3: 480–505.

Bull, Hedley and Watson, Adam (eds) (1984) *The Expansion of International Society*, Oxford: Oxford University Press.

Bull, Hedley (2002) *The Anarchical Society – a study of order in world politics*, 3rd edn, Basingstoke and New York: Palgrave.

Buzan, Barry (2004) *From International to World Society? English School theory and social structure of globalisation*, Cambridge: Cambridge University Press.

Buzan, Barry, Jones, Charles and Little, Richard (1993) *The Logic of Anarchy*, New York: Columbia University Press.

Buzan, Barry and Wæver, Ole (2003) *Regions and Powers – the structure of international society*, Cambridge: Cambridge University Press.

Buzan, Barry and Little, Richard (2000) *International Systems in World History – remaking the study of international relations*, Oxford: Oxford University Press.

Calder, Kent. E. (1988) 'Japanese foreign economic policy formation: explaining the reactive state', *World Politics* 40, 4: 517–41.

—— (2003) 'Asia's shifting strategic landscape – Japan as a post-reactive State?' *Orbis* 47, 4: 605–16.

Campbell, Laura B. (2005) 'The political economy of environmental regionalism in Asia', in T.J. Pempel (ed.) *Remapping East Asia: the construction of a region* (Cornell Studies in Political Economy), Ithaca: Cornell University Press, pp. 216–35.

Chalk, Peter (1998) 'Contemporary maritime piracy in Southeast Asia', *Studies in Conflict and Terrorism*, 21, 1: 87–112.

Cutler, Claire A. (1991) 'The "Grotian tradition" in international relations', *Review of International Studies*, 17, 1: 41–65.

Diamond, Jared (2005) *Collapse – how societies choose to fail or survive*, London: Penguin Books.

Eklöf, Stephan (2006) *Pirates in Paradise – a modern history of Southeast Asia's maritime marauders*, Copenhagen: NIAS – Nordic Institute of Asian Studies.

Elliott, Lorraine (2004) 'Environmental challenges, policy failure and regional dynamics in Southeast Asia', in Mark Beeson (ed.) *Contemporary Southeast Asia – regional dynamics, national differences*, Basingstoke and New York: Palgrave Macmillan, pp. 178–97.

Emmers, Ralf (2004) *Non-Traditional Security in the Asia-Pacific – the dynamic of securitisation*, Singapore: Eastern Universities Press.

Finnemore, Martha (2003) *The Purpose of Intervention – changing beliefs about the use of force*, Ithaca: Cornell University Press.

Finnemore, Martha and Sikkink, Kathryn (1998) 'International norm dynamics and political change', *International Organization*, 52, 4: 887–917.

Frécon, Eric (2002) *Pavillon noir sur l'Asie du Sud-Est – Histoire d'une resurgence de la piraterie maritime*, Paris: L'Harmattan.

Gilson, Julie (2007) 'Strategic regionalism in East Asia', *Review of International Studies*, 33, 1: 145–63.

Graham, Euan (2006) *Japan's Sea Lane Security, 1940–2004, A Matter of Life and Death?* London and New York: Routledge.

Green, Michael J. (2001) *Japan's Reluctant Realism – foreign policy challenges in an era of uncertain power*, New York: Palgrave.

Henmi, Masakazu (2006) *Umi o Mamoru Kaijō Hoanchō Jun shisen*, Tokyo: Seizando Shoten.

Herrmann, Wilfried A. (2002) 'Piracy-terror on the high seas', *The Indonesian Quarterly*, 30, 4: 441–55.

Hino, Keiichi (2000) 'Kaiyō anteika e tettei torikumi o!' *Sekai no Kansen*, 564: 104–06.

Honna, Jun (2006) 'ODA ni yoru hatsu no "buki" kyōyo to kaizoku taisaku', *Sekai Shūhō*, 87, 24: 52–53.

Hook, Glenn D. (1996) *Militarization and Demilitarization in Contemporary Japan*, London: Routledge.

Hook, Glenn D., Gilson, Julie, Hughes, Christopher W. and Dobson, Hugo (2001) *Japan's International Relations: politics, economics and security*, London and New York: Routledge.

Hughes, Christopher W. (2004) *Japan's Re-emergence as a 'Normal' Military Power*, Adelphi Paper No. 368–69, Oxford and New York: Oxford University Press.

Hurrell, Andrew (1995) 'Regionalism in theoretical perspective', in Andrew Hurrell and Louise Fawcett (eds) *Regionalism in World Politics*, Oxford: Oxford University Press.

—— (2002) 'Society and anarchy in international relations', in B.A. Roberson (ed.) *International Society and the Development of International Relations Theory*, London and New York: Continuum, pp. 17–42.

Hyslop, Ian R. (1989) 'Contemporary piracy', in Eric Ellen (ed.) *Piracy at Sea*, Paris: International Maritime Bureau, ICC Publishing.

ICC-CCS (2006) *IMB Releases Latest Piracy Statistics*, London. Online. Available: http://www.icc-ccs.org/main/news.php?newsid = 67 (accessed 3 May 2006).

JSA (2000) *Asia Anti-Piracy Challenges 2000*. Online. Available: http://www.jsanet.or.jp/e2–3/pi2-2-3.html (accessed 23 July 2006).

Kaijō Hōanchō Kokusaijika (2002) 'Kaizoku taizaku', *Sekai no Kansen*, 595: 144–5.

Kaijō Hōan Daigaku – Kokusai kōryū kikakushitsu (2006) 'Ryūgakusei no chishiki kōjyō o negatte', *Umi to Anzen*, 40, 528: 38–41.

Kang, David C. (2003) 'Getting Asia wrong: the need for new analytical frameworks', *International Security*, 27, 4: 57–85.

Katzenstein, Peter J. (2006) 'East Asia – beyond Japan', in Peter J. Katzenstein and Takashi Shiraishi (eds) *Beyond Japan – the dynamics of East Asian regionalism*, Ithaca and London: Cornell University Press, pp. 1–36.

Kim, Samuel S. (2003) 'Northeast Asia in the local-regional-global nexus: multiple challenges and contending explanations', in Samuel S. Kim (ed.) *The International Relations of Northeast Asia* (Asia in World Politics), Lanham, MD: Rowman and Littlefield, pp. 3–61.

Konaka, Satsuki (2006) 'Marakka Kaikyō no kaizoku kisei – kokusaiteki wakugumi no kōchiku to engankoku no taiō', *Ajiken Wa-rudo Torendo*, 132: 40–43.

Kuribayashi, Tadao (2003) 'Ajia ni okeru kaijōkōtsū no anzen kakuho no tame no kokusai kyōryoku ni tsuite', *Kaiji Kōtsū Kenkyū*, 52: 31–47.

Linklater, Andrew (1996) 'Rationalism', in Scott Burchill and Andrew Linklater (eds) *Theories of International Relations*, Basingstoke and London: Macmillan, pp. 103–28.

Liss, Carolin (2003) 'Maritime piracy in Southeast Asia', in Daljit Singh and Chin Kin Wah (eds) *Southeast Asian Affairs 2003*, Singapore: Institute of Southeast Asian Studies, pp. 52–70.

Little, Richard (2003) 'The English School vs. American realism: a meeting of minds or divided by a common language?' *Review of International Studies*, 29, 3: 443–60.

Menefee, Samuel Pyeatt (1996) *Trends in Maritime Violence*, Coulsdon, VA: Jane's Information Group.

—— (1997) 'Sharks of the sea', in Eric Ellen (ed.) *Shipping at Risk: the rising tide of organised crime*, Barking, Essex: International Maritime Bureau, ICC Publishing, pp. 29–46.

MOFA (2003) Online. Available: http://www.mofa.go.jp/mofaj/gaiko/kaiyo/kaizoku_3.html (accessed 21 October 2003).

—— (2005) *The Current State of the Piracy Problem and Our Country's Response*. Online. Available: http://www.mofa.go.jp/mofaj/gaiko/pirate/index.html (accessed 21 October 2003).

—— (2006) *Grant Aid to Indonesia for the Project for the Construction of Patrol Vessels for the Prevention of Piracy, Maritime Terrorism and Proliferation of Weapons*. Online. Available: http://www.mofa.go.jp/announce/announce/2006/6/0616–3.html (accessed 16 July 2006).

MLIT (2000a) *Model Action Plan*, Tokyo. Online. Available: http://www.mlit.go.jp/english/mot_news/mot_news_000428/mot_news_000428_3.html (accessed 23 July 2006).

—— (2000b) *Tokyo Appeal*, Tokyo. Online. Available: http://www.mlit.go.jp/english/mot_news/mot_news_000330/mot_news_000330_2.html (accessed 23 July 2006).

—— (2003) Online. Available: http://www.mlit.go.jp/english/mot_news/mot_news_000428 (accessed 27 October 2003).

Miyashita, Akitoshi (2003) *Limits to Power – asymmetric dependence and Japanese foreign aid policy*, Lanham MD and Oxford, UK: Lexington Books.

Mo, John (2002) 'Options to combat maritime piracy in Southeast Asia', *Ocean Development and International Law*, 33, 3–4: 343–58.

Mukundan, Pottengal (2002) 'Higashi Ajia kaiiki ni okeru kaizoku higai no genjō to keikō oyobi kaizoku mondai ni taisuru ICC-IMB no katsudō', *Kaiun*, May: 62–64.

Murphy, Martin N. (2007) *Contemporary Piracy and Maritime Terrorism*, Adelphi Papers No. 47, 388, Oxford and New York: Oxford University Press.

Nakamura, Hiromichi (2001) 'Kaizoku jiken no dōkō', *Umi to Anzen*, 35, 507: 16–19.

—— (2006) 'Kaijō hoanchō no kokusai shien katsudō – katsudō no gaiyō', *Umi to Anzen*, 40, 528: 22–27.

Ninushi to Yusō (2004) 'ISPS kōdō e no torikumi to genjō', 31, 6: 15–17.

Nippon Foundation (2004) Online. Available: http://www.Nippon-foundation.or.jp/eng/speeches/2004658/200446582.html (accessed 8 July 2004).

—— (2005) *Piracy Trends in East Asia*. Online. Available: http://nippon.zaidan.info/library/seikabutsu_print_view (accessed 19 December 2005).

Oceans and the Law of the Sea (1982) *Article 101 – Definition of Piracy in United Nations Convention on the Law of the Sea of 10 December 1982*, Division for Ocean Affairs and the Law of the Sea. Online. Available: http://www.un.org/Depts/los/convention_agreements/texts/unclos/UNCLOS-TOC.htm (accessed 14 March 2006).

Ogawa, Kazuhisa (2002) *Nihon no Kokkyō o Mamoreru ka?* Tokyo: Seishun.

Pempel, T.J. (2005) 'Introduction: emerging webs of regional connectedness', in T.J. Pempel (ed.) *Remapping East Asia: the construction of a region* (Cornell Studies in Political Economy), Ithaca: Cornell University Press, pp. 1–30.

Pugh, Michael C. (1993) 'Piracy and armed robbery at sea: problems and remedies', *Low Intensity Conflict and Law Enforcement*, 2, 1: 1–18.

Ravenhill, John (2002) 'A three bloc world? The new East Asian regionalism', *International Relations of the Asia Pacific*, 2, 2: 167–95.

ReCAAP ISC (2008) *Adding Value Charting Trends*, Annual Research Report 2007. Online. Available: http://www.recaap.org/index_home.html (accessed 28 February 2008).

Renwick, Neil and Abbott, John (1999) 'Piratical violence and maritime security in Southeast Asia', *Security Dialogue*, 30, 2: 183–96.

Rozman, Gilbert (2004) *Northeast Asia's Stunted Regionalism: bilateral distrust in the shadow of globalization*, Cambridge: Cambridge University Press.

Samuels, Richard (2007) *Securing Japan – Tokyo's grand strategy and the future of East Asia*, New York: Cornell University Press.

—— (2007/8) '"New fighting power!" Japan's growing maritime capabilities and East Asian security', *International Security*, 32, 3: 84–112.

Saunders, Elizabeth (2006) 'Setting boundaries: can international society exclude rogue states?' *International Studies Review*, 8: 23–53.

Scholte, Jan Aart (2000) *Globalization – a critical introduction*, Basingstoke and New York: Palgrave.

Shambaugh, David (2004/5) 'China engages Asia – reshaping the regional order', *International Security*, 29, 3: 64–99.

Singh, Bhubhindar (2002) 'ASEAN's perceptions of Japan: change and continuity', *Asian Survey*, 42, 2: 276–96.

Smith, Anthony L. (2006) 'Japan's relations with Southeast Asia: the strong silent type', in Yoichiro Sato and Satu Limaye (eds) *Japan in a Dynamic Asia – coping with the new security challenges*, Lanham, MD and Oxford, UK: Lexington Books, pp. 179–98.

Song, Yann-Huei (2003) 'Maritime security and international maritime instruments', *The Indonesian Quarterly*, 31, 4: 450–83.

Tagliacozzo, Eric (2001) 'Border permeability and the state in Southeast Asia: contraband and regional security', *Contemporary Southeast Asia*, 23, 2: 254–74.

Takai, Susumu (2002) 'Marakka Kaikyō Shūhen Kaiiki no Kaizoku to Kaigun no Yakuwari'. Online. Available: www.nids.go.jp/publication/kiyo/pdf/bulletin_j5–1_1.pdf (accessed 3 February 2010).

Tazaki, Yukio (2002) 'Kuraishisu intabyū kaijō Hoanchō chōkan Nawano Katsuhiko – kokusai hanzai, tero e no yokushiryoku toshite kaikoku Nihon no kōsutogādo "shitsukoi" kaihō, koko ni ari!' *Zaikaijin*, 15, 9: 46–51.

Terashima, Hiroshi (2001) 'Ajia no umi to kaizoku no Kyōi', *Gaikō Fōramu*, 14, 7: 38–41.

Tōi, Yoshitaka (2006) 'Kaijō hoanchō: chūmoku no misshyon – kaijō sekyuritei', *Sekai no Kansen*, 660: 124–29.

Tsunekawa, Keiichi (2005) 'Why so many maps there? Japan and regional cooperation', in T.J. Pempel (ed.) *Remapping East Asia: The construction of a region* (Cornell Studies in Political Economy), Ithaca: Cornell University Press, pp. 101–48.

Umezawa, Akima (2003) 'National Institute of Informatics (NII) Academic Society Home Village'. Online. Available: http://www.soc.nii.ac.jp/jsil/annual_documents/2003/autumn/houkoku-abstr/Panel%20C4%2Umezawa%20paper.pdf (accessed 20 December 2005).

Vagg, Jon (1995) 'Rough seas? Contemporary piracy in South-East Asia', *British Journal of Criminology*, 35, 1: 63–80.

Weatherbee, Donald E. (2005) *International Relations in Southeast Asia – the struggle for autonomy*, Lanham, MD: Rowman and Littlefield.

Weeks, Stanley B. (2003) 'Maritime terrorism: threats and responses', Paper Presented at the International Conference on Geo-Agenda for the Future: Securing the Oceans, Ship and Ocean Foundation.

Yamada, Yoshihiko (2003) *Umi no Terorizumu*, Tokyo: PHP Kenkyūjo.

Yamada, Yoshihiko (2006a) 'Ajia no kaizoku mondai ni taishite Nihon ga hatasu beki yakuwari', *Hōritsu Bunka*, 264: 26–29.

Yamada, Yoshihiko (2006b) 'Kaiyō sekyuritei to Kaizoku mondai', *Journal of World Affairs*, 54, 11: 2–14.

Yamada, Yoshihiko (2007) 'Gendai no kaizoku Mondai', *Senchō*, 127: 1–14.

Young, Adam J. and Valencia, Mark J. (2003) 'Conflation of piracy and terrorism in Southeast Asia: rectitude and utility', *Contemporary Southeast Asia*, 25, 2: 269–83.

5   Stronger political leadership and the shift in policy-making boundaries in Japan

Shinoda Tomohito[1]

Under the leadership of Prime Minister Koizumi Junichirō (2001–06), policy making in Japan changed drastically. During the 2001 Liberal Democratic Party (LDP) presidential election campaign, the prime minister publicly vowed to carry out structural reform of various aspects of the Japanese economy. The untraditional, top-down decision-making style he used to carry out reforms met with fierce resistance from LDP members. During the five and a half years of his term, however, Koizumi successfully streamlined the public sector, privatized the special public corporations, government financial institutions, and, most importantly, the postal services, while also resolving the problem of non-performing loans.

In the area of foreign and national security policy, Koizumi also took advantage of newly strengthened political institutions. After the 11 September 2001 incident, he expressed full support for US military action, and said Japan would do everything possible within the framework of its Constitution to help. Koizumi kept his promise by passing anti-terrorism legislation in an extraordinarily short period of time and dispatched Japan's Self-Defence Forces (SDF) overseas under wartime conditions for the first time in the country's post-war history.

What made these unprecedented achievements under Koizumi's leadership possible? In order to answer this question, this chapter first explains the traditional boundaries of policy making which made it difficult for the prime minister to exercise top-down leadership. Then, it explores what institutional changes were brought about by administrative reform under the leadership of Hashimoto Ryūtarō (1996–98) which helped set the playing field for Koizumi. In order to examine how Koizumi exercised top-down decision making, concrete examples are introduced in the area of fiscal and foreign policies. The final section discusses developments regarding these policy-making boundaries in the post-Koizumi era.

1. Traditional boundaries in policy making

Japan has a British-style parliamentary system, and the Constitution vests executive power in the Cabinet (Article 65). However, Japan's policy making for most of the post-war period was highly decentralized, and the Cabinet had seldom effectively played the role of 'core executive'. The Japanese government interprets narrowly the principle of the Cabinet's 'collective responsibility' (Article 66) to mean that all cabinet decisions must be made unanimously. This interpretation forced the prime ministers to build a consensus among cabinet members and ministries, and thus made it very difficult for them to exercise a top-down leadership style.

Although the prime minister held the authority to appoint cabinet members, intra-party factions served as a channel to allocate cabinet posts, bringing the LDP's decentralized nature into the Cabinet. At a time of cabinet reshuffling, the prime minister formed his cabinet carefully, considering the factional balance and requests from each LDP faction. Even strong prime ministers could not ignore completely such requests. Cabinet members, therefore, were often more grateful for their appointments and remained more loyal to their faction leaders than to the prime minister. As a result, cabinet members served as channels to represent their faction's opinions on government policy, making it more difficult to form a unified Cabinet.

The limited size of the support staff at the Cabinet Secretariat, or *Kantei* (the Japanese equivalent of Britain's 10 Downing Street or the United States' White House), exacerbated the situation. Although the Cabinet Secretariat listed nearly 200 officials, many of them were on loan from other ministries. Their loyalties usually belonged to their home ministry rather than to the prime minister. Prime Minister Murayama Tomiichi (1994–96) lamented in an interview, 'There were only three politicians, including myself at the prime minister's office. We were surrounded by bureaucrats' (Interview by author, 13 September 1996).

As a result, Japan's prime minister and his cabinet had not functioned effectively as a 'core executive' within the government. According to Dunleavy and Rhodes, core executives 'primarily serve to pull together and integrate central government policies, or act as final arbiters within the executive of conflicts between different elements of the government machine' (Dunleavy and Rhodes 1990: 4). Former Chief Cabinet Secretary Gotōda Masaharu, confirming this definition of a core executive, described the main responsibility in his former position as 'to mediate and settle disputes' between various government agencies participating in the policy-making process (Gotōda 1989: 3).

Since the prime minister's authority to initiate policies was not clearly defined in the Cabinet Law, the national leader rarely initiated policy in the traditional policy-making process. When he did provide policy direction, he usually instructed the related minister to follow up. The minister in turn gave instructions to his administrative vice minister, the bureau chief, and the director of the related section. If an officer in the chain of command sabotaged the measure, the policy did not survive.

In the traditional policy-making process, the main working level officers were deputy directors (*kachō hosa*). Their proposals were repeatedly discussed within the section before being brought to a meeting with other sections within the same bureau. If the other sections approved the proposal at a bureau meeting, it was finalized as a bureau decision. Before this finalization, however, the details of the policy had to be coordinated with officials from other bureaux and related ministries, examined in terms of legal and budgetary considerations, as well as put through ministry secretariat and political consultation with the government and opposition parties.

Former Deputy Chief Cabinet Secretary Ishihara Nobuo, who served in this core executive position for seven and a half years, described the bureau meeting as 'the actual decision-making organ' within the bureaucracy. According to Ishihara, official meetings at higher levels, such as ministry meetings, administrative vice-ministerial meetings, and ultimately cabinet meetings, are really nothing more than confirmation of policy (Ishihara 2001: 90–91). Japan's traditional policy making, thus, can be described as a bureaucracy-led, bottom-up process.

Some Japan scholars argue that a gradual structural change took place in this bureaucracy-led process. LDP Diet members accumulated knowledge and experience in specific policy areas and became known as *zoku*, or policy tribes (Muramatsu and Krauss 1987; Inoguchi and Iwai 1987). The power shift from the bureaucracy to the LDP Policy Research Council subcommittees (*bukai*) became evident especially after the two oil shocks of the 1970s. Lower economic growth after the oil shocks slowed down the increase of government revenues. With funds limited, bureaucrats became more dependent on the mediation and political decisions of the ruling party when reallocating funds among administrative pro-grammes (Nakamura 1984: 3–63). It became part of the official process for them to seek approval from the relevant *zoku* members of the LDP subcommittee before submitting proposals to the Cabinet.

Once the LDP subcommittee approved a policy, it was brought to the LDP's Policy Research Council for approval. The coalition government required approval from all coalition partners. But when the LDP was stable and in charge, Ishihara explains, 'We only needed to seek approval from the powerful figures within the subcommittees and the party. The deliberation at the Diet was close to a ceremony' (Ishihara 2001: 85). In this decentralized policy process, the core executive, including the prime minister and the Cabinet Secretariat, still played a very limited role.

In the sphere of fiscal policy, as well as for any policy involving government spending and revenue, the Budget and Tax Bureaux of the Ministry of Finance (MOF) played a central role. The Constitution does not give these MOF bureaux the power to create the budget. In fact, it only recognizes the authority of the Cabinet to draft the budget and of the Diet to enact it. The Fiscal Law, however, gives the MOF authority to form the government budget. In this sense, the bound-aries are here inscribed clearly. Throughout the post-war period, the MOF estab-lished a near monopoly on drafting the budget. With the power of the purse, basic macroeconomic and fiscal policies were formulated, and the MOF enjoyed much prestige over other ministries (Campbell 1977; Hartcher 1998).

Budget making is a very decentralized and cumulative process. Based on the economic forecasts made by the Economic Planning Agency, the MOF calcu-lated government revenue and set the budget spending ceiling for major func-tional spending categories by the end of July each year. Each ministry gathered requests from its regional offices from all over the nation and related government institutions, and consulted with LDP subcommittee members. All budget requests and tax proposals from various ministries were submitted by each ministry to the MOF by the end of August.

The MOF examined the initial proposals from the ministries between September and December. Playing a central role in the process were 11 budget examiners of the MOF's Budget Bureau, who were assigned to each ministry, plus their assistants or sub-examiners. Negotiations took place at both the bureaucratic and the political levels as it became part of the official budget process for ministries to seek approval from the relevant *zoku* members before submitting budget proposals. Every now and then, political compromises were made with strong pressure exerted by the *zoku* members. Major political battles over the budget took place in November and December (Sakakibara 1991: 71–76; Campbell 1977).

Then the final proposal had to go through political-level negotiations between the MOF and other ministries, and had to be approved by the LDP's executive members before Cabinet approval at the end of December. However, at this level there was very little room for negotiation. Throughout the process, the MOF played the leading role, and there was only a very limited role for the prime minister and Cabinet to play, illustrating how, at the time, the boundaries between and among the ministry, prime minister and Cabinet were clearly established.

In the area of foreign and national security policy, the prime minister's leadership was often sought, especially when controversies arose. As head of the Cabinet, the prime minister is authorized by Article 73 of the Constitution to conduct foreign affairs. The prime minister represents the Japanese nation in its relations with foreign governments, for example as Japan's chief diplomat at annual summit meetings.

Along with the role of chief diplomat, the prime minister is also in charge of military operations. Article 7 of the Self-Defence Force Law states that the prime minister is commander in chief of the SDF on behalf of the Cabinet. The prime minister can legally mobilize the SDF in case of external attack (Article 76) or when the public peace is disturbed (Article 78). Although their degree of interest and involvement in foreign and national security affairs has varied, all of Japan's post-war prime ministers have recognized their responsibilities in this area.

The ruling parties and the government recognized the prime minister's authority to represent the nation. Therefore, although the Ministry of Foreign Affairs (MOFA) has a minister, it requires the prime minister's involvement. As long as his foreign policy objectives do not conflict with domestic interests, the prime minister is given relative freedom in foreign affairs.

Thus, the traditional boundaries for domestic (or fiscal) and foreign policy making are different. The typical domestic or fiscal policy making was decentralized both within the government and the ruling party. The prime minister and the Cabinet Secretariat usually played marginal roles. In the foreign and national security policy area, MOFA wanted to involve the prime minister. But the decision-making process was usually bottom-up without the involvement of the Cabinet Secretariat.

2. Institutional changes brought about by the Hashimoto reforms

Under the Hashimoto Ryūtarō administration (1996–98), strong public sentiment against the national bureaucracy emerged in Japan. The factors which created this public sentiment were government scandals, which included two high MOF officials who received lavish treatment from a financially troubled credit union owner, and the *jūsen* problem, which involved seven housing loan companies that had gone bankrupt. In 1996, the *jūsen* crisis sparked heated debates about the need to reform the MOF and to divide its functions among independent agencies. Critics argued that the MOF's authority was too strong, and that its use of fiscal authority to regulate financial markets distorted government policy, creating problems such as the *jūsen* crisis.

During the October 1996 general election campaign, virtually all the political parties listed administrative reform as a top policy priority. After the election, Hashimoto inaugurated the Administrative Reform Council (hereafter the Reform Council). Hashimoto appointed himself as chairman of the Reform Council, thus forcing his government to act on its recommendations. After one year of discussions, the Reform Council published the final report in December 1997. Based on this report, the details of legal changes were introduced to the Diet under the leadership of Hashimoto's successor, Obuchi Keizō, and passed the Diet in July 1999 to bring about drastic organizational and institutional changes to the central government in January 2001.

Enhancing the political leadership of the prime minister and Cabinet was one of the major objectives of this administrative reform. First, the Cabinet Law was revised to bolster the prime minister's ability to initiate policy. While the national leader's authority at cabinet meetings was opaque under the old law, the revised Article 4 clarifies his authority to propose important, basic policies at such meetings. Technically, under the old law, it was possible for the national leader to propose a policy as a member of the Cabinet. But cabinet members, including the prime minister, rarely did so. With the revision of the Cabinet Law, institutional arrangements were clearly set for the national leader to initiate policies from the top. Second, the authority and functions of the Cabinet Secretariat were also reinforced. The revised Cabinet Law provides the Cabinet Secretariat with the authority to plan and draft important national policies. Third, the Cabinet Secretariat was enlarged, and the number of assistants to the prime minister was increased from three to five. To assist the chief cabinet secretary and his three deputies, three assistant chief cabinet secretary positions were created to replace the directorship of the former Cabinet Offices of Internal Affairs, External Affairs, and National Security Affairs. Fourth, the 'Guidelines for the Policy Coordination System' clearly defined the role of the Cabinet Secretariat: 'to present policy direction for the government as a whole, and coordinate policy strategically and proactively' (Cabinet decision, 30 May 2000). The guidelines also instructed other ministries to recognize that 'the Cabinet Secretariat is the highest and final organ for policy coordination under the Cabinet'. This placed the Cabinet Secretariat above other ministries and agencies.

The revisions to the Cabinet Law further strengthened the support system behind the prime minister, and were expected to change the budget process. The revised Cabinet Law identified fiscal and budget policies as important national issues. The law authorized the prime minister to form the Council on Economic and Fiscal Policy (CEFP) under the Cabinet Office as an advisory organ independent of the bureaucracy to advise the prime minister on macroeconomic and fiscal policy issues. Based on the recommendation of the CEFP, the prime minister is able to initiate the budget process by proposing the total size of the budget and prioritizing major spending items. According to former Deputy Chief Cabinet Secretary Ishihara Nobuo, this change moves the boundary of fiscal policy making by shifting 'the essential function of budget formation from the MOF to the Cabinet Secretariat' (Ishihara 1998: 189).

While Hashimoto's reform efforts reduced the role of the MOF, they did not have a dramatic effect on MOFA. The members of the Reform Council criticized the ineffectiveness of financial institutions in charge of Official Development Assistance (ODA) and the elitism of MOFA officials. After the reforms, the Overseas Economic Cooperation Fund and the Japan Export-Import Bank were merged into the Japan Bank for International Cooperation. This was the only MOFA-related change brought about by the administrative reform; MOFA itself remained basically untouched. In contrast to the fiscal policy area, the impact of the institutional changes brought about by administrative reform remained uncertain in the area of foreign policy.

Following these Hashimoto reforms, an important shift in boundaries took place during the Koizumi administration which strengthened political leadership in both domestic and foreign policy. The next section examines changes in fiscal policy making with the establishment of the CEFP, and in section 4 the discussion moves to foreign policy making with three case studies.

3. Boundary shifts in fiscal policy making under Koizumi

The CEFP was established in January 2001, with the prime minister, five other cabinet members, the governor of the Bank of Japan, and four experts from the private sector as members. At that time, it was not certain whether or not the newly established CEFP would actually change the budget-making process. Prime Minister Mori Yoshirō appeared to have no intention of taking advantage of the CEFP as a forum through which to demonstrate his leadership in the budget process.

The situation regarding the CEFP changed completely when Koizumi Junichirō took over the premiership. Koizumi was the first prime minister to be selected outside of traditional factional power struggles. He was elected by an overwhelming majority of LDP local branches, giving him legitimacy to form his own cabinet without consulting faction leaders. He appointed Takenaka Heizō, an economics professor at Keiō University, as the Minister of Economic and Fiscal Affairs in charge of the CEFP. Koizumi publicly promised that he would promote 'reform without sanctuary' and his support rate skyrocketed to the highest level on record (the records go back to 1949), to figures as high as 78 per cent according to *Asahi*

Shimbun, 85 per cent according to *Mainichi Shimbun*, and 87 per cent according to *Yomiuri Shimbun* (all figures published on 30 April 2001).

In his first policy speech on 7 May 2001, Koizumi publicly declared that his cabinet would conduct structural reform in the spirit of 'No fear, no hesitation, and no constraint'. As concrete plans for reform, he presented three main objectives: (1) the financial disposal of non-performing loans within the coming two to three years, (2) the creation of an economic system that will remain competitive in the twenty-first century, and (3) fiscal structural reform. For the fiscal reform, the prime minister announced that the target amount for new government bond issues would be kept under JPY30 trillion in the FY2002 budget.

Stressing the importance of the CEFP in carrying out his plans for reforms, Koizumi stated at the first CEFP meeting that he attended:

> It is no exaggeration to say that the Council on Economic and Fiscal Policy is the most important council for providing more substance to the broad principles introduced in my policy speech. . . . Following the belief that 'there will be no economic recovery without structural reform', the essential point is that we strive to carry out structural reform holding nothing sacred and to establish a society where people can move toward new goals with confidence and hope for the future development of Japan.
>
> (CEFP 2001a: 2)

While the CEFP was officially chaired by the prime minister, its proceedings were moderated by Economic Minister Takenaka. According to his memoirs, Takenaka had two important goals for the CEFP. The first goal was to drastically change the framework of macroeconomic management. Throughout the 1990s, the Japanese government had conducted a series of expansionary fiscal policies, which resulted in an inflated government debt without a significant contribution to economic recovery. Takenaka wanted to reduce public investment, and to focus on the disposal of non-performing loans. The second goal was to present a scenario of structural reform without concrete figures in order to avoid any shocks to the financial market (Takenaka 2006: 251). In order to improve the transparency of the CEFP's proceedings, Takenaka told the members that the summary of the discussions would be posted on the Internet three days after each meeting.

At the first meeting, Takenaka presented his idea of creating the Basic Policies (or *honebuto no hōshin*) in order to control fiscal policy formulation. He suggested that the Koizumi administration limit deficit financing bonds to JPY30 trillion. Finance Minister Shiokawa Seijūrō supported Takenaka's proposal, reflecting the thinking of the austerity-minded MOF officials. The MOF minister also suggested that the Basic Policies should include a bold plan to reallocate the budget, by cutting wasteful expenditures and increasing spending for priority programmes (CEFP 2001a: 7).

The CEFP held two more meetings to continue these discussions, and finalized the Basic Policies at the fourth meeting on 21 June. In the introduction of the 33-page document, the main items of Koizumi's reform were displayed – the privatization of postal services and special public corporations, and the JPY30 trillion ceiling of debt-financing bonds. In the document's first chapter, the disposal of non-performing loans within a few years was identified as the highest priority. The second chapter, which dealt with establishing a new social infrastructure, called for the revision of the traditional fiscal policy which focused on public investments, suggesting a substantial budget cut. The third and fourth chapters offered the CEFP's plan to tackle politically difficult issues, including reforms to medical insurance and the pension system, which changed the boundaries of national and local taxes.

Throughout the process, Takenaka and his staff formulated policies without consultation with the LDP policy subcommittees. It was Prime Minister Koizumi who had instructed them to ignore the traditional log-rolling process with the LDP subcommittees. Koizumi even told them not to contact *zoku* members of the relevant subcommittees even if called upon to do so. An explanation should be provided only to the chairman of the Policy Research Council, and it would be the chairman's responsibility to persuade LDP members (Iijima 2006: 62).

LDP *zoku* members strongly criticized this process. For example, former Deputy Chief Cabinet Secretary Suzuki Muneo said of the CEFP, 'The Council does not understand the parliamentary system' (Shimizu 2005: 250). According to many LDP members including Suzuki, prior consultation with the members of the ruling party was essential for policy making under a parliamentary system. But LDP *zoku* members did not choose to challenge the popular prime minister on this issue in the face of the forthcoming July upper house elections.

In the 29 July 2001 elections, Koizumi's high popularity brought a victory to the LDP with 65 out of 121 re-elected seats. At the press conference after the election, Prime Minister Koizumi reconfirmed his determination to push forward economic reform, and declared that his administration would introduce a detailed, three-step reform schedule: the first schedule by the end of August; the second during the fall Diet session; and the third during the year-end budget process.

On 3 August 2001, the first CEFP meeting after the election was convened, during which the MOF budget bureau chief reported that in order to achieve Koizumi's JPY30 trillion limit of debt-financing bonds, the government needed to reduce spending by JPY3 trillion. One of the private-sector members, Chairman Okuda Hiroshi of Toyota, stressed that the first CEFP budget overview should show a clear difference from the past fiscal policy-making style so that the public would know the significance of the policy changes. Another private-sector member, Professor Yoshikawa Hiroshi, then suggested an increase of JPY2 trillion in the priority policy areas, while cutting JPY5 trillion in the non-priority areas of expenditure to reach the goal of JPY3 trillion reduction. Finance Minister Shiokawa, who had stated the need for drastic reallocation of the budget at the previous meeting, expressed his support for this suggestion. Then, Prime Minister Koizumi stated:

> This is right after the election [victory]. Let's go for the idea of a JPY5 trillion cut with a JPY2 trillion increase. . . . Otherwise, the people will not have

a strong impression of change. . . . We need to 'strike while the iron is hot'. There certainly will be opposition [from the LDP]. But we had better show our determination that the CEFP will make the decision.

(CEFP 2001b: 14)

This became the decision of the Council. On the following morning (4 August), senior MOF officials visited the prime minister's office and expressed their concern about making a budget proposal with a drastic budget cut of JPY5 trillion without any consultation with the LDP. Koizumi, however, did not yield, and instructed the MOF officials to make a detailed proposal to follow the CEFP's decision. Assistant to Koizumi, Iijima Isao, declares that 'this was a historic moment when the budget initiative shifted from the MOF to the *Kantei*' (Iijima 2006: 67). Thus, the boundary was shifted in fiscal policy making. On 10 August, the Koizumi Cabinet officially approved the budget overview with a JPY2 trillion increase in the seven prioritized policy areas[2] and a 10 per cent cut in virtually all the other areas of spending, including public works investment and ODA.

Between August and November 2001, MOF officials had to negotiate with ministries and LDP subcommittees in order to draft the basic principles of budget formulation for the CEFP. The basic principles were presented at the 27 November CEFP meeting, and approved by the CEFP and the Cabinet on 4 December. As a result, in the FY2002 budget, the issuance of new bonds was kept under JPY30 trillion, expenditures in non-priority areas were reduced by JPY5 trillion, while JPY2 trillion was reallocated to priority areas. Among the key areas of reduction, public works, which have often been criticized as pork barrel projects benefitting LDP politicians, were reduced by 10.7 per cent. Fiscal expenditures for special public corporations were cut by 21.1 per cent, with a reduction amounting to more than JPY1 trillion. This created strong fiscal pressure for the forthcoming privatization of many special public corporations, including the four highway-related public corporations and the postal service (CEFP 2001c). On 24 December, the Cabinet approved the FY2002 budget to implement Koizumi's structural reform.

After the first year under the Koizumi administration, a new nine-step schedule for fiscal policy making was established: (1) By the end of January 2002, the CEFP produces 'Reform and Perspective' to present the medium-term macroeconomic outlook and policy goals. (2) At the end of June, the CEFP formulates 'Basic Policies', which describe major fiscal policies for the next fiscal year. (3) In July, the Cabinet Office provides an updated economic outlook and forecast for detailed budget formulation. (4) At the end of July or early August, based on this forecast, the CEFP produces a 'Budget Overview' to identify priority areas for budget allocation and non-priority areas for budget cuts. (5) By the end of August, the initial budget proposals are submitted by the ministries. (6) Negotiations and coordination between the MOF and the ministries as well as LDP politicians take place between September and November. (7) By the end of November or early December, the CEFP announces the 'Basic Principles for Budget Formulation' to present the basic principles of the budget in advance of the actual budget proposal. (8) By the end of December, the MOF finalizes the budget proposals for the next fiscal year for cabinet approval. (9) Then, in late December or early January 2003, the Cabinet Office provides an economic outlook for the next fiscal year based on the current economic and fiscal management (see Figure 5.1). Clearly, the decision-making boundary for the budget outline shifted from the hands of MOF officials to the CEFP.

As a result of fiscal policy reform initiated by the CEFP, the balance of the annual budget was significantly improved. The deficit in the primary balance (the budget balance, excluding interest payment and debt redemption from the expenditure side and bond revenues from the revenue side) of the central and local governments combined reached a high level at 5.7 per cent of the nominal GDP in FY2002. In FY2005, the deficit was reduced to 3.3 per cent. The expenditures of the central and local governments decreased from 23.2 per cent of the GDP in FY2002 to 21.6 per cent in FY2004 (Cabinet Office 2006a). The bond dependency ratio (the bond revenue to the total revenue) of the central government significantly decreased from 44.6 per cent in FY2003 to 30.7 per cent in the FY2007 budget proposal (MOF 2006).

The budget allocation had been inflexible due to sectionalism among the ministries and their bureaux. For example, the public works budget allocation had remained almost unchanged among the major categories for at least a couple of decades. The CEFP's scheme to prioritize the budget completely changed this situation. Between FY2001 and FY2006, the expenditure for public works was reduced by 22.6 per cent. Two other major budget categories which experienced a significant cut were ODA by 25.1 per cent and energy-related projects by 23.3 per cent. On the other hand, expenditures in the priority areas, such as social security (28.5 per cent) and the promotion of science and technology (19.7 per cent), were increased during the same period (Cabinet Office 2006b).

	Before 2001	*Since 2001*
end-Jan		CEFP drafts budget agenda, 'Reform and Perspectives'
end-June		CEFP establishes the 'Basic Policies' for budget drafting
July-Aug	MOF sets budget ceiling	CEFP drafts budget overview
end-Aug	Ministries draft budget proposal	Ministries draft budget proposal
Sept-Dec	Examination and negotiation period	Examination and negotiation period
Nov-Dec		CEFP issues 'Basic Principles for Budget Formulation'
end-Dec	MOF proposes budget for Cabinet approval	MOF proposes budget for Cabinet approval

Figure 5.1 Shift from MOF officials to the CEFP

Source: author

The CEFP's approach worked well; they successfully implemented economic structural reform through setting budget outlines. The reallocation of the budget brought significant advances in streamlining the public sector. It forced reforms and privatization of the special public corporations, government financial institutions and, most importantly, the postal service. The CEFP also successfully injected government funds into major banks to settle non-performing loan problems. It raised medical expenses for patients, thereby relieving the deficit in social security. Furthermore, the CEFP played an important role in bringing about tax reform to shift revenue sources from the central government to the local governments.

The CEFP has become a forum through which the prime minister, the economic minister and private-sector members present their plans for reform. The economic minister and the private-sector members lead the discussion to form the Basic Policies, which became a 'public roadmap for reform to the people' (Takenaka 2001: 1). In spring 2002, ministries and industry representatives began to lobby CEFP members so that their projects would be included in the Basic Policies. Deputy Chief Cabinet Secretary Furukawa Teijirō described this boundary shift, saying, 'It was at this time that I realized the budget-making power had truly shifted from the MOF into the hands of the *Kantei*' (Interview by author, 30 October 2003).

By forming the Basic Policies, the CEFP not only built a broad framework and set budgeting priorities for the next fiscal year budget, but also created momentum for major structural reforms such as the disposal of non-performing loans and the privatization of special public corporations. As the ministries had to respond to any reforms requested by the prime minister, the economic minister and the private-sector members of the CEFP, the entire decision-making process became open to the public. The CEFP's deliberation was available on its website soon after the meeting, improving the transparency of policy making. This new policy-making style became a tool for the prime minister and his economic advisers to set their domestic policy agenda and fiscal policy to pursue their goals. The MOF, which used to monopolize the traditional cumulative budget process, now had to formulate budgets following the instructions given by the CEFP. Thus, the fiscal policy-making boundaries shifted towards the Cabinet Office and closer to the prime minister.

At the same time, a similar shift occurred in the boundaries for foreign policy making, which is examined in the next section.

4. Boundary shift in foreign policy making

During his five and a half years of service, Prime Minister Koizumi successfully implemented a number of foreign and national security policies. In the area of national security, three major pieces of legislation were initiated and implemented by the Cabinet Secretariat. The first major piece was the anti-terrorism legislation. After the 11 September 2001 incident, Deputy Chief Cabinet Secretary Furukawa Teijirō quickly organized a task force in the Cabinet Secretariat to design the Japanese government's response. The task force was formed under the leadership of the assistant chief cabinet secretary from the Japan Defence Agency (JDA, now Ministry of Defence). MOFA officials had earlier dominated foreign policy making, but now found themselves forced to play subordinate roles on the task force. The new institutional arrangement of the Cabinet Secretariat avoided interagency conflicts between the JDA and MOFA, and enabled operations to run smoothly in the task force. As a result, on 19 September, Koizumi was able to announce his plan to support actively American reprisals for the terrorist attacks in a very timely manner.

His plan included the dispatch of SDF vessels to help the United States in collecting intelligence, shipping supplies, and providing medical services and humanitarian relief. He also pledged to strengthen protective measures for US bases in Japan. In addition, Koizumi announced non-military measures that included USD10 million to help fund the rescue and cleanup work after the attacks in the United States, a plan to provide emergency economic aid to Pakistan and India to help solicit their cooperation, and economic measures to avoid confusion in the international economic system (Koizumi 2001). In developing the plan, task force members carefully examined lessons from the Persian Gulf War, and recognized that financial contributions alone would not be highly appreciated by the international community, especially by the United States. On 25 September, Koizumi visited the United States to meet with President George W. Bush, and pledged to implement his plan as quickly as possible. Koizumi's plan elicited much praise from US policy makers as it was more than many experts in Japan and the United States had expected and was presented in a timely manner. The White House even provided a press release to show US appreciation (White House 2001).

Koizumi was keenly aware of the importance of the timeliness of Japan's response to the campaign against terrorism. A normal political process might delay the implementation and again invite international criticism of 'too little, too late'. As previously described, government policies were usually vetted first by the relevant policy subcommittee of the LDP's Policy Research Council. After approval at the subcommittees, policies moved to the LDP's General Council to build a party consensus, and then became the party's official policy. Under the coalition government, policies further require an agreement with the LDP's coalition partners, Komeitō and the then Conservative Party, before cabinet approval.

In the case of anti-terrorism legislation, however, Koizumi saved time by reversing this political procedure, seeking agreement from the coalition partners before consulting the LDP's policy committees. Once the three parties reached an agreement, it would be difficult for individual LDP members to oppose the decision. LDP *zoku* members, who had been consulted first in the traditional policy-making process, were kept outside the boundaries of the policy-making inner circle.

The Koizumi government needed to secure the passage of two key pieces of legislation in order to move ahead with the anti-terrorism plan. One bill would revise the Self-Defence Force Law to authorize SDF action to defend US bases in Japan against unexpected terrorist attacks. The existing law authorized SDF action only when a situation was already in progress and could not be handled by the police. A second law would authorize logistical support for US forces in the Indian

Ocean, including provision of supplies and medical services, transportation of personnel, search and rescue activities, and humanitarian assistance to displaced persons. The 1999 Regional Crisis Law strictly limited the area of such support to Japan's territory, or the sea and airspace surrounding it. The new law would allow support in foreign territory with permission from the relevant foreign government. More concretely, it would expand legitimate areas of activity to territories and seas between the Indian Ocean and Japan.

On 25 September 2001, the three coalition parties agreed on the outline for the new law. The following day, the government explained the legislation to representatives of the opposition parties. Just one day later, the outline was reported to LDP members through the party's General Council. The members of the LDP policy subcommittees were the last group to learn officially about the new legislation at a 28 September joint meeting of the Cabinet, Defence, and Foreign Affairs subcommittees.

During the passing of the anti-terrorism legislation, the task force in the Cabinet Secretariat played a central role. Meanwhile, MOFA was suffering from the stand-off between MOFA officials and Foreign Minister Tanaka Makiko. The Koizumi administration also questioned Minister Tanaka's ability to handle Diet deliberations competently. As a result, the Cabinet Secretariat took charge of the anti-terrorist legislation, and then Chief Cabinet Secretary Fukuda Yasuo answered questions in the Diet, symbolizing the Secretariat's leadership in pushing forward the legislation. The anti-terrorism legislation passed the Diet after just three weeks of deliberation. It was a considerably smooth passage for such a major piece of legislation that would authorize the Japanese government to dispatch SDF units abroad in times of combat for the first time.

After the passage of the anti-terrorism legislation, Prime Minister Koizumi tried to take advantage of the momentum to pass the contingency legislation. This legislation would provide a framework for dealing with an emergency in case of a military attack on Japan. The proposed bills clarified the government's decision-making process, strengthened the prime minister's authority, facilitated action by the SDF, and would allow for a limitation on the exercise of personal rights in times of national emergency. This was the first attempt since the end of World War II for Japan's Cabinet to pass new bills governing the nation's response to a military attack.

The Koizumi government simply followed the same strategy as in the anti-terrorism legislation. Basically the same task force within the Cabinet Secretariat restarted their original task of drafting the contingency bills. Although the bills were suspended during the Diet sessions in 2002, in May 2003 during the ordinary session of the Diet they passed the lower house after an agreement was reached between the ruling coalition and the Democratic Party of Japan (DPJ). A combined 90 per cent of the members who attended the session voted for one of the most controversial pieces of legislation in Japan's post-war history. This quick action was only possible because the boundaries of policy making had shifted so that power to initiate legislation moved from MOFA to the Cabinet Secretariat.

The same strategy was adopted again for the Iraq Special Measures Law (The Law Concerning the Special Measures on the Humanitarian and Reconstruction Assistance Activities in Iraq). The task force in the Cabinet Secretariat drafted the new laws that would enable the dispatch of the SDF to Iraq for active contribution to humanitarian and reconstruction activities in Iraq. The legislation passed the Diet in July 2003, and based on this legislation, the Japanese government dispatched the Self-Defence Forces to Iraq in February 2004.

In the aforementioned three case studies of national security policy, the *Kantei* played a central role. For the anti-terrorism legislation, the task force in the Cabinet Secretariat, instead of MOFA, drafted an important piece of national security legislation to be approved by the Cabinet within a short period of four weeks. These cases under the Koizumi administration demonstrated clearly a major change in policy-making boundaries, with the power shifting from MOFA to the prime minister and the Cabinet Secretariat.

5. Beyond the Koizumi administration

In the LDP presidential race to succeed Koizumi, Chief Cabinet Secretary Abe Shinzō won the election with broad support from across the LDP factions. When he formed his cabinet, Abe chose his friends and allies as cabinet ministers in order to reward them for their support. The first Abe cabinet, at the outset, received as high as a 65 per cent approval rating, according to a Kyodo News survey (Kyodo News Service, 28 September 2006).

In terms of fiscal policy making, Abe appointed Ōta Hiroko as the Minister of Economic and Fiscal Policy to head CEFP meetings. Abe aimed to continue Koizumi's policy to pursue fiscal reform without a tax increase. Abe believed that economic growth should come first, and that Japan's fiscal balance would improve with a higher growth rate without a tax increase. This position led Abe to clash head on with the MOF, which wanted to raise the consumption tax.

Abe and Ōta confronted the LDP construction *zoku* by announcing their intentions to use road-related taxes for broader purposes. Road-related taxes, about JPY3.5 trillion a year, were used only for road construction to meet the demands of LDP politicians for more roads in their home districts. Many critics pointed out that these taxes were being used for wasteful and unnecessary road construction projects and that the funds should instead go into the general revenue. At the 30 November CEFP meeting, Abe announced that he would like to shift the road-related taxes to the general revenue. After a fierce battle between the *Kantei* and LDP *zoku* members, a political compromise was reached. The government would put only the surplus road tax revenue into the general expenditures after the funds for necessary road construction projects had been spent. The failure to move all the money into the general account was a major setback for Abe's plan to cut the fiscal deficit. Chief Cabinet Secretary Shiozaki Tadahisa and his deputy Matoba Junzō did not have enough administrative skill or political resources to mobilize Abe's top-down policy initiative. The Abe cabinet could not fully take advantage of the boundary shift which took place under the Koizumi administration to push forward his reform for fiscal policy making.

On the other hand, Abe showed strong leadership in the area of foreign policy by moving quickly to improve relations with China and South Korea. During Koizumi's leadership, the prime minister's visit to Yasukuni Shrine offended Chinese and South Korean political leaders. Prime Minister Abe promised that, unlike Koizumi, he would not publicly visit the shrine in his official capacity of prime minister, though he refused to say whether he would visit it in private. In response, Chinese and South Korean leaders welcomed Abe's visit to Beijing and Seoul in October 2006, which significantly improved Japan's bilateral relationships with each of these countries.

Abe also pushed three major pieces of national security legislation forward. First, he successfully enacted the legislation to upgrade the Defence 'Agency' to a 'Ministry'. Second, Abe moved to establish procedures for a national referendum to amend the Constitution. Third, the Abe administration introduced a bill to facilitate changes regarding US forces in Japan. These legislative proposals were initiated and delivered with strong leadership from Prime Minister Abe. But these bills were not introduced by the Cabinet Secretariat in the top-down decision-making style of the Koizumi administration. The Defence Agency itself proposed that it be turned into a ministry. The referendum bill was proposed by LDP and Komeitō legislators. MOFA and the Defence Agency prepared the facilitation of US bases. The only national security-related bill introduced by the Cabinet Secretariat was one to establish a National Security Council. This bill, however, was not even discussed in the Diet during Abe's tenure, and eventually died under the Fukuda administration. Just as with the boundary shift for fiscal policy making, the Abe cabinet could not take advantage of the boundary shift in the national security policy area which had taken place under the Koizumi administration.

In September 2007, Abe suddenly announced his resignation on the grounds of his health, and Former Chief Cabinet Secretary Fukuda Yasuo won the LDP presidential election to become the prime minister. In the fall 2007 Diet session, the legislation to continue the SDF mission in the Indian Ocean for anti-terrorism activities became a major issue. Abe's sudden resignation made it logistically impossible to extend the existing Anti-Terrorism Special Measures Law before it expired on 1 November. The Fukuda administration introduced new legislation which would dispatch the Maritime SDF only for refuelling operations to support maritime inspections in the Indian Ocean.

DPJ President Ozawa Ichirō publicly announced his opposition to the legislation. He proposed an alternative idea to promote Japan's participation in the International Security Assistance Force (ISAF) on Afghanistan soil, an operation which had been authorized by the United Nations. However, Ozawa's idea was not widely accepted by other DPJ members as ground activities by the ISAF would be more risky than maritime operations. In November, Ozawa met with Prime Minister Fukuda, and agreed to form a coalition government with the LDP, although this idea did not reach fruition. Instead, it met with such strong opposition within the DPJ that Ozawa at once announced publicly his resignation as DPJ president.

Although Ozawa was persuaded to keep the presidency, this turmoil confused the DPJ's Diet operation regarding the anti-terrorism legislation.

In December, the ruling parties decided to extend the Diet session in order to pass the legislation with a two-thirds majority in the lower house, which would override the rejection by the upper house under Article 59 of the Constitution. On 11 January 2008, the legislation was enacted to authorize the government to restart maritime operations in the Indian Ocean.

Overriding legislative action was politically risky, and the Fukuda administration had to utilize this measure with caution. In January 2008, for example, LDP Secretary General Ibuki Bunmei tried to use this tactic when he introduced a proposal which would extend the controversial temporary gasoline tax. However, this attempt met with strong public resentment, and Ibuki had to withdraw the proposal at once, leaving the gasoline tax to expire at the end of March 2008. On April 30, the Fukuda cabinet passed legislation to revive the gasoline tax with a two-thirds majority in the lower house.

This incident, however, exemplified the vulnerability of the Fukuda cabinet with its unstable power base. As his job approval rate stayed in a low level (25 per cent, *Asahi Shimbun*, 30–31 August 2008), Fukuda announced his resignation on September 9, and hoped that his successor would be able to dissolve the lower house under a better political environment in order to improve the power balance in the Diet in the subsequent election.

When Asō Tarō took over the prime ministership, his cabinet initially received 48 per cent of public support (*Asahi Shimbun*, 11–12 September 2008). Asō, however, did not immediately dissolve the lower house as Fukuda had hoped. On 30 October, the prime minister declared that he would postpone the general election in order to achieve economic recovery. Asō delivered two economic stimulus packages: one of 5 trillion yen for FY2008 and one of 15 trillion yen for FY2009. On the national security front, he successfully passed the legislation to extend the SDF's refuelling activities in the Indian Ocean, and enacted the Anti-Piracy Legislation to dispatch the SDF vessels to protect foreign vessels from pirate attacks off Somalia. However, the public support for his cabinet steadily declined.

When Asō finally decided to dissolve the lower house in July 2009, his support rate was as low as 17 per cent (*Asahi Shimbun*, 18–19 July 2009). In the 30 August general election, the DPJ recorded a historic victory, capturing 308 seats in the 480-member lower house to bounce the LDP out of power. The new DPJ Prime Minister Hatoyama Yukio received a support rate of 71 per cent (*Asahi Shimbun*, 16–17 September 2009), the second highest in history next only to Koizumi in April 2001.

As the DPJ manifesto during the election campaign called for reducing the bureaucratic influence on the government, Hatoyama encouraged the ministers, the senior vice ministers and the parliamentary secretaries to take political initiative within each ministry. These DPJ politicians in the government frequently met with each other and made policy decisions. Thus, new boundaries seemed to have been established in each ministry and deemphasized the role of the bureaucrats. However, Prime Minister Hatoyama suffered from a financial scandal from the beginning of his term. Many experts claimed there was a lack of prime ministerial leadership under the DPJ government. As a result, the early stage of the Hatoyama administration demonstrated the decentralized nature with strong political leadership within each ministry but a lack of a core leader.

Conclusion

Traditional policy making in Japan before Koizumi could be characterized as a bureaucracy-led, bottom-up process with limited political intervention. However, the traditional boundaries for domestic (or fiscal) and foreign policy making were different in terms of the prime minister's involvement. The typical domestic or fiscal policy-making process was decentralized both within the government and the ruling party. The MOF monopolized the process, and the prime minister played a marginal role. In contrast, MOFA wanted to involve the prime minister in the foreign and national security policy-making process.

Important institutional changes were brought about by Hashimoto's administrative reform, which set the stage for the shift in boundaries for policy making under the Koizumi administration. In the area of fiscal policy, the newly established CEFP played a central role to set priorities for the fiscal year budget, and created momentum for major structural reforms. The MOF, which used to monopolize the traditional cumulative budget-making process, now follows instructions given by the CEFP. In the area of national security policy, the *Kantei* began playing a central role under the Koizumi cabinet with MOFA playing a subordinate role. Thus, the policy-making boundaries shifted towards the Cabinet Office and the *Kantei*, therefore closer to the prime minister and away from career bureaucrats.

The Abe cabinet could not fully take advantage of the boundary shift which took place under the Koizumi administration to push forward his reforms for fiscal policy making or national security initiatives. After the party's defeat in the 2007 election, the Fukuda administration had to face a new political situation with the upper house dominated by opposition parties. Fukuda had to pass major pieces of legislation, such as the new Anti-terrorism Law and the revival of the gasoline tax, through the lower house. Similarly, the unstable political environment also troubled Prime Minister Asō throughout his term. While he successfully delivered economic stimulus packages and important pieces of national security legislation, he suffered a low public approval rate. As a result, the LDP was forced out of power.

We have seen that the boundaries between the political leaders and the bureaucracy in the policy-making process within the government began to shift towards the prime minister under the Koizumi government after the path was laid by Hashimoto. Under the LDP governments after Koizumi, however, the political environment did not support top-down, centralized decision making. The newly established DPJ government brought about new boundaries within each ministry with more active DPJ members at the posts of ministers, senior vice ministers and parliamentary secretaries. While the prime ministerial leadership was not demonstrated during the Hatoyama government, and the new Kan Naoto government is still finding its feet, the new equilibrium for political leadership in policy-making will likely be put into practice under the DPJ government, which is expected to continue, at least, until 2013.

Notes

1 Acknowledgement. The author is grateful to the Japan Society for the Promotion of Science's Grants-in-Aid for Scientific Research for financial support of this research.
2 The seven areas are: (1) environmental issues; (2) the aging population; (3) the development of local facilities; (4) urban revitalization; (5) science and technology; (6) human resource development; and (7) information and technology.

References

Cabinet Office (2006a) 'Annual Report on the Japanese Economy and Public Finance'. Online. Available: http://www5.cao.go.jp/zenbun/wp-e/wp-je06/06–00000.html (accessed 5 September 2007).
—— (2006b) 'Koko made Susunda Koizumi Kaikaku'. Online. Available: http://www.kei-zai-shimon.go.jp/explain/pamphlet/0608.pdf (accessed 6 September 2007).
Campbell, John (1977) *Contemporary Japanese Budget Politics*, Berkeley: University of California Press.
CEFP (2001a) 'Heisei 13 nendo Dai 8 kai Gijiroku', 18 May. Online. Available: http://www.keizai-shimon.go.jp/minutes/2001/0518/minutes-s.pdf (accessed 9 August 2007).
—— (2001b) 'Heisei 13 nendo Dai 13 kai Gijiroku', 3 August. Online. Available: http://www.keizai-shimon.go.jp/minutes/2001/08038/minutes-s.pdf (accessed 5 September 2007).
—— (2001c) 'Heisei 13 nendo Dai 30FP, kai Gijiroku', 27 November. Online. Available: http://www.keizai-shimon.go.jp/minutes/2001/1127/minutes-s.pdf (accessed 5 September 2007).
Dunleavy, Patrick and Rhodes, R.A.W. (1990) 'Core executive studies in Britain', *Public Administration*, 68, 1: 3–28.
Gotōda, Masaharu (1989) *Naikaku Kanbo Chōkan*, Tokyo: Kōdansha.
Hartcher, Peter (1998) *The Ministry: How Japan's most powerful institution endangers world markets*, Boston: Harvard Business School Press.
Iijima, Isao (2006) *Koizumi Kantei Hiroku*, Tokyo: Nihon Keizai Shimbunsha.
Inoguchi, Takashi and Iwai, Tomonobu (1987) *'Zoku' Giin no Kenkyū*, Tokyo: Nihon Keizai Shimbunsha.
Ishihara, Nobuo (1998) *Kan Kakuarubeshi*, Tokyo: Shōgakkan Bunko.
—— (2001) *Kengen no Daiidō*, Tokyo: Kanki Shuppansha.
Koizumi, Junichirō (2001) 'Japan's measures in response to the simultaneous terrorist attacks in the United States', 19 September. Online. Available: http://www.kantei.go.jp/foreign/koizumispeech/2001/0919terosoti_e.html (accessed 9 August 2007).
MOF (2006) 'Highlights of the Budget for FY2007', December. Online. Available: http://www.mof.go.jp/english/budget/e20061224a.pdf (accessed 5 September 2007).
Muramatsu, Michio and Krauss, Ellis (1987) 'The conservative policy line and the development of patterned pluralism', in Kozo Yamamura and Yasukichi Yasuba (eds) *The Political Economy of Japan, vol. 1, The Domestic Transformation*, Stanford: Stanford University Press, pp. 516–54.

Nakamura, Akira (1984) 'Jiyūminshūtō no yottsu no kao', in Nakamura Akira and Takeshita Yuzu (eds) *Nihon no Seisaku Kettei: Jimintō, Yatō, Kanryō*, Tokyo: Azusa Shuppan.

Sakakibara, Eisuke (1991) 'The Japanese politico-economic system and the public sector', in Samuel Kernell (ed.) *Parallel Politics: economic policymaking in Japan and the United States*, Washington: Brookings Institution, pp. 50–79.

Shimizu, Masato (2005) *Kantei Shudō*, Tokyo: Nihon Keizai Shimbunsha.

Takenaka, Harutaka (2006) *Shushō Shihai*, Tokyo: Chūkō Shinsho.

Takenaka, Heizo (2001) 'The Economic and Fiscal Policy of the Koizumi Administration: achievements of the council on economic and fiscal policy and policies ahead', 27 December. Online. Available: http://www5.cao.go.jp/keizai1/2001/1227daijin-speech-e.pdf (accessed 6 September 2007).

—— (2006) *Kōzō Kaikaku no Shinjitsu*, Tokyo: Nihon Keizai Shimbunsha.

White House Press Release (2001) 'US Welcomes Japan's Anti-Terrorism Assistance Package', White House Press Release, 20 September. Online. Available: http://www.globalsecurity.org/military/library/news/2001/09/mil-010920-usia12.htm (accessed 18 September 2007).

6 Leadership strategies
(Re)drawing boundaries among and within parties in Japan

Uchiyama Yū

For years, scholars have attempted to define politics (or 'the political') in various ways. One of the most notable definitions may be that of German political philosopher Carl Schmitt. He defines the political as the distinction between friend and enemy:

> The political is the most intense and extreme antagonism, and every concrete antagonism becomes that much more political the closer it approaches the most extreme point, that of the friend-enemy grouping. In its entirety the state as an organized political entity decides for itself the friend-enemy distinction.
>
> (1996: 29–30)

There have been many historical examples in which political leaders utilized the friend–enemy distinction in order to consolidate their supporters *vis-à-vis* their opponents, effectively strengthening their positions in polities – Adolf Hitler and Mao Zedong are the extreme cases. By defining one part of society as a friend and the other part as an enemy, political leaders can mobilize support for themselves. In other words, political leaders often try to draw boundaries in society as a strategy to strengthen their leadership. Hereafter, such a strategy is called a 'boundary strategy'.

One leader who adopted explicitly this strategy in recent years is Prime Minister Koizumi Junichirō, who was in office from April 2001 through September 2006. As we will see in further detail later, when he undertook neoliberal reforms such as budget cuts and privatization, Koizumi was faced with furious resistance from those whose interests would be harmed by such reforms. In order to mobilize support for his reform and overcome resistance, Koizumi emphasized the friend–enemy distinction: he called his opponents 'the forces of resistance' (*teikō-seiryoku*) and gave the general public the impression that his opponents were going to damage the public's interests, whereas he was siding with the people. Thus Koizumi succeeded in gathering huge support from the public – he enjoyed extraordinarily high approval ratings throughout his prime ministership, and achieved reform goals to a significant degree. Such a confrontational strategy had rarely been adopted by the Liberal Democratic Party (LDP) leaders before

Koizumi. Considering that a number of preceding prime ministers who tried to initiate reforms were forced to withdraw their plans once faced with strong opposition, Koizumi's case shows how well this boundary strategy worked. (The point to be noted is that a boundary strategy like Koizumi's has been made possible by institutional reforms, as pointed out in Chapter 5.)

This chapter shows how recent Japanese prime ministers – namely, Koizumi and his successors Abe Shinzō and Fukuda Yasuo – used boundary strategies, and how the strategies worked.[1] It focuses particularly on how they drew boundaries *among* and *within* political parties, as the ways in which leaders drew such boundaries are representative of their leadership styles.

This chapter first classifies different types of boundary strategies, locating them in comparative contexts and linking each type to a certain prime minister. Then, each prime minister's boundary strategy is delineated chronologically: Koizumi, Abe Shinzō and Fukuda Yasuo. Finally, we examine the factors that affected their choice of strategies.

1. Types of boundary strategies

There are various ways for government leaders to draw boundaries among and within parties as strategies to reinforce their positions. Usually they draw dividing lines between the governing and the opposition parties, but some may try to create divisions within the opposition party itself. Some may even want to emphasize fissures within their own party. This section shows how boundary strategies can be classified (for a visual expression of each type of boundary strategy, see Figure 6.1).

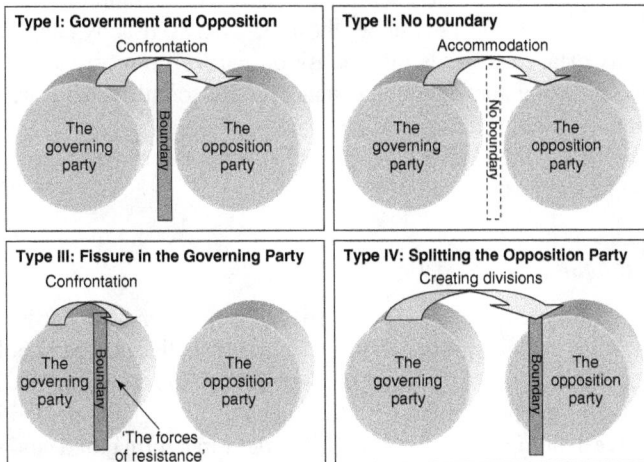

Figure 6.1 Types of boundary strategies

Source: author

Type I: government and opposition

The first and seemingly the most common strategy is to emphasize the dividing line between the government and the opposition. If we classify present democracies into two model types, the Westminster (or majoritarian) model and the consensus model (Lijphart 1999), this strategy tends to prevail in polities that belong to the Westminster model, most typically represented by the United Kingdom. In such polities, the two major parties compete with each other for votes, and the winner usually monopolizes cabinet positions. The electoral system (usually the single member district system) gives the winner a disproportionately large share of the seats.[2]

Although the policies of the two parties tend to be convergent as per the median voter theorem, the parties still try to stress their differences in electoral campaigns and parliamentary debates. They present their own manifestos to the constituencies in the campaigns, and commit themselves to implementing policies prescribed in the manifestos when they take office. The opposition party attempts to harshly criticize the government and point out the defects of its policies in order to appeal to the constituencies. Barring a few exceptions such as the wartime coalition government led by Winston Churchill, the governing party rarely cooperates with the opposition, and the opposition is usually excluded from the policy-making process.

In Japan, the long governing LDP seems to have been following this strategy. The Japan Socialist Party, the biggest opposition party under the 1955 system,[3] emphasized its confrontational position against the LDP, and advocated policies such as unarmed neutrality and abolition of the Self-Defence Forces (SDF), which the LDP would never have accepted. However, it is also incorrect to think that the LDP and the opposition parties confronted one another in the same way as their British counterparts. When we examine the Diet's deliberation process closely, we find that the LDP (especially under the 1955 system) usually adopted a rather accommodative stance towards the opposition parties. In most cases where the LDP seemed to take a confrontational stance, it did so only in appearance; truly confrontational stances were rare events.

Thus, the strategy the LDP usually pursued cannot be seen as Type I, but Type II, which we turn to next.

Type II: non-boundary strategy

In contrast to the Type I strategy, Type II tries to include as many parties as possible into the policy-making process. This strategy is usually adopted in polities that follow a consensus model.[4] Typified by Switzerland and Belgium, such polities generally have proportional representation, such as through an electoral system, and hence have a multiparty system. Major parties often form grand coalitions and share the executive power; the norm of decision making there is not majoritarian but consensual. The parties cooperate with one another as much as possible, and even the minority parties are usually included in the policy-making process.

When all major parties form a grand coalition, there exists no boundary between the government and the opposition, at least not in the same sense as in the majoritarian polities. Thus, the Type I strategy is not given higher priority in such polities. Some may think that the Type I strategy is universal, but such thought stems from the misconception that Westminster-style politics is the ideal. The majoritarian model, however, does not work well under certain conditions, such as in plural societies (i.e., societies with deep fissures regarding such matters as languages and religions) (Lijphart 1977). It is the consensus or consociational model that better fits such societies.

Although conflicts between the governing LDP and the opposition parties seem to have been fierce in Japan, the LDP's posture *vis-à-vis* the opposition had long been similar to that of the consensus model. When the LDP government intended to have its bills passed by the Diet, it tried to achieve as much consensus with the opposition parties as possible. As many scholars have pointed out, the political style of the LDP has been highly accommodative (Curtis 1988, 1999; Kuroda 2005; Richardson 1997).

Such an accommodative posture is best shown by the function of the Inter-party Relations Committees (IPRC, *Kokkai Taisaku Iinkai*). The IPRCs are not parliamentary standing committees, but organizations that belong to each party. Although the formal arena where parties negotiate parliamentary affairs is the House Management Committee (HMC, *Giin Unei Iinkai*), which is one of the parliamentary standing committees, important matters are often decided in informal meetings among representatives from the respective parties' IPRCs. Curtis characterizes the IPRC (*Kokutai*) politics as follows:

> The role of the *Kokutai* is not to negotiate the substance of policy, but to arrive at understandings about how to advance the parliamentary process . . . *Kokutai* negotiations emphasize informality, privacy, implicit understandings, and a willingness to make gestures that enable the other side to save face or to maintain an ostensible posture of opposition while in fact facilitating the passage of legislation.
>
> (1999: 119)

The LDP and the opposition parties collided with one another on the surface but, in reality, the former was prepared to concede to the latter in order to reach a consensus. What is interesting is the difference between appearance and substance. While Japan has a parliamentary system similar to Britain and the majority rule appears to be used in decision making, the actual decision-making process in the Diet is highly consensual. Kuroda explains this difference by his bilayer theory as follows:

> External forces created the Diet, including the HMC and plenary sessions where Diet members act in accordance with Western standards in appearance, debating pros and cons of issues, and deciding them by majority rule . . . This is called *tatemae*-level performance or ritual. The substance, however, was to

be processed by the IPRC, where members of the Diet can informally negotiate (through *honne*-level communication) and arrive at a consensus behind
closed doors in advance of formal proceedings.

(2005: 54)[5]

In sum, while the successive LDP governments seem to have adopted the Type I
strategy on the formal level, their informal but substantive strategy had been that
of Type II. Most Japanese prime ministers prior to Koizumi attached importance
to this non-boundary strategy. Having experienced Type III and Type IV strategies
under Koizumi and Abe, Fukuda's LDP seems to have returned to Type II.

Type III: emphasizing fissures within the governing party

The Type III strategy is unique in that it purposefully attempts to bring boundaries into the governing party and/or the government. In a presidential system, the
president can enact policies by becoming an ally of a majority of the lawmakers,
irrespective of their parties. Thus, it may be possible for the president to stand
against members of his or her own party. In a parliamentary system, however,
the power of the chief executive (the prime minister) is based on the support of
the majority party or parties; as a result, it is impossible for the chief executive to
keep his or her position without the support of the members of the governing party.
Hence, Type III seems to be unlikely in polities with parliamentary systems.

One of the rare political leaders who succeeded with this strategy is Koizumi;
he successfully adopted it and exerted strong leadership during his attempt to
implement neoliberal reforms. Since many LDP politicians were backed by the
sectors that benefited from regulative and protective policies, these politicians
thought that their interests were being threatened by Koizumi's reform. Some ministries also feared their budgets and organizations would be cut. In particular, *zoku*
politicians[6] such as construction *zoku* and postal *zoku* and related ministries
fiercely resisted Koizumi.

Faced with strong resistance from the inside, Koizumi introduced a clear
friend–enemy distinction into his own party, the LDP, and the government. He
called those who opposed him 'the forces of resistance' even though they were
members of the LDP. This strategy sought to gain the attention of the general
public by stressing conflict within the governing party, and obtain enough support
directly from it to overcome such resistance. How Koizumi used it and why it was
possible is explained in the next section, after defining the fourth and final type of
boundary strategy.

Type IV: splitting the opposition parties

This strategy type is the exact mirror image of the Type III strategy. It intends to
cause an internal division in the opposition party. The workings of this strategy
will be easily understood if one remembers that 'divide and rule' has been a traditional tactic of governing. If one party successfully raises issues about which

members of the other party deeply disagree, it is likely to cause a severe internal division in the latter and weaken its power.

A necessary condition for this strategy to be successful is that the targeted party lacks unity. If the opposition party is highly united around a certain ideology – that is, almost all members of the party share the same ideology – there are few issues that the governing party can exploit to induce internal divisions in the opposition. By contrast, if the ideological distribution in the opposition is wide – in other words, if the party has potential ideological fissures around some issues on the left–right political spectrum – opportunities exist for the government to take advantage of the fissures.

The biggest opposition party at the moment, the Democratic Party of Japan (DPJ), meets this condition. The DPJ is a combination of former parties that vary from conservative to social democratic. It was formed in 1996 by centre-right and centre-left politicians who seceded from existing parties, such as the LDP and the Socialist Party. The DPJ revamped itself in 1998 by merging with other parties. The Liberal Party led by Ozawa Ichirō, a leading conservative politician, joined the DPJ in 2003. Thus, the ideological distribution of the DPJ has become very wide. In particular, there is a deep divide in the party around issues concerning national security (e.g., the international role of the SDF, amending the Constitution) and conservative values (e.g., nationalistic education).[7] By contrast, the LDP is relatively cohesive regarding such issues.

Prime Minister Abe's leadership was illustrative of the Type III boundary strategy. After attempting to use the Type III strategy as Koizumi did, Abe came to instead emphasize conservative issues that were likely to consolidate his party and induce divisions in the DPJ. In the following section, we take a closer look at how the above-mentioned types of boundary strategies were used by prime ministers in recent years.

2. Koizumi's distinctive strategy

As mentioned earlier, the original boundary strategy in Japan had been that of Type II. But the leader serving as prime minister at the beginning of the twenty-first century broke this custom; Koizumi, emphasizing conflict within the LDP, used a boundary strategy that worked against his own party in order to reinforce his own leadership.

As soon as he took office, Koizumi expressed his firm intention to carry out 'structural reforms' that included a budget cut, deregulation, and privatization, as shown in his first keynote address delivered to the Diet. Although his reform plans were met with intense resistance within the LDP, he confronted that resistance rather than withdrawing the plans. In May 2001, he asserted at the plenary session of the Diet that all who opposed his policy should be regarded as 'the forces of resistance'. He is even known to have declared, 'If LDP members think of frustrating my reform plans, I will destroy the LDP!' during a speech he made on the advent of the upper-house election in July of that year (*Asahi Shimbun* [evening edition], 9 July 2001).

Koizumi's adversarial posture against his own party was really 'strategic' in that he expected it to provide him with enough public support to win over the resistance from inside his own party.

'Good' and 'evil'

Koizumi's distinctive boundary strategy was closely related to his peculiar political style, which can be characterized as populism. Otake defines populism as

> a 'theatrical' political style where, assuming a dichotomy between 'ordinary people' and 'elite', 'good' and 'evil', or 'friend' and 'enemy', a political leader takes the side of the ordinary people and performs the role of a 'hero' who fights against the enemy
>
> (Otake 2003: 118–19)

Through utilizing this style, Koizumi successfully infused into the minds of the public an impression that he himself represented 'good' and the forces of resistance were 'evil'.

This strategy of dramatizing conflict between Koizumi and his opponents within his own party appealed to those who otherwise would have paid little attention to politics, like housewives and the young. Thus Koizumi succeeded in gathering vast public support; he enjoyed an approval rating as high as over 80 per cent just after his inauguration, and the average rating throughout his prime ministership was 50 per cent.[8]

As implied earlier, one of the conditions that enable the Type III strategy is high popular support for the leaders. Japanese prime ministers other than Koizumi could not adopt this strategy because their power was based on their party's support. Since factions in the LDP had nearly autonomous power, politicians who were eager to be the LDP president (i.e., the prime minister) had to depend on the support of other factions; there was very little prospect for a candidate without factional support to win the party presidential election. The power relations in the LDP made it impossible for successive prime ministers to take an adversarial stance against another part of the LDP.

Koizumi, however, was elected without factional support; rather, it was a 'popular vote' that put him into power (Otake 2003). When the party presidential election was held in the spring of 2001, prefectural branches of the LDP conducted primaries by themselves.[9] Though most expected Hashimoto Ryūtarō (who was supported by major factions) to win, the result of the primaries was an overwhelming victory for Koizumi. This high popular support, in place of factional support, functioned as an effective power resource for Koizumi.

Four categories of environmental and institutional changes that occurred at the time should be noted as the factors that made Koizumi's strategy even more effective: (1) the increasing role of television in politics, (2) growing disaffection with the LDP among those who felt themselves badly treated by LDP policies, (3) the increasing number of floating voters, and (4) institutional changes such as electoral and administrative reforms. The first three created a favourable political environment for Koizumi to obtain high popular support, and the last factor provided him with greater institutional power over the LDP and the government.

Since the mid-1990s, television had been increasing its role as a medium of political communication in Japan – the breakdown of the LDP government in 1993 was often attributed to TV reports criticizing the LDP (Iwai 1996; Uchiyama 1999). Koizumi's populist style, characterized by dramatic confrontations, fitted well with this political environment called 'telepolitics'. Koizumi often appeared not only in TV news programmes but also in tabloid TV shows, and attracted the attention of a broad range of people.

As for disaffection with the LDP, the LDP governments tended to adopt policies that emphasized the redistribution and protection of vulnerable sectors like agriculture, construction, and small and medium-sized enterprises. In contrast, those who received little benefit from these policies – such as companies in competitive sectors of the economy and white-collar professionals – demanded more market-oriented policies. However, they continued to vote for the LDP, if rather reluctantly, because there were hardly any other credible alternative parties. Thus, a fissure was arising among those who supported the LDP (Pempel 1998). Koizumi took advantage of this fissure and appealed to those who demanded neoliberal reform.

These two changes are closely related to the increasing number of 'floating' voters (*mutōha-sō*), who are voters with little party affiliation and who switch parties from election to election. Voters who are disaffected with existing parties often become floating voters, and they tend to be influenced by the mass media, especially television. Floating voters now amount to nearly half of all voters. For example, in an opinion poll conducted by the *Asahi Shimbun* in April 2001 (just after Koizumi took office), 46 per cent of respondents said they had no party affiliation, while the percentage of those who supported the LDP and the DJP were 32 per cent and 7 per cent, respectively (*Asahi Shimbun*, 30 April 2001). Thus, the results of elections tend to be affected greatly by the attitude of this large number of floating voters. Koizumi's victory in the 2005 election can be explained from this standpoint, as examined in further detail later on.

Moreover, electoral and administrative reforms took place in the decade before Koizumi. First, the electoral system of the lower house was changed from a multi-member district (MMD) system to a combination of a single-member district (SMD) system and a proportional representation (PR) system in 1994. These reforms had several effects, but primarily, factions in the LDP began to be deprived of their power, and the power of the party executive *vis-à-vis* backbenchers was enhanced. Thus, Koizumi could exert greater control over his party; measures like 'assassins' tactics, as mentioned in more detail later on, would have been impossible without this electoral reform. Second, executive institutions were changed in order to increase prime ministerial leadership in 2001. Among them, the function of the Cabinet Secretariat was enhanced, and new organizations such as the Cabinet Office and the Council on Economic and Fiscal Policy (CEFP, *Keizai-zaisei Shimon-kaigi*) were created. These institutions provided Koizumi with considerable influence over policy making (for further information regarding these institutional reforms, see Chapter 5; see also Takenaka 2006 and Uchiyama 2007).

Koizumi's structural reform and postal services privatization

Backed by huge public support, Koizumi succeeded in overcoming resistance from the inside of the LDP and effecting reform to a significant degree. For example, he succeeded in cutting budgets substantially: the general account of the budget that amounted to JPY82.7 trillion in FY2001 was reduced to JPY79.7 trillion in FY2006. Among these cuts, funds for public works were the main target. These funds amounted to JPY9.4 trillion in FY2001, but were reduced to JPY7.2 trillion in FY2006 (a reduction of 23.7 per cent). Koizumi also successfully disposed of bad loans that had put restraints on the Japanese economy (though this was in part greatly helped by the economic revival at that time in Japan). His other achievements included: privatization of quasi-governmental corporations typified by the Japan Highway Public Corporation, reform of the social security system such as the pension system and healthcare system, regulatory reform such as introducing special deregulation zones and market testing, and reform of the financial system of local governments.

What best shows the effectiveness of Koizumi's strategy is the privatization of Japan's postal services. Koizumi had been eager to privatize postal services long before he took office. After he was re-elected as LDP president in September 2003, he began to pour his energy into postal services privatization. The basic policy for privatization was discussed at the CEFP so that the decision-making process would be insulated from the influence of the postal bureaucracy and *zoku* politicians. The postal service privatization bills were drafted based on the policy chosen by the CEFP, and these bills were submitted to the Diet in April 2005 (*Nihon Keizai Shimbun*, 28 April 2005).

However, a lot of LDP politicians strongly opposed the bills, with postal *zoku* at the core of the resistance. Koizumi made concessions and the bills were amended in June. When these amendments were approved by the Executive Council of the LDP, which had until then operated under the unanimity rule without vote, a majority rule and vote was introduced for the first time. Five members clearly opposed it (*Nihon Keizai Shimbun*, 29 June 2005).

The bills were put to the vote in the lower house, the House of Representatives, in July, which passed the bills by a narrow margin, as 37 members of the LDP voted against them, and 14 were absent. In August, the upper house, the House of Councillors, voted down the bills as 22 members of the LDP rebelled. Koizumi dissolved the lower house immediately, and a general (lower house) election was held the next month. What deserves attention in this election is the fact that the LDP did not endorse those who voted against the postal bills and ran other candidates, or 'assassins' (*shikaku*), in their districts. Thirty-three ex-LDP candidates (mainly postal services *zoku*) who had rebelled ran in the single-member districts as independents or formed new parties (*Nihon Keizai Shimbun*, 12 September 2005).

The result was an overwhelming victory for the LDP, which won 296 out of 480 seats. Faced with these results, those members of the upper house who had rebelled changed their minds, and the bills passed the Diet in October 2005, with LDP members unanimously consenting. Thus, the postal services were privatized in October 2007.

Measures like 'assassins' tactics had never been adopted in the previous history of the LDP, which had attached great importance to consensus within the party. By drawing a clear boundary within the LDP and dramatizing it, Koizumi succeeded in attracting the support of floating voters who otherwise would have voted for the Democratic Party. This is the main reason for the LDP's landslide victory in the 2005 election. In addition to this unprecedented victory, we should note that postal services privatization, which had been thought nearly impossible, was actually accomplished. All these examples show how well Koizumi's distinctive boundary strategy worked. Along with the institutional reforms mentioned earlier, this strategy made him a 'strong prime minister' in a country where prime ministers had been generally weak.[10]

3. Abe's shift in strategy

It is no exaggeration to say that Abe 'inherited' the prime ministership from Koizumi. What enabled Abe, a relatively young politician (he was 52 years old when he took office in September 2006), to become the prime minister is the fact that he enjoyed the highest popular support among the party presidential candidates. Abe became well known during the Koizumi administration, since both his soft and sweet image and contradictorily tough position against North Korea was appreciated on the popular level. Koizumi appointed Abe as the Secretary-General of the LDP in spite of his youth in 2003, intending to appeal to the constituencies by stressing the freshness of his party in the face of the lower house election. Moreover, it was evident that Koizumi himself thought of Abe as his successor.

With this background, Abe was destined to copy Koizumi in a sense. He had to act as a 'strong prime minister', which was the image that his predecessor impressed on the public. No sooner had he taken office than he appointed five assistants to the prime minister to reinforce the function of the Prime Minister's Office. Thereafter, Abe took various opportunities to emphasize a top-down style of policy making, especially in his attempt at continuing Koizumi's neoliberal reforms.

Inconsistent use of the Type II strategy

Abe also inherited the basic line of economic policy from Koizumi: neoliberalism. One of the tasks that Koizumi turned over to Abe was the issue of financial resources for road construction (*dōro tokutei-zaigen*).[11] This is a system where taxes imposed on gasoline and other automobile-related goods are allocated to a special account exclusively used for road construction. The reformers insisted that such resources should be used for general purposes, but it could not be achieved under the Koizumi administration.

In November 2006, when the FY2007 budget was compiled, Abe openly said that gasoline excise should be used for general purposes (*Asahi Shimbun*, 1 December 2006). The Chief Cabinet Secretary, Shiozaki Yasuhisa, even mentioned that the system should be changed from the beginning of FY2007 (*Asahi Shimbun*, 8 December 2006). But it naturally caused resistance from road *zoku* politicians and the Ministry of Land, Infrastructure, and Transport (MLIT), and the stance of the Prime Minister's Office began to waver. Just three days after his statement, Shiozaki said 'it is not the timing but the content that matters', which signified his partial retreat. The policy which was finally decided upon in early December prescribed that the government should construct 'really necessary roads', and that any amount of tax revenue exceeding such expenditure for road construction should be used for general purposes. Since the MLIT could define what would be considered as 'really necessary roads' and estimate how much would be necessary to construct them, the amount that would be allocated for general purposes was expected to be fairly small.[12] This indicated Abe's de facto withdrawal of his plan. Thus, though Abe seemed to be prepared to confront the *zoku* politicians at first, he did not keep a firm stance against them. Unlike Koizumi, Abe did not use the Type III strategy consistently, but instead chose to make concessions.

The second example that shows Abe's inconsistent stance on the boundary strategy is an annual policy document called the Basic Policies or 'Robust Policies' (*honebuto no hōshin*), which is deliberated at the CEFP around June each year and shows the administration's basic principles of policies and reforms. This document played a great role in promoting reforms under the Koizumi administration. A lot of reform agendas such as social security reform and postal services privatization were set by annual versions of this document.

The first (and the last) 'Robust Policy' in the Abe administration was decided upon in June 2007. Compared with those of Koizumi's, it seemed to be retreating from the reformist position. For example, the last such policy under the Koizumi administration in 2006 prescribed that the total expenditure should be cut by up to JPY14.3 trillion over five years from FY2007, and that the expenditure on public works should be cut by 1 to 3 per cent on an annual basis. Abe's 'Robust Policy', however, lacked such numerical targets. At the meetings of the CEFP, the members from the private sector repeatedly insisted that a numerical target for cuts in public works expenditures should be included, but Abe made a concession on that point as well (*Nihon Keizai Shimbun*, 20 June 2007).[13]

While Abe did not deploy the Type III strategy against the LDP to the full extent, his strategy instead targeted the bureaucracy. He commenced civil service reform that would strengthen the regulation of the 'descent from heaven' (*amakudari*), a practice in which high-level government officials obtain jobs in the private sector. He intended to ban the descent from heaven using the influence of ministries over the private sector. Of course, strong objections arose in the bureaucracy, and some LDP members sided with the bureaucrats. But Abe forced his way this time. Since the schedule of Diet deliberations was so tight that it seemed nearly impossible for the civil service reform bill to pass during that session, the members of the LDP's IPRC tried to persuade Abe to withdraw the bill. But Abe again expressed his firm intention to have it passed, and he extended the Diet session twice, despite the objections of LDP Diet members (*Nihon Keizai Shimbun*, 16 June 2007).

Thus, Abe is characterized by his inconsistent use of the Type III boundary strategy. What deserves attention here is that there is an interdependent relationship between the use of this strategy and popular support. A certain amount of popular support is a condition for the strategy to be effective. In turn, if the strategy works well, it increases popular support. In Koizumi's case, the relationship was a virtuous circle; he used the boundary strategy effectively backed by high popular support, which helped him gather further support. In contrast, Abe seemed to have fallen into a vicious circle. Though he enjoyed high public support before and right after he took office, the approval ratings continued to fall over time (see Figure 6.2). Besides some unfortunate events that occurred while he was in office (such as a scandal over thousands of missing pension records and the suicide of Minister of Agriculture Matsuoka Toshikatsu), unskilful use of this strategy decreased public support for him, and further prevented Abe from effective use of it.

Creating divisions in the DPJ

Seeing that the Type III strategy was not working well, Abe changed his focus regarding which issues he would emphasize. From around the spring of 2007, he began to stress ideological issues such as constitutional amendment and education instead of economic policy. While an economic policy based on neoliberalism is likely to cause divisions within the LDP because *zoku* politicians would object to

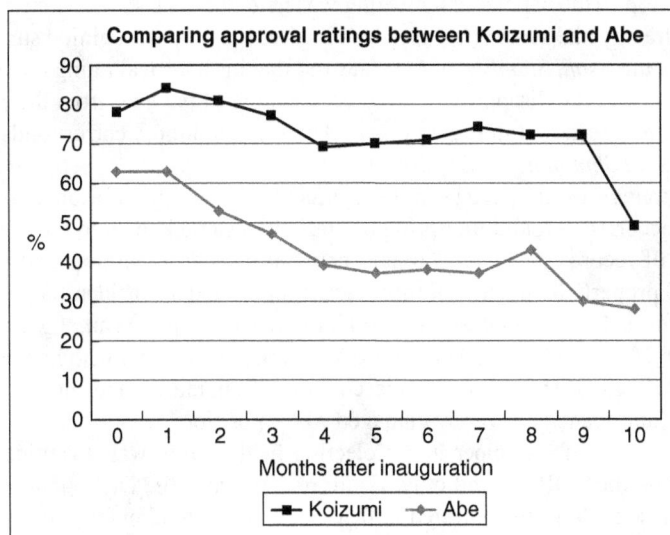

Figure 6.2 Approval ratings of Koizumi and Abe

Source: *Asahi Shimbun*

it, the LDP is relatively cohesive around ideological policy. Comparatively, the DPJ is less united on ideological issues and suffers from internal disagreements about them.

This disparity shows up well in the data garnered from questionnaires completed by candidates for the lower house conducted jointly by the University of Tokyo and the *Asahi Shimbun* in 2003 and 2005. In response to the question 'Do you think the Constitution should be amended?', 65.6 per cent of LDP candidates answered 'Favourable' in 2003, and 87.4 per cent answered so in 2005. When those who answered 'Moderately Favourable' are included, the numbers are 92.4 per cent and 96.8 per cent, respectively. Clearly, very little ideological division exists on this issue in the LDP. On the other hand, the ratios of DPJ candidates who answered 'Favourable' were 31.2 per cent in 2003 and 45.8 per cent in 2005. When those who answered 'Moderately Favourable' are included, the numbers are 61.7 per cent in 2003 and 70.9 per cent in 2005. Of the DPJ candidates responding, 21.2 per cent answered 'Unfavourable' or 'Moderately Unfavourable' in 2003, and 17.4 per cent did so in 2005.[14]

Abe attempted to take advantage of these circumstances and use the Type IV boundary strategy against the DPJ. At the beginning of 2007, Abe clearly stated that he would like to prepare to amend the Constitution under his administration. He accelerated this policy in late spring the same year (*Asahi Shimbun*, 15 May 2007). The national referendum law for amending the Constitution was enacted in May, and the education-related bills were passed through the Diet in June. In the party platform prepared for the upper house election, the amendment of the Constitution came first, and the revival of education came next. Moreover, Abe started discussing the right of collective self-defence, establishing a panel of experts to study the topic (the panel's first meeting was held in May).

This strategy had some effect on Abe's leadership. A public opinion survey conducted by the *Asahi Shimbun* in May showed that his approval rating recovered to 43 per cent and the disapproval rating dropped by 10 per cent from the previous month (this is reflected in Figure 6.2, as Abe's eighth month corresponds to May 2007) (*Asahi Shimbun*, 15 May 2007).

This strategy would have been more effective if several unfortunate problems had not occurred. Around the spring of 2007, it became known to the public that millions of records of those who paid national pension premiums had not been managed properly by the Social Insurance Agency, and a considerable number of the records had even been lost. This problem caused an outrage among the general public. In May, Minister of Agriculture Matsuoka Toshikatsu, who had been suspected of illegal use of political funds, committed suicide. As a result, pension and political fund scandals severely damaged Abe's position.

The outcome of the upper house election held in July was a routing for the LDP. While the LDP secured only 37 out of 121 seats, the DPJ obtained 60. As half of those seats were contested in that election, the total number of the LDP's seats, including uncontested seats, was 83 and that of the DPJ was 109. The result of the election was clear: the coalition government of the LDP and the Kōmeitō (the Clean Government Party) lost the majority in the upper house. Thus, there emerged a 'twisted' (or divided) Diet where the government controlled a majority in the lower house but lost the majority to the opposition parties in the upper house.

In spite of this abysmal outcome, Abe stuck to his position. However, he finally decided to step down in mid-September, claiming that his decision was due to health problems.

4. The non-boundary strategy of Fukuda

In September 2007, Fukuda succeeded Abe and began his prime ministership faced with a difficult situation. Since the upper house has nearly the same power as the lower house, it was very difficult for Fukuda to get his bills passed without the consent of the opposition parties. Although the lower house can override the decision of the upper house by a two-thirds majority (hereafter referred to as a 'supermajority') according to Article 59 of the Constitution, this measure had seldom been used.

An attempted grand coalition

One of the most important issues at that time was the extension of the Anti-Terrorism Special Measures Law (*Tero-taisaku Tokubetsu-sochi-hō*). The Law provided the legal basis for sending the SDF to the Indian Ocean to support the US-led anti-terrorism operation, through such actions as supplying fuel to foreign naval vessels and helping those who suffered in the conflict in Afghanistan. However, this law was expected to expire at the beginning of November 2007. While the DPJ objected to its extension, Fukuda proposed to the Diet a bill for another law focusing on fuel supply (*Hokyu-shien Tokubetu-sochi-hō*). The DPJ opposed this one as well. Seeking to maintain a good relationship with the United States, Fukuda needed to find some way to continue the activities of the SDF in the Indian Ocean. There were two alternatives for Fukuda: to persuade the DPJ to cooperate with him (the Type II strategy), or to force the bill through the Diet by a supermajority of the lower house (Type I).

On 30 October, Fukuda had a meeting with the DPJ's leader Ozawa. The content of their discussion was not disclosed at that time, but it was said that the two talked about a grand coalition of the LDP and the DPJ (*Asahi Shimbun*, 31 October 2007). They met again three days later, and agreed to prepare to form a coalition on the condition that the government would start discussing a permanent law that would enable the SDF to be sent overseas on the basis of United Nations' resolutions (Ozawa had long insisted that such a law should be enacted).

However, when Ozawa brought the tentative agreement back to his party that night, the party cadre strongly opposed it, insisting that they should instead seek to replace the LDP government. He talked with Fukuda over the telephone immediately afterward and confessed that he would not be able to keep the agreement. Thus, Fukuda's attempt to form a grand coalition with the DPJ was frustrated.

Shaking up the DPJ

Putting the issue of anti-terrorism legislation on the agenda also meant taking advantage of the ideological division within the DPJ. In other words, Fukuda continued to use the Type IV strategy as Abe did.

The DPJ has starkly contrasting opinions regarding national security issues. Ozawa, who has been serving as the party's leader since April 2006, argues that the SDF should be engaged in international peacekeeping activities that involve military action if they are based on UN resolutions.[15] But a considerable number of DPJ members who tend to have a centre-left ideology disagree with him on this, since they believe it would be against Article 9 of the Constitution.

One of the reasons the DPJ cadre opposed the idea of a grand coalition is their fear that forming a coalition with the LDP to pass the anti-terrorism bill would widen the ideological division within the DPJ. Indeed, a series of events occurred which had a similar effect.

Once the DPJ objected to the agreement Ozawa made with Fukuda, which was a vote of no confidence in him, Ozawa decided to resign from his post as party leader. Faced with his departure, the cadre agreed to persuade Ozawa to overturn his decision, since they feared that his resignation would further deepen the division within the party. Some of the members even feared that when Ozawa left, his followers would leave as well, effectively splitting the DPJ (*Asahi Shimbun*, 7 November 2007). It may have been that Ozawa's real intention was to stimulate the party members to consolidate unity for the forthcoming election. Whatever the reason, it is certain that the events concerning the anti-terrorism legislation had the effect of shaking up the DPJ.[16]

The fuel supply bill passed the lower house in mid-November. Right after the DPJ-led upper house rejected it in January 2008, the LDP-led lower house approved it by a supermajority. This means that Fukuda resorted to the Type I strategy which emphasized the government-opposition boundary.

The oscillation of Fukuda's strategy

So far, we have seen that Fukuda used multiple strategies. While he attempted to shake up the DPJ (Type IV), the basic line of his boundary strategy seemed to be an accommodative posture towards the DPJ (Type II), typified by the failed attempt to form a grand coalition.[17] The Type II strategy, however, bears no fruit if the other party has no intention to cooperate. When it was clear that the DPJ would not cooperate with Fukuda, he utilized the supermajority to get his bills passed (Type I).

In other words, Fukuda's strategy sometimes oscillated between Type I and II depending on the circumstances, notably the DPJ's attitude. This is best shown in the events surrounding the issue of financial resources for road construction, which was raised on the agenda after the new Anti-Terrorism Law was passed.

The rates of some of the taxes which were appropriated for the road construction resources include provisional rates (*zantei-zeiritsu*). For example, the provisional rate of gasoline excise is JPY48.6 per litre, twice as high as the original rate of JPY24.3. The DPJ insisted that the resources be used for general purposes and the provisional rates be reduced to the original rates. Since the article of the Special Taxation Measures Law that imposes the provisional rates was expected to expire at the end of March 2008,[18] the government would have lost a considerable amount of its tax revenue if it could not obtain the DPJ's consent to the revision of the Law.

At a question-and-answer session of the Diet in January 2008, Fukuda emphasized that the bill for revising the Law was so important to people's everyday life that he would make every effort to have it passed by the end of the fiscal year. He added that he would try to consult with the opposition parties in order to obtain good results for the people (*Asahi Shimbun*, 22 January 2008).

As the DPJ continued to refuse to compromise, the government submitted to the Diet a 'bridge bill' to extend the provisional rates for two months. It seemed at first that Fukuda intended to steamroll the bill through the Diet by resorting to the use of his supermajority. But the government and the opposition parties accepted the mediation of the speakers of both houses, and the former withdrew the bridge bill in late January. The parties agreed that they should reach 'a certain conclusion' on the bills concerning the budget by the end of the fiscal year on the condition that they be deliberated thoroughly (*Asahi Shimbun*, 31 January 2008).

However, the government forced the bills for revising the Special Taxation Measures Law through the lower house at the end of February.[19] The opposition parties resorted to a confrontational stance, insisting that the agreement had been broken, and refused to cooperate with Fukuda in deliberating the bills in the upper house (*Asahi Shimbun*, 28 March 2008). Thus, the provisional rates expired on 1 April, and in the end, the lower house passed the bills by a supermajority at the end of April.[20]

In sum, the need to deal with a 'twisted' (or divided) Diet prompted Fukuda to adopt a Type II strategy. But the success of this strategy depends on the oppositions' attitudes towards cooperation. When the DPJ decided not to cooperate, Fukuda was forced to resort to a Type I strategy. Meanwhile, he also continued to use Type IV to shake up the DPJ.

Conclusion

In examining how Japan's recent prime ministers chose and used boundary strategies, we see four main strategy types: Type I, which emphasizes the boundary between government and opposition; Type II, which attaches importance to consensus making among parties; Type III, which introduces fissures within one's own party; and Type IV, which induces division within the other party.

The strategy of traditional LDP prime ministers has been Type II. They emphasized the division between their governments and the opposition parties on the surface, but in reality, they tried to obtain a consensus from the latter when it came to policy making. Koizumi was distinctive in that he introduced the Type III strategy through defining his opponents within his own party, the LDP, as the forces of resistance. The fact that he effected reform to an unprecedented degree shows how well this strategy worked. Abe attempted to apply the Type IV strategy to the opposing party, the DPJ, by politicizing such issues as constitutional amendment, along with an inconsistent use of Type III. Fukuda, faced with a twisted Diet, was forced to return to Type II, while using Type I and IV as needed.

We have seen which factors affected Japanese prime ministers' strategy choices. The conditions that made it necessary for the LDP prime ministers under the 1955 system to adopt Type II were their weak institutional power over the LDP and the procedures of deliberation in the Diet. As those prime ministers had only a weak institutional foundation on which to depend, they could not exert strong leadership (Uchiyama 2007: 182–86). Furthermore, the procedures of Diet deliberation had such 'viscosity' that the governments were forced to pay great costs to have their bills passed (Mochizuki 1982). These factors have traditionally prevented prime ministers from adopting strategies other than Type II (see Table 6.1).

With the arrival of the twenty-first century, this accommodative strategy seems to have become obsolete. This was mainly caused by institutional changes such as the electoral and administrative reforms, as well as environmental changes such as the emergence of telepolitics, a growing disaffection with the LDP, and the increasing number of floating voters. The institutional reforms not only reinforced the power of the prime minister, but also increased the people's expectations for strong leadership.[21] Environmental changes made the public demand a new style of politics. In this way, the conditions under which Koizumi could adopt the Type III strategy were created. Also to be noted is that the use of the Type III strategy is difficult for those who have low public support. While high public support for Koizumi enabled him to overcome the resistance he faced within the LDP, Abe could not use the Type III strategy as effectively because of his lack of public

Table 6.1 Types of boundary strategies and factors that affect them

Types of strategies	Prime ministers using the strategies	Factors that affected the choice of strategy
Type I (Government and opposition)	Fukuda (as it was needed)	Supermajority in the lower house DPJ's refusal to cooperate
Type II (No boundary)	Fukuda (basically) Prime ministers under the 1955 system	The 'twisted' Diet Insufficient popular support Weak institutional foundation and viscous procedures in the Diet
Type III (Fissures in the governing party)	Koizumi (consistently) Abe (inconsistently)	High public support Strong institutional foundation
Type IV (Driving wedges into the opposition)	Abe Fukuda	Lack of unity in the opposition party

Source: author

support. In short, the factors that enable effective use of the Type III strategy are the prime minister's institutional strength and high popular support.

In addition to the inconsistent use of Type III, Abe used the Type IV boundary strategy against the DPJ. This was made possible by the organizational structure of the DPJ, which was characterized by a lack of unity; if the party had been sufficiently cohesive, Abe (and Fukuda) could not have used this strategy. Thus, a necessary condition for the effective use of the Type IV strategy is that the targeted (opposition) party is less cohesive than the targeting (governing) party.

Fukuda's return to the Type II strategy is mainly due to the existence of a 'twisted' Diet as well as his lack of high public support. When the DPJ refused to cooperate with him, he resorted to the Type I strategy by utilizing the supermajority. After Fukuda suddenly resigned in September 2008, Asō Tarō took over the position of prime minister. Asō's strategies seemed to be similar to those of Fukuda's (mainly Type I and II) as the situations the two leaders faced were also alike (the 'twisted' Diet). But because of the maladministration of the Asō government and his unpopularity, the LDP lost power in the lower house election of August 2009. The DPJ won a landslide victory, and Hatoyama Yukio, who had replaced Ozawa Ichirō as the party's leader in May 2009, became the new prime minister in September.

As soon as the DPJ achieved power, the Hatoyama government began an attempt to contain and weaken the LDP by, for example, reforming the budget the Asō administration had compiled and channelling less money to LDP supporters (At the centre of this attempt was Ozawa, now the Secretary-General of the DPJ). Thus, their main strategy can be judged to be Type I. If the DPJ also wins in the upper house election that is expected to be held in the summer of 2010, it will be highly probable that the government will continue to use the Type I strategy.

Notes

1 This chapter attaches special importance to the three prime ministers – Koizumi, Abe and Fukuda because each of them typifies each type of boundary strategy. More recent prime ministers such as Asō Tarō and Hatoyama Yukio are touched on in the concluding section.

2 According to Lijphart (1999: 9–30), the characteristics of the Westminster model include: (1) executive power concentrated in one-party and bare-majority cabinets; (2) cabinet dominance; (3) a two-party system; (4) a majoritarian and disproportional system for elections; and (5) interest group pluralism.

3 The 1955 system is a political system that was established that same year, when the Liberal Party and the Democratic Party merged to form the LDP and the Socialist Party reunified. Under this system, the LDP continued in its role as the dominant governing party, with the Socialist Party as its biggest opposition party. This party system collapsed in the mid-1990s.

4 According to Lijphart (1999: 31–47), the characteristics of the consensus model include: (1) executive power-sharing in broad coalition cabinets; (2) an executive–legislative balance of power; (3) a multiparty system; (4) proportional representation; and (5) interest group corporatism.

5 *Tatemae* refers to the position or opinion one expresses in public. *Honne* refers to one's real intention, which is seldom openly expressed. It has been pointed out that *tatemae* and *honne* often differ from each other in Japan.

Uchiyama Yū

6 *Zoku* politicians are politicians who specialize in certain policy areas and have great influence on policy making in these areas. *Zoku* politicians and corresponding ministries often form firm coalitions and exert great power on policy making in related areas.

7 Survey data provide evidence that ideological distribution is wider in the DPJ than in the LDP. The University of Tokyo and *Asahi Shimbun* jointly conducted a questionnaire survey to members of the House of the Representatives in July 2003. The survey included such questions as: 'Do you think the defence power of Japan should be strengthened?' and 'Do you think Japan should be a permanent member of the Security Council and take a more positive role in international politics?' Each respondent answered questions on a five-point scale (Favourable: 1; Moderately Favourable: 2; Neutral: 3; Moderately Unfavourable: 4; Unfavourable: 5). While the standard deviation of the LDP members' answers on the defence power was 0.93 (Mean = 2.0, N = 175), that of the DPJ members was 1.26 (Mean = 3.08, N = 103). As for the question on the Security Council, the numbers were 0.76 (LDP; Mean = 1.45, N = 177) and 1.11 (DPJ; Mean = 1.96, N = 103) respectively. See http://www.j.u-tokyo.ac.jp/~masaki/ats/atsindex.html (accessed 26 February 2008).

8 This rating comes second only to the 68 per cent approval rating enjoyed by Hosokawa Morihiro, who was in office or just nine months (from August 1993 through April 1994).

9 In the LDP presidential elections, Diet members of the LDP and delegates from prefectural branches cast votes. At first, the majority of Diet members supported Hashimoto, but, faced with Koizumi's overwhelming victory in the prefectural primaries, most of the members changed their minds.

10 For how Koizumi exerted leadership in policy making, see Uchiyama (2007).

11 The reason why Koizumi avoided touching upon the issue of financial resources for highway construction remains unclear. It might be that he preferred not to break the compromise that had been made between him and the highway *zoku* politicians around the issue of privatization of the highway pubic corporations.

12 Indeed, while financial resources for road construction in the FY2008 budget amounted to JPY3.3 trillion, only JPY192 billion of this amount is expected to be used for general purposes.

13 Abe's accommodative stance towards the LDP is best shown by his treatment of the 'postal rebels' who had been expelled from the LDP by Koizumi at the 2005 election: Abe reinstated them to the LDP. He admitted 11 of the expelled lower house members to the party in November 2006. He further allowed an expelled and failed candidate in the 2005 election to run in the upper-house election held in 2007 as an endorsed candidate of the LDP.

14 Each respondent answered the questions on a 5-point scale (Favourable: 1, Moderately Favourable: 2, Neutral: 3, Moderately Unfavourable: 4, Unfavourable: 5). The standard deviations of the answers also show that the DPJ was less cohesive than the LDP. Those of the LDP are 0.74 (Mean = 1.45, N = 291) in 2003 and 0.54 (Mean = 1.18, N = 309) in 2005. Those of the DPJ are 1.28 (Mean = 2.37, N = 269) in 2003 and 1.27 (Mean = 2.07, N = 275) in 2005. In this regard, while the LDP was getting more cohesive, unity among the DPJ remained basically unchanged. See http://www.j.u-tokyo.ac.jp/~masaki/ats/atsindex.html (accessed 26 February 2008. See also endnote 6).

15 When Ozawa served as the Secretary-General of the LDP in 1990, he was eager to contribute the Self-Defence Forces to the US-led multinational force in Iraq, but failed.

16 An article in the *Asahi Shimbun*, 5 November 2007, said:

> Though the DPJ tried to distract public attention from the issue of fuel supply by emphasizing the pension problem . . ., the LDP insisted that the DPJ should propose an alternative bill for anti-terrorism legislation with the intention to shake the DPJ.

17 Fukuda's choice of Type II certainly seems in line with his accommodative personality. Furthermore, the emergence of a twisted Diet made LDP members prefer a mild-mannered politician like Fukuda as their president.
18 Japan's fiscal year begins in April and ends in March.
19 Though Fukuda finally steamrolled the bills, the timing shows that he attached some importance to the Type II strategy. If he had not been considering the possibility of a compromise with the DPJ, he would have passed the bills through the lower house much earlier (most likely by the end of January). As it was, the delay in passing the bills led to the expiration of the temporary rates, and caused some confusion among the general public in regard to this issue.
20 Article 59 of the Constitution prescribes that if the upper house does not make a decision within 60 days after it receives a bill from the lower house, the latter can regard it as a rejection of the bill by the former.
21 This point is closely related to a process called the presidentialization of politics. Presidentialization is a political process characterized by increasing leadership power and autonomy within the political executive, increasing leadership power and autonomy within political parties, and increasingly leadership-centred electoral processes (Poguntke and Webb 2005). It hardly needs to be said that Koizumi was a typical example of this phenomenon.

References

Curtis, Gerald L. (1988) *The Japanese Way of Politics*, New York: Columbia University Press.
—— (1999) *The Logic of Japanese Politics: leaders, institutions, and the limits of change*, New York: Columbia University Press.
Iwai, Tomoaki (1996) '55-nen-taisei no Hōkai to Masu-media', *NenpōSeijigaku*, 67–88.
Kuroda, Yasumasa (2005) *The Core of Japanese Democracy: latent interparty politics*, Basingstoke and New York: Palgrave Macmillan.
Lijphart, Arend (1977) *Democracy in Plural Societies: a comparative exploration*, New Haven: Yale University Press.
—— (1999) *Patterns of Democracy: government forms and performance in thirty-six countries*, New Haven: Yale University Press.
Mochizuki, Mike M. (1982) *Managing and Influencing the Japanese Legislative Process: the role of parties and the National Diet*, unpublished dissertation, Harvard University.
Otake, Hideo (2003) *Nihon-gata Popyurizumu*, Tokyo: Chūō Kōron Shinsha.
Pempel, T.J. (1998) *Regime Shift: comparative dynamics of the Japanese political economy*, Ithaca: Cornell University Press.
Poguntke, Thomas and Webb, Paul (eds) (2005) *The Presidentialization of Politics: a comparative study of modern democracies*, Oxford: Oxford University Press.
Richardson, Bradley (1997) *Japanese Democracy: power, coordination, and performance*, New Haven: Yale University Press.
Schmitt, Carl (1996) *The Concept of the Political*, trans. George Schwab, Chicago: The University of Chicago Press.
Takenaka, Harukata (2006) *Shushō Shihai: Nihon seiji no henbō*, Tokyo: Chūō Kōron Shinsha.
Uchiyama, Yu (1999) 'Masu-media: Dai-yon no Kenryoku?' in Sasaki Takeshi (ed.) *Seiji-kaikaku 1800-nichi no Shinjitsu*, Tokyo: Kōdansha.
—— (2007) *Koizumi Seiken*, Tokyo: Chūō Kōron Shinsha.

7 The problem of boundaries for Japan's local authorities

Mergers, public services and the growing disparity in Japanese society

Muto Hiromi

Municipal mergers were promoted under the Koizumi administration (2001–06), which pushed neoliberal reforms in many fields such as highway management, the postal system, welfare, transportation, and employment, all in the name of 'structural reform'. Koizumi's neoliberal reforms called for a change in the style of government in Japan, and this included local authorities. Many smaller local authorities have been pressured into merging, and all local authorities have been pushed to contract out their public utilities. These local authorities have thus taken on a new role, which we examine in this chapter. As a crucial result of these changes, the disparity between the rich and the poor in Japan has been exacerbated, so much so that the phrase 'disparity in society' (*kakusa shakai*) has recently become widely used and discussed in Japan (Tachibanaki 2006).

Municipal mergers, especially those known as the 'Great Heisei Mergers' (or 'Great Heisei Consolidation'; see Yokomichi 2007), have taken place along with these Koizumi reforms. It is not necessarily the case, however, that municipal mergers are direct products of neoliberal reforms, which promote small and efficient governments. Therefore, it is essential to examine the following questions: Who sought to implement the municipal mergers, and how were they promoted to others? Even though mergers create a tremendous burden for local authorities, what has driven municipalities to merge? What has happened to the municipalities that have merged? What can be understood from this process? Finally, as a result of mergers and neoliberal reforms, what has happened to the relations between municipalities and their citizens?

In addressing the issue of municipal mergers, two major boundary problems arise for Japan's local authorities: the legal boundaries between different local authorities, and the metaphysical boundaries between the local authority and its citizens.

First, the legal boundaries between local authorities have changed considerably, yet only in some prefectures. The number of municipalities has been drastically reduced, but the number of people affected was relatively small, since the boundaries changed mainly among municipalities with relatively small populations. In big cities, few municipal mergers have taken place. The main impetus for these small-town mergers came from politicians (i.e., members of the lower house in the Diet), and it is for that reason that we focus on 'political process' (see also Imai 2008).

Second, there has been a fundamental change in the metaphysical boundaries of local authorities' activities. In other words, the boundaries between public service providers and public service consumers, or the boundaries between the local authority and citizens, have been newly inscribed.

In his book entitled *Politics in the 'Great Heisei Mergers'* (*Heisei Daigappei no Seiji-gaku*), published in April 2008, Imai discusses how mergers have been promoted by national-level politicians, and concludes that the Heisei mergers of local authorities were a failure from any point of view. This chapter takes up this discussion and, by analyzing the problem of boundaries, seeks to reveal whether, and if so, how and why this failure came about. The first section of this chapter analyzes the legal boundaries between different local authorities, focusing on the problems associated with merging municipalities, and the second section goes into further detail on the metaphysical boundaries between the local authority and its citizens, focusing on the problems arising from the changes in public service brought about by these mergers.

1. Boundaries of local authorities: municipal mergers and the decreasing number of local authorities

The first time that municipal mergers were promoted by the central government in Japan was in 1888–89, when the number of municipalities (towns and villages) decreased from 70,000 to 16,000. The second major transition started in 1953, and the number decreased from 10,000 to 3,392 by 1965. This number remained relatively stable for the next 30 years. By 1995, there were still 3,234 municipalities, a decrease of only around 150 since 1965. However, the third instance of such mergers began in 1999, and the number decreased from 3,200 to 1,821 by 2006 (see Table 7.1).

Municipal mergers may be necessary and in some ways desirable, but if mergers are to be successful, they must gain the support of the citizens, since municipalities are established and indeed exist for citizens. Before citizens will give their support, however, they must understand the purpose of, or reason for, the mergers. This was the case during both the Meiji and Showa era mergers. To start with, the purpose of the Meiji mergers was to create a system of modern local authorities able to respond to the basic needs of the citizens, such as compulsory elementary education, taxation and registration of the inhabitants, in accordance with the new local government system (*shisei chōson sei*) of 1888. The standard size of a village authority was 300–500 households, which was thought to be the minimum size needed to run an elementary school.

The Showa mergers, in turn, created the contemporary system of local authorities with a more extended range of duties. The duties included taxation, police and fire protection; compulsory education was extended to junior high school, and an Education Commission[1] was created in every local authority in accordance with the newly established local government law under Japan's Constitution of 1947. Junior high school was new, but the logic for running these schools was similar to that used for running elementary schools in the earlier mergers: it was thought

Table 7.1 The transition in the number of municipalities

Date	City	Town	Village	Total
1888	—	(71,314)		71,314
1889	39	(15,820)		15,859
1898	48	1,173	13,068	14,289
1908	61	1,167	11,220	12,448
1922	91	1,242	10982	12,315
1930	109	1,528	10292	11,929
1940	178	1,706	9614	11,498
Oct. 1945	205	1,797	8518	10,520
Oct. 1953	286	1,966	7616	9,868
April 1955	488	1,833	2885	5,206
Sept. 1956	498	1,903	1574	3,975
June 1961	556	1,935	981	3,472
April 1965	560	2,005	827	3,392
April 1975	643	1,974	640	3,257
April 1985	651	2,001	601	3,253
April 1995	663	1,994	577	3,234
April 1999	671	1,990	568	3,229
April 2005	739	1,317	339	2,395
March 2006	777	846	198	1,821

Source: The Ministry of Internal Affairs and Communications (see also Yokomichi 2007: 17).

that, for a junior high school to operate, a population and fiscal base of at least 8,000 inhabitants was required. It can be said, then, that the Meiji and Showa era mergers had a clear purpose that involved public services for citizens.

But what was the purpose and logic of the Heisei mergers that took place in the late 1990s and early 2000s? The next section turns to consider this question.

The decentralization committee and municipal mergers

The starting point for the Heisei mergers goes back to discussions led by the Decentralization Promotion Committee, established in 1995 by the Murayama Tomiichi administration, a coalition government between the Japan Socialist Party, the Liberal Democratic Party (LDP), and the New Party Sakigake. In the early discussions, the members of the committee decided to promote decentralizing the central and prefectural government's administrative powers and granting them to local authorities, on the premise that the existing boundaries of local authorities should be maintained. They realized that if they started discussions about changing the physical boundaries of municipalities, the discussions would most likely continue for a very long time, and the committee was, according to the law, to be dismantled after five years. Given their time limit, the committee chose not to address the local authorities' boundary problem.

This is not the first time, however, that Japan has grappled with the idea of boundary changes for local authorities, and past experience shows that addressing this problem directly has not led to success. A prime example of frustrated attempts to address such an issue is the ongoing discussion about imposing a new regional system (*Dō-Shū-sei*[2]), to replace Japan's existing prefectural system. In these discussions, the debates on prefectural mergers were protracted extensively, without any significant outcome in terms of actual boundary changes. Described in detail later on, the example illustrates the difficulties encountered when attempting to redraw existing boundaries.

The prefectural system versus the new regional system

There have been 47 prefectures in Japan since the Meiji prefectural system was established in 1888. This means that prefectural boundaries seem to be very stable, and debates about changing prefectural boundaries appear to be unfruitful. Nevertheless, such debates have continued for nearly a century. In 1927, under Prime Minister Giichi Tanaka, a regional system was proposed. Seven regions (Hokkaido, and the regions of Tokyo, Sendai, Nagoya, Osaka, Hiroshima and Fukuoka) would be established and the head of each would be appointed by the central government. Prefectures would be changed to local autonomous bodies and governors would be elected by the public. This proposal involved a three-tier system, with the central government, regional governments, and local governments. In the end, however, the proposed system was never implemented.

In 1947, a new local government system was introduced through post-war reform; prefectures became local autonomous bodies and the governors became elected by the public. Unlike in the 1927 proposal, however, prefectural boundaries were not changed. This new system was disfavoured by the old Ministry of the Interior, which tried to introduce the pre-war prefectural system, under which governors controlled prefectures, and these governors were not elected, but designated by the central government. One of the documents illuminating the intention of this ministry was the report by the 4th Committee to Investigate Local Government Systems (*Chihō Seido Chōsakai*) of 1957. A majority of the committee members, supported by the bureaucratic interest,[3] proposed that prefectures be turned into 'local regions'. The proposal argues that:

> A striking imbalance has arisen between prefectures in terms of the ability required to implement a modern system of administration, and there are many cases where the existing area of prefectures is too small to enable administrative projects that cover a wide area, such as resource development or land conservation, to be dealt with in a rational manner. Moreover, if we also look at this situation from the perspective of efficiently managing highly sophisticated administration as well as from that of reducing administrative costs, it is reasonable to presume that it is much more rational to deal with such administrative matters within the context of a much larger land area.
>
> (Committee to Investigate Local Government Systems 1957,
> and Yokomichi 2008)

In other words, prefectures were too small to be efficient, and should be expanded to become 'local regions'. As far as the character of prefectures was concerned, the report continues to say that:

The larger part of the work carried out by prefectures has the character of work that should be categorized as being part of the state as a whole, and despite the fact that this tendency is at last being seen as a trend to be taken forward, changes in the character of prefectures since World War II and accompanying these, the string of reforms of prefectural systems such as the public election of the prefectural governor, may be insufficient in terms of safeguarding cooperative relations between the central and local government and maintaining a set level of administration in the country as a whole.

The bureaucratic interest insisted that the newly introduced autonomous prefectural system did not work for cooperative central/local relations; they proposed to instead make a centrally controlled system of central/local relations, just like the pre-war system.

On the other hand, a minority group in the committee pointed out the importance of the democratic characteristics in the existing prefectural system and insisted that prefectures should continue to maintain their present role as local autonomous bodies. They then proposed a merger of three or four prefectures in order to expand prefectural functions and reduce the number of prefectures to between 15 and 17.

The government did nothing relating to the majority's report. However, two items from the minority's proposal were presented to the Diet; one was the merger of three Tokai prefectures (Aichi, Gifu and Mie), proposed by the Association of Business in central Japan (*Chubu Keizai Rengōkai*) in April 1963, and the other was the merger of three prefectures in the Osaka area (Osaka, Nara and Wakayama), proposed by the Association of Business in the Kansai area (*Kansai Keizai Rengōkai*). The government proposed an act to promote these prefectural mergers, but these prefectures rejected the plan and the act was not passed in the Diet.

In recent years, talk of a regional system has been revitalized once again, along with the discussion on municipality mergers. Political parties, business organizations and think tanks have been publicizing their ideas for promoting a regional system since 2000.

In November 2003, the 27th Committee to Investigate Local Government Systems presented a 'Report concerning the Future System of Local Government' and mentioned the regional system as a potential future system of government. In February 2006, the 28th Committee to Investigate Local Government Systems issued a 'Report concerning the Regional System', in which the committee declares that:

Wide-area local government reform will have to be located not simply in the context of responding to problems concerned with the prefectural system, but in that of re-evaluating the nature of the nation of Japan.

(Committee to Investigate Local Government Systems 2006)

The 28th Committee concluded that 'introducing a regional system can be thought of as appropriate in terms of a specific measure for realizing wide-area local government reform'. The committee found that prefectures are too small as individual bodies to take over the domestic functions of central ministries; therefore, the committees favoured creating regions larger than prefectures to move forward with the decentralization process.

The committee insisted that a concrete plan for a regional system should be carried out in line with the following three aims: (1) to develop decentralization and strengthen local autonomy, (2) to have land areas with autonomy and vitality, and (3) to construct an efficient administrative system running through the central and local governments. This vision of a regional system, which has regional autonomy as its goal, is different from the original concept of a regional system, proposed by the 4th Committee in 1957, which intended to maintain central control.

The 28th Committee proposed three separate plans for drawing boundaries: one plan divides Japan into 9 regions, the next plan uses 11 regions, and the final plan suggests creating 13. The 9-region plan would divide Japan into the regions of Hokkaido, Tohoku, Kita Kanto-Shinetsu, Minami Kanto, Chubu, Kansai, Chugoku-Shikoku, Kyushu and Okinawa (see Figure 7.1). The 11-region plan would have the regions of Hokkaido, Tohoku, Kita Kanto, Minami Kanto, Hokuriku, Tokai, Kansai, Chugoku, Shikoku, Kyushu and Okinawa. Finally, the 13-region plan would comprise Hokkaido, Kita Tohoku, Minami Tohoku, Kita

Area of Regions (Example 1:9 Regions)

Source: Yokomichi, 2008.

Figure 7.1 Nine-region plan

Source: Yokomichi, 2008.

Kanto, Minami Kanto, Hokuriku, Tokai, Kansai, Chugoku, Shikoku, Kita Kyushu, Minami Kyushu and Okinawa.

The committee put forth three different plans for drawing up regional boundaries because they could not arrive at a consensus on one plan. They disagreed, for example, about contested territories such as Niigata prefecture, the island of Shikoku, and the Tokyo area. As Niigata prefecture is located between Tohoku and Chubu prefectures, there was disagreement regarding with which of these two prefectures it should merge. Shikoku is problematic, as its population is too small to be considered an independent region, but because it is a separate island with a relatively large land mass, it would be awkward to merge it with another prefecture. Tokyo is the capital and has an enormous population, but has too small a land mass for a region, so it too is difficult to place within a regional system. This shows how difficult it can be to agree upon boundaries, and explains why there have been such long discussions without any results.

Despite the difficulty, however, discussions on the new regional system did continue. The government established the Council for Creating a Vision for Regional Systems (*Dō-Shū-sei Bijon Kondankai*) in January 2007, in order to formulate a 'vision for regional systems', including such basic matters as the shape of the local society, the shape of the economic society, and the new face of government in terms of central government and local government relations under a regional system. The council is also expected to bring together a vision of regional systems within a period of three years. They publicized the interim report in March 2008, which stated that 'the regional system is an effective way to invigorate the Japanese economy'. Given this focus on the economy, the council seems to reflect the views of business leaders like Nippon Keidanren (Japan Business Federation). They will continue these discussions and will issue the final report within a three-year period.

Compared to the goals set by other councils, this is an ambitious plan. Others who have tackled this issue have faced years of debates and discussions. In November 2004, for example, the Liberal Democratic Party set up the internal Investigative Committee on Regional Systems (*Dō-Shū-sei Chōsakai*), which issued a first interim report in July 2005, and a second interim report in June 2007 (Liberal Democratic Party 2007). They discussed many aspects of a regional system, but failed to propose any plans for drawing boundaries in specific areas. The report said they would continue to discuss the matter and that a regional system should be implemented within a period of 8 or 10 years; their main conclusion, therefore, seems to be that discussions and debates will inevitably continue for a long time.

If a regional system is introduced, prefectures will be directly and drastically affected, and since each prefecture has a governor, the National Governors' Association (NGA) has joined in the debates. In January 2007, the NGA publicized the document, 'Basic Thinking concerning a Regional System' (*Dō-Shū-sei ni Kansuru Kihonteki Kangaekata*), in which they proposed seven basic principles that should guide the creation of a new regional system. The first item is that 'the regional system must promote decentralization'. The proposals in this document are almost the same as those put forward in 2006 by the 28th Committee to Investigate Local Government Systems, but the NGA further stressed the importance of decentralization in creating a regional system (National Governor's Association 2007).

Thus, while there have been a plethora of discussions on a prospective regional system in recent years, the matters are so complicated that it will take a long time before any agreement is reached. One of the most difficult issues is the durability and continuing salience of legal boundaries between existing regions, currently in the form of prefectures, inhibiting the creation of new boundaries. It will take time to create and garner support for a feasible plan to draw and implement these new boundaries. This shows how matters of decentralization, whether on the prefectural or municipal level, can be time consuming and difficult. As discussions on a new regional system showed, however, matters of decentralization remain complex.

Decentralization and municipal mergers

The Decentralization Promotion Committee, established in 1995, took a two-tiered strategy: first, they planned to promote the decentralization of legal power and administrative activities, and second, they planned to promote financial decentralization. However, the committee was forced to suspend discussions on financial decentralization regarding local authorities.

After the bubble economy burst in the early 1990s, the central government's financial situation also suffered. The Ministry of Finance (MOF) therefore started to devise means of reducing the funds allocated to local authorities. It insisted on the importance of a 'saucer' theory of decentralization (*ukezara-ron*),[4] meaning that local authorities had to be a certain size to qualify as a 'saucer' for, or receptacle of receiving the decentralized functions, since decentralization required a relatively large local authority. But subsequent events revealed that this was just a negotiating ploy, since even when a local authority increased in size, no central departments transferred their powers. Moreover, the expenditures by local authorities include many important public services governed by national laws, so the effect of cutbacks would have been small, even if they had in fact been implemented. The MOF would have been better advised to review the expenditures of central government departments.

In 2001, the MOF resumed concentration on the financial decentralization of local governments, and tried to cut local government expenditure with their 'trinity reform' (*sanmi ittai kaikaku*). Trinity reform refers to the following three reforms: (1) transferring tax revenue sources from the central government to local governments, (2) having the central government subsidize local governments, and (3) allocating local tax. These reforms aimed to change the fundamental elements of the Japanese local financial system. The results, however, included big cutbacks in local government expenditure, but very little decentralization.

The Decentralization Committee first attempted to promote decentralization, as mentioned earlier, on the premise that the boundaries of local authorities should not be challenged, but pressure from the MOF as well as from LDP politicians made the committee consider promoting mergers. Faced with this pressure, the committee set up a task force in 1996, named the Review Group on Administrative Structures (*Gyōseitaisei Kentō Group*). The committee's second report, issued in July 1997, included the review group's declaration that mergers of municipal authorities were necessary and should be promoted, along with other proposals such as the promotion of administrative reform, the awakening of somnolent local assemblies, the enhancement of citizens' participation, and the promotion of fairness and transparency. But these recommendations alone were not enough to encourage any mergers, and the task was left to the Ministry of Home Affairs.

The ministry's research group on mergers

In 1998, the Ministry of Home Affairs set up a research group on mergers under a bureau chief, with academics as key members and the chair. The group discussed the purpose and advantages of mergers. According to the group, the purpose of the mergers should be to set a minimum size for municipalities, just as had been the case during the Showa mergers, which set a minimum population of 8,000 for towns. The group at one point proposed a minimum size of 20,000 for municipalities, but, in the end, neither the group nor the Ministry of Home Affairs accepted this proposal as the purpose or goal of the mergers.

Nevertheless, the group divided municipalities into the following five size categories, and clarified the advantages of increasing a municipality's population through mergers:

(1) Major cities: A city with a population of 500,000 can be designated a 'major city' (*seireishitei toshi*) to which certain powers, such as the welfare of children and the disabled, are ceded by the prefectural government. The Heisei mergers led to the designation of five new major cities: Saitama City in 2003, Shizuoka City in 2005, Sakai City in 2006, and Niigata and Hamamatsu Cities in 2007.

(2) Core and special case cities: Since the 'core city' (*chūkaku-shi*, cities with populations of over 300,000) scheme was introduced in 1995, 35 cities have been so designated, 14 of them since 2000. 'Special case' cities (*tokurei-shi*, cities with populations of over 200,000) were introduced following the recommendation of the Decentralization Committee in 2000, and since then, 44 cities have become special case cities. These schemes are good incentives to mergers, as core and special cities can have the administrative power of a health office (*hoken-jo*), can introduce a large-scale waste incinerator which suppresses dioxin emissions, and can involve education advisers (*kyōiku shuji*) on all subjects in the education committee.

(3) Medium-sized cities: A city with a population of 100,000 can set up a fire service, run a senior high school, and establish an independent office of women's affairs.

(4) Small cities: The minimum population required to become a city is 50,000, though when the population of a merged municipality passes 40,000, it can

become a small city according to the Special Law on the Merger of Municipalities (*Gappei Tokurei Hō*) of 1995. Compared with a town or village,
a small city can have a welfare office (*fukushi jimusho*) and an education
adviser, and can set up an independent environmental administration office.

(5) Towns: If small municipalities wish to merge to form a town, the post-merger
population must be at least 10,000, a slightly higher population than that set
for towns during the Showa mergers. Among other things, a town with a population of 10,000 or more differs from a village in a number of ways. It can,
for instance, run a day care service for the elderly, or the smallest kind of
home for the elderly, or appoint a construction engineer.

Mergers can result in a number of other advantages, such as a special bond issue
for essential public works following the merger, a special 10-year local allocation
tax system, not to mention the lower cost of local assemblies following the reduction in the overall number of local councillors.

Mergers also come with disadvantages. First and perhaps the most obvious disadvantage is that certain local officeholders will lose their positions. For example,
only one mayor can be elected per municipality. If both mayors of two potentially
merging towns wish to continue in office, a merger movement usually encoun-
ters strong resistance; and to counter similar resistance from local councillors, a
special merger rule was created by law.[5] Administrative staff members also face a
great amount of challenging work and added stress when dealing with mergers.

A more crucial disadvantage, one could argue, is that small merging municipalities are likely to face a decline in revenue from the local allocation tax. Since
the local allocation tax is not proportional to the population, it tends to benefit
smaller municipalities, because every municipality has the same statutory duties,
regardless of size, under the 'grade adjustment' (*dankai hōsei*) for the local allocation tax. According to the grade adjustment system, smaller municipalities are
allocated more funds in terms of amount of funds per person from the central government than the larger municipalities. When a municipality grows, the amount
of funds allocated to it per person decreases. Therefore, under the current grade
adjustment system for local allocation tax, revenue actually declines for formerly
small municipalities.

After pinpointing this disadvantage, the research group further examined this
grade adjustment system, and recommended that it be greatly diminished, or even
abolished, if the government wanted to promote mergers. However, the Ministry
of Local Government informed the research group that they would not change
the grade adjustment of local allocation tax, prompting observers to think that the
ministry did not really intend to encourage mergers at that time. Later on, however, the ministry did not maintain their policy views, because they realized that
abolishing the grade adjustment would be an effective way to stimulate mergers.

Over time, the advantages of mergers seemed to outweigh the disadvantages,
especially after the Ministry of Home Affairs added certain special merger rules
by law. However, these advantages were still not enough to persuade many municipalities to merge. Research to discover the consequences of mergers continued.

The National Institute of Research Advancement (NIRA) started its 'Research Project on the Governance of Local Governments'.[6] Economists were invited to be members of this project and reviewed the consequences of mergers from a purely economic point of view. Not surprisingly, they found that smaller municipalities are more expensive than bigger ones.

However, the major obstacles are often the geographical situation of Japanese municipalities. Physical boundaries between different local authorities, such as rivers and mountains, create a natural separation of these communities; from that separation there also often follows the additional boundary of differing identities. These boundaries of geography and identity serve as obstacles to mergers. There are many isolated villages in Japan, like small islands or small communities in semi-mountainous areas. It is very difficult to merge those small villages because the physical boundaries, that is, the sea and/or mountains, make it difficult for people to have a sense of a joint community or common identity with those in other areas. Even if those small municipalities merged, citizens do not feel they belong to the same municipality. On the other hand, municipalities in Hokkaido are too dispersed to have a large population. If those municipalities merged, the land area of the local authority would become very large, but the population would still be small; moreover, the citizens would not gain the feeling of living in the same community or of sharing a common identity. Mergers in such areas are very difficult, and it is for that reason that the ministry supported small municipalities by maintaining the grade adjustment system. A merger would not solve any of the problems in those small villages as, even if the legal boundaries were to change, the salience of physical barriers and boundaries of identity would remain.

Learning from the English experience of the nineteenth century

It is instructive to look back at the case of England in considering the case of local authority boundaries in Japan. In England, *ad hoc* authorities were set up ubiquitously in the eighteenth and nineteenth centuries. They were, for example, the Court of Sewers, the Incorporated Guardians of the Poor, the Improvement Commissioners, and Turnpike Trusts. Later, an all-purpose authority was thought to be necessary, and in the nineteenth century, those *ad hoc* authorities started to be dismantled (see Muto 1995 and Webb and Webb 1913).

Turnpike Trusts went bankrupt after the railway was laid along the turnpike road. Turnpike roads were then returned to local parishes, but the parishes could not maintain them. Counties assumed the responsibility of maintaining de-turnpiked roads at the end of the nineteenth century when county councils were established. Before this solution was implemented, however, the highway districts were set up by area parishes, but they did not have resources or knowledge to perform that duty.

On other issues, such as health and sanitation, problems in urban areas were so severe that new ways of handling the problems had to be sought. A general board of health and local boards of health were established. On the issue of laws regarding the poor, the Incorporated Guardians of the Poor still worked. Finally the Gordian

Knot was cut by the Public Health Act of 1872. The Local Government Board was set up and became responsible for public health, relief of the poor, and highway administration. An all-purpose authority was set up in all areas, in the form of boroughs and urban authorities in urban areas and rural sanitary authorities in rural areas. One can conclude from this English experience that the most important factor to consider in deciding who should hold administrative authority is whether a candidate is capable of carrying out the relevant responsibilities; that capability stems from having adequate finances, and the amount of funds available depends on the appropriate size, mainly in terms of population, of the local authority. Local authorities should provide local government service on the one hand, but should also promote citizens' autonomy on the other hand. If a local authority is too large, it is difficult to promote citizens' autonomy. Thus, larger local authorities are not always more competent to hold broader administrative authority.

In this sense, the Research Group on Mergers' five categories of municipalities, based on size, are important, and these categories can be used to promote mergers, but they can also be used to argue against mergers. As far as administrative difficulties are concerned, smaller municipalities like villages with population of less than 10,000 are the targets of mergers. As mentioned earlier, however, the group was unable to convince itself and the Ministry of Home Affairs to set the minimum population for a town at 20,000.

Further, the financial difficulties of local authorities are not insuperable. The financial situation of every local authority differs from others, since their revenue depends upon their own tax base. This is the reason that the Ministry of Home Affairs introduced the local allocation tax. The trinity reform targeted the diminution of this allocation tax and central grants, while supporting an increase of local tax revenue, by a tax transfer (*zeigen ijō*). Parts of the consumption tax and income tax were transferred to local authorities. This transfer not only made poor authorities a bit less poor; it also made rich authorities much richer by far, so some richer authorities are not given the allocation tax (*fukōfu dantai*). This transfer increased the number of those non-allocated authorities, but it has very considerable disadvantages since it encouraged many extravagant and unnecessary projects. Some kind of horizontal adjustment by local authorities in mutual agreement is necessary, but no effective proposal of this kind has yet found much support.

Political demands for mergers: the meaning of 3300–1000–300

In his book entitled *Decentralization Reform*, Nishio Masaru relates a heated discussion with LDP politicians in December 1996 (Nishio 2007). The Decentralization Committee went to the LDP and outlined its first recommendation, which included the abolition of the 'delegated function system' (*kikan inin jimu*) under which local authorities were subordinates to the Minister, with the premise that the existing boundaries of local authorities should be maintained, as mentioned earlier. Politicians, however, insisted that mergers should be promoted at once (Nishio 2007: 38–39). When Nishio replied that politicians should first explain their wishes to mayors and local councillors as well as citizens in each constituency, one politician observed, 'Mr. Nishio, you do not know politics in Japan at all, do you? If we made such a speech in our constituency, do you think we could ever be elected again?' Nishio answered by saying that this was why Japanese politics had become so obscure; politicians manage to communicate two different messages, in a style referred to as 'formal and informal' or 'front and back' (*omote* and *ura*), far too expediently.[7] He went on to say that if the majority of the LDP believed in more mergers, this policy should be stated in their party's platform for the next election. This argument ended, however, with the LDP changing the committee's direction. The committee was asked to abandon their crucial initial premise that the existing boundaries of local authorities should be maintained, and start instead to promote mergers.

In August 1998 the LDP and the Komei Party reached an agreement that the number of municipalities should be reduced from 3,300 to 1,000 within several years (*Asahi Shimbun*, 27 August 1999), and in fact, the number has thus far been reduced to 1,785, to date. In February 1999, the Economic Strategy Council (*Keizai Senryaku Kaigi*), an advisory council to the Prime Minister Obuchi Keizō, presented the report, 'A Strategy for Regenerating the Japanese Economy'. The report said:

> One of the reasons for the depression in the Japanese economy can be traced to the depression in local economies. Unless the local economies and local cultures become autonomous, instead of being dependent upon the central government, the future of the Japanese economy will be grim. It is imperative that local sovereignty is established. To do this, the number of municipalities should be reduced to less than 1,000.
>
> (Economic Strategy Council 1999)

The chairperson, Higuchi Hirotarō, was the honorary chairperson of Asahi Beer Breweries Limited and the council seems to have a strong business interest.

Decentralization is desirable for business in terms of business regulations because an enterprise can send its applications for any business regulations to the local, decentralized office, instead of to the ministry in Kasumigaseki. The concentration of government ministries in Kasumigaseki is not favourable for local business. Under the centralized system, each enterprise must send its application to the relevant ministry, but under a decentralized system it can submit its application at the nearest office. In this sense, deregulation and decentralization was thought of as the necessary wheels for reforms.

Aside from business interests, the reasons given for mergers were to promote administrative efficiency, to strengthen municipalities as 'saucers' of decentralization, to reduce expenditures, and so on. If politicians truly believed those reasons, however, it is unclear why they recommended 1,000 municipalities rather than, for example, taking on the Liberal Party's recommendation of having only 300 municipalities. If it can be said that the municipalities should be bigger, and that bigger is better, they should have recommended the lowest number possible. The

Liberal Party led by Ichirō Ozawa had clearly stated that there should be only 300 municipalities in their manifesto (Liberal Party 1998). This manifesto was adopted by the Democratic Party of Japan, with which the Liberal Party merged in September 2003.[8]

There are exactly 300 single-member constituencies in Lower House national elections. If the number of municipalities was reduced to 300, the boundaries of municipalities and the boundaries of single-member constituencies would become almost the same in many areas. In those areas, both the Diet member and the mayor would be elected from the same area. The Diet member would therefore become a competitor, perhaps even a strong rival, of the mayor, and vice versa. No politician wants such a strong rival. Why did the Liberal Party favour it? There are currently only a few areas that are both a municipality and a single-member constituency. For example, in Iwate prefecture, the Diet member is Ozawa, and he is amazingly popular there. There is no rival in sight, but his situation is exceptional. If a municipality's boundary was the same as that of a national election constituency, intense competition would occur in almost every constituency. It might be good for the people, but it would make life very difficult for politicians.

There are, on average, about 10 municipalities in every national constituency. The actual number per constituency varies, however, since rural areas tend to have more municipalities than urban areas. In a typical rural constituency, there are more than 10 mayors and several hundred local councillors. National-level politicians must communicate with all of the local-level politicians who belong to the same party. Of course, local politicians will usually support their party's national-level politician, but since there are so many of them, it seems difficult for national-level politicians to control local politicians.

If the number of municipalities was reduced to 1,000, there would be, on the average, about three or four municipalities in each rural constituency. National politicians seemed to be able to control their supporters much more easily than at present, without the threat of competition that they would face from local politicians if there were only 300 municipalities. A mayor might emerge as a rival to a national politician, but the national politician can take advantage of having a wider constituency than the mayor's. It seems, then, that national politicians have chosen the number 1,000 because it would create a desirable situation for themselves, though they cannot of course admit it formally.

Nonaka Hiromu was the Chief Cabinet Secretary of the Obuchi administration from July 1998 to October 1999. Looking back at his role in merging municipalities, he wrote:

> I think I did too much. I regret what I did. At that time I did not think that there would be over 1,000 mergers. However, to date there have been 1,800, and mergers are still going on, even though the act to promote mergers has not been put into effect. This means that small municipalities are forced to be dependent and merged because the trinity reforms introduced a financial system disadvantageous to small municipalities. This is the worst point of

the Koizumi administration, which caused the collapse of local autonomous government from its base.

(Nonaka 2006: 113)

After examining merger problems and reviewing related documentation thoroughly, Imai argues that two main factors led municipalities to merge: the decrease of local allocation tax in 2001, and the relaxation of the grade adjustment of local allocation tax in the early 2000s. He further argues that the most striking defect of the mergers was the special merger fund for public works to merged municipalities. In comparing merged and non-merged municipalities, Imai shows that merged municipalities have lost financial discipline because of extravagant public works expenditure and because their financial situations have actually become worse than non-merged municipalities. Another defect of the mergers is the effect of the widening distance between town halls and citizens. He concludes that the Heisei mergers of local authorities were a failure from any point of view (Imai 2008: 272).

The change of legal boundaries between local authorities does not necessarily wield great influence over citizens' lives directly. If managed properly, a merger would simply mean a change of postal address. Public services could be maintained at the same level as before the merger, with lower service charges. However, the ways of supplying public services have in fact changed, as discussed in the next section, and this change of the metaphysical boundary between citizens and their local authority does wield a great influence over citizens' lives.

2. Boundaries of public services: privatization of public administration and changes in public services

Privatization and other Thatcherite reforms (see Muto 1989 and Muto 1991: 26–36) finally reached Japan in the form of the Koizumi administration's structural reform. Before Koizumi, the Nakasone government of the 1980s (1982–87) inherited the Commission on Administrative Reform set up by the Suzuki Zenkō administration (1980–82) in 1981 and, in line with the commission's recommendation, three public corporations were privatized in the mid-1980s. After that, administrative reform continued to be sought under the three consecutive administrative reform promotion committees, though it is difficult to identify the results specifically significant to the topic at hand.[9] Koizumi resumed administrative reforms by means of privatization. His main targets were the Japan Highway Corporation and the postal system. In the area of local administration, his government introduced the designated manager system (*shiteikanrisha seido*) in 2003, under which local authorities must select a designated manager to be in charge of a public utility, like a public library or gymnasium, by contract.

While the designated manager system was a major new reform introduced by the Koizumi administration, Japan's local authorities have a long history of outsourcing certain duties. In post-war Japan, local authorities entrusted their public services to public corporations. One such example is 'the council of social welfare' (*shakaifukushi kyōgikai*), which was set up in every local authority and has provided various welfare services, whose costs were paid by the local authority and whose administration was controlled by the local authority, under the provisions of Article 89 of the Constitution.[10] Before Koizumi came to power, 'outsourcing' and the 'NPM', or new public management, had been gaining popularity and both had a great influence on local authorities; to some degree, these systems prepared local authorities for using the new designated manager system.

In 2006, the Koizumi administration introduced market testing in the central government, as Britain had also done, but resistance from central departments was so strong that there were only a few cases of competitive tendering of their services. Local authorities, however, were required by law to introduce the designated manager system by September 2006. Before this system was introduced, local authorities managed public services such as libraries and gymnasiums by hiring their own public servants, or contracted the work out only to public organizations (*kōkyōteki dantai*), such as public corporations. Under this new system, however, local authorities are allowed to contract out the management of public services to private companies and non-profit organizations.

In the same year this system was required to be set in place, there were a number of accidents involving public utilities managed by designated managers. The *Asahi Shimbun* reported an accident where a high school student was killed by an elevator managed by a designated manager on 3 June 2006 (*Asahi Shimbun*, 4 June 2006), and that a seven-year-old girl had been sucked into a water intake and died in a swimming pool managed by a designated manager on 1 August 2006 (*Asahi Shimbun*, 1 August 2006). The causes of these accidents were deemed as the designated manager's carelessness or lack of responsibility, and in some cases, their use of low-cost labour. These incidents highlighted a dangerous drop in the quality of services provided to citizens; by outsourcing their public services at the highest level in post-war history, it can be said that local authorities are promoting 'disparity in society' (Tachibanaki 2006).

Boundaries between government service and public service

Civil society services can be categorized by service provider, as follows (see Figure 7.2):

(1) Civil society services: These public services are provided in the market without government grants. They are, for example, nursery services run by non-approved nurseries (*muninka hoiku*) and private companies, public transportation (taxi services and air transportation) and medical services.[11]
(2) Public services: These services are thought to be necessary in civil society and are provided by voluntary organizations and private companies, which are subsidized in part by local authorities. They include, for example, nursery services provided by certified nurseries (*ninshō hoiku*), meals-on-wheels, transport services for the elderly, minibus services for citizens, private schools, public transportation (railway and bus services), gas and electricity.

Services: Direct Government, Government, Public, and Civil Society

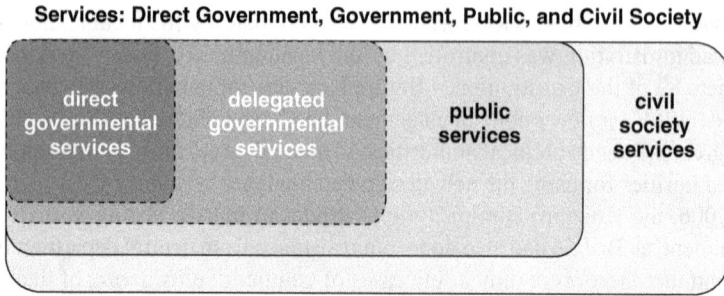

Figure 7.2 Services: direct government, government, public, and civil society
Source: Author

(3) Delegated governmental services: These public services are considered to be important and are delegated by the governments so that they are provided by public corporations. These services include welfare services provided by the council of social welfare, nursery services provided by the approved nursery (*ninka hoiku*, a nursery run by a private organization), school meals, and public utilities like water, gas, and so on, run by the local authority corporations.

(4) Direct governmental services: These public services are considered to be the most important, and are provided by public servants. Although we use the term 'direct', these services are not always provided by the public servants directly, but can be outsourced as well. They include numerous services, such as compulsory education,[12] school meals,[13] public libraries, taxation, hygiene control, parking enforcement and other police services, some nursery services provided by the direct nursery (*chokuei hoiku*, a nursery run by the local authority), public hospitals and water.

According to the Constitution, delegated governmental services must be controlled by 'the public authority'. In this context, public authority means the government. In other words, governments (both central and local) have decided what should be considered 'public'; in other words, governments have monopolized 'the public', and have been able to define the boundary between the public and the private. This has been the standard notion since the 1950s.

The central government set up the 'special legal organization' (*tokushu hōjin*) in the 1950s, and so-called 'third-sector organizations' (*daisan sekuta*) in the 1970s. Those organizations are considered to be publicly controlled organizations, and they undertook delegated governmental activities such as motorways, multi-purpose dams, housing, and railway construction. Local authorities also set up third-sector organizations in order to manage delegated governmental projects such as toll roads, local railways, recreational utilities, and housing. Kobe city was a striking example of the use of these organizations in the area of transport, urban development, and the like, so much so that it was sometimes called 'Kobe city company' (see Miyazaki 1979). The designated manager system is an extension of this idea and has drastically reduced direct governmental services.

Conclusion: two outcomes of the changes

In post-war Japan, we may observe that direct governmental services have been reduced continuously and transformed into delegated governmental services, while the delegated governmental services have, in turn, been transformed into subsidized public services. In other words, the work force for these services has shifted from being predominantly public servants to being predominantly non-public servants, changing the boundaries between the public and the private sectors in the process. This change has produced two important outcomes that will influence citizens' lives:

(1) Bureaucracy is being suppressed.[14] The number of local public servants had been growing since the local government system was established after World War II until 1994, peaking at 3,280,000 that year. Since then, however, the number has been decreasing, which is desirable from the citizen's point of view, as it indicates that the government's monopoly on 'the public' has started to be dismantled. In other words, local bureaucracy is decreasing.

The Japanese government has traditionally made a clear boundary between the public servant and the citizen. In this distinction, the public servant is supposed to transcend the various interests in civil society, whereas every citizen may pursue their own private interests. Moreover, the public servant in the central government has been, and is, called '*kan*', while the public servant in a local authority has been, and is, called '*kō*' (Ide 1982). '*Kan*' is higher than '*kō*' in terms of social status. The citizen, by contrast, has been called '*min*' and this social rank is the lowest. This notion was popular in pre-war Japan, but the influence of this ranking has survived to some degree even to the present time. It is only recently that citizens have come to be considered part of the public. In other words, the boundary of 'the public' has changed, and now consists of both public servants and citizens. Citizens are no longer content to remain categorized as merely the private sector, and instead claim that they too are part of the public sphere, can provide public services, and can help to define the public interest.

(2) Citizens provide public services, but for less pay. There are positive aspects of citizens working to provide public services, in that the people are playing a part in implementing public administration, and that it is a form of citizens' participation in local government. However, one of the major problems with this system is that when citizens do work to provide public services, their pay is incredibly low. Since the competitive tendering system drives prices down, it necessarily influences levels of pay. Local authorities therefore make citizens work for low pay. In Japan there is a large disparity between full-time, regular employees and part-time, non-regular employees. Moreover, the number of part-time employees has increased recently. According to the 2008 White Paper issued by the Ministry of Health, Labour and Welfare, the proportion of non-regular workers was 38 per cent in 2001 and has risen to 44 per cent in 2008. The White Paper said that

workers who cannot become regular workers often experienced anxiety and frustration over their working conditions. Using non-regular workers is effective in cutting costs, but not good for raising employability and productivity (*Mainich Shimbun*, 22 July 2008). Many observers think this is damaging because it has produced the phenomenon of the 'working poor'.

It is important to note that local authorities are one of the groups who are promoting this kind of gap in society. This is not the normally expected role of local authorities. On the contrary, local authorities are expected to resist this disparity, taking the view that, as a national population, no boundaries exist between the rich and the poor, but all are citizens to be served by the local authority. If local authorities do not acknowledge their responsibility in this respect, they will exist only for the elite or the rich. Thus, the low wages of working citizens should be controlled, while the suppression of bureaucracy should be accelerated. In the present situation, however, the low wages of working citizens has been accelerated instead.

There are various ways in which Japan might try to deal with this situation. The first option is for the Japanese government to ratify the International Labour Organization (ILO) convention 94.[15] This convention has so far been ratified by 59 member states, though in 1982 the UK revoked its earlier ratification. Some local authorities in Japan tried to introduce a bylaw, which contained the same regulation as this ILO convention 94, and the All-Japan Prefectural and Municipal Workers Union (*Jichirō*) started a movement to support ratification of the convention.[16]

The second option might be the introduction of a living wage. The term 'living wage' is different from the minimum wage regulated by law. The minimum wage is too low to secure a decent life even if an employer works 40 hours a week.[17] For example, the minimum wage in Tokyo is JPY791 per hour, the highest in Japan, and in Okinawa and two other prefectures it is JPY629, the lowest. With such a low level for the minimum wage, the advent of a class known as the 'working poor' was inevitable, even in an industrialized country like Japan. However, there is no movement to promote the living wage in Japanese government circles, except that the Japanese Trade Union Confederation (*Rengō*) has proposed a Japanese version of the living wage, along the lines of that defined by the Living Wage Unit in the Mayor of London's office in 2006.[18]

A third option might be to apply the principle of 'equal pay for equal work', but this principle is not yet legally enforceable in Japan. In the UK, the Equal Pay Act was established in 1970 and became legally enforceable in 1975. In the same context, one must also consider the Dutch model of work sharing, which is considered a practical application of the principle of 'equal pay for equal work'.

In conclusion, we may say that the boundary between government services and public services has been blurred. In other words, the boundary between the public servant and the citizen has become obscure, which points to two important implications: on the one hand, the suppression of the bureaucracy should be accelerated in order to strengthen the citizens' commitment to public services and the independent voluntary sector in civil society, but on the other hand, the citizens' wages should be controlled by the principle of 'equal pay for equal work' in order to secure a fair deal in society. It would be difficult in reality to apply the principle of 'equal pay for equal work' fully in the near future; in the long run, however, we must introduce the principle and resolve the problem of disparity.

Notes

1 This commission system stemmed from the American system and is an administrative commission that has executive power.
2 '*Dō-Shū-sei*' is a proposed system of regions, which would be larger than, and replace, prefectures. *Dō* and *Shū* are names for regions and *Dō-Shū-sei* is a kind of federal system. There has been a lot of discussion about adopting such a system, but no action as of yet. If the government is serious about realizing this type of system, a trial case could easily be applied to Hokkaido, which is a prefecture as well as a *Dō* in size.
3 The bureaucratic interest means interest of bureaucrats who prefer the old system in which governors are centrally designated bureaucrats.
4 *Ukezara* means the 'saucer' or the 'receiver', with which a person can get something. In this context, an *ukezara* should be a bigger municipality that is capable of receiving the responsibility for performing wider functions.
5 Merged municipalities can have twice as many councillors as the number stipulated by law. A councillor must serve for a minimum of 12 years before being eligible to receive a pension. If a merger cuts a councillor's career to shorter than 12 years, however, any third-term councillors would still be considered eligible for a pension.
6 See http://www.nira.go.jp/pubj/output/dat/3306.html (accessed 16 September 2010).
7 '*Omote*' means front or head, and '*ura*' means back or tail, literally. Colloquially, *omote* means in the formal life, and *ura* means in the informal life. Nishio pointed out that politicians should say the same things when speaking formally and informally (Nishio 2007).
8 There is no statement about 300 municipalities in the DPJ manifesto 2009, but the DJP did not give up that target of 300 municipalities.
9 The Hashimoto Ryūtarō government (1996–98) carried out important political and administrative reforms: (1) to strengthen the prime minister's leadership in the cabinet, and (2) to reorganize central departments. It can be said that the first point is significant in the sense that it made it possible for Koizumi to carry out his reforms.
10 Article 89 of the Japanese Constitution states: 'No public money or other property shall be expended or appropriated for the use, benefit or maintenance of any religious institution or association, or for any charitable, educational or benevolent enterprises not under the control of public authority'.
11 Except for public hospitals, medical service organizations are not given direct government grants; it can be said, however, that health insurance systems run by local authorities support medical organizations.
12 There are many private schools from the elementary level to higher education in Japan and they are given government grants under the name of a 'private school grant' (*shigaku-josei*). But the percentage of the grants compared to total costs is not high. For example, Hosei University's grant covers less than 10 per cent of its total expenditure.
13 Meals for compulsory schools were mainly provided by the direct service in the 1980s, but they have long faced pressure to outsource this service.
14 The phrase 'suppression of bureaucracy' is used here in close alignment with the concept of suppression of bureaucratic control over public services.
15 Article 1 of the International Labour Organization, C94 Labour Clauses (Public Contracts) Convention, 1949, states the following:

1. This Convention applies to contracts which fulfill the following conditions:

   (a) that at least one of the parties to the contract is a public authority;
   (b) that the execution of the contract involves:

      (i) the expenditure of funds by a public authority; and
      (ii) the employment of workers by the other party to the contract;

   (c) that the contract is a contract for:

      (i) the construction, alteration, repair or demolition of public works;
      (ii) the manufacture, assembly, handling or shipment of materials, supplies or equipment; or
      (iii) the performance or supply of services; and

   (d) that the contract is awarded by a central authority of a Member of the International Labour Organization for which the Convention is in force.

2. The competent authority shall determine the extent to which and the manner in which the Convention shall be applied to contracts awarded by authorities other than central authorities.
3. This Convention applies to work carried out by subcontractors or assignees of contracts; appropriate measures shall be taken by the competent authority to ensure such application.
4. Contracts involving the expenditure of public funds of an amount not exceeding a limit fixed by the competent authority after consultation with the organizations of employers and workers concerned, where such exist, may be exempted from the application of this Convention.
5. The competent authority may, after consultation with the organizations of employers and workers concerned, where such exist, exclude from the application of this Convention persons occupying positions of management or of a technical, professional or scientific character, whose conditions of employment are not regulated by national laws or regulations, collective agreement or arbitration award and who do not ordinarily perform manual work.

16 In September 2009 Noda City passed the bylaw of public contract (*Kōkeiyaku Jōrei*), which requests contractors to pay their workers more than the amount regulated by the Noda City. This bylaw has the same idea as ILO convention 94. Noda City, located in the northern part of Chiba prefecture, has a population of about 160,000.
17 A statement about minimum wage in the DPJ manifesto 2009 proposes a target of JPY 1,000 per hour.
18 See http://www.london.gov.uk/view_press_release.jsp?releaseid = 8090 (accessed 1 July 2008).

References

Committee to Investigate Local Government Systems (1957) Dai 4 ji Chihō Seido Chōsakai, 'Chihō Seido Kaikaku ni kansuru Tōshin', 18 October.
—— (2003) Dai 27 ji Chihō Seido Chōsakai, 'Kongo no Chihō Jichi Seido no Arikata ni kansuru Tōshin', 13 November.
—— (2006) Dai 28 ji Chihō Seido Chōsakai, 'Dōshūsei no Arikata ni kansuru Tōshin', 28 February.
Economic Strategy Council (1999), Keizai Senryaku Kaigi Tōshin, 'Nihon Keizai Saisei e no Senryaku'. Online. Available: http://www.kantei.go.jp/jp/senryaku/index.html (accessed 26 February 2008).

Ide, Yoshinori (1982) *Nihon Kanryōsei to Gyōsei Bunka*, Tokyo: Tokyo University Press.

Imai, Akira (2008) *'Heisei Daigappei' no Seijigaku*, Tokyo: Kōjinsha.

Liberal Democratic Party (2007) Project Team on Dōshūsei, 'Dōshūsei ni kansuru Dai 2 ji Chūkan Hōkoku'. Online. Available: http://www.jimin.jp/jimin/seisaku/2007/seisaku-011.html (accessed 14 June 2008).

Liberal Party (1998) 'Nihon Saisei no Shinario', the Liberal Party, June.

Miyazaki, Tatsuo (1979) *Toshi no Keiei*, Tokyo: Nikkei Shimbunsha.

Muto, Hiromi (1989) 'Igirisu ni okeru gyōsei kaikaku', in Gyōsei Kanri Kenkyū Senta (ed.) *Seiō Shokoku no Gyōsei Kaikaku: Igirisu, Furansu, Nishi Doitsu, EC*, Vol. 2, Tokyo: Gyōsei Kanri Kenkyū Senta, pp. 1–38.

—— (1991) 'Igirisu chihō jichi no dōkō: zaisei kaikaku to kyōsō nyūsatsusei no dōnyū o chūshin ni shite', *Gyōsei Kanri Kenkyū*, 56: 26–36.

—— (1995) *Igirisu Dōro Gyōseishi*, Tokyo: Tokyo University Press.

National Governors' Association (2007) 'Dōshūsei ni kansuru Kihonteki Kangaekata'. Online. Available: http://www.nga.gr.jp/upload/pdf/2007_1_x04.pdf (accessed 18 January 2007).

Nishio, Masaru (2007) *Chihō Bunken Kaikaku*, Tokyo: Tokyo University Press.

Nonaka, Hiromu (2006) 'Ninagawa kakushin Kyoto fusei to no taiji', *Toshi Mondai*, 97, 12: 113.

Tachibanaki, Toshiaki (2006) *Kakusa Shakai: nani ga mondai na no ka*, Tokyo: Iwanami Shoten.

Webb, S. and Webb, B. (1913) *The Story of the King's Highway*, reprinted in 1963, London: Frank and Cass.

Yokomichi, Kiyotaka (2007) 'Nihon ni okeru Shichōson Gappei no Shinten', COSLOG, Up-to-date Documents on Local Autonomy in Japan, No.1, March. Online. Available: http://www.clair.or.jp/j/forum/honyaku/hikaku/pdf/up-to-date_en1.pdf. (accessed 1 July 2008).

—— (2008) 'Nihon ni okeru Dōshūsei no Dōnyū Rongi', the Council of Local Authorities for International Relations (CLAIR), March. Online. Available: http://www.clair.or.jp/j/forum/honyaku/hikaku/pdf/up-to-date_en3.pdf. (accessed 1 July 2008).

8 Boundaries in Japan's business and government relationship

Regression, change and façades

Peter von Staden

A business and government relationship does not emerge *ex nihilo*. Its defining boundaries and related mode of operation, rather, is a function of its past and the forces that shape the present. In the case of Japan, their interaction is fettered by the legacies of the domestic economy's sclerotic institutions and pulled by the logic of global production processes. Now leaving its developmentalist past, the relationship has also taken on new complexities. The voice of business has become much less unified and, in those domains where it is most internationally competitive, a new balance with government has taken place. From the political perspective, reform-minded law-makers have found it expedient to advance their change agenda. But, at the same time, under the cosh of the current economic crisis, Japan descends deeper into debt, making economic reform more painful and consequently less likely that the relationship's boundaries will be re-inscribed. It is thus that with one foot in the past, Japan's business and government relationship moves forward.

This then quickly brings us to the issue of what constitutes 'change' and, in turn, how to pinpoint its telltale signs. Though there may be signs that flag change, taken in isolation it is often difficult to argue that any particular sign, in itself, accurately signals that something larger is afoot. An important distinction is to be made between change in the factors that make up a political economy and change in the matrix of factors as an interrelated whole. Though a boundary may shift in the business and government relationship, that is, if a change occurs in one aspect of the social, economic, political or cognitive structure in which the relationship operates, this does not necessarily translate into a change in the relationship itself. Actors, too, may play an important role in determining the degree to which a boundary shift may alter the interaction of business and government. Whether bureaucrat, politician or businessman, they all bring to the relationship individual characteristics and each is vested with authority and influence to respond to or potentially ignore the forces of change that they individually and collectively confront. However, the degree to which those constraints are stretched is a matter importantly influenced by personality (Samuels 2003). The age-old oscillations in the debates over structure and agency suggest that change incorporates aspects of both. More to the point, though, what we are seeking here is enduring change, that is, change that is a product of both sustained alteration in the boundaries that make up the structure and an alteration in the patterns of behaviour of the actors themselves.

Without the aid of hindsight, it is often difficult to know whether any particular juncture is a significant turning point or but a smaller step along a continuum of change. For example, it remains unclear whether former Prime Minister Koizumi Junichirō's period in office (2000–06) will come to be seen as a significant departure point or not. However, we know that he was the benefactor of change already afoot and, in this sense, boundary shifts during the tenures of Koizumi, the ensuing brief prime ministerial appearances of Abe Shinzō (2006–07), Fukuda Yasuo (2007–08), Asō Tarō (2008–09), and the rise of the Democratic Party of Japan under first Prime Minister Hatoyama Yukio and now Prime Minister Naoto Kan, need to be understood from a broader perspective. With this in mind, history may come to our aid, not as the prognosticating muse but as a more sober judge of past events which, in turn, may afford us a clearer perspective on the trajectory of Japan's business and government relationship.

This chapter proceeds in five parts. The first section considers two different frameworks which may be used to understand the business and government relationship. The second section differentiates between and characterizes the business and government relationship in the domestic and international realms. The third section considers the impact of the global economic crisis on how these actors interact; the fourth section considers the issue of personality and, finally, in the fifth section we return to the central question of the change in the boundaries of the government and business relationship.

1. Frameworks for understanding the relationship between government and business

On the interaction of business and government in Japan, the literature primarily focuses on the second of these two actors. Two important frameworks, however, which give a comparatively greater voice to business in this relationship are that of the 'iron triangle' (Johnson 1982) and 'reciprocal consent' (Samuels 1987), both of which are founded on research that spans from Meiji Japan to the end of the post-1945 high growth period. Although the focus of these works does not specifically include the contemporary, they both provide a historical perspective to understanding the current boundary change in Japan. These frameworks also emphasize different but important features of the business and government relationship and provide a solid foundation to begin to evaluate the changes in how these actors have interacted since Koizumi.

The iron triangle

Johnson argues that the success of politicians, bureaucrats and business (the three key actors in the 'iron triangle') in coordinating their efforts to achieve Japan's post-war economic miracle was not accidental; nor was the process teleological or one that implied a future terminal point. On the contrary, he provides a historically based evolutionary explanation of how the relationship between these three key actors arrived at a particular mode of interaction in the post-1945 period that gave rise to Japan's economic success. Although his analysis ends during the heydays of Japan's economic strength, it does not imply that a subsequent new mode would not emerge; rather, it is implicit in his argument that the government and business relationship is adaptive. The state of economic development, though not in itself unique to Japan, arises from a particular set of conditions which have shaped Japan's economic and political institutions. Having transcended this phase of catching up with, and surpassing, many world economies, Japan is now, as a mature economy, still working out a new mode of business and government interaction.

Conceptually, Johnson sees the relationship as one that is exogenously shaped by the economic and political context in which the relationship is located and yet, at the same time, also importantly directed by key actors. According to Johnson, the environment frames the set of opportunities and actors make their choices accordingly. He sees these actors as playing pivotal, leading roles in the formulation of Japanese industrial policy. The actors are talented individuals who find themselves in key positions within ministries and who consequently command and orchestrate the national industrialization effort. Importantly, some of these actors enter these positions at a relatively young age and remain within the government throughout their careers. This continuity, stretching from the late Taishō (1912–26) days of the Ministry of Agriculture and Commerce (MAC) to the post-war halcyon days of the Ministry of International Trade and Industry (MITI) a half-century later, is critical to the government's development of its relationship with business. In conjunction with business, Johnson contends, these government actors engage in what is effectively a trial-and-error process of learning how to interact. At any given point, government and business interaction operates in a particular mode and, over time, the relationship moves onto the next phase, inscribing boundaries in the process.

Self-control

The origins of the first mode of interaction – self-control – are traced to government and business relationships in the Meiji period (1868–1912), notably with the sale of publicly owned plants to the private sector (Johnson 1982: 310). Subsequently, the Meiji government proposed the creation of a new economic ministry which later took the form of MAC, established on 7 April 1881. Although in its first years, the ministry had relatively little active involvement in the economy, this was attributable to a decision by the government to adhere to a *laissez-faire* policy and the fact that the connections between MAC and industrialists were relatively weak. Certainly Kansai industrialists, and in particular those from the Osaka textile firms, were 'fiercely independent and suspicious of Tokyo' (Johnson 1982: 88). The degree of independence exercised by business changed through the economic tumult in the 1920s, the growing militarism of the 1930s and finally the Sino-Japanese and Pacific Wars. Although the emphasis of Johnson's analysis is on the bureaucracy, he does not consider the role of business to have been unimportant in the relationship, as the central issue, he contends, was the striking of a balance between control and latitude of action. The place where this boundary is drawn to separate these two aspects of control and latitude of action shifts with the changing political and economic environment and, indeed, is a characteristic of each mode of interaction. As Johnson puts it: 'Industry is quite willing to receive governmental assistance, but it does not like government orders . . . Government is often frustrated by the excessive competition' (Johnson 1982: 312).

State control

In Johnson's view, the 1930s marked a shift in the latitude afforded business by the government and its implementation of policy to manage the economy. As historical events unfolded and Japan moved towards war, the state increasingly created and applied levers of control to shift Japan to a war-time footing. Johnson's analysis indicates that business responded through both formal and informal channels to the tightening grip on the economy pointing out that, despite increased nationalization efforts, the 'business sector was still strong enough to withstand state and public pressure and to insist on private ownership and a large measure of private management' (Johnson 1982: 133).

It is understood that this second mode of interaction, here referred to as state control, does not imply either total state domination or business obsequience but a condition where business operated in newly established boundaries of greater government constraint. From the business perspective, the overall implication of Johnson's analysis is that there was more continuity than discontinuity than the delineation in the relationship between 'self-control' and 'state control' suggests. To be sure, the shift to a centrally managed economy and the growing military presence did distinguish the 1930s from the 1920s. Fundamentally, however, business continued to desire self-management and a minimum of government interference while, at the same time, recognizing the constraints of the time.

State guidance

The final mode of interaction, referred to here as state guidance, covers the postwar and high growth period until approximately 1975, during which, as Johnson argues, a particularly efficacious balance was struck between the latitude desired by business in controlling its own activities and the guidance that government exercised in directing business. Effectively, this 'balance' was but one point, he suggests, in the evolution of government and business interaction. As with the other modes of interaction, it is also shaped by contemporaneous political and economic conditions which both constrained and provided the opportunities for politico-business interaction. Central to Johnson's perspective is the vaunted role of MITI as the perspicacious central directing agency of Japan's industrialization efforts. Business, to follow Johnson's line of argument, was guided through incentives and the influence of personal ties with ministry elites and politicians to shift its resources into industries of greatest promise. Politicians, closely aligned with the ministry, and business through *amakudari* or 'descent from heaven' and the ties bound through generous financial donations interlocked these three key actors (Johnson 1982: 11, 21, 63–73).

Johnson's analysis shows that in Japan, at least, business and government interaction is evolutionary and adaptive. In this sense, his greatest contribution was to provide a framework which identified the key actors and their conduits of interaction. His historical analysis reminds us that these actors learn to work together through interaction itself. Shifts from one mode to the next occur in response to the economic and political construct of the boundaries of the business and government relationship. That said, the business and government relationship, though adaptive to the context in which it is located, reflects considerable continuity. In particular, we see the continued desire on the part of business to gain access to the locus of policy making in order to shape policy outcomes and, at the same time, to retain as much control over itself as possible. How and to what degree that access may be gained varies. Interaction will vary according to practices in the government, either those established in legislation or through informal channels, on the one side, and the personalities involved, on the other. In circumstances where there is constancy in actors, close interaction can be anticipated. Throughout Johnson's analysis, the government's *laissez-faire* approach to market intervention in the Meiji period, the militarist 1930s and the post-war period, the milieu comprising family, educational and professional networks was an important facilitator of interaction. Business and government interaction is not only a matter of locating the actors in a particular economic and political construct, which may or may not draw them together in pursuit of particular aims, but is also about particular personalities.

This, however, is not to suggest that conflict is absent in the relationship or, for that matter, trust will necessarily develop through repeated interaction. With regard to such issues which more closely reveal the dynamics of the relationship, Johnson is less clear. His concern is with the main lines that describe the 'iron triangle' and its relationship to the shifting political economic construct over time. It is here that 'reciprocal consent' allows us to go beyond Johnson's thesis of evolutionary change to more closely consider the dynamic of the boundaries of the business and government relationship. In particular, our concern is in understanding how they operate together as they move through the history of modern Japan, and to then use this as a guide to help us distinguish between fundamental changes in the relationship and smaller alterations that do not transform the overall structure of the relationship.

Reciprocal consent

Through his analysis of Japan's energy industries, Samuels' shows that a *modus vivendi* or 'understanding' was struck between government and business, in which government exercised its influence over business according to its jurisdictional remit, while business, accepting this, maintained control of industry. As a case

in point, government would establish legislation such as the Important Industries Control Law (1931), which provided a framework for industrial development and facilitated the formation of cartels.[1] But the operation of these cartels was left to business itself. In each instance, the negotiations were repeated though there was no change in the essential boundary between jurisdiction and control. This 'iterative process of reassurance . . . works better where the parties to these negotiations are stable and where the institutions that guarantee their compacts are enduring' (Samuels 1987: 8). Stability, however, should not be misconstrued as the absence of conflict; in the case of the energy markets, for example, friction between government and business was not uncommon. Neither should the concept of 'reciprocal consent' be seen to imply trust, but rather an established mode of interaction (Samuels 1987: 261).

What is critical for our purposes here is that, regardless of the degree of trust, an 'understanding' nevertheless existed between government and business which framed their interaction according to mutually acknowledged tenets. This 'point of compact', according to Samuels, is a specific moment in the development of the relationship when the roles of each are made explicit and their willingness to adhere to the implied rules of that compact. As he illustrates through comparison with the energy industries in a number of Western countries, once the mode of operation is set, the relationship operates within the established boundaries.

Samuels is less clear, however, on whether the relationship develops over time. Where Johnson has separated the pre-war era into two periods in which different modes of interaction occur, the implication of Samuels' 'point of compact' thesis is that the historical juncture sets up the understanding of 'reciprocal consent'. Thereafter, this is voluntarily reinforced through repeated interaction. Here, akin to the *seishō* (politically well-connected businessmen) relationship, family, financial and other ties bind business and government actors together, fostering stability and trust, and thus ensuring the continuity of the mode of operation.

As both Johnson and Samuels show, business seeks to steer a path between accessing governmental actors, whether they be political figures or bureaucrats, and retaining independence. Although this observation is undoubtedly not unique to Japan, the location of this balancing act within the framework of Japan's state of economic development and Japan's sustained goal of catching up with and surpassing other world economies sets it apart from others. Johnson's emphasis on the deliberateness of this particular goal-oriented pursuit underscores the importance of the dominant mindset which framed the conception of Japan's industrial policy, and is reinforced by his argument that this mentality was infused in industrial policy formulation throughout much of modern Japanese history. That said, industrial policy in the 1930s was located within the military's aims for Japan's expanded presence in Asia. As such, the aims of industrial policy deviated from the goal of catching up by means of its alignment with industrial success alongside Western powers. However, if international benchmarks of industrial success were sought, then the comparator would have continued to have been Western, serving as a reminder that a gap remained in many industrial sectors. By implication, then, once this century-old gap was closed and the overarching aim which has framed the modal transitions in the boundaries of the government and business relationship is found anachronistic, the moorings that underpin the relationship are called into question. The primary concern of these authors is the business and government (or in its inverse order) relationship from Meiji Japan through to the end of the high growth period. It is important to remember that contemporary Japan – one that is inexorably drawn into a global economy and where MITI (now METI, Ministry of Economy, Trade and Industry) has, in turn, taken on a very new and different role – is different. The period of economic catch-up and the constancy of the Liberal Democratic Party (LDP) as the party in power is over.

2. Distinguishing between business and government interaction in the domestic and international realms

With thespian panache, Koizumi's tenure as prime minister captivated the media's attention both at home and abroad in ways rarely seen in Japanese politics. He transfixed us, brought hope to an otherwise bleak economic and political landscape and, with stalwart determination, baffled us and incensed Asian neighbours. During his years in office 'reform' was his mantra and in this pursuit, he said, there would be no sanctuaries.[2] That said, he was as much an instigator of change as he was an inheritor of reform already afoot along the continuum of modal transitions. But, as has been underscored, this is more than a transition from one mode to the next in the interaction between government and business within the overarching paradigm of Japan's state of development; rather, the changes that have occurred indicate the creation of something entirely new.

The political economy of the high growth era with its attendant protectionist policies was increasingly untenable in the decade or more prior to Koizumi. China – both economically and militarily – loomed large on the near horizon. The logic of international wage differentials and strategic outsourcing in the increasingly integrated global economy has had an important influence on the business and government relationship. Business, too, though never the single entity that this term suggests, has become more stratified. Where the nascent and recovering industries in the post-war years were largely in need of protection from international competitors, not only had a marked bifurcation between weaker domestic industry and those internationally oriented emerged but greater differentiation within these broad categories can be seen as well. Trade associations too have become less capable of representing all voices at once and internal divisions have become marked. On the other hand, the seemingly inexorable logic of the market drove the once dominant LDP in new directions that placed a strain on its relationship with the ministries and called into question how business would operate given the shifting boundaries of the iron triangle, or whether, indeed, this tripodal configuration would even remain intact.

This distinction between the domestic and international has led to, broadly speaking, two different kinds of business and government relationships. Internationally competitive firms largely represented by the Keidanren have lobbied government hard for freer markets, been more cautious in supporting political parties and have shared the task of forging Free Trade Agreements, shifting the balance of power between the two actors to a more equal footing. While at the domestic level continued protective policies remain essential not only because many firms are not internationally competitive but also it is in their very uncompetitiveness that they contribute to sustaining Japan's informal social security network.

The domestic level

Reform in favour of a 'Westminster system' was one of the most significant structural changes that Koizumi brought to political decision-making and, by extension, the business and government relationship (Estevez-Abe 2006). Koizumi's snap election in 2005 that ousted anti-postal reform party members is seen as a manifestation of increased central party control at the expense of intra-party factions (*habatsu*). Reform processes set in motion under Hashimoto Ryūtarō in the late 1990s and later under Obuchi Keizō took effect in 2001 as Koizumi came into power. Central in the process of change from '*kanryō shudō*' (bureaucratic leadership) to '*kantei shudō*' (leadership from the prime minister's residence) was the role of the *Zaisei Shimon Kaigi* (Council on Economic and Fiscal Policy) (Sakiyama 2005: 174). Hashimoto's reforms expanded the Cabinet Office and strengthened the prime minister's position, thereby greatly enhancing the centrality of these institutions and, in turn, undermining the hitherto more diffuse political decision-making process. Through these and other structural changes that Koizumi inherited, Estévez-Abe argues, the once critical power-broker role played by factions in policy formulation had been reduced to the 'point of no return' (Estévez-Abe 2006: 633). This is not to suggest that Koizumi was but a political opportunist riding on the reform efforts of predecessors, for he, too, advanced the cause of political reform. For example, his initial attempts to reduce the decision-making power of the LDP's Policy Affairs Research Council (PARC) were stymied and he was forced to compromise. However, emboldened by his 2005 victory, he later managed to push through reforms that significantly undermined the position of the *zoku* (policy tribes) and PARC itself.

Following Koizumi's departure in 2006, the LDP failed to sustain the momentum for change. Holding office for approximately 12 months each, steerage of the nation was passed among LDP Prime Ministers Abe, Fukuda and Asō. The brevity of their successive tenures was too short either to advance the inherited reform initiatives or to make significant change in their own right (Arase 2009). Indeed, 'girding for the next election battle, some of "Koizumi's children"', that is those 83 Diet members ousted for resisting Koizumi reform were returned to LDP ranks (Arase 2009: 114).

> The Koizumi government was at once a high water mark for this struggle [between bureaucracy, the LDP and cabinet] and for the strength of the prime minister and the cabinet in this conflict; the three years since Mr Koizumi left office have witnessed a steady decline in the ability of the prime ministers to corral party members and bureaucrats. Rather than building a Westminster

system, Mr Koizumi strengthened the position of cabinet within the tripartite governing system without fundamentally transforming the system.

(Harris and Murphy 2009: 12)

While the combination of prime ministerial ineptitude and, later, the withering challenge of economic crisis steadily lead the LDP to its defeat in the election of August 2009, the then DPJ leader, Ozawa Ichirō, seized the opportunity to sway the disaffected voters to his party. In short, structurally based reform quickly passed into limbo as the LDP party focussed on its survival.

Current indications of the Hatoyama government, however, suggest that the DPJ is serious about living up to its electoral manifesto to change the political deci-sion-making process. Although early signs suggested otherwise, the Government Revitalization Unit (GRU) and National Policy Unit (NPU) have been put into place which should prove to strengthen the prime minister's office. Reportedly, 'high on the [GRU's] list of priorities will be reining in Japan's public utility organizations, traditional employers of retired bureaucrats in a practice known as "descent from heaven"' (*The Mainichi Daily News*, February 10, 2010). By per-mitting retired top bureaucrats to assume positions in business, this practice, also known as *amakudari*, has been a key means by which business has gained access to political decision-making. Although details of this plan are not clear at this point, if this linkage was broken, the business and government relationship would lose an important informal conduit of communication. Government plans are also underway to strengthen the NPU by adding 3 vice ministerial and 12 parliamen-tary secretarial positions, 11 of which will be either in the Cabinet Office or the Cabinet Secretariat. Similarly, the group of special advisors to the prime minister will be strengthened from 5 to 10 (*Kyodo News*, 15 January 2010). Ostensibly, if the locus of the current bureaucracy controlled policy-making process was shifted into the hands of cabinet and the ministries would be content to accept an advisory role, political decision-making would change fundamentally. In itself, this would not necessarily eliminate pork; however, the more that decision-making is cen-trally controlled, the easier it becomes for such change to occur.

Yet, notwithstanding Koizumi's structural reform attempts and its attendant change to vested bureaucratic interests – and the implications for the boundar-ies of the business and government relationship – pork barrel politics remained a reality. For all of his apparent reformist zeal and his 'clean' image portrayed in the media, some would argue that the contrary is in fact true. Writing in the *New Left Review* in 2002, McCormack charges Koizumi with underhanded actions. Rather than the arch-enemy of Tanaka Kakuei's honed system of patronage, as Koizumi would wish us to believe, he would appear to be an adept practitioner of that very system. McCormack writes:

While Koizumi constantly reiterates his 'structural reform' and 'no sanctions' slogans – to general applause – he offers no credible programme. Indeed, the brokering system of interest politics is so deep-rooted that he [Koizumi] is said simultaneously to be securing high pork funds in order to construct the

world's longest bridge in his own electorate: across Tokyo Bay from Yokosuka City in Kanagawa Prefecture to Futtsu City in Chiba Prefecture.

(McCormack 2002: 22)

Under Koizumi and the LDP's trio of successors, the iron triangle of the 'construction state' (*doken kokka*) composed of politicians and bureaucrats, financial institutions and the construction industry – as opposed to the manufacturing industry of Johnson's configuration – was largely unassailable to would-be reformists. While the manufacturing sector has had to adapt under the weight of the 1990s economic downturn and the neoliberal order, 'the core construction sector has, if anything, tightened its grip on the state' (McCormack 2002: 21).

This picture, though, has changed under the DPJ. The Hatoyama government's decision to suspend the construction of the Yamba Dam is a signal that there are limits to which the state will – and indeed can – maintain high levels of pork. As a legacy from a period of economic robustness, this closure has symbolic significance but, as will be discussed later, it is still too early to call an end to the construction sector's close association with government. In December 2009, the Hatoyama government published its interim 'New Growth Strategy' outlining plans for the revitalization of the nation. Conceptually, it is a demand-led strategy targeting the environment, health and tourism sectors to create 4.76 million new jobs. Apart from whether this is possible, it worryingly 'smacks of LDP-style pork-barrelling' in that many of its target investment proposals, such as airports and ports, would provide questionable economic gain but for the related construction firms (George Mulgan, 4 February 2010). Reform of political decision-making since Koizumi has changed, but it is unlikely that government will be able to wrest control from bureaucracies in the short term if for no other reason than that it is they who often have the depth of knowledge to formulate policy and that mindsets are hard to change.

The international realm: a new balance of power

As Japan's economy expanded in the post-war period, its complexity grew as well. Part of the diversification process and the need to reduce production costs has been its integration into the Asian economy and the corresponding transformation of MITI from a regulatory to a deregulatory agent. The MITI of Johnson's view of the state of development which was premised on the pursuit of 'national interest' is no longer accurate. MITI's greater access to information and expertise that formerly brought business under its sway has been of less consequence since the mid-1980s. Japan's economic integration in East Asia has eroded MITI's autonomy and forced the reinterpretation of its mission to include 'the recovery and expansion of the Asian regional economy as a whole' (Kohno 2003: 99). But regional integration is part of a larger process which has been critical in shifting Japan from its 'developmental' frame of reference. Hatch and Yamamura argue that the continued close cooperation between MITI and business, in particular with regard to regional business initiatives, stems from institutional path dependency and the reduction of transaction costs. Indeed, from their perspective in the late 1990s, the 'logic of cooperation will transcend the moment, driving Japan's developmentalist political economy well into the future' (Hatch and Yamamura 1996: 64). This is not to suggest that all is the same as the liberalization of financial markets that started in the 1970s, the bending of the state to foreign pressure demands for greater transparency in politico-business communication, among other factors, has reduced government ability to direct industry.

This change in coordination has been furthered by the growing expression of varied business interests and the associated fragmentation of trade associations. This argues, in turn, that communication between business and government has become more complicated and that the potential for competition between them for access to government has increased. When Johnson writes of business, he is primarily referring to big business and, in the high growth period, that was manufacturing. Trade associations, as well, are not fixed entities. Ostensibly, the logic of an association's inception and the rationale for its continued existence is based on a collective need for voice. As much as Meiji industrialists increasingly found the Chambers of Commerce inadequate to express their particular interests – and so gave birth to the Industrial Club of Japan – by the 1920s bankers too had formed their own specific representative group. In this sense, the waxing and waning of such groups parallel change in growth and diversification of an economy (Tsujinaka 1988). In the post-war period, interest groups in general have become less loyal to government, more fragmented and have increased in number from 10,000 in 1960 to 36,000 in 1991. Similarly, diversity of voice among businesses increased dramatically with the number of associations leaping from 169 to more than 800 during the same time period (Pempel 2000: 159). Although the need to better coordinate their interests underpinned the merger in 2002 of Keidanren (Federation of Economic Organizations) and Nikkeiren (Japan Federation of Employers' Association), internal fragmentation within the new Nippon Keidanren remains a problem. Issues such as Koizumi's reform initiatives impact differently according to sectoral interests and pulling associations in opposing directions (Vogel 2006).

But change in the business and government relationship is not only a matter of fragmentation but also evaluating the impact of the emergence of new industries in the later years of high growth. Expressed from the business perspective, the associated jurisdictional issues have made government interaction more complicated. Seen through the lens of 'bureau pluralism', government and business interaction is depicted in terms of a coordinating activity between ministerial bureaux and representatives of assigned industries. At this micro-level, bureau members represent the interests of an individual or a group of associations under its jurisdiction in negotiations within government. Issues may straddle the interests of a number of ministries and, as deliberations progress, discussions may include other ministries as well (Aoki 1988). The efficacy of this system is argued to be that it reduces delays. For example, in the early post-war period, the competitiveness of the machinery industry was hampered by a series of interrelated issues in the chain between the cost of iron and steel production to freight rates and further along

the line. Given the complementarity of the industries, coordination of interests between MITI and the Ministry of Transport were soon reached. However, in the case of the information and telecommunications industry, regarding an amalgam of the computer, telecommunications and broadcasting industries, intractable conflicts over jurisdiction arose between MITI and the Ministry of Postal Services which 'retarded the development of Japan's information and telecommunications industry' (Okazaki 2001: 338).

Increasingly, as firms have been able to finance themselves through access to international sources of funds, not only did they undergo a process of disintermediation with domestic banks, albeit not entirely, but ministerial sway diminished as well (Vogel 2006; Hatch and Yamamura 1996; see also Fukao 2002 and Kamikawa 2002). The government's former reliance on coercive tools has given way to 'softer' approaches relying on mutual understanding and negotiations. Nippon Keidanren's involvement in Japan's free trade agreements with Singapore, Mexico and South Korea through and beyond the 1990s reveals the varied roles it plays. As a pressure group, an information provider and an interest coordinator, it has led Free Trade Agreement (FTA) initiatives, as with Mexico concluded in March 2004 (Yoshimatsu 2005). Conversely, weak political leadership has hindered the formation of such agreements and, in turn, business determination has been critical in their realization (Hatakeyama 2003). The emerging picture is thus not just one of growing diversity within business but also change in the relative balance of power and boundaries between government and business. This is not to suggest that all business groups have equal access to governmental actors or agencies or that equality now prevails. Rather, as Japan's economy has matured, albeit perhaps still beleaguered by institutional vestiges of the catching-up era, the business and government relationship, in line with this change, has grown closer to what might be called a partnership of 'equals'.

3. The global economic crisis and Japan's fiscal noose

With the announcement on 7 September 2008 that the two US firms Fannie Mae and Freddie Mac would be nationalized, the global financial crisis was brought squarely into the forefront of the business world. For Japan, this came at a time when its economy was beginning to show signs of recovery from the 1990s downturn and the LDP was in the midst of its post-Koizumi leadership crisis. Although the in-house 'cleansing' of Japan's banks placed them in a comparatively healthy and less exposed position to weather the global storm, the economy as a whole was weak (Grimes 2009: 107). The stimulus measures that followed have helped prevent what would have been far worse. But, the expenditures have also rendered market restructuring politically unviable until economic recovery is in full swing. This, as we shall see, is increasingly difficult given the tightening fiscal noose.

A legacy of Japan's post-war growth strategy based on exports to the US is the current tepid domestic demand. Although this asymmetric trade relationship is changing with Japan seeking to stimulate consumers spending, declining real wages suggest that in the near future domestic demand will not be able to take up the slack. If the long-term forecast of 0.5 to 1 per cent GDP growth is correct, then not only will the government have to walk a tight-rope to be able to payback its largesse but will also have to find new ways of expanding economic output. Arguing that without fundamental restructuring of the domestic market, Richard Katz asserts that it will be difficult for Japan to achieve strong long-term growth (Katz 2010). If growth is sought by freeing up the domestic market, unemployment would follow which potentially would be tolerable if new jobs were generated and the government could afford the costs of dislocation and, at the same time, increase household income, support the aging population and pay back debt. This is – at least for the moment – unrealistic. Under current economic conditions, it is more likely that firms will continue to keep worker numbers above efficiency levels and fund construction firms that otherwise would be forced to fold. Here, business and government need each other – as does this nation as a whole – for this Catch-22 relationship is a key aspect of Japan's informal social safety net (Murphy 2009). As long as gains from restructuring are less than the political backlash of change, the relationship will at least keep a foot in its past ways of the high growth period.

In assessing what the foregoing discussion suggests about the trajectory of the boundaries of the business and government relationship, two salient points emerge: (1) initiatives to concentrate power in the prime minister have begun to embed themselves in political decision-making processes under Koizumi and then Hatoyama. To be sure, the rise of special interest groups has, among other factors, had a countervailing influence; and (2) the voice of business has increasingly become diversified and, in internationally competitive industries in particular, it has developed greater autonomy from ministries such as MITI (as well as METI). How these forces combine to form a new mode of interaction is less clear. Given the long-term trend of greater integration of Japan in the Asian and the global economy and Japan's continued manifold links with the United States, business and government will remain intertwined. It is clearer, though, that in the international realm this realignment of boundaries in the business and government relationship will be drawn along lines akin to a more balanced partnership of 'equals' in which fixed roles do not define the contours of the relationship. Although in principle METI's aim is deregulation, in practice, the responsibility for leadership in initiatives varies and, as has been seen, business may decidedly drive matters.

While Japan's economy has transcended its catching-up phase which underpinned Johnson's view of Japan's state of development, this does not imply that we have come full circle back to the *laissez-faire* approach of government during the first mode of interaction. As much as the nature of politico-business interaction is a function of the environment in which it operates, Johnson reminds us that the experience of actors is passed from one mode to the next and in this sense we can anticipate institutional continuities as we have seen in the domestic economy. Having undergone the subsequent dark years of militarist government and the horrors of war, only to forge a new business and government relationship of the economic 'miracle', it is unlikely that the value of interest coordination will be soon lost. Certainly, as Samuels' understanding of the relationship seen through reciprocal consent argues, coordination does not imply the absence of conflict but rather accommodates the inevitability of disagreement. However, this is contained within the larger understanding of trust and mutual respect of defined terrains of control and activity. But this depiction of politico-business interaction is suggestive of fragility as well. If the analytical lens is restricted to this binary configuration, the forces that draw the entities together operate in a one-dimensional plane and we miss the surrounding factors that enmesh the actors together.

Although greater plurality of voices within business has emerged, the business and government relationship remains embedded within the political decision-making process, and is part of Japan's elite power structure. Lincoln and Gerlach point out that much of the literature on Japan's post-war state-industry interaction is framed as a dyadic relationship. They argue that this focus misses the wider network in which the relationship is enmeshed. Stakeholders in business and government are no more than actors – albeit important ones both argue – in a 'web with *many* spiders, none of them dominant' (Lincoln and Gerlach 2004: 14, emphasis added). The outcome of Hatoyama's current initiatives notwithstanding, Colignon and Usui argue that *amakudari* remains alive and well in Japan's contemporary political economy, fulfilling a key role as an inter-institutional link in the formation of a network of cooperation. Such networks should be seen as:

> conduits of information and negotiation among politicians, bureaucrats, and businesspersons. At its broadest conception, these networks provide the structural substance of a power structure based on an association of bureaucratic, political, and business elites, or an 'iron triangle'.
>
> (Colignon and Usui 2001: 866)

In their survey of the positioning of retired elites, they use Johnson's distinctions of *yokosuberi* ('sideslip' from a central ministry or agency to a public corporation), *chii riyō* ('position exploitation' by ex-bureaucrats moving into political office) and *amakudari* ('descent from heaven' by bureaucrats to private corporations). In contrast to this depiction of a single linear move of the ex-bureaucrat to a new position, they also observe that some retirees move several times, which they call *wataridori* (migratory bird), thus forming four categories. Their research identifies that between the 1970s and 1990s the representation of ex-bureaucrats in cabinet posts diminished from 50 per cent to 20 per cent and that during the same time period only one ex-bureaucrat became prime minister. Further, movement to public corporations dramatically dropped from 80 per cent of *tokushū hōjin* (special legal organizations) board positions to 45 per cent. Although the implication is that *amakudari* is on the wane – at least in terms of *chii riyō* and *yokosuberi* – the movement of ex-bureaucrats to the top 100 largest firms has increased over the same period from 35 per cent to 67 per cent and more than a doubling of those in board positions from 2.1 per cent to 5 per cent (Colignon and Usui 2001: 890).[3] Colignon and Usui stress that the importance of their findings is much less in the identification of change in any particular sector but more in the broader implications. The composite picture argues for the resilience of the institution of *amakudari* despite significant political and economic change throughout the period of observation. Both as an explanation for its persistence and the character-ization of the phenomenon, *amakudari* should be seen from the perspective that 'interinstitutional cooperation is an inherent part of society constantly interacting with other forces in that society' (Colignon and Usui 2001: 890). Invoking a meta-phor of the game Go, they urge us to think of the impact of *amakudari* in terms of structuring the 'expectations and choices' of corporate policy decisions.

4. Personalities: Koizumi and beyond

Accepting that the business and government relationship is located within the larger construct that shapes choice, this raises, in turn, the question of how much freedom actors can exercise. To what degree did Koizumi's reformist policies shape the relationship and, given Abe's inclinations, did business correspondingly steer a different course? It is argued here that the broader trends outlined earlier continue but within that structure, actors play a role; however, such key figures as the prime minister may change frequently and the potential gains achieved by one actor may be undermined by the next. Indeed, according to Curtis:

> Koizumi is the first prime minister who actually breathed life into this new structure. And the new structure changed the dynamic of policy making and shifted the centre of gravity away from the LDP and into the prime minister's office. That new institutional context for policy making is going to continue, but how it gets implemented is *hugely* dependent on personality.
>
> (Curtis 2006: 12, emphasis added)

If the embedment of change is influenced by actors, it also suggests that, though new trends appear in the business and government relationship, the institutional-ization of the emerging new mode of interaction may remain an ongoing process for some time. As a case in point, consider the difference in approach to economic reform under Koizumi and Abe.

A key decision in Koizumi's privatization strategy was the appointment of Takenaka Heizō, an academic and a man reportedly 'uninterested in the influ-ence-peddling game that dominates Japanese politics', as the Minister of State for Economic and Fiscal Policy (Moffett 2004: 13). Backed by Koizumi, Takenaka tackled reform and ran the Council as the 'government's primary economic decision-making body' (Katz and Ennis 2007: 83). Under Koizumi the reform message was clear, particularly after his 2005 election, although his successor struck a more conciliatory cord (Stockwin 2007: 228). In an interview with *Chūō Kōron* in 2005, still as party secretary, Abe signalled that, notwithstanding the success of Koizumi's 'strong' leadership style, 'during times of large reform there remained even within the ranks of the ruling party the need for the widespread agreement' (Abe 2005: 107). Abe's selection of Omi Kōji, as Minister of Finance, Yamamoto Yūji, as Minister of Financial Services, Shiozaki Yasuhisa as Chief Cabinet Secretary and Ōta Hiroaka, as Minister of State and Fiscal Policy as his economics team seemed to signal that the reform drive may soon fade. Ōta was seen as a 'lightweight' and though Shiozaki was considered reform-minded, Abe's personal commitment, if not interest, in matters economic was questioned, undermining the chances of reform (Curtis 2006: 10; Katz and Ennis 2007: 83). In fact, shortly before his inauguration one pundit suggested that Abe's arrival 'may well be a return to the "normal" Japan where insiders rule and dictate the consensus' (Koll 2006: 36). Indeed, the brevity of his tenure and that of Fukuda and Asō argue that LDP had returned to its traditional practices.

In the case of the DPJ, the traditional tale of leadership has taken a new twist. Riding on the wave of public disenchantment with the LDP, Hatoyama was elected and party strategist and Secretary-General Ozawa Ichirō was to stay out of the public eye. Early signs of Hatoyama's political acumen suggest that *de facto* control of the party would remain in Ozawa's hands reminiscent of traditional LDP factional politics but this would not appear to be true. Ozawa has proven himself to be anything but inconspicuous. Hatoyama was at pains to distance himself from the corruption scandal that embroiled Ozawa and show that his party was led by the Prime Minister. Although the choice of 'anti-Ozawa' group member' Edano Yukio as head of the GRU may have been influenced by the need for Hatoyama to demonstrate his leadership strength prior to the next Upper House elections, his presence was part of a growing influence of cabinet power (*The Mainichi Daily News*, 10 February 2010).

Such peak associations as Nippon Keidanren and *Keizai Dōyūkai* (Japan Association of Corporate Executives) have been vocal in their objections to government economic policies underscoring that, though the iron triangle may remain as a general statement of business and government configuration, the nature of the ties that bind have changed. Although Keidanren's resumption of soliciting political donations was, ostensibly at least, intended as a means to exercise greater influence in shaping government policy, the emphasis was to promote the whole economy and society and not more narrow interests, thereby setting it apart from former practises (Furukawa 2004). In the main, funding would be given directly to the party executive rather than the former practise of direct distribution to party members, thereby strengthening central 'authority' (*kengen*) in inter-party politics (*Nihon Keizai Shimbun*, 13 May 2003). Importantly, its chairman, Okuda Hiroshi, argued that donations were envisaged as a way of underpinning the forging of a relationship with policy makers based on 'cooperation [and] sometimes through confrontation' (Okonogi 2003). Quick to reassure that this was not a ploy to prevent the emergence of a two-party system, he added that if 'the party [LDP] fails to deliver on its platform or promises, there will naturally emerge calls for giving both votes and money to other parties' (Okonogi 2003).

Although a top executive of the internationally competitive Toyota Motor Corporation, a member of the Council on Economic and Fiscal Policy and an advocate of market liberalization, Okuda would seem not to carry enough sway in Keidanren to convert reform naysayers. A bill drafted by the Fair Trade Commission to revise the Anti-Monopoly Law and so invigorate competition was met with vigorous opposition from Keidanren on the argument that the ministries themselves should first clean up their own improper practises. The Japanese media and others, though, found this little more than a ploy to divert attention from the lobby group's own vested interests. In unambiguous terms, the *Asahi Shimbun* lambasted the business community as a whole for its continued role in fettering competition in Japan's flagging economy.

> Japan's industrial community is still awash with collusive relations between bureaucrats unwilling to lose their regulatory control over industries, symbolized by administrative guidance, and businesses tethered by protectionist restrictions. This back-scratching climate continues to foster anti-competitive practices like cartels and bid-rigging.
>
> (*Asahi New Service*, 23 April 2004)

It comes as no surprise that pork barrel politics remain a reality in Japan and that cosseted relationships between firms and government officials continue to influence political decision making. Less clear, though, is how much has changed.

Conclusion

In an article entitled 'Why Japan Keeps Failing', *The Economist* declared that Japan's 'structural change is on hold' and that under Prime Minister Fukuda Yasuo, 'power has flowed back to the factions and the party gerontocrats' (*The Economist*, 23 February 2008). To be sure, navigating legislation through the Democratic Party of Japan-controlled upper house and the turmoil of Abe's sudden side exit from power would never be easy for the LDP. It was hoped that a more sure and steady hand would be found in Fukuda eschewing radical change and, that having failed, stronger stewardship under Asō. Some hoped that the attitude of 'steady on' and 'business as usual' would buy time for the LDP to regroup. Although structural change in the period between Koizumi and Hatoyama was on hold, it is important to remember that the impetus for change comes from before Koizumi's arrival and is linked with dynamics that will drag Japan along. To be sure, actors play their role and can slow the rate of change but Japan has moved from its developmental state to something new and, in turn, the boundary of the business and government relationship has been reinscribed.

As an organic entity, the relationship is redefined as it moves along the path of change in the political and economic framework and, larger, the evolution of the nation itself. In this multifaceted construct, some boundaries are essentially static and resistant to change, potentially leading to institutional sclerosis. As Johnson has argued in his historical examination, the business and government relationship in Japan is evolutionary in nature. To be sure, though, continuities do remain. Despite reform, pork barrel politics is not gone but neither its current presence nor its long-standing existence is unique to Japan. That said, the comparative proximity of business and government in their interaction and their ability to reinscribe modes of operation speaks to the relationship's receptiveness to change. Johnson emphasizes the nexus point between the exogenous factors of the politico-economic construct and its link to the underlining developmentalist drive of the nation; Samuels, on the other hand, draws our attention to the inner mechanism of the relationship itself. The shifting boundary here is the on-going negotiation of interaction located within the framework of the original 'compact' and guided by the premise of reciprocity. For Johnson, the evolution of the relationship has been traced from the perspective of 'control and latitude' while Samuels speaks of 'reciprocal consent'. Although emphasizing different aspects of business and government interaction, both authors see the relationship in terms of boundaries that shift.

At this stage, then, the signs indicate that more than one mode of interaction may emerge. The diversity of voices within the business community and the differences between industries suggest that a pluralistic depiction may better capture developments. If business heeded government in the early post-war years because such ministries as MITI could offer protection from international competitors and had greater access to information, the boundaries that defined that mode of interaction have changed only for small and medium-sized enterprises. Large internationally competitive firms operate with government as, comparatively speaking, 'equal' partners. Although the role of MITI (and that of METI) has altered dramatically since Johnson's era of the iron triangle, and business now exercises greater latitude, these actors remain entwined in the fabric of corporate Japan. Within this framework they exercise the degrees of latitude afforded to them in pursuit of their aims. Corruption and abuse of privileged access to decision makers will remain, but such activities do not belie the fundamental shifts in the boundaries that have fostered change in the relationship.

Notes

1 The Important Industries Control Law, among others, helped *zaibatsu* gain dominant positions within numerous industries which later came under the scrutiny of Supreme Commander of the Allied Powers (SCAP). In 1947 the Anti-Monopoly Law and the Deconcentration Law were passed, the former prohibiting the formation of cartels and the latter dissolving *zaibatsu* holding structures.
2 Koizumi's era follows the economic turmoil of the 1990s and much of his attention was devoted to addressing the associated issues. However, the primary concern here is his political reforms and their implications for government's relationship with business. For detailed discussions on his economic and fiscal initiatives, see Muramatsu and Okuno (2002) and Amyx (2004). For more on the '55 System' see the comprehensive five volume series of Kitamura *et al.* (2003).
3 Note that the authors do not have comparative statistics for the 1970s to the 1990s regarding the category of *wataridori*.

References

Abe, Shinzō (2005) 'Ōkii na kaikaku no tame ni wa tōnai tasūha keisei mo hitsuyō da', *Chūō Kōron*, 9: 104–09.

Amyx, Jennifer A. (2004) *Japan's Financial Crisis: institutional rigidity and reluctant change*, Princeton: Princeton University Press.

Aoki, Masahiko (1988) *Information, Incentives, and Bargaining in the Japanese Economy*, Cambridge and New York: Cambridge University Press.

Arase, David (2009) 'Japan in 2008: a prelude to change?', *Asian Survey*, 49, 5: 107–19.

Colignon, Richard, and Usui, Chikako (2001) 'The resilience of Japan's iron triangle: amakudari', *Asian Survey*, 41, 5: 865–95.

Curtis, Gerald L. (2006) 'Assessing the new Abe administration in Japan', New York: Centre on Japanese Economy and Business, Columbia Business School, 1–15. Online. Available: http://digitalcommons.libraries.columbia.edu/japan_event/45 (accessed 5 May 2007).

Estevez-Abe, Margarita (2006) 'Japan's shift toward a Westminster system', *Asian Survey*, 46, 4: 632–65.

Fukao, Mitsuhiro (2002) '1980 nendai kōhan no shisan kakaku baburu hassei to 90 nendai no fukyō no genin – kinyū shisutemu no kinō fuan no kenten kara', in Muramatsu Michio and Okuno Masahiro (eds) *Heisei Baburu no Kenkyū: baburu no hassei to sono haikei kōzō*, Vol I, Tokyo: Tōyō Keizai Shimpōsha, pp. 87–126.

Furukawa, Takahisa (2004) 'Keidanren no sōshikiteki seiji kenkin saikai: sono nerai wa nani ka?' *Sekai*, 4: 133–40.

George Mulgan, Aurelia (2010) 'Will Japan's new economic growth strategy deliver?', 4 February. Online. Available: http://search.japantimes.co.jp/cgi-bin/nn20100115a5.html (accessed 15 February 2010).

Grimes, William W. (2009) 'Japan, the global financial crisis, and the stability of East Asia', in Ashley J. Tellis, Andrew Marble, and Travis Tanner (eds), *Strategic Asia 2009–2010: economic meltdown and geopolitical stability*, Washington: The National Bureau of Asian Research, pp. 105–29.

Harris, Tobias and Murphy, Colum (2009) 'Can the DPJ bring democracy to Japan?', *Far Eastern Economic Review*, July/August: 8–14.

Hatakeyama, Noboru (2003) 'Nihon Mexico jiyū bōeki kōshō ketsuretsu senryaku no fuzai', *Chūō Kōron*, 12: 50–55.

Hatch, Walter, and Yamamura, Kozo (1996) *Asia in Japan's Embrace: building a regional production alliance*, Cambridge: Cambridge University Press.

Johnson, Chalmers (1982) *MITI and the Japanese Miracle: the growth of industrial policy, 1925–1975*, Stanford: Stanford University Press.

Kamikawa, Ryūnoshin (2002) 'Baburu keizai to Nihon ginkō no dokuritsusei', in Muramatsu Michio and Okuno Masahiro (eds) *Heisei Baburu No Kenkyū: baburu no hassei to sono haikei kōzō*, Vol I, Tokyo: Tōyō Keizai Shimpōsha, pp. 127–94.

Katz, Richard (2010) 'Japan's fake economic reforms: why Tokyo could use a little more creative destruction', *Foreign Policy*, 8 January. Online. Available: http://www.foreignpolicy.com/articles/2010/01/08/japans_economic_reforms (accessed 10 February 2010).

Katz, Richard, and Ennis, Peter (2007) 'How able is Abe?' *Foreign Affairs*, 86, 2: 75–91.

Kitamura, Kimihiko, Ito Daiichi, Uji Toshihiko, Uchida Mitsuru, Ōhashi Toyohiko, Kanazashi Masao and Satake Goroku. (eds) (2003) *55 Nen Taisei Zenki no Seitō Seiji*, Vol I–V, Tokyo: Daiichi Hōki Kabushiki Kaisha.

Kohno, Masaru (2003) 'A changing Ministry of International Trade and Industry', in Jennifer Amyx and Peter Drysdale (eds) *Japanese Governance: beyond Japan Inc.*, London: RoutledgeCurzon, pp. 96–112.

Koll, Jesper (2006) 'Japan turns its back on reform', *Far Eastern Economic Review*, September, 33–36.

Lincoln, James R. and Gerlach, Michael L. (2004) *Japan's Network Economy: structure, persistence, and change*, Cambridge: Cambridge University Press.

Mainichi Daily News, 'Anti-Ozawa group member Edano appointed head of Government Revitalization Unit', 10 February 2010. Online. Available: http://mdn.mainichi.jp/mdn-news/news/20100210p2a00m0na018000c.html (accessed 15 February 2010).

McCormack, Gavan (2002) 'Breaking the iron triangle', *New Left Review*, 13: 5–23.

Moffett, Sebastian (2004) 'A premium on postal reform', *Far Eastern Economic Review*, October, 12–13.

Muramatsu, Michio and Okuno, Mashiro (2002) *Heisei Bubble no Kenkyū: baburu no hassei to sono haikei kōzō*, Vol I and II, Tokyo: Tōyō Keizai Shin Shuppankai.

Murphy, R. Taggart (2009) 'The Financial Crisis and the Tectonic Shifts in the US-Japan Relationship', *The Asia-Pacific Journal: Japan Focus*, 32, 2. Online. Available: http://www.japanfocus.org/-R_Taggart-Murphy/3200 (accessed 10 February 2010).

Okazaki, Tetsuji (2001) 'The government-firm relationship in post-war Japan: the success and failure of bureau pluralism' in Joseph E. Stiglitz and Shahid Yusuf (eds), *Rethinking the East Asia Miracle*, New York: Oxford University Press, pp. 323–42.

Okonogi, Kiyoshi (2003) 'Hiroshi Okuda', *Asahi News Service*, 28 August.

Pempel, T.J. (2000) *Regime Shift: comparative dynamics of the Japanese political economy*, Ithaca: Cornell University Press.

Sakiyama, Hiroshi (2005) 'Seijibu kisha ga mita Koizumi seiji: nani ga kawatta no ka?' *Sekai*, 9: 171–77.

Samuels, Richard J. (1987) *The Business of the Japanese State: energy markets in comparative and historical perspective*, Ithaca New York: Cornell University Press.

—— (2003) *Machiavelli's Children: leaders and their legacies in Italy and Japan*, Ithaca New York: Cornell University Press.

Stockwin, J.A. (2007) 'From Koizumi to Abe: same bed, different dreams?' *Japanese Studies*, 27, 3: 223–30.

Tsujinaka, Yutaka (1988) *Rieki Shūdan*, Tokyo: University of Tokyo Press.

Vogel, Steven K. (2006) *Japan Remodeled: how government and industry are reforming Japanese capitalism*, Ithaca: Cornell University Press.

Yoshimatsu, Hidetaka (2005) 'Japan's Keidanren and Free Trade Agreements: societal interests and trade policy', *Asian Survey*, 45, 2: 258–78.

9 Adjusting the boundaries between Keidanren and labour unions in Japan

A critical reappraisal

Hasegawa Harukiyo

During the Koizumi Junichirō administration (2001–06), the Japanese government implemented structural economic reforms that were heavily influenced by neoliberal ideology. The main impact of those reforms has been a reduction in welfare provision, privatization of public enterprises, deregulation, a lower level of state protection for employees and the implementation of measures aimed at adjusting the boundaries[1] between the state and the market. This neoliberal trend reflected the growing influence of the Japan Business Federation, Nippon Keidanren (hereafter Keidanren), over government policy. The reforms have pushed the boundaries of capital and labour into confrontations across Japan, in the form of struggles between companies/management associations and workers/labour unions. The boundaries of capital have continued to expand under the momentum of the Koizumi-era reforms, even after Prime Minister Asō Taro's inauguration in September 2008 and the change of governing party to the DPJ (Democratic Party of Japan) in September 2009. A significant number of Japanese employees still face declining working conditions, in some cases even approaching levels of relative poverty, a measure of income inequality defined by the Organization of Economic Cooperation and Development (OECD) (OECD 2007). In response to the ongoing reinscription of labour boundaries and what some observers regard as the concomitant threat posed to democracy[2] in Japan, some new countervailing forces have emerged from civil society seeking restitution of labour rights, and it may be argued that the sea change in the political *status quo* represented by the DPJ victory also reflects this new area of public concern. This chapter aims to provide an explanation of the confrontational relationship between management and worker/labour unions within a capitalist society in the context of the boundaries of capital and labour. The first section provides a historical overview of the dynamics of these boundaries throughout the development of post-war Japanese capitalism. This is followed in section 2 with an analysis of the expanding boundaries of capital in scope and intensity during the last two decades. Section 3 moves on to examine the close connection between Keidanren and Japanese political parties, which underlines the strength of the boundaries of capital. Section 4 then turns to labour's boundary expansion, which is followed by an examination of the boundaries of labour and labour unions in section 5. Section 6 examines the relationship between labour unions and political parties. The final section assesses the dynamics between capital and labour in terms of legislative, economic and corporate boundaries. This chapter argues that these boundaries are linked to the future status of democracy in Japan, with far-reaching consequences for ordinary citizens.

1. Boundaries between capital and labour: Japanese post-war capitalism and the characteristics of boundaries

The history of capitalism has been dominated by the dynamic interplay of liberalism and democracy. Liberalism as an ideology has tended to be fostered by the interests of capital, while the cause of promoting democracy has been consistently championed by labour. These ideologies and interests reflect how boundaries are defined through modern capitalist development. Yet, throughout the emergence of modern industrial societies, these boundaries have not necessarily been at odds with each other. The interdependence and complementarities of liberalism and democracy also apply to capital and labour. When capitalist development is considered as a nexus of competing and complementary boundaries, the social outcome of modern industrial society has depended on the dynamic strengths and weaknesses of the boundaries demarcating the interests of capital and labour. Historically, social turmoil emerged in societies where the dynamic equilibrium between these boundaries has tipped excessively towards the interests of either capital or labour.

Figure 9.1 provides a schematic view of the development of civil society under capitalism and shows that the dynamic between capital/liberalism and labour/democracy shifts like a pendulum, determining the boundaries of these two major social interest groups. Civil society, within the framework of the competing but complementary ideologies of capital and labour, develops as the role of the state

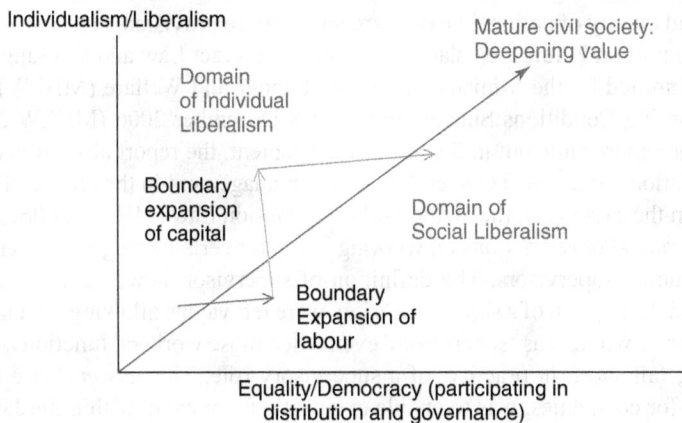

Figure 9.1 Development of civil society under capitalism

Source: author

is reduced and democracy is diffused and embedded among various institutions and practices within society. This serves to enable liberal values. As liberalism and democracy develop in tandem, the majority of citizens in advanced industrial democracies ideally should be able to live free from economic, political and social fear (Bauman 2004).

In Japan, the boundaries of labour expanded as important advances for workers were achieved in the immediate post-war decade (1945–55). During this period, large-scale strikes took place on a regular basis and the advancement of labour rights played a central role in domestic politics (Hasegawa 1993). The second stage (1960–73) witnessed rapid economic growth that averaged annually 10.6 per cent. During this time, capital and labour tended to compromise, working to raise their respective shares of the national pie through collaboration (Hasegawa 1993). Boundaries were still unsettled at this time, but both labour and management sought to avoid confrontation in the common interest of rapid economic growth. The third stage (1973–85) was a period of transition before the economic slowdown. The adjustment of boundaries became a pressing issue for both labour and management as the rate of economic growth dropped to only 3–4 per cent, but capital interests (thus, management) gained the upper hand.

Since the 1990s, the boundaries of labour have been on the defensive, under pressure from an intensely individualistic and competitive form of liberalism generally known as neoliberalism. The reforms of the Thatcher government in Britain, which spearheaded the rise of the neoliberal agenda, appeared in Japan with a time lag of 10–15 years. The erosion of the boundaries of labour in Japan was already evident in a 1995 report from Nikkeiren, the Japan Federation of Employers' Associations (Nikkeiren 1995), but further large-scale reforms began with the Koizumi administration in 2001, and the momentum of these policies persists (Nippon Keidanren 2008).

These shifts in boundaries came to be reflected in various official reports and indicators measuring the quality of life, level of average income as well as pensions, and quality of national health care and welfare provision. A recent example is the 'Report on Future Legislation of Labour Contract Law and Working Hours Law' submitted by the Ministry of Health, Labour and Welfare (MHLW) at the 70th Working Conditions Subcommittee on 8 December 2006 (MHLW 2006a). While the report came out in favour of management, the report also observed the confrontational relations between labour and management in the House of Councillors. In the same year, the White-collar Exemption Law (MHLW 2006c) called for the removal of restrictions on working hours for certain categories of employees, including supervisors. The definition of supervisor, however, and even the scope and description of a supervisor's job, were left vague, allowing management to categorize workers as 'supervisors' even when those workers' functions, by any measure, fall short, in practice, of a supervisory role. The *raison d'être* behind this bill, for companies, was to enable expectations (or even, within the Japanese context, obligations) of longer hours from employees. The social consequences of such pressures would seem to have included a higher risk of poor health, even in extreme cases *karōshi* (death from overwork), and declining birth rates (Japan

Institute for Social and Economic Affairs 2008). All in all, the vagueness of the bill principally opens the whole legislation to an interpretation favourable to the interests of capital.

Japan ratified the International Labour Convention No. 100 (equal pay for work of equal value) in 1967, but it has not yet ratified the International Labour Convention No. 175 (the part-time labour law). This has allowed management to continue to apply lower wages for part-time labour. The Equal Employment Opportunity Law established in 1985 no longer makes direct discrimination an option, but indirect discrimination continues in the manipulation of human resource management strategies. As suggested earlier, struggles concerned with the boundaries of capital and labour are now widespread, though frequently the results, via legal process, tend to favour corporate rather than employees' or citizens' interests.

The bubble economy, which followed the Plaza Accord[3] and the increased valuation of the Japanese yen in 1985, triggered the full-scale globalization of Japanese companies. Japanese capitalism was forced to undergo significant structural changes, which entailed a 'hollowing out' of the economy. Japan maintained an annual economic growth average of 4.8 per cent from 1985 to 1990 (Ministry of Internal Affairs and Communications, MIAC 2008b), but capital export (in the form of foreign direct investment, or FDI) increased remarkably, and the overseas production rates of major Japanese manufacturers rose to 29.8 per cent of their total production by 2003 (METI 2004). In particular, Japanese FDI focused upon China, where the number of Japanese companies in operation reached over 22,000 in 2005 (Inagaki 2006). Globalization has led to changes to both corporate management and employment systems. The boundaries between capital and labour have extended beyond the boundaries of the Japanese territorial state, but within Japan, the result has been to push back the boundary of labour that workers had previously attained. The strategy used by large corporations, as supported by Keidanren, was to weaken the labour unions and decrease labour costs by increasing the proportion of non-regular employees,[4] such as part-time or temporary workers, agency workers and contract workers, to as much as 30 per cent of the entire workforce. The result of this targeted policy has been that the boundaries (and influence) of capital have expanded and intensified from the late 1990s to the present day (2009), giving more flexibility to large corporations; however, this has created difficulties for small and medium-sized enterprises, as their business with large corporations declined as those corporations moved overseas. In practice, as seen in the section on corporate boundaries, increases have been observed in the number of non-regular workers, working hours and overtime hours, depreciating working conditions and living standards for well over half of all employees in a country with the world's second largest economy (Labour Research Council 2008). The increased expansion of capital's boundaries and intensity of its influence are also reflected in cutbacks in social security and welfare provision and the growing number of working poor, that is, employees living on the margins of official standards of poverty (*Kyoto Shimbun*, 18 May 2006).

2. Expanding the boundary of capital: domain expansion and intensification

The expansion of capital's boundaries takes place in two ways: through expanding its domain or intensifying its influence. Capital's domain can be expanded at the macro (or government) level (Nippon Keidanren 2008), while its influence can be intensified at the micro (or company) level (Hasegawa 2005). At both levels, the boundary of capital can be expanded through the promotion and prevalence of neoliberal ideology, the introduction of new systems, or changes and reforms in existing systems. The agent pushing these activities forward in Japan is Keidanren, a federation of large corporations that are remarkably open about their objectives and strategies. The 2008 'Report of the Management Labour Policy Committee', released in December 2007 (Nippon Keidanren 2007), indicates the strategies that corporations have for expanding the boundaries of capital. However, we should note that the boundaries of capital here are limited to those of large corporations. The boundaries of small- and medium-sized enterprises remain unchanged, as the primary beneficiaries of Keidanren's strategy are its 1300 member companies at the heart of corporate Japan.

Chapter 1 of Keidanren's report identifies the two main trends of the Japanese economy: globalization and a rapidly ageing society with a low birth rate and overall population decrease. To companies, these changes mean tougher competition and potential labour shortages. For these reasons, Keidanren is calling for reforms to be carried out at the macro (government) level, with two main goals: (1) raising competitiveness through the improvement of productivity; and (2) fostering a change in society so that all members are able to participate in labour. Achieving the first goal requires an emphasis on innovation and an increase in productivity in the service sector. For the second goal, Keidanren aims to widen the participation in the labour force of youth, women and older people, in order to maximize the efficient utilization of labour. The federation proposes the following specific measures at the macro (government) level:

(1) Improving the operation of the external labour market. This will have a particular focus on employment issues relating to youth, women and older people, and will include: (a) strengthening the supply–demand adjustment function; (b) developing policies through cooperation with the government and private sector to improve vocational skills; and (c) cooperation in executing plans such as the 'job card plan', which would specify the skills/knowledge of each potential worker.
(2) Facilitating legislation and infrastructure to allow diverse working styles. This includes: (a) plans for labour management allowing appropriate and diversified employment modes; (b) plans for systems allowing styles of work that are self-determined and self-sustaining; and (c) measures to help families with young children.
(3) Pushing up the bottom line of productivity. This includes (a) reviewing the minimum wage system; (b) boosting the vitality of regional economies

through consolidation and development of various government policies, as well as the introduction of the regional (or *Dō-Shū*) system (see Chapter 7); and (c) taking measures to support management of small and middle-sized businesses. These businesses supply 70 per cent of Japan's employment, but are faced with a difficult economic situation; therefore, targeted measures to support them are essential. Keidanren suggests, for example, promoting investment in equipment and human resources, and facilitating smooth business succession.

Once Keidanren names these macro-level goals, it goes on to list goals on the micro-(company) level. In seeking to revive the economy, the core goal on this level should be to restructure the Japanese-style employment system (Nippon Keidanren 2007). Keidanren suggests that companies take the following specific steps:

(1) Change the focus from recruiting new graduates to recruiting and utilizing a diverse range of 'human resources'. This includes promoting recruitment throughout the year (not just at times coinciding with university graduations) and mid-career recruitment, and active utilization of female and older workers.
(2) Maintain long-term employment as the fundamental practice, but utilize the external labour market as well. Keidanren promotes long-term employment in support of management that stresses human dignity. At the same time, companies can consider an employee's work–life balance or needs, and utilize temporary employees, part-time employees and agency workers.
(3) Shift from a seniority wage system to one based on tasks, roles and contributions.
(4) Secure labour–management relations within the company and improve communications. In other words, good labour–management relations within the company should be firmly maintained.

Further, as a means to readjust the dynamics between capital and labour with a view to expanding capital's boundaries, Keidanren's 2007 report proposes basic management policies, particularly in preparation for labour–management negotiations and discussions. Keidanren proposes that companies manage and control the cost of labour based on productivity, and restructure wage and assessment systems, by:

• Ensuring that the total cost of labour is in line with productivity. (As decisions on the cost of labour are still based on the company's ability to pay wages, efforts to increase added value will be an issue for both labour and management)
• Providing for an open wage system. (This entails shifting to a wage system based on tasks, roles and contributions. Fixed wages for a job or seniority are against the trends of a flexible labour market and advanced industrial structures)

- Establishing transparent and reasonable assessment systems for human resources. (Such systems ensure that an individual's treatment matches the assessments of that individual's performance and contributions)
- Offering education to develop a highly skilled workforce, and encouraging the transfer of skills and expertise. (Supply training to nurture self-reliant workers, while securing and recruiting a workforce with practical skills)
- The three key points that influence a company's decisions on working conditions (including wages) are: tougher global competition, relentless practice of total labour cost management and the goal of sustaining steady economic growth.

Finally, Keidanren asserts that companies can aim to help workers realize a good work-life balance in order to improve productivity, secure a good workforce, and promote a fulfilling life for the people (Nippon Keidanren 2007), by taking the following steps:

- Promoting efficient working styles. The emphasis should be on work results. This system can facilitate productivity by encouraging workers to take effective breaks, including scheduled annual paid holidays.
- Promoting flexible working styles. Such working styles can depart from fixed hours or fixed workplaces, including short-time work, 'teleworking' and working from home.
- Having senior management take on the crucial role of facilitating cooperation between labour and management to help employees realize a good work-life balance.

Yet, beneath Keidanren's rhetoric, the key issues remain: (1) the efficient use of the workforce; (2) the search for a growth-driven society; and (3) the tacit acceptance of social fragmentation. On the whole, these growth-driven strategies are still based on the typical linear economic growth paradigm in line with the logic of capital, which constantly seeks to self-increase, pushing forward the boundaries of capital in both scope and intensity. The policy also reflects the domestic effects of the logic of capital derived from the globalization of Japanese business and the consequences of an ageing society within Japan. If continued, these may result in deepening the economic and social gulf between those who benefit from the logic of capital and those left behind, unprotected by the countervailing power of democracy (Tachibanaki 2006; Kumazawa 2007; Goto *et al.* 2007).

3. Keidanren and political parties

To expand the boundaries of capital, Japan's corporate giants make substantial annual financial donations to Keidanren. Until 1993, the large sums of money donated (approximately JPY10 billion in total) were allocated automatically to the governing Liberal Democratic Party (LDP) (*Akahata Shimbun*, 30 November 2003). This practice came to an abrupt end in 1994, following the corruption scandals that hit LDP politicians in cases involving companies such as Tokyo Sagawa Kyubin, Recruit and Zenekon. These high-profile corruption cases led to a brief hiatus in the LDP's long post-war reign as well as corporate donations to Keidanren. Nevertheless, donations resumed in 2004 under a new allocation plan. This new method involves the allocation of money to political parties whose policies reflect those of Keidanren. This practice aimed to establish two stable, pro-business political parties, the LDP and the Democratic Party of Japan (DPJ). (Until late 2009, Japan remained a one-party democracy, and the initial intention of Keidanren to create two major parties had yet to be realized; whether the effect of the DPJ electoral victory in September 2009 will meet Keidanren's expectations has yet to be seen.)

Most of the donated money has been directed to the LDP via the People's Political Association (*Kokumin Seiji Kyōkai*) (Kabunushi Ombudsman 2004). LDP policies, which prioritize big businesses, promote a business-oriented government. One point of view runs that a close corporate–government relationship serving the interests of big corporations may be hard to square with the interests of ordinary citizens (*Asahi Shimbun*, 6 January 2008); the basic values of democracy may be at risk when the interests of small- and middle-sized businesses and ordinary citizens are compromised in the interests of corporate giants. It may be a question of democratic maturity; some observers remark that while formal electoral democracy is well established in Japan, its system of governance has strayed from democratic principles (*Asahi Shimbun*, 6 January 2008).

In this perspective, the ways in which large corporations exert influence on politics through Keidanren have arguably corroded the foundations of democracy. When a company's donation to the party in power is in some way linked to its profits (see Table 9.1), it is not altogether a social contribution. Should the company in question be under the influence of and accountable to social stakeholders, then a social case could be made, but the point is inevitably weakened where it involves corporations with appointed executives controlled by profit-motivated shareholders.

When Keidanren resumed the practice of serving as a mediator for political donations in 2004 (Kabunushi Ombudsman 2004), it reportedly offered JPY2.22 billion to the LDP, JPY60 million to the DPJ, and nothing at all to other parties (*Sankei Shimbun*, 24 August 2007). Large companies provide the donations to Keidanren, which subsequently assesses each party's policies. Quite simply, the political party with the most favourable policies for corporate interests receives the largest contribution (Kabunushi Ombudsman 2004). The LDP distributes these contributions to individual politicians. At the same time, the LDP seeks to cooperate with the bureaucracy to promote policies and implement laws in line with Keidanren interests. This practice has resulted in high-profile corruption cases at the Ministry of Defence (MOD) (2006), Green Resources Institute (2006), Yamada Yoko (2007) and national universities (2008).

Table 9.1 shows the correlation between munitions orders from the MOD and donations to the LDP. For example, Mitsubishi Heavy Industries obtained

Table 9.1 Munitions contracts with the Ministry of Defence, donations to the Liberal Democratic Party, and the number of former MOD officials employed by company (2006)

	Contract amounts (JPY billion)	Donations (JPY million)	Number of former MOD officials employed
Mitsubishi Heavy Industries	277.6	30	62
Kawasaki Heavy Industries	130.6	5	49
Mitsubishi Electric	117.7	18.2	98
NEC	83.1	18	40
IHI Marine United	44.6	N/A	16
Fujitsu	44.1	16.8	16
Toshiba	42.3	28.5	35
IHI (Ishikawajima-Harima Heavy Industries)	36.5	10.9	34
Komatsu	36.3	10	21
Fuji Heavy Industries	19.9	18	26
Hitachi	19.4	28.5	59
Nakagawa Bussan	14.8	N/A	N/A
NOC (Nippon Oil Corporation)	14.3	N/A	N/A
Daikin Industries	13.3	3	17
Cosmo Oil	13.1	N/A	2

Source: *Akahata Shimbun*, 28 October 2007. Online. Available at <http://www.jcp.or.jp/akahata/aik4/2006-02-19/2006021902_02_0.html> 9 August 2008

Note: Table produced based on materials from the Ministry of Defence and Reports on Political Funding and Expenditure. Donations indicate the amounts sent to the People's Political Association in 2006. Numbers of ex-official employees are as of April 2006, except the figure of Fujitsu (October 2005).

JPY277.6 billion worth of contracts (its donation to the LDP was JPY30 million). It appears that 62 former government officials of the MOD who had joined Mitsubishi Heavy Industries were mediators (see Table 9.1). The same situation applies in the case of Mitsubishi Electric; the company donated just JPY18.2 million, but won JPY117.7 billion worth of orders, facilitated by 98 former officials who had joined the company. There were 475 former officials employed in the defence industry in 2006, and the top 15 companies were awarded 70 per cent of the contracts (see Table 9.1). In this way, the collusion among Keidanren, the LDP and government officials expands the boundaries of capital, benefitting a particular group of corporations.

A bill to revise the Political Fund Control Law was passed on 1 December 2006, at a special committee meeting of the House of Representatives and the House of Councillors, by a majority of the committee members from both the governing and opposition parties, except the Japanese Communist Party (JCP) and Social Democratic Party (SDP). Although its purpose was to strengthen political ethics and revise the Public Office Election Law, it contained a provision to relax restrictions on political donations by foreign companies and other organizations. The bill allowed companies with foreign capital ratios of over 50 per cent to make political donations. As a result, major Keidanren member companies whose foreign capital rates exceed 50 per cent, such as Canon and Sony, may now make political donations (*Asahi Shimbun*, 11 May 2006). The new legislation thus potentially opens a route for foreign capital to influence Japanese domestic politics. Should this occur, far from strengthening political ethics, the Political Fund Control Law would serve to undermine democratic civil society and national sovereignty.

4. Boundary expansion for labour: domain expansion and intensification

The boundaries of labour are represented by labour unions in terms of their activities and values. In Japan, 10.14 million employees, or 18 per cent of the total workforce of 54.16 million, were unionized in 2006. Union membership is split into the following: 6.67 million members in Rengō (Japan Trade Union Confederation), 950,000 members in Zenrōren (National Confederation of Trade Unions), and 160,000 members in Zenrōkyō (National Trade Union Council) (MHLW 2006b). For labour interests, boundary expansion is effected by expansion in labour union organizations and countervailing movements in civil society. Boundary intensity is measured by the influence exerted by the unions and other forces, including political parties; such influence is manifested in the improvement of working and living conditions and the development of welfare provision, medical care and education for employees and ordinary citizens. In principle, labour unions work for the benefit of their members, but in reality the gains and losses of union campaigns take effect among both members and non-members at both corporate and national level, directly or indirectly. If unions succeed in raising wages and improving working conditions, such benefits will accrue also to non-union members in the same corporation. If industry-level improvements are achieved through the federation of unions, then with time such benefits will be shared by all member unions as well as non-union employees. Thus, the continued decline of union membership reduces their effect as a countervailing force, and this will affect not only union members, but also non-union members and ordinary citizens as well.

Bearing that in mind, in quantitative terms the boundaries of labour have been shrinking since the 1980s or earlier. The annual rate of unionization began to decline heavily after 1999, peaking in 2002 and reaching 18.1 per cent in 2008 (MHLW 2008c). This inevitably has a follow-on effect on working conditions, welfare provision, medical care and education for most employees (Labour Research Council 2008).

Table 9.2 lists the different employment types, showing the demarcation of the current boundaries of labour. Compared to the 2000 figures, 2008 shows a decrease in the proportion of regular staff and employees, and an increase in the number of non-regular employees (which include part-time or temporary workers, agency workers and contract workers). This indicates that a mechanism has been established for capital to secure cheap, non-regular workers in large quantities from diverse sources.

Table 9.2 Percentages of workers by employment type

Employment type	2006	2000
Regular staff/employees	67.2	74.2
Part-time/temporary workers	22.5	21.9
Agency workers	2.3	0.7
Contract workers and other non-regular workers	8.1	3.3

Source: The Ministry of Health, Labour and Welfare (MHLW) (2001 and 2007) *Rōdō Keizai no Bunseki*, Tokyo: MHLW.

5. Boundaries of labour and labour unions

As mentioned earlier, labour unions represent the organizational boundaries of labour, in the form of Rengō, Zenrōren and Zenrōkyō. This chapter does not analyze the last-named, but focuses on the first two major federations, which are more integrated national centres. While federated on an industry basis, most unions in Japan are company-based. Labour unions are also an integral part of the entire socio-economic system in Japan and interact organically in various ways. At times, however, even a top national union may be co-opted, as shown later in this section.

Rengō (Japan Trade Union Confederation)

When Rengō was founded in November 1989, it embraced 78 industrial unions and 8 million union members. By 2008, this figure had decreased to 52 unions and 6.7 million members (Rengō 2008). For the past two decades, in fact, Rengō has weakened as an organization, which has contributed to the shrinking of the boundaries of labour. Rengō sought to protect and expand the boundaries of labour, but has had little effect, if at all. Rengō's rhetoric is on a par with that of Keidanren; its mission is to 'protect all the people's employment and life' and to facilitate 'the scrutiny of management and to realize social fairness' (Rengō 2005). Policy agendas include preventing tax increases, reforming social security systems, enacting workers' protection laws, preventing unfavourable reform in regulations, eliminating socio-economic gaps, promoting equal treatment, protecting basic labour rights for workers in the public sector, and fostering the realization of fair globalization. Rengō has targeted the following issues:

-   alleviating the increasing stress at workplaces;
-   changing the government's strong market orientation;
-   increasing consumers' demands;
-   fostering conditions in which people can realize fulfilled lives;
-   moving away from a divided society;
-   creating a labour-centred welfare society;
-   providing jobs;
-   promoting fairness in wages and working hours;

- equal treatment;
- creating a safety net for industrial injuries, unemployment, sickness and old age;
- developing a recycling-based society, thereby sustaining the environment;
- developing a society based on citizen participation and decentralization of power;
- creating a society which may promote international cooperation and world peace;
- achieving solidarity in international labour activities;
- encouraging joint efforts among small and middle-sized company unions as they confront struggles;
- encouraging joint efforts among part-time workers as they confront struggles;
- demanding policies and social systems protecting employment and people's life;
- ensuring the existence of annuity insurance, medical insurance and employment insurance systems;
- addressing labour issues;
- promoting social security, job placement and skill training; and
- developing schemes to support childcare and care for elderly people (Rengō 2008).

Rengō has also been actively working on the following tasks:

- setting up strike organizations (through its central strike committee, strategy committee, expansion strategy committee, and joint struggle centres for middle and small-sized company unions or part-time workers);
- submitting union requests and establishing a target date to obtain the employer's response;
- organizing joint efforts among small and middle-sized company unions, and among part-time workers, for those faced with struggles;
- conducting year-long activities (including workplace inspections, consultation on labour issues, abolition of unpaid overtime hours, and activities relating to working hour reduction policy).

Even with these goals and activities, however, Rengō's success in checking the advance of capital's boundaries remains questionable.[5] There are several reasons for Rengō's uneven record as an effective labour union. First, it was established as an organization composed of company unions. Company unions by their very nature are restricted in their options as countervailing forces due to the logic of their role as part of the company. As the pressures of globalization intensify, tougher competition leads company logic to prioritize survival.

Nevertheless, new forces within Rengō have emerged to expand the boundaries of labour, as in the Rengō leadership election of 6 October 2005, for which there were two main contenders: Takagi Tsuyoshi of the Textile, Chemical, Food,

Commercial, Service and General Worker's Union, and Kamo Momoyo of the Japan Community Union Federation (JCUF). Takagi won the election, 323 to 107 (with 42 votes for other candidates). This was not, however, the landslide victory that it may at first seem. Kamo's JCUF has a membership of 3300, just 0.4 per cent the size of Takagi's organization, and yet Kamo obtained nearly one-third the number of votes that his opponent received. This indicates increasing support for Kamo's defiant stance on labour–management relations and reflects the voices of non-regular employees that are JCUF members (JCUF 2008). Not surprisingly, therefore, by October 2007, Takagi promised that he would tackle non-regular employment issues decisively. He expressed support for the three labour laws, including the Minimum Wage Law and the Labour Contract Law, on the condition of additional amendments. As for the proposed revision of the Labour Standards Law, he indicated that his response would be dependent on the outcome of the amendments for the Minimum Wage Law. The specific content of the Labour Contract Law is examined in Section 7, later on.

Zenrōren (National Confederation of Trade Unions) was founded on 21 November 1989 with a membership of 1.34 million. By 2006, this number had declined sharply to 710,000. Zenrōren's mission includes protecting workers' dignity as human beings, fighting for peace, democracy and social progress, independence from capital, independence from political parties, united action in achieving common goals, and acting a union that will fight for workers' rights. The organizational base is not at company level, but at the level of industrial unions and regional organizations (by prefecture) that accept individual membership. Zenrōren's prevailing principles are 'independence from capital', 'independence from political parties' and a 'united front based upon common demands' (Zenrōren 2008b).

Zenrōren's policies focus on securing big pay rises, establishing national standards for a minimum wage, reducing working hours, opposing rationalization, strengthening employment security, improving working women's positions and implementing international labour standards, including the International Labour Conventions (Zenrōren 2008a). Its activities include economic and political struggles, policy proposals, workers' education, workers' welfare, and the struggles of industrial unions based on workplaces, regional struggles and cooperation with political parties to realize common objectives. Zenrōren also works on the following:

–   independence from capital, the government and political parties;
–   thorough practice of democracy in trade unions;
–   democracy at workplaces;
–   eradication of unfair labour practices;
–   fully secured rights to organize for workers and labour unions, rights for collective bargaining and rights for collective action;
–   abolition of any discrimination due to status, race, nationality, etc.;
–   trade based on equality and reciprocity;
–   establishing economic democracy;
–   taxation for the people;

- democratic, efficient and fair government;
- establishing new international economic orders based on respect to national sovereignty; and
- preserving the global environment (Zenrōren 2008a).

Zenrōren negotiates with the government, management and management associations as a means to promote its policy and goals. In comparison with Rengō, Zenrōren is a labour union more inclined to fight for its principles, aiming to protect and expand the boundaries of labour through struggles rather than compromises.

6. Labour unions and political parties

Given the nexus among Keidanren, the LDP and government officials that has to date protected and expanded the boundaries of capital, what is the situation on the labour side of the fence? Have they forged any comparable political alliances or established any kind of relationship with existing parties? To some extent, this question is ideological; the relations of capital are forged through money and interests, but on the labour side, relationships are based on principles and shared values.

Rengō is now connected with the DPJ, but in the 1989 election won 11 seats in the upper house for its own candidates (*Rengō-no-kai*); however, all lost their seats in the 1992 election. In 1993, the Democratic Reform 'Rengō' Party was formed, which was integrated into the DPJ in 1998. Since then, Rengō has become the largest supporter of the DPJ, although some Rengō unions support New Kōmeitō or the Social Democratic Party (SDP). In 2005, Maehara Seiji, the then leader of the DPJ, called for a review of the party's relationship with Rengō due to its negative image and declining membership (*Kyōdō Tsūshin*, 10 October 2005). Maehara is no longer leader, but holds a ministerial post and is still an ideological influence on the party; he favours revision of the Japanese Constitution, advocates overseas deployment of the Japanese Self-Defence Forces and views China as a threat – positions normally associated with far right politics (Maehara 2008).

In 2006, Ozawa Ichirō took over the DPJ leadership and restored the party's relationship with Rengō (Rengō 2006). Ozawa was originally a powerful figure within the ruling LDP, working for stronger links between corporate interests and Rengō. Although the DPJ has teamed up with Rengō, its biggest supporter at election time, the DPJ is a political party more than willing to compromise with the logic of capital, as illustrated by the receipt of Keidanren funds, as discussed earlier. Since the DPJ's victory in the 2007 upper house elections, the party has had a positive influence in promoting democracy and Rengō policies, and its resistance to the ruling LDP in the House of Councillors is said to have played an important role in the resignation of Prime Minister Fukuda Yasuo in September 2008 (Fukuda 2008).

While Rengō has been affiliated with the DPJ, Zenrōren has maintained strong ties with the Japanese Communist Party (JCP). The foundation of their relationship lies in a common ethos of opposition to the expansion of capital's boundaries.

Zenrōren does not envisage much improvement in working conditions through compromise; the JCP has a similar expectation over social reform. Such principles and shared perspectives derive from a commitment to Marxism (Japanese Communist Party 2008). In Japan, Marxist ideology receded in the 1980s with the emergence of neoliberal ideology, and the General Council of Trade Unions of Japan (Sohyo) and the Japan Socialist Party (JSP) have gradually weakened their organizational foundation. Sohyo in fact dissolved in 1989 and merged with right-wing union federations to form Rengo in the same year. The JSP also disbanded in 1996, their members being absorbed into the SDP and DPJ.

Thus, its uncompromising attitude and collaboration with the JCP have made Zenrōren Japan's only radically countervailing union force. However, Zenrōren has only a small influence on society and on its own has been unable to stem the spread of neoliberalism under the Koizumi and successive governments.

After the dissolution of the JSP in 1996, the SDP was established in the same year. The SDP has since cooperated with Zenrōren and the JCP in certain areas to maintain the clearly demarcated boundaries of labour.

Table 9.3 shows party support for labour legislation. The LDP, New Kōmeitō and DPJ have consistently supported measures that allow for the expansion of capital's boundaries. The SDP and JCP have opposed some of these measures.

7. Dynamics between capital and labour

Legislative boundaries

In a situation where labour's field of action is becoming increasingly limited, attention needs to be paid to the venues of campaign and conflict at the capital–labour boundary. On 28 November 2007, the Labour Contract Law, which determines the conditions of work, was passed by the House of Councillors with the approval of three parties: the LDP, New Kōmeitō and the DPJ (*Yomiuri Shimbun*, 28 November 2008). The law, in its entirety, is relatively short, consisting of only five chapters, but its passage was extremely controversial. Prior to the vote, heated discussions took place in the MHLW Committee of the House. The LDP and New Kōmeitō, and even the DPJ and Rengō, supported this law, while the JCP, SDP and Zenrōren opposed it. It has yet to be seen whether this legislation will in effect favour one side or the other of the labour–capital duality.

However, there are some pointers as to likelihood. First, the law may contribute to demolishing collective labour–management relations, which could favour capital. The Labour Contract Law was devised in response to increasing labour–management conflicts deriving from divergent perspectives on the nature of employment. It replaced the Labour Standards Law, management infringements of which had instigated a number of the conflicts; although it could be argued that they were thus essentially management issues, under the new law they are considered on an individual basis. Article 10 of the law was also introduced retroactively to settle existing labour conflicts, a *post hoc* intervention which some have argued is arbitrary. A potential point of contest also exists in an inconsistency between Articles

Table 9.3 Japanese political parties' attitude to legislation regarding labour laws

Name of laws	Liberal Democratic Party (LDP)	New Komeito	Democratic Party of Japan (DPJ)	Social Democratic Party (SDP)	Japanese Communist Party (JCP)
Revision of Labour Standards Law (1998: Introduced discretionary labour system and modified working schedule system.)	Y	Y	Y	Y	N
Revision of Manpower Dispatching Business Law (1999: Dispatched work liberalized in principle.)	Y	Y	Y	Y	N
Amendment of Employment Measures Law (2001: Promoting organizational restructuring in the name of support formid-carrier employment shifts.)	Y	Y	Y	N	N
Amendment of the Labour Standards Law (2003: Expanding the temporary employment system and relaxing limitations to the discretionary labour system.)	Y	Y	Y	N	N
Amendment of the Manpower Dispatching Business Law and Public Employment Security Law (2003: Increased the agent work done in the manufacturing sector.)	Y	Y	N	N	N
Amendment of the Labour Safe Sanitation Act (2005: Relaxed the restrictions on total annual working hours and overtime work.)	Y	Y	Y	Y	N
Labour Contract Law (2007: Effective from 1 March 2008.)	Y	Y	Y	N	N
Minimum Wage Law (2007)	Y	Y	Y	Y	N

Source: *Akahata Shimbun*, 21 February 2007

1 and 10, whereby Article 1 insists on contracts, but Article 10 disregards them. Further, Article 4 states that contract terms should be 'confirmed in writing wherever possible', implying that not all contracts are expected to be set out in writing. Implementing this article in a society such as Japan, where people have relatively little experience with written contracts compared to the West, could lead to verbal confirmations being accepted as normal practice, undermining the validity of written contracts themselves. There is also a real risk that workplace regulations may equally come to be seen as terms of contract, subject to change at any moment under the terms of Article 10. A pessimistic view of the potential effect of this law, then, is that working conditions may well deteriorate. There are reasons, therefore, to suspect that the new law may operate more in the interests of corporate capital than labour (Labour Contract Law 2007).

For the Labour Contract Law to be an agent of the extension of labour boundaries, on the premise that labour–management relations are changing from the collective to the individual, then Article 10 would need to reflect terms more favourable to employees. The JCP, Zenrōren and SDP alone, however, would not have sufficient influence to revise the law without some shift in DPJ thinking. Although some DPJ parliamentarians are known to sympathize with the SDP and JCP, they will no doubt follow the party line in voting and seek a compromise with the logic of capital under the influence of Keidanren; DPJ voting patterns tend to show a proclivity towards such a procedure (see Table 9.3). The result tends to be that the DPJ ends up helping to make bills and systems that push back labour boundaries and the party's support for the new legislation underscores this tendency.

Economic boundaries

The economic landscape over the past two decades has been characterized by an expansion of the boundaries of capital. For employees, this has meant lower wages, declining incomes and longer, intensified working hours. The expansion in the boundaries of capital has been legitimized in the name of 'reforms' to existing labour laws, which have resulted in a steady rise in the number of non-regular employees earning significantly less than regular employees and with less secure job tenure.

According to the MIAC, the number of non-regular employees in 2007 accounted for 35.5 per cent of the total workforce; compared to 20 years ago, there are now twice the number of female non-regular employees, and 2.5 times the number of male non-regular employees (MIAC 2008a), accounting for 19.9 per cent of working men and 55.2 per cent of working women.

Employees under the age of 35 account for 33.6 per cent of the non-regular workforce. By industry sector, the figures are: food/beverages/hotel (32.3 per cent), wholesale and retail (27.1 per cent), medical/welfare (23.3 per cent). The geographical distribution by prefecture is: Okinawa (40.7 per cent), Kyoto (40.0 per cent) and Osaka (38.6 per cent). The detailed figures for non-regular employees are: part-time workers, 8,850,000; casual or temporary workers, or employees taking on a second job (classed as *arbeit* in Japan), 4,080,000; contract employees,

2,250,000; and dispatched agency workers, 1,600,000 (MIAC 2008a). Both recent graduates and former full-time regular employees who have been made redundant are among the increasing number of non-regular employees. The expansion of capital's boundaries can be observed across a broad spectrum of the economy, yet the overwhelming burden of non-regular employment is falling disproportionately on female and young employees. The rise in the number of non-regular employees with low wages and long working hours may also have knock-on effects on the wages and working conditions of those in regular employment.

The same income statistics published by the Ministry of Internal Affairs and Communications (2008) revealed that 76.8 per cent of employees earned less than JPY5 million (excluding executives), while 53.1 per cent earned less than JPY3 million. The average income of part-time workers and other non-regular workers amounted to only JPY1.2 million and JPY2.2 million respectively. The average number of working days per week for part-time employees amounted to 4.7 days and the average working time to 5.8 hours per day. The corresponding figures for other non-regular employees stand at 5.1 days and 7.7 hours. The income of non-regular employees has remained low in spite of working hours that are not much different to those of regular employees.

As 76.8 per cent of all employees earn less than JPY5 million each year, this means that a majority of the Japanese working population is living on a low income relative to the cost of living in Japan and the size of GDP. At the same time, declining income has also contributed to a widening wealth gap. The Gini index figure indicating the income gap, taken in the mid-1980s, was 0.278; a decade later, this figure had risen to 0.295, and by the year 2000 had reached 0.314, a clear reflection of the widening income dispersal across Japan (OECD 2006: 219). As Figure 9.2 illustrates, in 2005, a greater number of people were sharing a smaller total income compared to a decade earlier. Annual incomes of above JPY12.5 million accounted for 10 per cent of the total national income, but only 4 per cent of employees fell in this upper stratum of income levels. The fact that the average annual income in 2005 was JPY4.5 million, and that even by 2008, over two-thirds of the working population (76.8 per cent) earned less than JPY5 million, means that the rate of relative poverty (income inequality) in Japan is now one of the highest in the OECD (OECD 2007). More than half of all single working parents found themselves in relative poverty in 2000, compared with an OECD world average of around 20 per cent (OECD 2007).

A large number of regular employees can also be found among the 76.8 per cent of employees earning under JPY5 million each year. Deducting 35.5 per cent of the workforce made up of non-regular employees still leaves 41.3 per cent of regular employees in this stratum. The same government statistics reveal the astonishingly long working hours of low-income earners. Of all employees in the 25–44 age bracket, 20 per cent were found to work over 60 hours a week. Indeed, it is not uncommon to hear of young employees starting their daily commute around 6:00 a.m. in order to arrive at work by 8:00 a.m., returning home in the evening between 10:00 p.m. and midnight. A recent study carried out by the MHLW (2006a) found that over half of all employees interviewed had complained of work-related stress

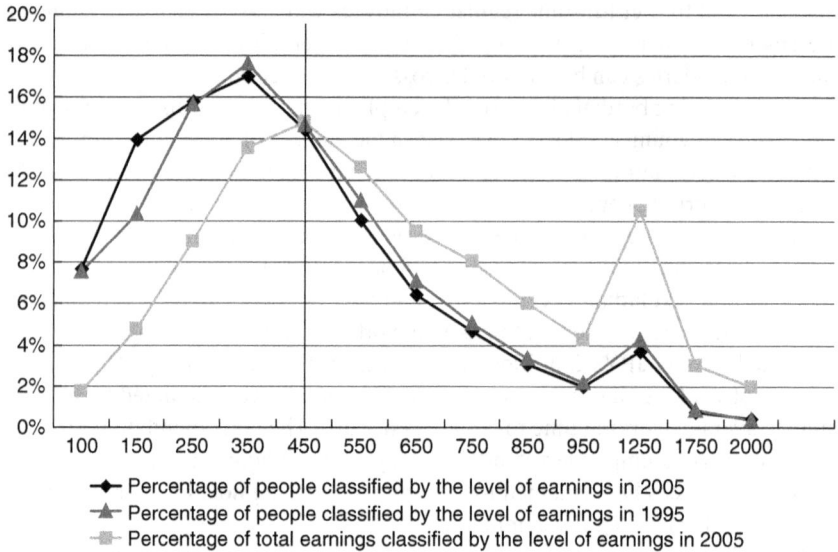

Figure 9.2 Level of earnings

Source: Compiled from the statistics of the MHLW (2006) *Rōdō Keizai no Bunseki*, 288.

due to long working hours and excessive work. The accumulation of work-related stress over a long period of time is one of the primary causes of workplace fatalities and work-related suicide in Japan (The numbers of employees reported as dying from overwork and suicide were 142 and 81 respectively in 2007) (MHLW 2008a).

Corporate workplace boundaries[6]

It is misleading to suggest that the expansion in the boundary of capital is forcing a wedge between executives and employees. The majority of those in management positions (executives, departmental heads) responsible for implementing the expansion of capital earn less than JPY10 million each year. In reality, these executives earn only slightly double the average national income. A significant number of these employees, along with non-regular employees, regular employees and low to mid-level managers, are not protected by labour unions and confront deteriorating working and living conditions. A common feature among all these employees, regardless of disparities in income levels, is an inferior quality of life compared to their counterparts in other industrialized countries.

The deterioration in working conditions for all employees, but especially in non-managerial positions, can be attributed to a series of labour reforms adopted during the 1990s following lobbying by powerful employers' federations such as Nikkeiren and Keidanren on behalf of large corporate interests. The Manpower

Dispatch Business Law (*Haken Hō*) of 1996, which affected 16 industrial sectors, led to the creation of thousands of low-wage contract agency workers. The industrial sectors affected by the law were subsequently liberalized in 1999, and the scope of the law expanded to include the manufacturing industries. By October 2007, the number of employees working on the frontline (i.e., with low wages and under poor conditions) of the ever-expanding corporate workplace boundary came to some 1.6 million (MIAC 2008a).

Human rights as currently understood are infringed on a daily basis for many non-regular and non-Japanese employees working in Japan, who receive low wages for long hours at corporate workplaces. Over half of these part-time and casual employees earn less than JPY1 million a year, whereas employees from dispatch agencies earn on average JPY2.2 million a year. Again, the working hours of these non-regular workers are barely different from their regular counterparts. In 2005, 41.8 per cent of these non-regular employees worked on average over 35 hours a week (MIAC 2006). As of 2008, the minimum monthly living wage in Tokyo was JPY230,000; this means that close to half the working population in Japan is living precariously close to the poverty line (Rengō 2008).

Among non-regular employees in Japan, non-Japanese workers are most likely to be subject to the worst working and living conditions. The majority of these workers come from Brazil, Vietnam and China as labourers or technical internship trainees. According to the MHLW, there were over 750,000 non-Japanese workers in Japan in 2006 (MHLW 2007). These workers often perform work that is 'heavy', 'dirty' or 'dangerous', where the turnover rate is very high. Human rights infringements faced by these non-Japanese workers tend to be worse than those faced by their Japanese counterparts (*Akahata Shimbun*, 21 October 2006).

Working and living conditions in recent years have also been deteriorating for regular employees at corporate workplaces. In 2001, the average male regular employee worked 9.5 hours per day, whereas in 2005, this average had risen to 10.2 hours. The proportion of all male regular employees working over 10 hours a day also rose from 40 to 60 per cent over the same period. During this time, average annual incomes declined by JPY100,000, and the number of acknowledged work-related injuries and illnesses, including fatalities, rose 2.3 times to 330. Close to half of these cases involved death from overwork (*Asahi Shimbun*, 1 October 2006). The Japan Research Institute of Labour Movement (JRILM 2008) survey also found that up to 50–60 per cent of regular employees worked up to 20 hours of overtime per month, and 4 per cent of all employees worked over 80 hours of overtime per month. The main reason given for this was the quantity of work to be finished. According to a recent Labour Policy Research Council survey, the number of overtime hours worked each month in the service industry is 37.4 hours for male employees and 38.5 hours for female employees (*Asahi Shimbun*, 1 October 2008).

As these statistics clearly show, the emergence of the 'working poor' extends well beyond workers on the margins of the economy. The expansion and intensification in the scope of the boundaries of capital have come at the expense of the boundaries of labour that have traditionally protected employees' working conditions and basic human rights.

The continued impoverishment of a large majority of employees in Japan may well give rise to unstable social conditions. As examined in section 1, the emergence of organized social movements calling for the reinvigoration of democracy is a hallmark of mature civil societies. The consolidation of democratic networks of non-Japanese employees, non-regular employees and likewise of regular employees in Japan is a first step towards regaining a meaningful democracy that serves the majority of citizens rather than a small minority of corporate interests.[7] Formal parliamentary democracy is to retain its legitimacy as the most desirable form of government, the expansion of capital boundaries needs to be challenged by a countervailing power, namely organized labour and various democratic forces within civil society.

Conclusion

The boundaries between capital and labour are found at various sites within Japanese society. Certain conflicts – whether between Keidanren and trade unions or between political parties funded by Keidanren (LDP, DPJ) and those receiving no funding (JCP, SDP) – are discussed in the Diet, and these discussions reveal the social systems that the government intends to implement. Since 1980, the boundaries have been adjusted in favour of capital and Keidanren, and the pressure of globalization has become more pronounced since 2000. The rise of neoliberalism as the state ideology has been accompanied by efforts to roll back labour regulations. A tougher competitive environment has not only legitimized these reforms, but also made profit-taking 'short-termism' the prevailing mode of thought. Labour system reforms have emphasized diversification of labour and of labour markets. Informed by neoliberal rhetoric, the market for non-regular labour has grown. The low wages and long working hours of non-regular employees have also dragged down the average wage and working conditions of those remaining regular employees. This has brought about a rapid acceleration of social divisions and disparity in society.

The new Labour Contract Law (MHLW 2008b) is unlikely to reverse this trend. Rather, it seems the law may simply legitimize the outcome of individual labour–management conflicts in favour of management, as may have been intended. To make substantial improvements to working conditions and living standards, a reinforcement of collective labour–management relations is required. In other words, unless Zenrōren, Rengō, the JCP, SDP and DPJ work together to push forward the boundaries of labour, working conditions for the majority of workers in Japan can only deteriorate. Although with the 'regime change' of 2009, the DPJ is expressly keen to swing the pendulum towards democracy, as long as they continue to receive funds from Keidanren, the party can never credibly pursue policies independent of the logic of capital. The priority must be to enact a law to promote major improvements in working conditions, including wages and working hours. However, before this can happen, workers and citizens need to recognize not only a commonality of interest, but their relatively disadvantaged positions both in their own society and in comparison with other comparable industrially advanced democracies, especially in Europe. Without this awareness, labour boundaries will remain passive and unassertive against challenges.

Our analysis and discussion on the concrete boundaries of capital (as established by Keidanren) and labour (as established by labour unions and their federations) reflects the boundary of individual liberalism and social liberalism at an abstract level, as shown in Figure 9.1. Japanese civil society still has some way to go before it sees a proper balance between individual liberalism and social liberalism, and a higher effective level of democracy in civil society.

Notes

1 Lamont argues that the idea of 'boundaries' has come to play a key role in studies across the social sciences (Lamont and Molnar 2002). According to Lamont, the 'social boundary' denotes the boundary between capital and labour which represents the concept of class in a capitalist society. In its concrete form of expression, this boundary separates the capitalist and working classes. The objective of this chapter is therefore to analyze the roles played by the federation of corporations that thinks and behaves according to the logic of capital and the roles played by the federation of trade unions that thinks and behaves according to the logic of labour. A 'social system' refers to capitalist society, which incorporates two forms of logic, that of capital and that of labour; that society's development is achieved through their dynamic interaction. The emergence of social democracy depends upon the nature and balance of this interaction.

2 'Democracy' as used in this chapter refers to broad values of citizens' involvement in issues pertaining to liberty and representation, which can manifest in various ways. While formal parliamentary democracy may be a part of social democracy, formal electoral and parliamentary politics are insufficient in themselves for a fully democratic society. A more mature democracy requires a balance of countervailing powers to government or corporate policies that might otherwise serve minority interests; such countervailing powers would include unions, non-governmental organizations (NGOs), civil movements, media, the arts and other manifestations of a pluralistic society.

3 The Plaza Accord is an Agreement concluded in 1985 at the Plaza Hotel in New York City among five nations (France, West Germany, the United Kingdom, the United States and Japan), with the aim of devaluing the US dollar and thus contributing to reducing the US trade deficit and helping it emerge from the recession in that period.

4 'Non-regular employees' are defined by the Ministry of Health, Labour, and Welfare (MHLW) as including the following workers:

(1) Part-time workers: employees whose working hours are lower than those of regular employees;
(2) Retired part-time workers (*shokutaku*): retired employees re-employed (often by the same company and without time off between retirement and re-employment) under different working conditions;
(3) Contract workers (*keiyaku shain*): employees whose contract is limited by time;
(4) Dispatch workers (*haken shain*): employees who, through a dispatching agency, take up a particular job when and for the term that the job opportunity arises, and are dispatched to other companies.

5 A final report from the Rengō Assessment Committee, which consisted of seven members including a lawyer, Nakabo Kōhei, was submitted on 12 September 2003. This

report described the current situation of Japanese trade unions, and included comments such as: 'Rengō only speaks for the interests of male regular employees working in big companies and is soaked in policies for harmonious labour–management relations', 'Go back to the principal ideology of the labour movement, and reconstruct your concept' and 'Maintain the stance of struggle against irrationality in society and take action' (Rengō 2003).

6 Corporate workplace boundaries are the interface where labour is actually used to produce surplus value for capital, namely companies.

7 Not only the regeneration of existing unions (Rengō, Zenrōren, etc.), but also new unions such as the Labour Union of Migrant Workers, General Union, Coordinating Committee for the Problem of Foreign Workers, Metropolitan Area Youth Union and Executive Unions; and also various citizens' movements, such as co-operatives, environmental movements, human rights mobilizations, Osaka Net for decent work, Ombudsmen, non-profit organizations (NPOs) and NGOs have developed and countervailing powers are emerging at various levels and spheres. NPOs and NGOs may not directly expand the boundaries of labour, but they contribute indirectly to advance the democratic consciousness in civil society.

References

Bauman, Zygmunt (2004) *Wasted Lives: modernity and its outcasts*, Cambridge: Polity.

Fukuda, Yasuo (2008) 'Shushō Jinin o uke Kongo no Taiō o Kyōgi'. Online. Available: http://www.dpj.or.jp/news/?num = 13984 (accessed 2 September 2008).

Goto, Michio, Takeuchi Akio, Nakanishi Shintaro, Watanabe Norimasa and Yoshizaki Shoji (2007) *Kakusa Shakai to Tatakau*, Tokyo: Aoki Shoten.

Hasegawa, Harukiyo (1993) 'Japanese employment practices and industrial relations: the road to union compliance', *Japan Forum*, 5, 1: 21–35.

—— (2005) 'The political economy of Japanese "corporate governance": a metaphor for capitalist rationalization', in Glenn D. Hook (ed.), *Contested Governance in Japan*, London: RoutledgeCurzon.

Inagaki, Kiyoshi (2006) *Chūgoku Shinshūtsu Kigyō Chizu*, Tokyo: Sōsōsha.

Japan Institute for Social and Economic Affairs (2008) 'The declining birth rate in Japan', *Japan Economic Current*, 69: 1–10.

Japan Research Institute of Labour Movement (JRILM) (2008) *Shuto ken Jakunen Tanshin Rōdōsha Sō no Saitei Seikatsuhi Shisan Chūkan Hōkoku no Gaiyō*, Tokyo: JRILM.

Japanese Communist Party (2008) 'Nihon Kyōsantō Kōryo'. Online. Available: http://www.jcp.or.jp/jcp/Koryo/index.html (accessed 22 October 2008).

JCUF (2008) Rengō Kaikaku e no Watakushi no Ketsui. Online. Available: http://www.zenkoku-u.jp/rikkouho/rikkouho1.htm (accessed 8 August 2008).

Kabunushi Ombudsman (2004) 'Current state of political donations of listed companies and opinions about it'. Online. Available: http://kabuombu.sakura.ne.jp/archives/040430–32.htm (accessed 9 August 2008).

Kumazawa, Makoto (2007) *Kakusa Shakai Nippon de Hataraku to Iu koto*, Tokyo: Iwanami Shoten.

Labour Research Council (2008) 'Kinrōsha no seikatsu no genjō to kongo no kadai', *Rōdō Chōsa*, Tokyo: Labour Research Council, 2: 3–40.

Lamont, Michele and Molnar, Virag (2002) 'The study of boundaries in the social sciences', *Annual Review of Sociology*, 28: 167–95.

Maehara, Seiji (2008) 'Maehara Seiji'. Online. Available: http://www.maehara21.com/kiji/kiji080427.html (accessed 22 October 2008).

METI (2004) 'Major survey on activities of overseas corporations in 2004'. Online. Available: http://www.pref.osaka.jp/aid/naniwa/naniwa2006/n2006_06_05.pdf (accessed 20 September 2008).

MHLW (2006a) *Labour Policy Council, Materials pertaining to the 72nd Meeting of the Subcommittee on Working Conditions*, Tokyo: MHLW. Online. Available: http://www.mhlw.go.jp/shingi/2006/12/s1227–15a.html (accessed 8 August 2008).

—— (2006b) *Outline of the Basic Survey on Trade Unions for 2006*, Tokyo: MHLW.

—— (2006c) 'Report on future legislation of Labour Contract Law and Working Hours Law', report presented by the MHLW at the 70th Meeting of the Subcommittee on Working Conditions, 8 December. Online. Available: http://www.mhlw.go.jp/shingi/2006/12/s1208–12a.html (accessed 8 August 2008).

—— (2007) *Gaikokujin Koyō Jōkyō Hōkoku*, Tokyo: MHLW.

—— (2008a) *The Current State of Health and Safety Compensation for Brain, Heart and Mental Disease, etc*, Tokyo: MHLW.

—— (2008b) *Labour Contract Law*. Online. Available: http://www.eonet.ne.jp/~ninjya-sr/rodokeiyakuhou%20(2007.12.1).pdf (accessed 8 August 2008).

—— (2008c) 'Basic Survey Results on Trade Unions', Tokyo: MHLW. Online. Available: http://www.mhlw.go.jp/toukei/itiran/roudou/roushi/kiso/09/index.html (accessed 28 December 2009).

MIAC (2006) *Rōdōryoku Chōsa*, Tokyo: MIAC.

—— (2008a) *Basic Survey of Employment Structure for 2007*, Tokyo: MIAC.

—— (2008b) 'Gurafu de Miru Tokei'. Online. Available: http://www.stat.go.jp/data/nihon/g0703.htm (accessed 10 September 2008).

Nikkeiren (1995) *Shinjidai no Nihonteki Keiei*, Tokyo: Nikkeiren.

Nippon Keidanren (2007) *2008 nen ban Keiei Rōdō Seisaku Iinkai Hōkoku Gaiyō*, Tokyo: Nippon Keidanren.

—— (2008) *2008 Nippon Keidanren Kisei Kaikaku Yōbō*, Tokyo: Nippon Keidanren.

OECD (2006) *Factbook*, Paris: OECD.

—— (2007) *Economic Survey of Japan 2006*, Paris: OECD.

Rengō (2003) *Rengō Hyōka Iinkai*. Online. Available: http://www.jtuc-rengo.or.jp/rengo/hyoukaiinkai/index.html (accessed 8 August 2008).

—— (2005) *Rengō Kōdō Hōshin*. Online. Available: http://www.jtuc-rengo.or.jp/rengo/about_us/koudou_shishin.html (accessed 8 August 2008).

—— (2006) *Monthly Rengō*, June. Rengō.

—— (2008) *Shutoken Kyojū Shotai ni Hoshō Sarerubeki Saitei Seikatsuhi wa Ikura ka?* Online. Available: http://www.yuiyuidori.net/soken/ape/2008/2008_1209.html (accessed 8 February 2009).

Tachibanaki, Toshiaki (2006) *Kakusa Shakai nani ga Mondai na n oka?* Tokyo: Iwanami Shoten.

Zenrōren (2008a) 'Kōdō Kōryō'. Online. Available: http://www.zenroren.gr.jp/jp/index.html (accessed 8 August 2008).

—— (2008b) 'Kiyaku'. Online. Available: http://www.zenroren.gr.jp/jp/shokai/kouryou.html (accessed 2 September 2008).

10 Shifting boundaries in Japan's criminal justice system[1]

Patricia G. Steinhoff

This chapter examines ways in which the boundaries of the Japanese criminal justice system have been shifting as a result of the interaction between three elements: external forces that impinge upon Japan as part of the global effort to harmonize laws and impose universal standards; internal forces arising from both domestic political agendas and bureaucratic actors with roles in the system; and pressures arising out of the experiences of ordinary citizens, which become organized and visible through the activities of social movement organizations.

The Japanese government initiated a comprehensive review of the entire justice system in 1999, under Prime Minister Obuchi Keizō. When the Justice System Reform Council produced its final report in June 2001 (The Justice System Reform Council 2001), the new administration of Prime Minister Koizumi Junichirō immediately established a special office in the Cabinet Secretariat to oversee implementation of the council's recommendations. Over the next eight years the administrations of Koizumi and his successor, Prime Minister Abe Shinzō, passed a series of laws that dramatically transformed many aspects of the justice system, including new forms of legal training and legal support, the introduction of a lay judge (*baishin-in*) system, and several new systems for adjudicating or resolving specialized types of cases (Ministry of Justice Government of Japan 2006). These reforms have been widely discussed by legal scholars. Some other changes in the criminal justice system enacted during the same time period have attracted less attention, but are particularly interesting because they reveal the complex pressures that impinge upon the state from global forces, on the one hand, and civil society forces, on the other (Sassen 2007).

Although the criminal justice system can be viewed as a set of institutions and the laws that establish and govern them, it can also be understood as a set of practices and processes that are triggered by specific acts of individuals. These acts set in motion the activities of police, prosecutors, defence attorneys, judges, and prison officials, which take place primarily in the physical places specific to the criminal justice system: police stations, courts, and prisons. Every step in this process is deeply shaped by the specific practices and procedures that are used. What happens in and out of the courtroom, and before and after the trial, profoundly affects the outcome of individual cases and over time may institutionalize new practices. Other people who are not formal actors in the criminal justice system may become involved in particular cases and they, too, may have direct or indirect effects on the practices and procedures, and even the formal laws governing the criminal justice system.

The problem of shifting boundaries is approached here by tracing some specific instances that have worked through the criminal justice system.[2] Two contemporary criminal cases serve to focus the analysis in this chapter. The first case, the trial of Shigenobu Fusako, highlights the steadily increasing severity of the Japanese criminal justice system and its expansion beyond Japan's borders over the past four decades. These shifts occurred largely through new policies and procedures applied within existing laws. They were related to the conflict interaction between justice system personnel and New Left social movement groups, on the one hand, and to Japan's response to global initiatives and external pressures regarding terrorism, on the other. The second case, the Hikari City mother–child murders, highlights the forces underlying the rapid passage of major revisions to basic laws affecting the criminal justice system during the Koizumi and Abe administrations, and also shows Japan's response to conflicting domestic and international pressures regarding the death penalty. The first two sections present the cases and their civil society and social movement contexts. The following sections discuss how boundaries in the criminal justice system have shifted through state–civil society interactions and global pressures on Japan.

1. The case of Shigenobu Fusako

The arrest of Shigenobu Fusako in Osaka on 8 November 2000 was front-page news. TV news reports and major newspapers all showed pictures of the 55-year-old woman, smiling and giving a thumbs-up sign despite her handcuffs, as she was transported under heavy guard to police headquarters in Tokyo. She had not been seen publicly in Japan since early 1971, when she went to the Middle East as a member of a radical student organization called the Red Army Faction, to work with the Popular Front for the Liberation of Palestine (PFLP).[3] Shigenobu had initially arranged for a Japanese film crew to make a film about the cooperation between PFLP and the Red Army Faction, in order to promote the Palestinian cause in Japan and also to recruit young Japanese for military training in Lebanon through PFLP. The young Japanese who followed her to the Middle East first served as international volunteers with PFLP and later formed their own organization called the Japanese Red Army. Shigenobu was widely viewed as the leader of the group, which took credit publicly for a string of international incidents in the 1970s. During her long years in exile, she remained well-known in Japan through her own writings, along with books and mass media accounts about her, but she was never photographed. The middle-aged woman with glasses in the November 2000 news photos contrasted sharply with the photograph of a long-haired young beauty that had been distributed widely on wanted posters of Japanese Red Army members since the mid-1970s.

On several occasions since the late 1980s, other Japanese Red Army members whose pictures were on the same international wanted posters were arrested trying to enter Japan or were found abroad and sent back to Japan to face criminal charges. Most of those trials had already been completed when Shigenobu was arrested, but several recent returnees from the Japanese Red Army were being tried separately in Tokyo on charges ranging from passport violations to felony charges for airline hijackings and embassy invasions. The passport charges related to falsification of Japanese passports, but all of the other charges concerned acts committed overseas by Japanese citizens, over which the Japanese government claimed jurisdiction anywhere in the world.

Wakō Haruo, who had originally gone to the Middle East as a PFLP military volunteer in 1973, was already on trial for hostage-taking and attempted murder for two international embassy hostage-taking incidents. The first was an invasion of the French Embassy in the Hague, Netherlands, in September 1974, in order to negotiate the release of a Japanese associate who had been arrested in France. The basis for the attempted murder charge in the Hague Incident was the fact that two guns had been brought into the embassy invasion, and a shot fired by one participant had grazed the ear of a security guard in the building. The prosecution argued that under the prevailing interpretation of Japanese law, bringing a gun to the place where a crime is committed constitutes intent to murder and justifies a charge of attempted murder. Attempted murder carries a sentence of up to life imprisonment, whereas the other charges related to taking hostages carry a maximum sentence of seven years.[4]

After the Hague Incident, the Japanese government had placed Shigenobu and several other Japanese residing overseas on the International Police Agency (Interpol) wanted list in connection with the incident. As they were found and brought back to Japan more than 20 years later, some were charged with offenses related to the Hague Incident, while others were only charged with passport violations because there was insufficient evidence for more serious charges. Shigenobu was initially arrested on suspicion of hostage-taking in connection with the Hague Incident, and was rearrested on suspicion of attempted murder the following day. She was formally indicted for hostage-taking and attempted murder 23 days after her initial arrest, and rearrested the next day on passport violations. She was held at police headquarters in Tokyo for five months and then was transferred to unconvicted detention at the Tokyo House of Detention a week before her first trial session on 3 April 2001.

At the time, it was technically illegal to hold a prisoner in a police station jail after the initial interrogation period of three days, which can be extended to 23 days with a judge's permission.[5] Lawyers are never present during interrogations, which may be carried out for 12 hours a day and are primarily aimed at obtaining a confession (Foote 1995). Most suspects confess within the first three days. They have the right to remain silent, but most do not exercise it. Suspects who resist confession or refuse to talk are routinely held in such police station jails, known as 'substitute prisons' (*daiyōkangoku*) for much longer periods of intensive interrogation through the simple device of rearresting them on another charge. Since the clock begins again with each such arrest, official statistics do not reveal the actual length of time that resistant suspects spend in interrogation.

As Shigenobu was indicted on various charges, her name was added as a co-defendant in three other Japanese Red Army trials that were pending in Tokyo for the same incidents. One was a relatively minor offense of conspiring with Yamamoto Mariko to obtain a Japanese passport under a false name, in order to facilitate another person's departure from Japan. She was also added as a co-defendant in the ongoing trials of Wakō Haruo and Nishikawa Jun, both of whom were charged with attempted murder in connection with the 1974 Hague Incident. Shigenobu acknowledged the passport offenses, but contested those related to the Hague Incident.

Emphasis on confession and contrition is central to a criminal justice system that has long been considered to be oriented to rehabilitation and reintegration of offenders after relatively short prison sentences (Castberg 1990; Foote 1992b; Haley 1991). If a person confesses to a crime and does not contest the prosecution's version of events, a brief trial is held so a judge can accept the guilty plea, hear whether the perpetrator regrets or apologizes for the act, and then impose the sentence. However, if the defendant contests the charges, the trial in open court becomes a lengthy affair. Such trials are not continuous, but meet before a panel of three judges, usually once a month for half a day. Witnesses are called to testify, but the deliberations place greater weight on the documentary evidence that is submitted. The prosecution is not required to disclose any of the results of its investigation to the defence, so defence lawyers only learn about evidence as the prosecution introduces it in court when particular witnesses are called, and never learn about exculpatory evidence that the prosecution does not submit in court. The slow pace of the trial prolongs the time a defendant spends in unconvicted detention, but it also gives the defence some opportunity to rebut prosecution claims or find exculpatory evidence as the trial proceeds.[6] Shigenobu's first trial lasted nearly five years, from 23 April 2001 until 23 February 2006.

In both his own trial and in Shigenobu's, Wakō Haruo testified that Shigenobu had nothing to do with the Hague Incident (Wakō 2001; Wakō 2003). She had not been present and had not been involved in planning the incident. Wakō described in detail how he had initiated the effort to rescue his associate who had been arrested in France. Under instructions directly from his Palestinian military commander, he had gone to Europe to meet with the famous Carlos the Jackal (Ilyich Ramirez Sanchez, a Venezuelan who was also associated with PFLP), who supplied the weapons and outlined the attack plan that Wakō, Nishikawa, and a third Japanese man subsequently carried out. Wakō took full responsibility for the Hague Incident, and was angry and insulted that the prosecution was giving the credit to Shigenobu. Although Shigenobu was convicted as a co-defendant in Yamamoto's false passport case, prosecutors made little effort to implicate her directly in Wakō and Nishikawa's trials except for a lengthy argument by the prosecutor in his final statement in Wakō's trial. Wakō received a life sentence for the combined charges against him in two major embassy invasions, but the judge in his trial rejected the co-defendant charges against Shigenobu. The decision said that while she might have been involved, the prosecution had not shown that in

Wakō's trial (Shigenobu 2005). The judge in Nishikawa's trial also dropped the co-defendant charges against Shigenobu.

Evidence was presented in Shigenobu's trial documenting that she had not been in Europe during the time the Hague Incident was planned and carried out. She had a one-year-old child, and for part of the time she was attending a celebration in Libya as a guest of Libyan leader Muammar Khadafi. The only evidence linking her to the Hague Incident was a confession statement from another Japanese Red Army member who had been arrested in Sweden six months after the Hague Incident and deported back to Japan, where he was immediately arrested. After intensive interrogation he had confessed to attending a meeting some time after the Hague Incident, during which Shigenobu led a discussion that the prosecution claimed had implicated her.

In Japan, confession statements are not actually written by the person who is confessing. The police or prosecutor conducting the interrogation writes up a statement summarizing the results of the interrogation and tries to get the person to sign it, often by persuading a reluctant suspect that he can later tell the judge that it was not true. Such a signed statement is treated as a confession in court and is usually accepted even if the person has subsequently recanted it. In this case, the person was called as a reluctant prosecution witness in Shigenobu's trial, whereupon he testified that the confession was both coerced and inaccurate (author's field notes of Shigenobu Fusako trial session in the Tokyo District Court, 28 June 2001). The defence also submitted in evidence two versions of the supposed confession statement that demonstrated prosecutors had doctored it by changing the character for a key word to implicate Shigenobu more strongly.

The prosecution continued to insist that Shigenobu had been involved in the Hague Incident and demanded that she receive a life sentence, reiterating the logic that because a gun was used in the incident, she was guilty of attempted murder. The defence argued that she had neither been present nor involved in the planning of the incident, and therefore was not guilty of the attempted murder charge. The judge gave her a 20-year sentence, far more than the passport charges alone warranted, which was possible only by finding that she had been involved in the Hague Incident. In the decision, he wrote that she must have been involved in the Hague Incident: although it was completely unclear 'where, when, or with whom, one can infer that there was some sort of contact' (Shigenobu san o Sasaeru Kai 2006).

Both sides appealed the decision, the defence because the sentence was too heavy, and the prosecution because it was too lenient. Unlike the Anglo-American common law tradition, in Japan and most civil law countries the prosecution can appeal if it is not satisfied with the severity of the judge's decision. There are at least two felony cases currently on appeal in Japan in which the prosecution has appealed a verdict of not guilty. Under Anglo-American common law, that would constitute a clear case of double jeopardy and would not be permitted. Despite the fact that the Japanese Constitution contains a provision prohibiting double jeopardy, in practice the prosecution's appeal of a not guilty verdict is not considered double jeopardy and the prosecution is permitted to try the case over again in the appeals court, where they frequently prevail. In recent years, Japanese prosecutors have routinely appealed cases in which the sentence is lighter than they asked for (Hamai and Ellis 2008; Johnson 2002). A defendant who has been found guilty in the first trial generally remains in unconvicted detention for the duration of all appeals.

Shigenobu's appeal trial began on 19 May 2007. Her lawyer had travelled to France, where Carlos the Jackal is currently serving a prison sentence, and obtained a deposition from him confirming that Shigenobu was not involved in the Hague Incident and that he did not meet her until many years after the incident. During the lawyer's meeting with Carlos, he told her that a Japanese prosecutor had interviewed him some years earlier, and he had told the prosecutor the same things (author's field notes of Shigenobu Fusako appeals trial sessions in the Tokyo High Court, 19 April 2007 and 10 July 2007). The defence lawyer tried to introduce the new deposition in evidence and to have the judge require the prosecution to submit its earlier exculpatory evidence from Carlos, but she was only partially successful. The defence emphasized that Shigenobu could not be guilty of attempted murder in the Hague Incident because she had nothing to do with that event, while the prosecution continued to insist that she was the leader of a terrorist group and therefore was responsible for the Hague Incident, was guilty of attempted murder, and should be sentenced to life in prison. On 20 December 2007, the appeals court confirmed the 20-year sentence she had received in the first trial. Both sides appealed to the Supreme Court, and the final decision was confirmed in 2010.

From the time of her arrest in November 2000, Shigenobu was held essentially incommunicado, allowed limited communication only with her lawyer. In the police station jail shortly after her arrest, she wrote a document concerning her daughter's birth and upbringing in the Middle East, which her lawyer used to establish the stateless daughter's claim to Japanese citizenship and to bring her to Japan (Steinhoff 2008). Once Shigenobu's adult daughter was in Japan she was accorded limited visitation rights with her mother, but all other outside communications were prohibited. After Shigenobu was moved to the Tokyo House of Detention, she continued to be held incommunicado.

Persons held in unconvicted detention in Japan are kept in solitary confinement day and night, but normally can have daily visitors and can send and receive mail. A judge can prohibit communications at the prosecution's request, on the grounds that allowing communication would give the defendant an opportunity to conceal or destroy evidence. That rationale ends when the prosecution completes the presentation of its case, and any communications restrictions are generally lifted at that time. However, in Shigenobu's case the communications ban continued not only to the end of her trial, but beyond it. The ban was not lifted until June 2007, after all testimony in the appeal trial was completed.[7] Ironically, while Shigenobu was being held incommunicado, her story about her daughter's birth was published commercially in Japan with the assistance of her lawyer and supporters. The publication date was the day of her first trial session, 23 April 2001 (Shigenobu 2001).

Shigenobu has a large and active support organization, *Shigenobu Fusako-san o Sasaeru Kai*. Its participants include family members, her old friends from high school and college, fellow participants in the protests of the late 1960s, associates and supporters of the Red Army groups, and ordinary Japanese who find her a sympathetic figure. Support group members pay monthly dues, attend trial sessions, assist defence lawyers in various ways, and organize special events and publications to support Shigenobu's defence. As is customary for such support groups, they produce a newsletter, *Oriibu no Ki* (the Olive Tree) that serves to maintain communication between the isolated prisoner and supporters outside. During the long period when she was held incommunicado, the support group received its materials through her lawyer and daughter. Once it became possible to visit her in the summer of 2007, the support organization took charge of managing the schedule, since the demand for visits with her was very high. Although Shigenobu is a strong person with a deep commitment to the causes she has devoted her life to, she is undoubtedly sustained during her long struggle in the criminal justice system by the efforts of her support group.

Late 1960s protest and trial support as a social movement

The severe practices of the Japanese criminal justice system that were revealed in this case are quite common today for contested cases. They contrast sharply with the image of the post-war Japanese criminal justice system as a model of reintegrative and rehabilitative justice because of its emphasis on confession, apology, and short sentences. They are the product of a long, contentious process of interaction between state actors connected to the criminal justice system and social movement organizations working with case lawyers to protect the constitutional rights of persons arrested for criminal acts in the context of political activity. Although there are important historical antecedents, the current harsh practices can be traced to the period of violent political protest in the late 1960s, when young people in Japan were protesting in the streets and on college campuses along with their counterparts in Germany, France, Italy, and the United States. As violence escalated, the state cracked down with mass arrests at demonstrations, holding students in police jail cells rather than releasing them after a day or two, and indicting them for a variety of criminal offenses.

In response to the sudden need for legal and social support for large numbers of arrested students, volunteers developed a support system that maintained a telephone hotline for arrested students and provided lawyers, taught students that they could resist police pressures to confess by exercising their constitutional right to remain silent, and helped groups of family and friends build their own trial support groups to assist the lawyers and help defendants survive the long process of a contested trial. That system, which still exists today, created a large new venue for social movement activity through trial support groups and brought large numbers of civil society actors into direct involvement with the workings of the criminal justice system (Steinhoff 1999). The professionals in the criminal justice system did not remain passive in the wake of these sudden challenges to their routine practices, but began to apply available methods to increase the pressure: extending the length of time students were held in detention; bringing more serious charges whenever they could; and holding the young defendants in unconvicted detention instead of releasing them to a guarantor while they awaited trial. The support groups responded to this escalation by providing continuing support to defendants in unconvicted detention through regular prison visits, sending in supplies, and publishing newsletters that maintained communication between the prisoners and a wide circle of supporters outside.

The crackdown of 1968–69 did break the momentum of the protest cycle, but it had the unintended consequences, in Japan as elsewhere, of pushing a fraction of the protesters underground or into exile and thus creating new forms of protest that were much more difficult to anticipate and whose perpetrators were more difficult to apprehend (Zwerman and Steinhoff 2005). Shigenobu had belonged to one of the main New Left student organizations, but as the crackdown continued, the organization split and she ended up in the smaller, more radical, Red Army Faction. Under severe police pressure, one group of Red Army Faction members hijacked a plane into exile in North Korea and others went underground in Japan and later ended up in a disastrous internal purge, while Shigenobu pursued her assignment to find another international base for the group. It was in this context that Shigenobu went to the Middle East in 1971 and encouraged other young people to join her there.

During the 1970s, first as individual volunteers with PFLP and later on their own as the Japanese Red Army beginning in late 1974, this group became involved in a series of international terrorist attacks. Shigenobu came to be known as the public face of the Japanese group, which had a protected status in the Middle East after an attack on Lod Airport in Israel in 1972 carried out by three Japanese under PFLP direction resulted in the death of two of its participants and the capture of a third. Following the Hague Incident, the newly independent Japanese Red Army carried out two more attacks that used international leverage to obtain the release of prisoners from Japan, including both members of their own group and others. In each case, after considerable agonizing, the Japanese government authorized the release of the prisoners in order to avoid harm to the international hostages. Over the years, the Japanese police and mass media constructed an image of Shigenobu as the beautiful, powerful, and elusive leader of a hierarchical international terrorist organization (Steinhoff 1996). Japanese authorities could do little except place the names of known associates on the Interpol list, try to find out where they were, and enlist the cooperation of local authorities to arrest and deport them back to Japan. As soon as persons on the wanted posters were arrested on Japanese soil, their supporters would organize a trial support group to help them through the long criminal justice process.

Shigenobu's treatment within the Japanese criminal justice system, as well as her ability to continue to resist it, thus must be understood within the domestic context of three decades of contention between the criminal justice bureaucracy and the New Left's trial support system.

2. The Hikari city mother–child murder case

A young mother and her 11-month-old baby were murdered in their apartment in Hikari City, a small city in southwestern Japan, in April 1999. A few days later, an

18-year-old was arrested and confessed to the crimes. Although the age of majority in Japan is 20, the juvenile authorities turned him over to be prosecuted as an adult because he was older than 15. He was charged with the murders and, at the initial court session in December 1999, the prosecutor asked for the death penalty. This was a brief trial because the youth had confessed, and the issue was simply determining the length of the sentence. Despite the prosecution's demand for the death penalty, the Yamaguchi District Court sentenced him to unlimited imprisonment (*mukikei*),[8] in March 2000. The court found that he had just turned 18 (the age at which he became eligible to receive the death penalty) when the crime was committed, he had not broken into the apartment with the intention of murdering either the mother or the child, and he had expressed some degree of remorse.

The prosecutor appealed to the Hiroshima High Court and again demanded the death penalty. Yasuda Yoshihiro, a prominent lawyer who handles many death penalty cases and other high-profile political cases, and heads the anti-death penalty organization Forum 90 in Japan, became the youth's lead defence lawyer for the appeal. The Hiroshima High Court rejected the prosecutor's appeal in March 2002, reiterating the findings of the first trial decision and adding that there was a potential for rehabilitation. The prosecutor appealed to the Supreme Court, again seeking the death penalty.

During the time the initial decision in the case was pending in early 2000, the grieving husband and father joined forces with an attorney whose wife had also been murdered, to found a victim's rights organization called *Hanzai Higaisha no Kai*, nicknamed *Asu no Kai*,[9] and began campaigning for increased participation of crime victims in the criminal justice process. Their movement grew rapidly and soon was directly involved in the government's deliberations concerning the passage of a new victims' rights law and the revision of basic criminal laws. The husband and father became a public spokesperson for the victims' rights movement, advocating severe retributive justice to assuage the emotional pain of crime victims. Consequently, there was considerable public attention focused on the continuing appeals seeking the death penalty in the Hikari City case in which he was the victim as the surviving family member.

There was heightened media coverage when the Supreme Court agreed to hear the case and scheduled oral arguments, since agreeing to hear oral arguments is often the signal that a lower court decision will be overturned. On the first day of oral arguments the defence lawyers were absent, so the oral arguments had to be postponed for a month. This is a common tactic of defence lawyers when there is a dispute about trial procedures, but by then the case was in the public eye and the tactic was criticized heavily in the media. In June 2006, the Supreme Court rejected the appeals court's decision and remanded the case back to the Hiroshima Appeals Court for a new trial, expressing doubts about the lower courts' findings that there were sufficient mitigating circumstances to preclude the death penalty. In effect, the Supreme Court was ordering the appeals court to rehear the case in order to raise the sentence from unlimited imprisonment to the death penalty.

There are only three previous cases in post-war Japan in which a youth under the age of 20 at the time of the crimes was given a death sentence. Each of the three cases involved four murders, and two involved guns, which are rarely used in Japanese murders. In the first of these prior cases in 1983, the Supreme Court had articulated the standard that a minor should be given the death penalty when anyone viewing the case would agree that no punishment other than the death penalty could be applied. The Japanese criminal justice system, unlike the Anglo-American common law system, does not rely on precedent but rather focuses on careful application of the letter of the legal code. There is quite high consistency in Japanese higher court decisions, which scholars attribute to the single national judicial system under the authority of the Supreme Court, and the fact that the procedures for assignment and promotion of professional judges encourage conformity in decisions (Miyazawa 2001). However, these same conditions can lead to shifts in decisions over time, and there is clear evidence that the number of death penalty decisions has grown steadily since the 1980s. In remanding the Hikari City case back to the appeals court, the Supreme Court was implicitly tightening its own standard for minors to imply that the death penalty was the most appropriate sentence unless there were special mitigating circumstances.

The opening of the retrial in Hiroshima High Court on 24 May 2007 sparked a media frenzy. All of the major television news programmes featured heavy coverage of the event, framing it as a battle between the victim seeking justice and retribution for the murder of his wife and baby and the 'politically motivated' group of 21 anti-death-penalty lawyers who were defending the murderer. Quick shots of the cluster of defence lawyers entering the courtroom alternated with long full-face clips from the young widower's press conference, at which he denounced both the murderer and the lawyers defending him, insisting that only the death penalty was the appropriate punishment for the heinous crime that had taken his wife and daughter from him. The clear implication was that such a murderer did not deserve to be defended, and that it was improper for lawyers who opposed the death penalty to be appearing in court on the defendant's behalf.

Television commentators and Internet bloggers quickly took up the call and began demonizing the defence lawyers, who received numerous personal death threats over the next few days (author's field notes of *Stop Shikei Shikkō* public meeting and demonstration, 2 June 2007). Three days after the trial began, a celebrity lawyer named Hashimoto Tōru (who subsequently was elected governor of Osaka prefecture) talked about the case on the Osaka-based television talk show 'Takajin no Soko Made Itte Iinkai', where he was a regular commentator on legal matters. He denounced the defence lawyers for inappropriate conduct and urged the television audience, 'If you think what that group of lawyers is doing is impermissible, I want you to submit a disciplinary complaint to the bar association'. In response, several thousand viewers actually submitted formal complaints to the bar association demanding that the defence lawyers be disciplined. In September that year, four of the defence lawyers who had been targeted sued Hashimoto for damages in Hiroshima District Court.[10]

The defence team contended that both the prosecutors and the media had presented a highly distorted picture of the facts of the Hikari City case. The defence lawyers said they had joined the case *pro bono* not because of shared anti-death-penalty sentiments, but because they felt the case itself was important and the facts needed to be fully aired. They contended that the lurid picture painted by the prosecutor and taken up by the media did not match the medical examiner's findings, which supported the defence contention and the defendant's own account that this was not a premeditated murder but rather a situation that went out of control. They described the perpetrator as a youth from a dysfunctional family whose mother committed suicide when he was 12, and whose emotional development stopped at that point, and that the evidence can be found in the original psychological examination report on the youth (Hikari-shi Jiken Bengodan 2007; Hikari-shi Saiban Bengodan 2007). However, as expected, the Hiroshima Appeals Court this time found no mitigating circumstances that would preclude the death penalty, and sentenced the defendant to the death penalty on 22 April 2008.

The victims rights movement and justice system reform

As noted earlier, the victim in the case is a founding member and national board member of *Asu no Kai*. At the time the organization was founded in early 2000, Japan already had a victim compensation law that made modest payments to crime victims, and victim support centres had already been established. *Asu no Kai* had a broader agenda, based on the concept of victims' rights. They argued that the Japanese state was protecting the rights of criminal offenders and spending a great deal of money on their upkeep, but at the same time was not recognizing victims' rights and providing only a small amount of money to take care of the harm they continue to suffer because of the crime. The criminal justice system and the courts should not only administer justice for the purpose of maintaining social order, but also should be actively taking the side of crime victims (Zenkoku Hanzai Higaisha no Kai 2000b). They asserted the right of crime victims to participate in criminal justice processes, and proposed to conduct research based on their own experiences and those in foreign countries and to propose new laws, procedures, and administrative regulations and work to get them passed (Zenkoku Hanzai Higaisha no Kai 2000a).

Established just as the Justice System Reform Council released its interim report and invited public participation, *Asu no Kai* participated actively in the judicial reform process. After the Koizumi administration established an office in the Cabinet Secretariat to manage the implementation of the changes to the justice system, *Asu no Kai* presented its opinions on several different parts of the reforms. They lobbied successfully for a new law establishing the rights of crime victims (*Hanzai Higaisha nado Kihon Hō*) which passed the Diet in late 2004. Subsequently they were invited participants in government deliberations on other measures related to victims' rights. Revision of the Criminal Procedure Law passed the Diet on 20 June 2007. *Asu no Kai* had put forward a proposal to structure criminal procedures around three equal parties: the prosecution, the victim and the defendant. The changes did not go that far, but they do allow victims to participate by sitting with the prosecutors in the courtroom rather than in the observers' section, with the right to question the defendant and witnesses in court, and to present a final statement of their views (*saishū iken benron*) to the court paralleling the statement made by the defendant. They also won a new system for claiming damages following the guilty verdict with a simple lawsuit and a provisional declaration from the court, which is simpler than a regular civil lawsuit for damages. *Asu no Kai* also participated actively in recommending changes to the laws and procedures governing juveniles who commit serious crimes.

The *Asu no Kai* director Okamura Tsutomu credits the Koizumi and Abe administrations' leadership for changes beginning with the Crime Victims Basic Law to respect victims' rights (Okamura 2007). These dramatic changes in the Japanese criminal justice system were facilitated by a broader administrative reform of the Japanese government, which shifted from a traditional bottom-up decision-making system that vested strong power in government ministries and their bureaucracies, in favour of a top-down system centred on the Cabinet Secretariat and Chief Cabinet Secretary that gave the prime minister much greater power to initiate and coordinate designated policy areas. Shinoda (2007) traces the origins of the shift to Prime Minister Nakasone Yasuhiro's attempts to exert more independent authority through his chief cabinet secretary in the 1980s. During his tenure as prime minister in 1996–98, Hashimoto Ryūtarō initiated an administrative reform commission, which began to develop the formal structure to vest more authority in an expanded Cabinet Secretariat. The central posts of chief cabinet secretary and the deputy chief cabinet secretaries were strengthened, with greater autonomy from the ministries and enlarged staffs. The changes also permitted the creation of *ad hoc* policy offices outside of the ministries, at the discretion of the prime minister. The two parliamentary deputy chief cabinet secretaries could then oversee the rapid passage of new legislation that had been developed in the Cabinet Secretariat (Shinoda 2007).

This structure became law in 2001, but it appears that some of the changes had been implemented even earlier for specific issues. The Koizumi administration took over just when these broad administrative reforms went into effect, and simultaneously when the Justice System Reform Council issued its final report. One of the Koizumi government's first initiatives was to establish an *ad hoc* headquarters office in the Cabinet Secretariat to oversee the implementation of the recommended justice system reforms, above and outside the Ministry of Justice, the Ministry of Home Affairs, and the Supreme Court, the three bureaucracies that administer various parts of the justice system. The recommendations of the Justice System Reform Council were far-reaching but quite general, so the new headquarters established 12 advisory councils to assist in the development of specific legislation to implement the various reforms. One of these councils dealt with victims' rights, and *Asu no Kai* was involved with it from the start. After the new victims' rights law passed in 2004, their role was further institutionalized within the Cabinet Office for Victims' Rights that was established through the law.

Even more fundamentally, one of the Justice System Reform Council's three guiding principles was to open the justice system to greater public participation. This resonated with Koizumi's political strategy of working outside the traditional political factional structure, where his position was relatively weak, and making a direct appeal to the public for support of his policies. The Koizumi administration was eager to invite compatible civil society groups into the justice reform process as well as other new policy areas that were established within the expanded Cabinet Secretariat. *Asu no Kai* was one of many conservative civil society organizations newly created under the umbrella of the 1998 non-profit organization (NPO) law (Pekkanen 2003; Pekkanen 2006) that quickly stepped into this opening. The fact that the NPO legislation requires an organization to be sponsored by or linked to a particular government ministry in order to achieve legal NPO status has meant that conservative organizations that government ministries find compatible can achieve NPO status, while civil society organizations that are critical of government policies are far less likely even to seek NPO status. The Japanese NPO law is thus fundamentally different than the neutral provisions that provide incorporated status and tax benefits to NPOs in many other countries.

The largest of these conservative civil society organizations, *Nippon Kaigi*, was formally established in 1997, gained NPO status and quickly developed a national network of local chapters as well as an affiliated Diet members' organization in which over 200 Diet members participate. It promoted itself as a grass-roots organization interested in a range of issues on Koizumi's neoconservative agenda, including constitutional reform, educational reform, and promotion of Yasukuni shrine visits (Masshardt 2009: 187). *Nippon Kaigi* mobilizes its members through petition campaigns and other activities to provide popular support for its own agenda. It serves as a model of grassroots organization for other conservative groups, and often lends support to more specialized social movement organizations such as *Asu no Kai* when they conduct national petition campaigns. Both *Nippon Kaigi* and *Asu no Kai* were heavily involved in promoting more severe treatment of juvenile offenders, sparked by some sensational murders of young children by juveniles in the 1990s.

The way the criminal justice system responded to the Hikari City mother–child murder case must be understood against the backdrop of the recent involvement of conservative civil society and social movement organizations in justice system reform. Moreover, the activities of *Asu no Kai* can be seen as one aspect of a much broader move by the Koizumi administration to implement a neoconservative agenda through a top-down approach that skirted the traditional foot-dragging of the bureaucracy and was facilitated by neoliberal administrative reforms. Koizumi gathered momentum for his agenda with the support of conservative civil society organizations, whose rapid growth had been facilitated in turn by the 1998 NPO law that encouraged the development of non-profit organizations (NGOs) affiliated with specific government agencies as part of the neoliberal privatization of many functions previously carried out directly by government.

3. State–civil society interaction and boundary shifts

Close study of these two cases reveals that the boundaries between the criminal justice system and civil society have shifted as a result of the involvement of two quite opposing types of social movement organizations and their engagement with the state at different levels. One type has been building since the 1960s as an outgrowth of the New Left protest movements, while the other has emerged recently as part of the neoliberal and neoconservative trends that gained strength in the 1990s and came to fruition during the Koizumi administration.

On one front, New Left trial support organizations working with defence lawyers since the late 1960s have institutionalized a system of support for persons arrested for acts related to their political activity and have won some small victories in individual cases. Their strategy encourages arrestees to utilize their constitutional rights to remain silent when arrested, to seek legal counsel and to contest the charges with a full trial, by providing group support to the defendant during a long period of unconvicted detention. It constitutes a deliberate strategy of resistance to the standard criminal justice system procedures that encourage confession and contrition and reward them with short sentences. The criminal justice system has responded to each component of this trial support system and each new move of these organizations, escalating the pressure on those who resist by employing available but little used procedures. Initially these procedural innovations were used only on resistant political offenders, but over time they have become generalized practices that increase the severity of treatment not only for individuals involved in political trials, but for any individual who exercises the constitutional right to remain silent and pursues a full trial with a strong defence against the charges.

This long, contentious interaction between the criminal justice system and trial support organizations can be viewed as a sustained effort by a powerful bureaucracy to maintain the boundaries between the criminal justice system and civil society organizations that support defendants, and to reduce the already limited power of defence lawyers to defend criminal cases. It has been carried out largely without formally changing laws, through incremental changes that fall within the boundaries of administrative discretion, are legitimized by new internal regulations, or are simply ignored when they push beyond legal limits. A major consequence, certainly unintended on the part of the civil society organizations, has been to make the routine practices of the Japanese criminal justice system significantly more severe in the treatment of offenders than they were two or three decades ago. These same procedures have also been used to narrow the range of political dissent and escalate its cost, by extending the reach of the criminal justice system to harass people who have not committed a criminal act, and to criminalize everyday actions when certain people commit them (Steinhoff 2007: 21).[11]

On a different front, victims' rights organizations have emerged recently in civil society seeking more government support for crime victims and their families to address physical, social and psychological needs. Significantly, they also advocate more severe treatment of offenders, under the banner of assuaging the emotional pain of the victims through retributive justice. The Koizumi and Abe governments invited these social movement organizations into policy deliberations concerning revisions of the basic laws governing the criminal justice system, which were then quickly passed by the Diet. Reforms heavily promoted by crime victims' rights organizations have resulted in a restructuring of the boundaries of the criminal justice system to allow crime victims to sue for civil damages in conjunction with a criminal prosecution, to lower the age at which juveniles are tried as adults from 16 to 14, to allow police to investigate crimes committed by juveniles younger than 14 before turning them over to the family court, to allow victims of crimes by juveniles under 14 to receive full documentation of the family court case (redacted to remove personally identifying information) in order to pursue a civil suit for damages against the family, and to allow crime victims to participate directly in criminal trials alongside prosecutors. Thus it is not simply that the government opened its doors to hearing the opinions of these civil society actors; the reforms actually gave the people these organizations represent, crime victims and their surviving family members, a formal place as legitimate actors within the criminal justice system.

During the 1990s there were a series of sensational criminal acts in Japan, including some heinous murders committed by juveniles, crimes committed by foreign residents of Japan, and the sarin gas attacks in the Tokyo subway system carried out by members of the religious cult Aum Shinrikyō. Sensational mass media coverage of these events whipped up public sentiment to construct a moral panic about crimes, particularly crimes by foreigners and youth, as threats to personal security. The perceived remedy was '*gembatsuka*' or tougher punishment for offenders (Hamai and Ellis 2006; Hamai and Ellis 2008; Miyazawa 2008; Yamamoto 2008). Much of the media coverage focused on the sympathetic victims of these crimes, and led the media to embrace organizations such as *Asu no Kai* and to promote their demands for more punitive justice, as we have seen with the Hikari City murder case.

Although academic analyses have debunked the notion of spiralling crime increases in Japan, there has been an apparent decrease in the percentage of crimes that police are able to solve, although some scholars trace this to more scrupulous police recordkeeping of crimes rather than an actual increase in crime (Hamai and Ellis 2008). Since the major source of information about crimes and their prosecution is the criminal justice agencies themselves, the moral panic is in part created by, and certainly serves the interests of, these agencies. Representatives of victims' rights organizations provide an attractive means of promoting ideas and advocating actions that government bureaucrats cannot express publicly, and that even elected politicians might find sensitive. In addition to whipping up public support for more use of capital punishment, the victims' rights organizations have condemned lawyers who defend criminals and incited actions to silence them. Moreover, construed as public opinion, these demands for more severe and retributive punishment of criminals then factor into the decisions made by prosecutors and judges about what penalties are appropriate for various types of offenses, leading to a gradual judicial escalation of punishment.

In contemporary Japan, these two very different kinds of civil society and social movement involvement in the criminal justice system come into direct confrontation over criminal cases in which the prosecution demands capital punishment and lawyers associated with the anti-death penalty movement defend them. The anti-death penalty movement itself grew in part out of a series of death penalty cases with active civil society groups on the defence side. Four of these were criminal cases involving false confessions and wrongful convictions that were overturned by the Supreme Court in the early 1980s (Foote 1992a; Foote 1993). The defendants were set free after spending many years on death row, and new light was cast on the practices of the criminal justice system that produce false confessions and wrongful convictions. There was of course no DNA testing at the time, and the defendants were released only after extensive work by their lawyers and support groups demonstrated that they could not have committed the crime in question and had instead been victims of excessive pressure to confess to crimes they did not commit. Shortly after these four reversals of the death penalty, four other defendants in political trials supported by New Left trial support groups were given death sentences at their first trials, which were then confirmed in subsequent appeals. The support groups for all of these cases attracted people with a specific interest in opposing capital punishment, along with those who supported the defendants for other reasons. Through trial support activities they worked closely with a group of defence lawyers who in turn were involved in defending death penalty cases. By 1990 they had created an anti-death penalty movement led by a lawyer who has defended a number of very high-profile death penalty cases, both political and non-political.

On the other side, the most prominent spokespersons for the best-known victim's rights association are two men whose wives were murdered. In the Hikari City mother–child murders, the husband and father of the murder victims actively advocated the death penalty for a youthful offender who was defended by 21 lawyers linked by the media to the anti-death penalty movement, a movement whose leader was the lead defence attorney in the case. Although the revisions to the criminal procedure law that give crime victims a direct role in the trial had not yet gone into effect, the mass media gave this particular victim an even larger spotlight and joined him in demonizing the anti-death penalty movement and lawyers who defend death penalty cases. The conflict between these two organized segments of civil society over the location of the boundaries of the criminal justice system has played out both in the courtroom and in the mass media, and thus entered living rooms all over Japan.

4. Global pressures on the Japanese criminal justice system

The boundaries of the Japanese criminal justice system have also been shifting in response to globalization pressures, but not always in consistent ways. In some areas the Japanese government appears to be cooperating with external demands and trying to demonstrate its active compliance, while in other areas it seems to be pushing back defiantly. Yet when we look more closely, Japan's response has not always been consistent in following either trajectory.

The case of Shigenobu Fusako reflects the difficulties Japan has faced over its handling of international terrorism. Virtually all of Japan's direct involvement with international terrorism traces back to two branches of the Red Army Faction, which was itself a direct by-product of the 1968–69 crackdown on student protest.

The Japanese government was deeply embarrassed by the numerous international incidents carried out by its citizens under the banner of the Red Army in the 1970s, but was powerless to prevent them. When Japanese citizens associated with the group used the leverage of embassy invasions and airplane hijackings overseas in order to obtain the release of prisoners from Japanese custody, the Japanese government's first priority was the safety of the hostages. The government on two occasions released prisoners from Japanese custody to the Japanese Red Army in exchange for the release of hostages, and on other occasions provided planes to take the perpetrators to international destinations as part of negotiations to end a hostage-taking incident. These decisions were hotly debated within Japan, with the criminal justice agencies vehemently opposed but ultimately overruled. When persons released in these hostage incidents subsequently were implicated in other international incidents, Japan was condemned internationally for being soft on terrorism and was pressured to follow the declared Western hard line of refusing to negotiate with terrorists.

As Japanese citizens were identified as possible participants in the various overseas incidents, their names were placed on the Interpol wanted list, along with the people who had been released from Japanese custody in hostage exchanges. At that point the Japanese authorities could only advertise their wanted posters widely and hope the persons depicted on them would be found. After the surviving participant in the 1972 Lod Airport attack was released by Israel in an international prisoner-of-war exchange with the Palestine Liberation Organization in 1985, he was also placed on the Interpol wanted list, but like Shigenobu and other wanted persons, he remained overseas and beyond reach. In the late 1980s the first two Japanese who were on the Interpol list were found inside Japan and prosecuted, which further embarrassed Japanese officials who had believed they had full control over their borders. Under international pressure, Japan became more committed to international anti-terrorist activity prior to the 1988 Seoul Olympics. In that environment, Japan began more actively circulating the wanted lists of the Yodogo group of former Red Army Faction members in North Korea and the Japanese Red Army group based in the Middle East. For several years the two wanted posters were posted on the wall of every immigration officer's station at Narita International Airport. In the 1990s some of the persons on the wanted lists were found outside of Japan, and the Japanese government participated aggressively in bringing them back to Japan for arrest and trial, sometimes with questionable methods.[12]

During all this time the Japanese Red Army had openly taken credit for the international incidents of the 1970s and issued proclamations, books, and other publications in the name of the organization (Nihon Sekigun 1978; Nihon Sekigun 1993). Shigenobu Fusako wrote of her own personal experiences in the Middle East (Shigenobu 1983; Shigenobu 1984a; Shigenobu 1984b), edited some group publications and frequently presented herself as a spokesperson for the group, but never claimed a formal leadership title. Yet the Japanese government, criminal justice system, and mass media all viewed her as the supreme leader of a hierarchical organization and the presumed mastermind of its terrorist acts.

Her arrest in November 2000 was regarded as a major achievement, despite the embarrassment of having found her already inside Japan. As her trial unfolded it became increasingly clear that the prosecution's case for her involvement in the Hague Incident was weak, and that the organization itself was much looser and less hierarchical, and her own role less dominant, than outsiders had assumed. It was equally clear that although serious charges could not be pressed against some of the other returnees who had been on the wanted list for over 20 years, the government simply would not let Shigenobu off lightly, even if they could not actually prove the charges against her. She was convicted because of who she was imagined to be, rather than for what she actually had done. Her long sentence based on her conviction for attempted murder is a symbolic gesture with significance domestically as a vindication of the criminal justice system, and internationally as a token of Japan's firmness against home-grown terrorism.

It is noteworthy that the Japanese government's increasingly tough stance against its returning terror suspects in the 1990s coincided with the increased severity of treatment of criminal offenders in general and of political offenders in particular. The internal conflict between the criminal justice system and the New Left's trial support system provided the procedural mechanisms, but the arrest and prosecution of high-profile returnees from exile provided the opportunity to show the outside world that Japan could indeed be tough on terrorists. The same impetus to meet global expectations regarding terrorism justified the passage of other terrorism-related measures during the Koizumi–Abe and later years, although these have not involved the domestic criminal justice system directly.[13]

These efforts to meet global anti-terrorism pressures also coincided with the rise of a combination of neoliberal economics and neoconservative political and moral views associated in Japan, as in other Western industrialized countries, with a more punitive and retributive approach to criminal justice (Garland 2001). It was in this ideological climate that the Koizumi government developed its plans to revise the basic laws governing the criminal justice system and opened its doors to the victims' rights movement to participate. The punitive and retributive aspects of the Japanese victim's rights movements also resonated in the neoconservative environment, paralleling a similar development of victims' rights movements in the United States and United Kingdom.

The linkage becomes apparent if we look more closely at the nature of the rights discourse of the victim's rights movement and how it has played out in relation to the global human rights pressures for Japan to adjust its criminal justice system in line with the International Covenant on Civil and Political Rights (The United Nations 1966), the Standard Minimum Rules for the Treatment of Prisoners (First United Nations Congress on the Prevention of Crime and the Treatment of Offenders 1955), and other international documents relating to persons awaiting the death penalty, as well as the United Nations Convention on the Rights of the Child.

Asu no Kai does not invoke human rights, but rather the special rights that crime victims have that entitle them to participate in the criminal justice system. Contrasting the lack of rights that crime victims have and what they view as the massive protection that the Japanese legal system accords to criminal defendants, they advocated a system in which there were three main and equal parties to a criminal trial: the prosecutor, the defendant and the victim, as noted earlier. Missing in this equation is the defence attorney. *Asu no Kai* documents also emphasize the need for retributive justice as the basis for healing from the devastation of being a crime victim (Okamura 2000). With respect to juveniles, they argue that as victims they have a special right to attend family court proceedings and see the legal documents, and they carefully distinguish this from the general public's rights. They mistrust the closed proceedings and feel that their presence as the victims is needed to correct factual errors or slanted information that might be presented by the juvenile in family court. In the same context, they have argued strenuously for the right to appeal the judge's decision when they feel it is not adequate to the harm that has been done to them. Hence they not only confirm the prosecutor's right to appeal a decision that is not sufficiently harsh; they wish to add their own right as victims to make such an appeal (Okamura 2003; Zenkoku Hanzai Higaisha no Kai 2005). They have also sought and won the right to seek civil damages in addition to the criminal proceedings, in both adult and juvenile cases. This in turn reflects not only a more conservative and punitive approach, but accords with the neoliberal economics of making the offender pay for the crime quite literally. It must also be viewed in the context of their successful efforts to lower the age at which cases are tried in the regular criminal justice system from 16 to 14.

Scholars have pointed out that these changes to the juvenile law are in conflict with the United Nations Convention on the Rights of the Child, which Japan has signed. The UN committee that oversees compliance with the convention has criticized Japan for the use of police jail cells to hold juveniles and lowering of the age of criminal responsibility from 16 to 14, pointing out that criminal procedures are not appropriate for children (Sasaki 2005). The subsequent revisions of the juvenile law in 2007 moved even farther against the principles in the international convention, by allowing police to investigate crimes committed by children under the age of 14, including searching their homes and conducting police interrogations, before turning them over to the Family Court.

Japan has also been criticized for human rights violations in connection with its procedures for handling persons awaiting the death penalty. In 1980, only 26 persons with confirmed death sentences were awaiting the death penalty in Japan. It was against that backdrop that four death sentences of the 26 (15 per cent) were overturned as wrongful convictions, and death sentences were anticipated in four pending political cases. At that time persons awaiting the death sentence remained in unconvicted detention, with access to daily visitors and outside communications. That access had made it possible for support groups to work for the release of those wrongfully convicted, just as such outside access enabled trial support groups to sustain the spirits of persons in unconvicted detention during trials that continued intermittently for many years. At precisely that moment the prison administration resurrected a 20-year-old internal memorandum that said prisoners awaiting the death penalty should be sheltered from outside contacts in order to prepare themselves spiritually for death. This argument was used to institute a dramatic shift in the treatment of persons awaiting the death penalty, under which they were permitted only very limited visits and mail communications with designated immediate family members, and all other outside communications were prohibited.[14]

The severe isolation has created psychological problems for persons who wait many years before the death sentence is carried out.[15] In addition, the prison authorities have long maintained a policy of complete secrecy regarding executions. Japanese law requires that the Minister of Justice personally authorize the execution of the death penalty; some ministers would not sign death warrants, while others did. Executions were never announced publicly, and family members were not notified until after the death sentence had been carried out, when they were told to collect the deceased prisoner's personal effects. The severe isolation of persons awaiting the death penalty and the secrecy surrounding executions prompted human rights organizations to complain to the international monitoring committees, which in turn have issued several reports critical of Japan's treatment of persons awaiting the death penalty.

The criminal justice system and the government have largely ignored these criticisms and judges have also generally ignored defence lawyers who attempt to introduce human rights standards into trials by arguing that these standards are supposed to supersede national law because Japan has signed the international conventions and agreed to observe them. Instead, Japanese courts have been handing down increasing numbers of death penalty decisions at the urging of prosecutors (Hamai and Ellis 2008). The number of persons with confirmed death sentences awaiting execution rose steadily from 46 in 1990 to 99 in 2007, despite 53 executions during that time. In 2007, the Minister of Justice in the Abe cabinet announced that several executions had been carried out to keep the number from reaching 100. Several more executions have been announced since then, but an increased flow of death penalty decisions at all three court levels ensures that the number will remain high for some time, as shown in Table 10.1.

It is difficult to correlate judicial decisions with crime rates because of the varying length of time it takes cases to move through the courts. However, there is clear evidence that the rate of homicide in Japan has been low and steady since the late 1980s, and the rate of penal code violations by minors has been low and dropping (Johnson 2005). Although prosecutors and judges are supposed to be professionals making decisions strictly according to the law, the data suggest that both groups of professionals have been responding to societal pressures for more severe penalties as well as to the increased involvement of victims and victims' rights groups in the criminal justice process (Hamai and Ellis 2006; Hamai and Ellis 2008).

Table 10.1 Annual average of new death penalty decisions, by court level

	District Courts	*Appeals Courts*	*Supreme Court*
1990–9	4.8	3.5	4.2
2000–6	13.4	12.7	6.9

Source: Author's recalculation of data from Yasuda and Ogura 2007: 17.

Recent changes to the Prison Law have addressed some of the issues for which the Japanese criminal justice system has been criticized, again in conflicting ways. On the one hand, the longstanding issue of holding people illegally in police jail cells for extended periods of interrogation was addressed not by halting the practice, but by changing the law to make it legal. On the other hand, new rules in 2006 broadened visit and mail privileges for persons serving prison sentences. In 2007, additional revisions to the Prison Law increased both the frequency of visits and the range of visitors permitted to persons awaiting the death sentence. However, in line with Frank Upham's classic observation that Japanese legal reforms always end up leaving critical matters to bureaucratic discretion (Upham 1987), the new rules still leave a great deal to the discretion of prison officials. Initial tests of the new system found that about half of the requests to visit persons awaiting the death penalty were being refused (author's field notes of *Stop Shikei Shikkō* public meeting and demonstration, 2 June 2007). At the Tokyo House of Detention, which houses many death row prisoners as well as persons in unconvicted detention, prison officials responded to the new 2007 rules by announcing that they could not handle the expected increase in visits, so they arbitrarily cut the length of a standard visit in half, from 15 minutes to 8.[16] As of the author's last visit in November 2009, the allotted visit time was 10 minutes.

Thus the convergence of global anti-terrorism pressures and global neoconservative and neoliberal policies has contributed to increasing severity in the Japanese criminal justice system, which may be understood as an expansion of the system's boundaries. The global impact cannot be easily separated from the domestic forces advocating the same shift towards more punitive and retributive criminal justice policies. Moreover, the ability of the Japanese government to resist some globalization pressures while actively embracing others makes it clear that there is interplay between domestic and global forces rather than the one-way process that hyper-globalists imagine. The Koizumi and Abe administrations responded only to those global pressures for neoconservative social policies and neoliberal economic and administrative reforms that resonated with their own domestic political agenda and with conservative civil society organizations. Other global pressures associated with human rights, which resonated with certain civil society organizations but have not had strong domestic political and bureaucratic backing, have been studiously ignored or actively resisted by successive Japanese administrations.

Conclusion

This chapter uses an exploration of two recent criminal trials to examine the interplay of global, state and civil society forces that have reshaped certain aspects of the Japanese criminal justice system. This strategy precludes consideration of some other significant reforms such as the lay judge system, but permits a deeper examination of the role played by specific social movement groups as civil society actors and clarifies how the state has managed global pressures on its criminal justice system.

Within this limited approach, the following shifts in the boundaries of the Japanese criminal justice system may be identified.

(1) The criminal justice system has become harsher at all stages, keeping more people in the system for longer periods of time, with greater isolation from society and with an expanded use of the death sentence.
(2) The criminal justice system has expanded its reach to crimes committed by Japanese citizens beyond its national borders, and to intimidate dissidents who have not actually committed a crime.
(3) The sphere of family court procedures that protect juveniles has shrunk and the boundary for adult criminal procedures has correspondingly expanded downward from the age of 16 to 14; police criminal investigations have also been extended to children under the age of 14.
(4) Crime victims and their family members have been inserted into criminal justice procedures and have been accorded a number of specific new rights, in addition to receiving new forms of government support.
(5) Japan initially ignored and then began actively demonstrating its cooperation with global anti-terrorism efforts in the area of criminal justice.
(6) Japan has actively resisted the imposition of global human rights standards in the areas of capital punishment and treatment of children by extending its domestic criminal justice system in the opposite direction.

These boundary shifts have been the result of complex domestic interactions that open the doors of the criminal justice system to certain civil society actors and at the same time try to close them against others. They also reflect complex domestic responses to global efforts to harmonize legal regimes and impose global standards. These particular boundary shifts in the criminal justice system also parallel shifts in criminal justice in the United States and United Kingdom that have been linked to the rise of neoliberal economic policies and neoconservative political views in those countries (Garland 2001). Those societies have also experienced mass media-promoted moral panics about crime and personal insecurity, have undergone a shift to more punitive criminal justice practices and an orientation to raising the economic 'price' of criminal behaviour, have invited victims' rights organizations into the criminal justice system, and have come to view victims as clients of the system. The irony is that although those same boundary shifts in the two major common law countries have been analyzed as a reaction to chronic high crime levels, in Japan they have occurred despite continuing low rates of crime, under a quite different legal tradition. These comparisons suggest the penetrating power of the economic and social ideologies underlying globalization to override other differences; yet the analysis also demonstrates the highly nuanced and selective way the Japanese criminal justice system has responded to certain kinds of pressure and resisted others.

There are some new indications that the global tide of neoconservative and neoliberal ideas may not be as irreversible as it has seemed for the past decade. At one time, the Anglo-American criminal justice system could have been held up as the model of fairness against which the Japanese system ought to be judged, despite the greater concern of the latter for reintegration and rehabilitation and many other differences between the two systems. Unfortunately, since the terrorist attacks of 11 September 2001, the American criminal justice system has been deeply tarnished by the Bush administration's relentless anti-terrorism crusade and the use of extra-legal methods against non-citizens that put even the harshest practices of the Japanese criminal justice system to shame. Yet the US Supreme Court has intervened in several instances to curb these excesses and assert that basic Anglo-American legal rights and international rules governing the treatment of prisoners of war must apply even in these cases. Subsequently, one of the very first acts of newly inaugurated President Barack Obama was to firmly renounce any use of torture by any agents of the US government, including the Central Intelligence Agency, and to order that the Guantanamo Bay facility housing captured terrorist suspects be closed. Moreover, in both Europe and the United States, just as earlier doubts about rehabilitation led to pressures for a more punitive criminal justice system, there are now growing doubts about the effectiveness of an increasingly punitive and retributive system as well as its enormous economic and social costs. Those voices are still quite weak in Japan, but they do exist and new political and social conditions may energize them.

The overwhelming victory of the Democratic Party of Japan (DPS) and defeat of the conservative coalition in the Japanese election of August 2009 has brought to power a far more centrist political party which has some roots in the post-war Japanese left and in civil society organizations of the left. While this new government is just getting its footing, the signs of change in the area of criminal justice are already apparent. The prominent victims' right materials have disappeared from the cabinet secretariat's website where they used to be prominently displayed. More significantly, the new Minister of Justice, woman lawyer Chiba Keiko, has a long record of opposition to the death penalty and support for a variety of issues that the left has long advocated. In her first public message, she announced three major initiatives: the establishment of a new independent human rights agency that would provide citizens with recourse for redress of human rights violations outside the control of the Justice Ministry and courts; ratification of the "optional protocols" in international human rights treaties that Japan has steadfastly refused to acknowledge; and the promotion of greater transparency in criminal interrogations through video recording of all interrogation sessions (Repeta 2009). These initiatives, if actually enacted, would bring about a substantial reversal of Japan's current criminal justice practices.

More broadly, the global financial collapse of 2008 has called into question the fundamental economic principles of neoliberalism, while simultaneously revealing how heavily intertwined the global economy has become. Faced with the sudden collapse of major financial institutions, governments have rapidly abandoned their neoliberal free market ideals to intervene in markets and institutions that were previously off-limits as a matter of basic ideological principles. As governments work together to rebuild new global economic and financial institutions for the twenty-first century, they will also be irrevocably reducing the dominance of the ideological foundations of neoliberalism. That in turn may also temper the neoconservative social policies that have accompanied the rise of neoliberal economic principles to global dominance in recent years. While the institutional changes in criminal justice systems that have been inspired by neoconservative and neoliberal social ideas are not likely to collapse as quickly as the financial institutions have, they, too, may shift direction over time. Boundary shifts are, after all, evidence of the inherent flexibility and impermanence of institutions.

Notes

1 Yamazato Kinuko provided research assistance in the preparation of this chapter. The University of Hawaii Japan Studies Endowment, the Fulbright Commission, and the University of Tokyo Institute of Social Science supported the fieldwork, which also relied on the generosity and cooperation of many Japanese individuals and groups. My thanks to all of these individuals and institutions, but any errors are of course my personal responsibility.

2 The author's unorthodox angle of vision derives from more than 35 years of following the global activities of a relatively small number of Japanese who began as student activists in the social movements of the late 1960s. The research strategy is always to examine the most extreme cases, which reveal conflicts and practices that are obscured in more routine operations. This research led straight to the criminal justice system and to practices that were diametrically at odds with the prevailing view of how that system worked. Following individual cases over a long period of time and pursuing related issues and movements as they arose has provided a ringside seat to observe how global, state and civil society forces actively shape the Japanese criminal justice system and shift its boundaries.

3 PFLP was a new guerrilla organization that operated within the Palestine Liberation Organization and had settled in Lebanon after being ousted from Jordan.

4 The actual Japanese crime is called *taihō oyobi kankin,* the same words as arrest and imprisonment when carried out by legal authorities. To avoid confusion, this chapter uses the term 'hostage-taking', although the crime also includes other forms of kidnapping and holding people.

5 There have been recent changes to some criminal justice system procedures that this chapter also addresses. The chapter uses the procedures that applied at the time a case was being prosecuted.

6 A new system of 'lay judges' who will sit with the three professional judges will begin shortly for certain types of cases. Under the rationale that discontinuous trials would inconvenience the lay judges, trials under the new system (called *baishin* or jury, although it is not a jury) are to be held continuously. In order to accommodate that unaccustomed speed, such trials will involve a preliminary hearing at which the judges, prosecutors, and defence attorneys agree on what evidence will be presented, and no further evidence will be admissible. This system resembles the pre-war inquisitorial system with its preliminary trial investigation document (*yoshin shūketsu ketteishō*) that became the only material submitted in evidence at the trial. However, under this new system there is a limited form of discovery. Only if the defence asks for it, the prosecutors must hand over exculpatory evidence.

7 Among Red Army-related defendants, she now holds the record for having been held incommunicado the longest, at six and a half years. The previous record-holders were Shiomi Takaya in 1970–71 for 18 months, and Maruoka Osamu in 1987–90 for three years.

8 Technically, Japan does not have 'life sentences'. It has 'unlimited sentences' (*mukikei*) in which release from prison on parole is theoretically possible, and death sentences.

Those who advocate abolition of the death penalty in Japan acknowledge that this would only be feasible with the concurrent creation of a true life sentence without parole.

9 The official English name of the organization is the National Association of Crime Victims and Surviving Families. The name *Asu no Kai* (Tomorrow Society) was chosen with the idea that the lives of crime victims are very hard now, but that they will be better in the future (Zenkoku Hanzai Higaisha no Kai 2000a).

10 Hashimoto, who did not submit a complaint to the bar association himself, had neglected to warn people that the complainants could be sued and that courts have awarded substantial monetary damages for irresponsible complaints. Meanwhile, the various bar associations that received the complaints against the defence lawyers rejected them as being without merit and no defence lawyer has been disciplined. Consequently, since nothing had happened despite thousands of complaints, the complaint system and the bar associations became the target of criticism on the same talk show in December that year.

11 Arrests on trivial charges are a common pretext for harassment and intimidation of known political activists who have not committed any crime. The arrest not only allows the police to hold the person for an extended time in a police jail cell, but also justifies extensive searches of residences and offices in any way connected with the 'suspect'. If the person is then released without charges, civil liberties lawyers associated with the New Left trial support movement are happy to file suit for false arrest against the police, prosecutor and judge responsible for the arrest warrant. In a much more egregious case, prominent defence lawyer Yasuda Yoshihiro was arrested in December 1998 on charges related to legal advice he had given a client regarding a business deal and held for nine months in unconvicted detention. He was then the lead lawyer for Asahara Shoko (born Matsumoto Chizuo), the leader of Aum Shinrikyō who was facing a death sentence for charges stemming from his role in the Tokyo subway sarin gas attacks. Yasuda's arrest was viewed by many as an attempt to get him removed from the case. He was charged and prosecuted on felony criminal charges for what would ordinarily be treated as a minor civil matter, which meant that he faced prison time as well as loss of his license to practice law if he was found guilty. The charges were so blatantly false and the investigation had made so many obvious errors that he was found not guilty and the judge chastised the prosecutor in the decision. Despite the not guilty ruling, the prosecutors appealed, and he had to fight the case all over again on appeal. In a decision handed down the day after the Hikari City murder case re-trial ended with a death penalty verdict, Yasuda was found guilty of the business-related charge and sentenced to a fine (which would have been the usual verdict if the case had been handled as a civil matter) and a prison sentence equivalent to the time he had served in unconvicted detention. The appeals court may have felt this was a face-saving solution, but Yasuda has appealed that decision to the Supreme Court in a final attempt to clear his name and preserve his license to practice law.

12 In March 2000, four Japanese Red Army members were forcibly returned to Japan after serving jail terms in Lebanon for passport violations. Japanese authorities had arranged to have them flown to the Amman airport in Jordan blindfolded and under guard at gunpoint, as soon as they were released. After an Australian airline refused to take them because its officials thought the forcible deportation was illegal under international law, they were whisked off to Japan on a Russian Aeroflot charter. It was, in contemporary American terror-speak, a 'rendition' (recounted by Yamamoto Mariko, one of the four persons deported, in author's field notes of Wakō Haruo appeal trial decision and informal meeting afterwards, 9 May 2007).

13 In the wake of 9/11 and the United Nations resolutions calling on nations to support anti-terrorism activities, Japan quickly passed the Anti-Terrorism Special Measures Act in October 2001. The new law, which has been renewed several times but became particularly contentious after the Democratic Party's upper house victory in summer 2007, has enabled Japan's self-defence forces to provide cooperation and logistical support as

well as material supplies to US forces outside Japan's borders despite the constraints of Article 9 of Japan's Constitution, provided there was no combat taking place in the areas involved, and the activities were either on the high seas and airspace above, or were in land areas with the consent of the countries whose territory was involved (Shinoda 2007). The Koizumi and Abe governments also tried unsuccessfully for several years to pass a very extensive conspiracy law with the justification that it was needed to combat international activity by criminal groups and the use of new communications media for criminal purposes.

14 Prisoners awaiting the death penalty actually remain in cells on the same floors as persons in unconvicted detention. All the cells are completely closed and there is virtually no communication among the prisoners. Although the death row prisoners do not have the visiting privileges of those in unconvicted detention, they are allowed to watch a movie three times a month. A cart with a television set and VCR is wheeled to their rooms. In a prison interview with the author, prisoner Wakō Haruo reported that he was able to identify certain cells and their occupants as awaiting the death penalty because the cart stopped at their cell door (author's field notes of visit with Wakō Haruo at the Tokyo House of Detention, 22 May 2007). A more extended report appears in a letter from Wakō Haruo published in the newsletter of the support group for Daidoji Masashi, who is awaiting the death penalty at Tokyo House of Detention and whose wife was released to the Japanese Red Army in a 1977 incident (See Wakō 2005).

15 It is no coincidence that the measures to isolate death row prisoners from outside contact were instituted just before the defendants with strong New Left trial support groups received death sentences. None of the four persons awaiting the death sentence for crimes related to their political activity has been executed. This is believed to be because they have co-defendants who remain at large after having been released in hostage incidents in the 1970s.

16 The length of visits to persons in unconvicted detention has decreased from 30 minutes in the 1980s to 20 minutes in the 1990s, and 15 minutes for the past several years. The author's first, long-awaited visit to Shigenobu Fusako occurred right after the new rules came into effect, and the visit was cut short after only eight minutes.

References

Castberg, A. Didrick (1990) *Japanese Criminal Justice*. New York: Praeger.

First United Nations Congress on the Prevention of Crime and the Treatment of Offenders. (1955) 'Standard minimum rules for the treatment of prisoners'. Online. Available: http://www.unhchr.ch/html/menu3/b/h_comp34.htm) (accessed 3 February 2008).

Foote, Daniel H. (1992a) 'From Japan's death row to freedom', *Pacific Rim Law & Policy Journal*, 1:11–103.

—— (1992b) 'The benevolent paternalism of Japanese criminal justice', *California Law Review*, 80:317–90.

—— (1993) '"The door that never opens"?: Capital punishment and post-conviction review of death sentences in the United States and Japan', *Brooks Journal of International Law*, XIX:367–521.

—— (1995) 'Confessions and the right to silence in Japan', *Georgia Journal of International and Comparative Law*, 21:415–88.

Garland, David (2001) *The Culture of Control: crime and social order in contemporary society*, Oxford: Clarendon.

Haley, John Owen (1991) *Authority Without Power: law and the Japanese paradox*, New York: Oxford University Press.

Hamai, Koichi and Ellis, Thomas (2006) 'Crime and criminal justice in modern Japan: from re-integrative shaming to popular punitivism', *International Journal of the Sociology of Law*, 34:157–78.

Hamai, Koichi and Ellis, Tom (2008) '*Genbatsuka*: growing penal populism and the changing role of public prosecutors in Japan?' *Hanzai Shakaigaku Kenkyū*, 33:67–91.

Hikari-shi Jiken Bengodan (2007) 'Hikari jiken Q & A (Bengodan e no shitsumon ni kotaeru)', *Forum 90*, 29 August: 10–14.

Hikari-shi Saiban Bengodan (2007) 'Hikari-shi jiken bengonin kōshin iken chinjutsu', in N.S.H.H. Iinkai (ed.) *Anata mo Shikei Hanketsu o Kakasareru*, Tokyo: Inpakuto Shuppankai, pp. 90–173.

Johnson, David T. (2002) *The Japanese Way of Justice: prosecuting crime in Japan*. Oxford and New York: Oxford University Press.

—— (2005) 'The vanishing killer: Japan's postwar homicide decline', *Social Science Japan Journal* 9:73–90.

Masshardt, Brian (2009) 'Demonstrating democracy: citizen politics in Japan and Yasukuni Shrine, 2001–6', unpublished thesis, University of Hawaii, Honolulu.

Ministry of Justice Government of Japan (2006) 'Ensuring that the results of the justice system reform take root'. Online. Available: http://www.moj.go.jp/ENGLISH/issues/issues01.html) (acccessed 20 February 2008).

Miyazawa, Setsuo (2001) 'Administrative control of Japanese judges', in C.J. Milhaupt, J.M. Ramseyer, and M.K. Young (eds) *Japanese Law in Context: readings in society, the economy, and politics*, Cambridge and London: Harvard University Asia Center, Harvard University Press, pp. 79–83.

—— (2008) 'The politics of increasing punitiveness and the rising populism in Japanese criminal justice policy', *Punishment & Society* 10:47–77.

Nihon Sekigun (1978) *Danketsu o Mezashite: Nihon Sekigun no sōkatsu*, Vol. 1. Osaka: Jinmin Shimbun Henshūbu.

—— (1993) *Nihon Sekigun 20 nen no Kiseki*. Tokyo: Hanashi no Tokushū.

Okamura, Tsutomu (2000) 'Goaisatsu'. Online. Available: http://www.navs.jp/introduction/introduction.html (accessed 20 February 2008).

Pekkanen, Robert (2003) 'Molding Japanese civil society: state-structured incentives and the patterning of civil society', in F. Schwartz and S. Pharr (eds) *The State of Civil Society in Japan*. New York: Cambridge University Press, pp. 116–34.

—— (2006) *Japan's Dual Civil Society: members without advocates*, Stanford, California: Stanford University Press.

Repeta, Lawrence (2009) 'Transfer of power at Japan's Justice Ministry', *The Asia-Pacific Journal*, 44-2-09. Online. Available: http://www.japanfocus.org/-Lawrence-Repeta/3244 (accessed 20 February 2008).

Sasaki, Mitsuaki (2005) 'Amending the juvenile law in Japan: ignoring the UN Committee on the Rights of the Child recommendations', in *HURIGHTS Osaka*, (ed.) Osaka: HURIGHTS OSAKA. pp. 1–4.

Sassen, Saskia (2007) *A Sociology of Globalization*. New York: W. W. Norton & Company.

Shigenobu, Fusako (1983) *Jūnenme no Manazashi kara*, Tokyo: Hanashi no Tokushū.

—— (1984a) *Beirut-1982 nen Natsu*, Tokyo: Hanashi no Tokushū.

—— (1984b) *Taichi ni Mimi o Tsukereba Nihon no Oto ga Suru*, Tokyo: Aki Shobō.

—— (2001) *Ringo no Ki no Shita de Anata o Umō to Kimeta*, Tokyo: Gentōsha.

—— (2005) 'Hidakyou no Ishi o Shinayaka de Tayō na Chikara ni', *Oliibu no Ki*, p. 24.

Shigenobu san o Sasaeru Kai (2006) 'Seiji hanketsu o hihan shimasu', *Oriibu no Ki*, 15, March 15, p. 24.

Shinoda, Tomohito (2007) *Koizumi Diplomacy: Japan's kantei approach to foreign and defense affairs*, Seattle and London: University of Washington Press.

Steinhoff, Patricia (2007) 'Resisting repression through trial support groups in the Japanese new left cycle of resistance', paper presented at *Collective Behavior and Social Movements Workshop on Movement Cultures, Strategies, and Outcomes*, Hofstra University, Long Island, New York.

Steinhoff, Patricia G. (1996) 'Three women who loved the left: radical woman leaders in the Japanese red army movement', in A.E. Imamura (ed.) *Re-Imaging Japanese Women*, Berkeley, Los Angeles and London: University of California Press, pp. 301–23.

—— (1999) 'Doing the defendant's laundry: support groups as social movement organizations in contemporary Japan', *Japanstudien, Jahrbuch des Deutschen Instituts fur Japanstudien*, 11: 55–78.

—— (2008) 'Mass arrests, sensational crimes, and stranded children: three crises for Japanese new left activists' families', in A. Hashimoto and J. Traphagan (eds) *Japanese Families in a Global Age: conflict and change*. New York: SUNY Press, pp. 77–109.

The Justice System Reform Council (2001) 'Recommendations of the Justice System Reform Council – for a justice system to support Japan in the 21st century.'

The United Nations (1966) 'International Covenant on Civil and Political Rights'. Online. Available: http://www.hrweb.org/legal/undocs.html (accessed 20 February 2008).

Upham, Frank K (1987) *Law and Social Change in Postwar Japan*. Cambridge: Harvard University Press.

Wakō, Haruo (2001) 'So-in henben seikyū ni taisuru ikensho', *Kokkyō no nai Kishidan*, 30, 30 June, p. 7.

—— (2003) '"Hagu Jiken" ni kakawaru hansho kaishi ni atatte no ikensho', *Kokkyō no Nai Kishidan*, 24 March, pp. 1–30.

—— (2005) 'Mawari ga shikei kakutei no hitotachi ni nattemasu', *Shienren Nyūsu*, 277, May: 8–10.

Yamamoto, Ryoko (2008) 'Policing strangers: the convergence of immigration law enforcement and crime control in contemporary Japan', unpublished dissertation, University of Hawaii, Honolulu.

Zenkoku Hanzai Higaisha no Kai (2000a) 'Mokuteki to katsudō'. Online. Available: http://www.navs.jp/introduction/introduction.html) (accessed 20 February 2008).

—— (2000b) 'Setsuritsu no shuisho'. Online. Available: http://www.navs.jp/introduction/introduction.html#s (accessed 20 February 2008).

—— (2005) '2000 nen kaisei shonen hō 5 nengo minaoshi no ikensho o teishutsu'. Online. Available: http://www.navs.jp/report/1/opinion2/opinion2_10.html (accessed 20 February 2008).

Zwerman, Gilda and Steinhoff, Patricia G. (2005) 'When activists ask for trouble: state-dissident interactions and the new left cycle of resistance in the United States and Japan', in C. Davenport, H. Johnston, and C. Mueller (eds) *Repression and Mobilization, Social Movements, Protest, and Contention*, Minneapolis: University of Minnesota Press, pp. 85–107.

11 The rapid redrawing of boundaries in Japanese higher education*

Roger Goodman

The February 2008 issue of the influential journal *Chūō Kōron* was dedicated to the discussion of higher education reform in Japan. An article by Nakai Kōichi (2008: 80–81) described in detail a division which has arisen between what were dubbed the *'Genjitsu Rosen-ha'* (literally, the 'Practical Faction', but perhaps best translated as the 'Professional Training Faction') and the *'Han-Shikkōbuha'* (literally 'Anti-Service Function Faction', but possibly best translated as the 'Academic Training Faction') in the University of Tokyo's Faculty of Education, a division stemming mainly from the problem of finding jobs for the Faculty's graduate students. According to the article, Education faculties across Japan were having increasing problems placing their graduate students into jobs. In order to deal with this, in the previous five years, five new graduate professional training courses (including clinical psychology and higher education management) had been established in the Tokyo University Faculty and, according to the Head of the Faculty, Professor Kaneko Motohisa, the 'professional training orientation' that had been established had already led to a tripling in the number of student applications which, in turn, has meant that the Faculty had been able to establish seven new lectureships. At the same time, the article reported that the new orientation had led to the departure of several senior staff before their retirement age, including Professor Hirota Teruyuki, who was quoted as expressing concern about the new direction in which graduate work in educational studies in general was going in Japan: 'Today's graduate students are no longer able to become part of a community of knowledge-seekers in the unhurried, wandering manner of earlier times'. Education faculties at other universities were also reported to be unhappy with the change in direction at the University of Tokyo; as an unnamed source in the article asked, 'Why does the University of Tokyo need to train practitioners? It should keep to its role of educating academics and not jeopardize our jobs'.

Nakai's (2008: 74–76) article in *Chūō Kōron* also examined what he described as a 'sudden epidemic of research fraud and misconduct' taking place in Japanese universities. Examples cited included:

* An almost identical version of this chapter has been published in *Japan Forum*, 32, 1–2, March–June, 2010: 65–87.

(a) January 2003: University of Tokyo Medical School Professor Tsutsumi Osamu, the Crown Princess' gynaecologist, suspended for embezzling state subsidies;

(b) August 2003: University of Tokyo vice president Professor Nitagai Kumon (who ironically had announced the suspension of Professor Tsutsumi a few months earlier) forced to resign for misappropriating state subsidies through falsified business trips;

(c) June 2006: Waseda Professor Matsumoto Kazuko, a high-profile researcher and a member of a number of leading scientific research policy-related committees, forced to resign over the misuse of around ¥212 million of public money;

(d) October 2006: University of Tokyo Professor Taira Kazunari and research associate Dr Kawasaki Hiroaki dismissed after Kawasaki's papers in journals such as *Nature* were found to be based on fabricated data;

(e) December 2006: Osaka University Professor Sugino Akio dismissed for the use of fraudulent data.

All of these scandals were described as the side-effects of an increasingly competitive research environment and the pressure on universities to 'survive' exacerbated by conflicts of interests (*rieki sōhan*) experienced by researchers who were increasingly taking part, with university encouragement, in joint university–industry projects (*sangaku renkei*).[1]

A third article in *Chūō Kōron* (Kobayashi 2008: 64–73) examined the changing role and expectations of university presidents in Japan, starting with the story of Yūki Akio, a former administrative minister of education, the most senior bureaucratic position in the Ministry of Education and Science. In 2006, Yūki received a call from the then-president, Sendō Fujiro, about the presidency of Yamagata University. After some contemplation, Yūki decided to run in the election for the post. There was uproar in the institution. Many university faculty complained of 'a member of the Ministry of Education elite being "parachuted in as president" (*amakudari gakuchō*)' and argued that this constituted 'state control and threatened academic freedom'. When the election took place in 2007, Yūki lost, 355 to 378. In earlier times, his opponent would have become president at that point. However, in 2004, reforms had been introduced that turned national universities, such as Yamagata, into quasi-private corporations *(dokuritsu gyōsei hōjin)*, and the president was henceforth required to be appointed by a Presidential Election Committee; the election results of the faculty were only 'for reference'. The Committee chose Yūki as president, and he immediately proposed the introduction of a bureaucratic vertical management model with the president appointing senior administrators (*riji*) in various areas. In response, those who had opposed him from the very beginning continued airing their views that it was dangerous to leave university management to people who did not understand academia.

In a thoughtful article which sets the context for these (and other) articles about the changes occurring in Japanese higher education, Hasumi Shigehiko (president of the University of Tokyo, 1997–2001) described the European universities of the eighteenth century as the 'first generation' and the nineteenth century universities (which functioned as institutions of the nation-state) as the 'second generation' of higher education institutions historically (Hasumi 2008: 29). He saw the trends outlined in the other articles in the journal as symptoms of what he felt was the development of the 'third generation' of universities. These are institutions which have to generate their own profits and can no longer rely either on an automatic influx of students who must come to them (because of their monopoly over degrees and certificates) or on government funding to provide human resources for the nation. William Cummings (2006) has called this third type of university the 'service university' and it is the development of this service university culture that is leading to the increasing diversification of Japanese higher education, which is the focus of this chapter.[2]

The chapter proceeds as follows. After a brief history of the development of Japanese higher education, we look at the pressures on the contemporary system and how different sectors of society (the state, students, employers and universities themselves) have responded to these pressures. In the final section, we examine how the boundaries in the higher education sector have been rapidly redrawn in the past few years in the light of the pressures which have come to bear on the system.

1. The history of Japanese higher education

The history of Japanese higher education is very short by European standards. There were no great medieval universities along the lines of Bologna, Paris, Oxford or Cambridge. Whilst there were high levels of literacy in medieval and feudal Japan long before the Meiji Restoration of 1868 – mainly due to the widespread system of local private schools (*terakoya*) – the study of subjects such as medicine, mathematics and applied sciences, which has long been part of European curricula, were studied instead through apprenticeships. The development of higher education in Japan can therefore be legitimately taken as having started in the last third of the nineteenth century, when the Meiji oligarchs, recognizing that education was the key to preventing the country from being colonized, developed a system that would produce workers to drive the country's modernization. The emphasis of the oligarchs was on the primary level of education (by 1905, 90 per cent of young Japanese were receiving at least five years of education) but at the other end of the system, a small number of higher education institutions were established and charged with producing the bureaucrats and officials who would work in government. At the pinnacle of – and largely dominating – the system sat the imperial universities, which were charged with training the teachers for lower-order institutions and whose graduates were preferentially employed by state institutions. National universities, therefore, had always received their funding from the state and saw themselves as part of a state project. They were good examples of Hasumi's 'second generation' of higher education institutions described earlier.

During its early years, the private university system in Japan stood in large part in opposition to the state control over the imperial universities. As an official history of Japan's Private Colleges and Universities has put it:

Under the absolutist regime centred on the Emperor Meiji, the original ideals of a liberal education were suppressed. . . . But these ideals . . . remained alive in the private schools not officially recognised by the state, and over time they grew and eventually forced the state to concede.

(Nihon Shiritsu Daigaku Renmei, ed. 1984, 12–13)

Institutions such as Keiō, Dōshisha and Waseda were founded in 1858, 1875 and 1882 respectively by the anti-government liberal figures Fukuzawa Yukichi, Niijima Jo and Okuma Shigenobu, but were denied official recognition until the University Ordinance of 1918. In the 20 years following the Ordinance, however, higher education in Japan experienced impressive growth, particularly in the private sector, which catered to around two-thirds of the total university and college population of students by 1938, a pattern that has remained more or less the same to this day. In the post-war period, private universities were established increasingly to meet the excess demand that the national universities could not – or would not – meet, as individuals realized the value of self-investment in higher education for career prospects. Higher education in Japan expanded rapidly and continually throughout the post-war period. Over a 45-year period it moved from being, to use the categories of Martin Trow (1973), an elite system through being a mass system to becoming a universal system. In 1960, only 10.1 per cent of high school graduates went to some form of higher or further full-time education; by the 1980s this had risen to 49.9 per cent and by 2005, to 76.2 per cent, which was one of the highest rates in the world (Takeuchi 2007: 45).[3] As mentioned, the vast majority of this expansion has been in the private sector – around 80 per cent of Japan's higher education institutions are private – and resources remain, as at the system's beginnings, unequally distributed across the public/private divide. Today, private institutions receive only just over 10 per cent of their running costs from government sources (down from a high of almost 30 per cent in the early 1970s),[4] but since they were operating until the early 1990s in a rapidly expanding market (where demand far outstripped supply) they have had a very minimal service orientation. At their worst, they have been characterized as institutions which have served the interests of their owners and their staff more than their students (e.g., critiques by McVeigh 2002, Kinmonth 2005).

The way in which Japan's higher education system developed led to a higher education sector that is divided by several relatively clear-cut internal boundaries. There is, for example, a major boundary between national and private universities.[5] The average cost of attending national universities, which are generally considered to have higher academic status, is roughly half that of attending private institutions (see Newby *et al.* 2008, Chapter 4 for a full account of financing of Japanese higher education). Students who enter national universities have usually participated in the supplementary education systems of *juku* and *yobikō* and, since not everyone can afford to invest in these supplemental systems, students who gain entrance to national universities tend to come from higher social class backgrounds (see LeTendre, 1995 for a good overview of the research on the relationship between educational attainment and social background in Japan and

Roesgaard, 2006, for an overview of the different types of 'shadow educational' institutes which exist in Japan). The system is also divided into four-year institutions and lower-level two-year junior colleges known in Japanese as 'short-term universities' (*tanki daigaku*), which have largely catered to young women but are fast disappearing from the higher education scene. Finally, there is a boundary between the academically oriented universities (four or two-year *daigaku*) which collectively cater to around 50 per cent of high school graduates, and the vocationally oriented, generally three-year, higher education professional training colleges known as *senmon gakkō* in Japanese, which cater to around a further 20 per cent plus of high school graduates, including a significant proportion of students who 'double school' by attending university during the day and vocational school in the evenings (see Kinmonth 2005: 125; Abe 1989: 76).[6] Within each of these groups of institutions (national four- and two-year institutions, private four- and two-year institutions, and vocational schools), the spread of resources has historically been relatively static. It is the recent diversification within these sectors which is the main focus of the 'redrawing of boundaries' that is the focus of this chapter.

2. The pressures on Japanese higher education

The pressures on Japan's higher education sector are well documented, in both the academic and the popular press (see Hawkins and Furuto 2008, for a brief historical account of the development of these pressures). These can therefore be summarized in fairly short order.

Political pressures

The rhetoric of the market and deregulation (*kisei kanwa*) – spurred in particular by the belief that deregulation was the best means to restimulate the faltering economy – led to a 31 per cent increase in the number of four-year universities in Japan between 1992–2004 as more and more organizations entered the sector. Ironically, but by pure chance, this growth in the number of institutions coincided exactly with the number of 18-year-olds in the population (who constitute 95 per cent of new entrants at universities) decreasing by 31 per cent. The net effect was that the success rate for those applying to university increased from 55 to 80 per cent. By 2010 it has reached virtually 100 per cent as supply and demand have come into balance.

At the same time, as fallout from the 'bubble economy', there was increasing interest in how exactly public money was being spent. In the case of higher education, this became linked with the new international league tables of universities, which did not reflect well on Japan. In the QS/THE 2005 List of Top 200 Universities, there were only nine from Japan (of which only three were in the top 90), whilst Anglophone countries such as the United States had nine in the top 14, UK nine in the top 73 (and six in the top 30) and Australia nine in the top 80 (and five in the top 40). In 2007, the situation for Japanese universities had not changed much, with four in the top 90 and ten in the top 200, with the tenth university ranked at 199.[7]

Given the high status of Japanese secondary education in international tests such as the Programme for International Student Assessment (PISA) and the huge combined family and state financial investment in their higher education system, these figures suggested to many in Japan that something was not right with the higher education system in the country.[8] It was often pointed out that Japan's is the second most expensive system in the world after the US and that objectively Japan appeared to be getting a poor return for its investment, both public and private.

Economic pressures

In times of high economic growth, it was possible to sustain the argument that universities were a 'moratorium' or 'liminal' space for social growth between the rigours of high school and company life. Indeed, universities were largely characterized, up until the end of the 1980s, as adding social education to the academic education which high school had already provided (see Tsuda 1993). Such an argument, however, was no longer considered sustainable during the recession of the 1990s when universities, as with all other arenas of life in Japan, needed increasingly to demonstrate greater 'productivity' and 'efficiency'.

Demographics

The biggest pressure on universities, however, has been the declining number of students of the age to start university and structural obstacles to replacing students of that age with new markets. The bursting of the Japanese economic bubble coincided almost exactly with the peak of the number of 18-year-olds in the Japanese population. This generation, the second post-war baby boom, peaked at 2,050,000 in 1992 and then began a steady decline in numbers to around 1,410,000 in 2004 (a decline of 31.2 per cent). Due to the rapidly decreasing birth rate in Japan since the late 1980s, there is no third baby boom on the horizon, and the number of 18-year-olds will decline to 1,183,000 by 2012 (an overall decrease of 42.3 per cent over 20 years). The effects of this demographic shift on higher education have been dramatic, especially on lower-level and newer institutions. Every university has a government-regulated quota (*teiin*) which, if met, makes them eligible to receive government funding. In 2008, 47.1 per cent of Japan's private higher education institutions were under-enrolled (a condition known as *teiin-ware*) despite the government continually relaxing the method by which they calculated the benchmark (Fitzpatrick 2008: 37).[9] To give just one example of the rapid decrease in university applications, at a large mid-level university in the Kansai region with a total student intake each year of 3,000, there were in 1991, at the height of the second baby boom, 41,344 applicants; in 2006 (only 15 years later), its number of applications was down to around 800 (a drop of almost 93 per cent). Its attached two-year college had suffered an even more severe drop, from 5,871 applicants in 1992 to only 76 in 2005 (a drop of almost 99 per cent).

Similar demographic challenges, of course, have been faced by other countries, such as the US in the 1970s and the UK in the 1980s. Indeed, the UK is facing some of the same issues over the coming decade,[10] as the following quote from Shepherd suggests:

> The number of 18-year-olds (in the UK) will drop dramatically between 2010 and 2019 because of fewer births in the 1990s. Universities bank on steady numbers of students for fees . . . [The n]umber of international students [is] likely to fall as countries such as China develop their own institutions . . . In future, universities might not be able to rely on the government for funds . . .
>
> (Shepherd 2008)

The situation in Japan is much more severe than in the UK, however, for a number of reasons: with a 75 per cent participation rate in higher education, there is very little room for increasing participation among the current cohort of high school graduates;[11] Japan has a very low rate of immigration and hence little demand for higher education among a newly arrived population; it has a comparatively low level of international students, mainly because of the lack of demand for education in Japanese and lack of supply of higher education in English and, as a result, a dangerous over-dependence on students from mainland China;[12] a lack of demand for adult education because of the seniority employment system which discourages retraining at mid-career and the excellent provision of adult education courses through institutions such as *bunka kaikan* run by local governments (see Dugmore 2008) and Asahi Cultural Centres; and, finally, a very undeveloped system of part-time higher education, perhaps related to the preference of Japanese companies to do their training in-house rather than rely on external organizations. Graduate education (with the notable exception of engineering) has been limited by the preference of corporate Japan to train their own recruits in-house; in 2002, the number of graduate students was equivalent to 8.9 per cent of the undergraduate population, compared to 21 per cent in the UK (Newby *et al.* 2008: 64). In short, the US and the UK were able to deal in the 1970s and 1980s with their demographic problems by expanding their incoming cohorts and developing new markets, particularly by targeting overseas, mature, graduate and part-time students. None of these options appears to be easy to implement in the Japanese case.

Responses to the 'University Crisis' *(*daigaku kiki*)*

By government reform:

From 1 April 2004, Japan's national universities (which account for less than 20 per cent of the students in higher education but 80 per cent of the national higher education budget) were turned into independent agencies; their staff members were no longer national civil servants (*kokka kōmuin*) guaranteed jobs for life; and the power of the heads of these national universities was greatly strengthened.[13] The *Chūō Kōron* special issue, which we examined at the start of this chapter, described this process of universities becoming more independent from the Ministry of Education as the 'separation of mother-and-child (*oya hanare*, *kohanare)*', and the start of universities 'making contact with the real world' (Nakai 2008:77).

In order to stimulate institutions into being more entrepreneurial, the government shifted its emphasis from *ex ante* to *ex post facto* evaluations (in Japanese, this is described as moving from *jizen kiseigata shakai* to *jigo shorigata shakai*). This meant that institutions were much freer to try out ideas on the market and see if they worked. The new reforms were designed to reduce the difficulty in obtaining the external accreditation needed to establish new departments and courses (and to some extent new institutions) and replace it with much tougher *ex post facto* assessments. The flip side was the development of a rigorous assessment system, which was another major plank of the 2004 reforms. All national universities, for example, are now required to produce six-year plans and targets against which their performance will be judged and on the basis of which their subsequent funding will be determined; in 2006, eight national universities were assessed as falling behind on their six-year plans (Newby *et al.* 2008: 35). Third-party evaluation agencies, accredited by the Ministry of Education, Culture, Sports, Science and Technology (MEXT), have been set up in order to evaluate institutions' teaching and research.

As a further means of stimulating new activity and new ideas, funding has increasingly shifted from a historical to a competitive basis. As we shall see, substantial funds have been funnelled, over the past five years, into teaching-based Centres of Learning (COL) and research-based Centres of Excellence (COE) which in turn have led to the development of new hierarchies based on how universities have fared in these competitions, just as the Research Assessment Exercise and Teaching Quality Assessments introduced in the UK in the 1980s led to new ways of ranking universities there (see Nakai 2002; *Yomiuri Shimbun* Ōsaka Honsha 2003).

By industry:

Japanese industries responded to the 'university crisis' (*daigaku kiki*), as the current situation is often called, in two distinct ways. First, they began to evaluate students on skills rather than institution (though commentators note that it is important to separate rhetoric from reality here); industries claim that they are less interested in where students have studied and more in what they have done during their studies.

Second, industries have begun to treat universities as research partners. This was clearly not the case in the past. In the 1990s, money available for new equipment per university scientist was only 20 per cent of that available for peers in non-university government research institutions and only 25 per cent of that available in corporate laboratories; indeed, the national proportion of research and development (R&D) expenditure in universities slipped from 18.2 per cent in 1970 to 11.6 per cent in 1990 (Yamamoto 1995: 27, 34). As we discuss in further detail below, however, the new money that has come into the university sector to support research in science and technology, though extremely unequally distributed, reveals a new partnership between industries and universities and is playing a major role in the diversification of the higher education sector.

By students:

One result of the collapse in competition to get into lower ranked universities, which we will examine later, has been that students can opt for either a competitive or non-competitive route to higher education. The biggest effect on schools has been the amount of work that students need to do in order to enter different types of higher education institutions. This has been well documented by the sociologist Kariya Takehiko (see Kariya 2001, and, in English, Kariya and Rosenbaum 2003), who has examined how the amount of homework done by students from different types of schools has changed over the past 20 years. Whilst students at the top high schools are working as hard, if not harder, than ever before to pass examinations and get into top institutions that provide the increasingly valuable ticket to a secure job, those in lower-level high schools, knowing that they have a 'free pass' into a university at roughly the level they would expect to enter in any case, have virtually stopped working altogether. These two streams of students can be seen increasingly in junior high schools where many students are already opting out of what used to be called Japan's 'examination hell'. Kariya's research shows a very strong correlation between students' social class background and their choice of either competitive or non-competitive institutions. Rather as the sociologist Paul Willis demonstrated with his classic account of the relationship between class and education in Britain in his book *Learning to Labour* (1977), Kariya suggests that the increasingly conspicuous relationship between social class and educational success in contemporary Japan is likely to rapidly undermine the consensus that education in Japan is a meritocratic system and further reduce the effort that those from disadvantaged backgrounds invest in order to succeed through the education system.

By universities:

The manner in which individual universities have responded to the new conditions and incentives offered to them has varied hugely. Many have concentrated their attention on attracting as many of the dwindling pool of 18-year-old entrants as possible. To attract students, universities have bolstered public relations offensives, cut fees and accepted students through direct entry initiatives (universities may accept up to 50 per cent of their students without any entrance examination at all). To retain students, universities have revised curricula and changed teaching styles through faculty development programmes, since non-retention rates in the 1990s became as big a problem as dwindling entrance rates. Universities have cut unpopular programmes and have begun to diversify both what they offer and how they offer it.

Many universities have also moved to become more entrepreneurial. Many national universities – generally thought to be the most conservative institutions in the sector – have introduced reforms designed to increase current and develop new income streams. Oba Jun (2007) lists many of the reform initiatives which have taken place in national universities, most of which stem from the appointment of strong presidents prepared to introduce new ideas, presidents who have sometimes, as we saw at the beginning of this chapter, been appointed against the wishes of the majority of the faculty. Whether these often much-heralded reforms and practices that Oba describes will prove to have a major or lasting effect on the actual practice of the institutions concerned remains, of course, to be seen but their introduction is in itself of interest. Oba's account includes the following:

(a) Changing resource allocation policies: presidents have used their new control over resources to attract world class faculty (e.g., Tohoku University) as well as using the fact of governmental reductions in operational funding to review all costs (e.g., Mie University) and the more effective use of facilities, including charging departments for their use (e.g., Kyushu Institute of Technology).

(b) Creation of incentive funds, for example, to encourage departments to put in more applications for research funding (e.g., Niigata University), and the ending at many universities of the automatic granting of research funds to departments on a historical basis.

(c) Promotion, at most national universities, of income-generating activities through enhanced technology licensing offices.

(d) Introduction of more flexible staffing arrangements: for example, Gifu University has introduced a system of deans having points which allow them teaching resources within a fixed quota; Yamaguchi University has introduced a system where the vice president, not the department, has control over future appointments so as to prevent the automatic replacement of retiring or leaving staff.

(e) Recruitment of professional experts and managers to help with administration: in 2004, the University of Tokyo hired 10 experts from the business community as associate managing directors (*fukuriji*) or specially appointed experts (*tokunin senmonin*) including a patent attorney to help with intellectual property issues.

(f) Introduction of staff development programmes: instead of relying on Ministry of Education officials (whose loyalty was often thought to be split between the Ministry and the university), universities have begun to train and recruit their own staff. The University of Tokyo filled several senior appointments in 2004 through an internal advertising and recruitment process.

(g) Development of public relations (PR) activities: most universities have dramatically enhanced their PR. Hokkaido University, for example, hired a publicity agent in order to help them do so and Hiroshima University has opened branches in Tokyo, Osaka, Fukuoka and Beijing.

(h) Development of audit offices: these have been set up not only to conform to new government regulations over internal transparency but also to improve their own performance and understand their systems better. Yokohama

National University has established an audit office with eight staff reporting directly to the president for both internal and external audits.

(i) Establishment of public staff and unit-level evaluation: Osaka University has published unit level staff evaluations (and left individual evaluations to the unit level) whilst Okayama University conducted a recent university evaluation of all of its 1350 academic staff – of whom 897 were rated excellent, 332 good, 31 fair, and 20 as poor (70 did not participate) – and intimated that future reviews might be linked to pay.

(j) The provision of external leadership training programmes for presidents and vice-presidents to allow them to introduce many of the types of ideas discussed earlier has been introduced by organizations such as the Japan Association of National Universities (JANU) and the Centre for National University Finance and Management.

Many of these local initiatives in national universities foreshadowed the proposals which emerged from Prime Minister Abe's Educational Reform Council in mid-2007 which, in the context of higher education, indicated the need for competition, performance-based pay, rationalization, selection and concentration, and made a number of specific recommendations including the end of seniority pay in universities, the reduction of the salaries of professors currently over 60 by up to 30 per cent, the elimination of the domination of professors' meetings (*kyōjukai*) in decision making, higher fees for science-based courses, more flexibility around the age at which students could start at university, multiple entry systems and administrative reform (see *Yomiuri Shimbun*, 14 March 2007 and 26 May 2007).

Private universities were often even more responsive to the new pressures they found themselves under during the 1990s and 2000s. At the Kansai university and junior college that had faced such a dramatic collapse in applications following 1992 as mentioned earlier, major reforms were enacted in the early 2000s to stave off collapse: fees were slashed; bonuses (which had historically constituted around 30 per cent of total annual salaries) were cut by half; both enrolment targets and faculty numbers were reduced; two departments were closed down and two new departments and a Law School were opened; an educational reform centre (*Kyōiku Kaihatsu Shien Sentā*) was set up and monthly lectures by outside speakers on faculty development were introduced; an annual 'Open Class Month', when all faculty were expected to observe at least three other classes and write reports on them, was started; and the complete revision of several programmes, which had been running for many years with virtually no changes, was introduced. There is little doubt that the student experience was considerably improved in this period, though whether the university can survive in such a competitive environment remains to be seen.

Outcomes of the reform process

It should be no surprise that the shift from historically based to competitive funding has led to a much greater concentration of government and industry money being channelled to a small group of research-intensive universities. Positive and negative circles operate: universities which do good research receive more money which enables them to put in stronger applications and thereby receive more support. The Centres of Excellence (known in Japanese as 'COE') exercise is particularly conspicuous in this regard, as Table 11.1 demonstrates. Perhaps of greater concern to the general public, though, has been the reluctance to apply serious sanctions against Centres which have not met the objectives which were laid out in their original proposals. Eades (2005), one of the few non-Japanese members on the COE First Review Panel, describes how the attempts to impose such sanctions (including the withdrawal of funds altogether in two cases) were overruled by MEXT officials.[14]

Whilst the figures for the COE projects are well known in Japan, those for the total amount of competitive grants in aid funding are less well disseminated (see Table 11.2). In line with other countries, around 50 per cent of the total national research budget goes to clinical research. More significantly, though, whilst private universities received 13.2 per cent of the total available funding (Keio received 1.32 per cent), Tokyo and Kyoto alone receive 10.3 per cent and

Table 11.1 Ranking of leading Japanese universities by number of centres of excellence awarded (2002–4) (* = private University)

Institutions	Projects	Grants (JPY billion)
Tokyo	28	4.3
Kyoto	23	3.4
Osaka	15	2.5
Nagoya	14	1.8
Tohoku	13	2.0
Tokyo Tech	12	1.8
Hokkaido	12	1.75
Keio*	12	1.75
Waseda*	9	1.0
Kyushu	8	1.2

Source: author

Table 11.2 List of largest scientific grants-in-aid to Japanese universities – 2005 (JPY million) (* = private University)

Tokyo	20,111
Kyoto	13,114
Tohoku	9,479
Osaka	8,929
Nagoya	6,455
Kyushu	5,683
Hokkaido	5.614
Tokyo Inst of Technology	4,544
Tsukuba	3,020
Keio*	2,486

Source: author

6 per cent respectively (Takeuchi 2005: 67). The top 15 higher education institutions (out of more than 1,250 four- or two-year higher education institutions)
receive half of all governmental research grants.[15]

Even greater imbalances can be seen in external income generation. If one looks
at the total higher education external income (including research and donations) in
2004, this constituted only 6.2 per cent of total sector revenue, but, of this, 60 per
cent went to just 10 institutions (including all seven former imperial universities)
(Oba 2007: 30).

As a result of these increasingly large differentials (and despite the fact that
national universities have been under pressure to increase their fees to bring them
in line with those of private ones, which they can currently undercut in the market
due to their government subsidies), the composition of funds in the public and
private sectors as a whole remains very unbalanced (see Table 11.3).

If the example from the UK is anything to go by (and the UK has provided
much of the model for the current Japanese reforms), the concentration of funding in the leading research-intensive universities is set to get much stronger. Table
11.4 shows the direct grants for 2008/09 for three geographically close pairs of
universities in the UK (all nationally funded, as is the case for all 130 universities
bar one) with roughly similar student numbers for which they receive per capita
income (the differences are due to the proportion of part-time students) but dramatically different levels of direct government research grant support. When one

Table 11.3 Composition of funds (percentages)

	National Universities	*Private Universities*
Government subsidies	52.8	10.0
Tuition fees	13.9	76.1
Donations	2.0	1.6
Business income	28.2	1.6
Loans	2.4	1.7
Others	0.5	8.8

Source: author

Table 11.4 Government grant allocations for teaching and research at selected neighbouring
universities in the UK (2008–9)

Universities *(Student Numbers)*	*Funding allocations for teaching and research* *(GBP million)*		
	Teaching	**Research**	*Total*
UCL (22,000 students)	64.5	**101.3**	165.0
Westminster (24,000)	56.6	**2.2**	58.8
Oxford (20,000)	64.8	**110.1**	174.9
Ox Brookes (19,000)	35.7	**2.7**	38.5
Manchester (40,000)	98.3	**81.9**	180.2
Man Metro (31,000)	86.9	**3.3**	90.5

Source: author

adds in competitive (non-direct) grants, the differences in research funds are much greater still. This has been due to a conscious government policy which has been designed to maintain a number of world class research-intensive universities in the UK. There is no doubt, if one takes the British example as a case study, that the gap between research-intensive and non-research-intensive institutions in Japan will also grow exponentially in future years due to the positive and negative funding circles that have been consciously created by government policy. As the OECD report chaired by Howard Newby, who was previously head of the Higher Education Funding Council of England (HEFCE) as well as a Vice-Chancellor of three different British universities, puts it: 'the reforms are likely to produce two major consequences: the concentration of scientific research in fewer universities and a focus in these universities on research and post-graduate training at the expense of undergraduate training' (Newby *et al.* 2008: 27).

The division between research-intensive and teaching-only universities in Japan will grow not only due to government funding but also because of the developing relationship between industry and higher education and the move in the former to undertaking an increasing amount of applied research (see Hatakenaka 2004). At Japanese national universities, patent applications increased from 609 in 2000 to 4,152 in 2004. At the University of Tokyo, 31 per cent of income by 2004 already came from external resources; it had 1,600 joint projects with industries, annually bringing in JPY21 billion in income. The fact that this has led to serious conflicts of interest and cases of fraud and misappropriation of funds (as mentioned at the beginning of this chapter) demonstrates how fast this area is expanding, and how quickly people are having to adapt to a new entrepreneurial culture in Japanese universities.

The new financial realities are beginning to lead to increasing searches for economies of scale through mergers, takeovers and buyouts of institutions. One can already see an interesting shift from the mergers and acquisitions of public universities which took place in the period leading up to the *hōjinka* incorporatization process (when the number of national universities dropped by 10 per cent from 98 to 88) to strong private universities (e.g., Keiō, Kwansei Gakuin) beginning to take over neighbouring and more specialist institutions to broaden their portfolio (e.g., in this case, Kyōritsu Department of Pharmacy and Seiwa University respectively) and within the large private university conglomerations (known as *gakkō hōjin*) such as Tokai University which are consolidating their range of previously independent institutions (*Asahi Shimbun*, 2 April 2007). Overall one can foresee a dramatic reduction in the number of higher education institutions over the next decade.

Some future trends in Japanese higher education?

Higher education in Japan is going through a revolution as it moves from what Hasumi (2008) called in his *Chūō Kōron* article the second to the third generation of universities. Not only does the new third generation of universities incorporate greater diversity across the sector, but even within the same institution one can see

Research University	Service University
Arts and sciences focussed	'Professional schools'
Year-long courses	1-week to 4-month courses
Life-long personnel	Many adjuncts/part-time teachers
Research undertaken on top of teaching	Service carried out in parallel research and teaching units
Decentralised choice of research agenda	Central planning and contracting of service
Funding by grants and endowments	Funding by contracts

Figure 11.1 The 'research' and the 'service' university compared

Source: author (based on Cummings 2006)

operations working alongside each other based on two sets of different assumptions described by William K. Cummings (2006) as the research and service university functions (see Figure 11.1).

As the idea of the 'service university' is introduced alongside that of the 'research university' there are bound to be tensions, and it is these tensions that *Chūō Kōron* picked up in the example of the University of Tokyo Faculty of Education with which we started this chapter.

Not only will universities increasingly enter into, and compete in, different niches but within universities we will see the development of parallel cultures and the job of management will be to enable these to work alongside each other. It is inevitable that, at the beginning of the process, the new service orientation will have a lower status, but over time the balance of power is likely to change. The emergence of the service elements in universities will lead to changes in staffing patterns which we can see indications of in the already increasing flexibilization of the Japanese professoriate.

The ratio of part-time to full-time faculty has shifted from around 0.7 (1980) to 1.05 (2001). This involves a wide range of factors (including the fact that many full-time faculty in one institution earn a second income by teaching part-time in other institutions, a practice known as *kakemochi*) but it is also related to the growth in fixed-term contract employees in research-intensive universities. At the University of Tokyo, the proportion of contract research staff has grown from almost nothing to 3 per cent in recent years and is set to increase dramatically in the next few years.[16]

The proportion of women teaching in higher education has almost doubled since structural reforms – in particular the abolition of the faculties of Liberal

Arts and Sciences in almost all universities and the relaxation of the University Accreditation Standards – were introduced in 1991. But Japan still has the lowest female academic staff participation rates in the Organization for Economic Cooperation and Development (OECD). Its figure of 14.1 per cent of staff being female is far below half of the OECD average of 35.9 per cent (OECD, *Education at a Glance*, 2004). The figures also continue to disguise huge discrepancies as to where changes have taken place: the proportion of women, especially those above junior ranks, teaching in the elite former imperial universities remains, for example, less than half of the average in Japan. Until very recently, the government has taken a *laissez-faire* attitude towards gender employment in higher education, even when the Ministry of Education had direct control over recruitment in national institutions. In 2006, however, the Ministry introduced a JPY150 billion fund for gender equality in Japanese universities following the same competitive process as the Twenty-first Century COE Programme for research and the GP Programme on Teaching. By June 2006, 36 universities had applied for support under the programme (Yamanoi 2006a: 75, 78, 81). The logic behind introducing gender policies into Japanese universities is obvious; Japan cannot continue to ignore the potential among half of its population for reinvigorating its higher education system if it wishes to be competitive on a global stage. This economic reality alone will almost certainly see a major shift in the gender balance and boundaries between the sexes in Japanese universities over the next decade.

Another major change which can be foreseen is in the proportion of academics with foreign highest degrees. A foreign undergraduate degree has sometimes historically been seen as a disadvantage when applying for posts in Japan (see Hall 1998). This was not because of the quality of the degree itself. Rather it was due to the fact that studying overseas often took individuals out of the system of personal contacts and university factions and cliques through which appointments were often based; even today around one-third of new hires in universities in Japan gained a degree from the university which is employing them. The different set of skills that a foreign degree confers on individuals, however, is likely to lead to this attitude changing. In particular, the fact that higher education training in the US and Western Europe can mean both teaching and also grant application experience is likely to be increasingly highly valued in universities in Japan, which are beginning to place more importance on both of these areas.[17] For exactly the same reasons, it is likely that the proportion of foreign staff will increase substantially from the current very low (by global standards) figure.[18] Indeed the increase in over 50 per cent in the number of foreign staff in Japanese universities between 1995 and 2003, despite the general budgetary stagnation during this same period, implied that this trend may already be beginning (see Arimoto 2006a: 190). Certainly, there has been a growing trend of universities beginning to offer courses in English. Both International Christian University and the Faculty of Comparative Culture at Sophia University have offered programmes in English for many years. More recently, Ritsumeikan University (which is based in Kyoto) has opened a whole new campus called Asia Pacific University in Beppu where all the teaching, research and administration is carried out bilingually in

Japanese and English, and Waseda University has opened a School of International Liberal Studies which teaches its 600 students (one-third from overseas) only in English (Fitzpatrick 2008: 38). Perhaps most significantly, because of its capacity to set the trend for the rest of the sector, the University of Tokyo has begun to offer courses in English, for example in its Graduate School of Interdisciplinary Studies.[19]

As the trend accelerates, there is little doubt tensions will emerge between younger academics trained overseas and older academics trained in Japan and the boundaries between the generations will come to change. Whether those tensions are managed constructively or not, of course, is much harder to predict. What is clear is that after five or so decades of Ministry-controlled relative stability and stasis, Japan is now going through a period of increasing diversification and change in its higher education system and its new cadre of managers and presidents, however they came to their positions, will encounter many challenges as they steer the system through these changes. They may even look back nostalgically to the day when universities needed to seek Ministry guidance and support for every minor reform that they wished to implement.

Notes

1 Without wishing to defend the actions of individual researchers, some of the cases which involved the misappropriation of state funds may have been due to the inflexibility in the way in which government funds are allocated in Japan and the difficulty of transferring funds from one category to another for the sake of the research project rather than for personal gain. In the past, such virement seems to have been tolerated and some senior researchers may have been caught out by the change in culture of what was acceptable.

2 There is a large, and growing, literature on the idea of the 'third generation university', much of which is well summarized in Wissema (2009: xiii) who describes them as institutions which 'actively pursue the exploitation or commercialisation of the knowledge they create, making it their third objective, equal in importance to the objectives of scientific research and education'.

3 The literature on higher education tends to conflate the terms 'higher', 'further' and 'tertiary' education which can make the comparison of statistics over time within the same country or, even more, comparison between countries very problematic. For example, when the Dearing Committee (1997: Appendix 5; 49) reported on Japan, it gave two figures: 62 per cent of the 18-year-old cohort going 'to some form of post-secondary education' and the official figure of 44 per cent since the Japanese Government 'tends to refer to the universities and junior colleges as higher education provision'. For reasons to do with the high quality of vocational higher education which are argued elsewhere (see Goodman, Hatakenaka and Kim, 2009), this paper believes that it is proper to take the broader of these two definitions in this paper. Higher education is taken to include all 716 four-year universities (*daigaku*), 415 two-year junior colleges (*tanki daigaku*), 63 colleges of technology (*kōsen*) and 2,973 professional training colleges (*senmongakkō*).

4 See Kiyonari (2001, 103–33) for a historical analysis of government funding support for private universities and junior colleges in Japan. The original plan, when government funding was first introduced in the 1970s in order to respond to the student unrest throughout the country of the previous two years, had been that this subsidy would rise gradually to meet exactly half the costs of all private institutions. In actual fact, while

funding did rise steeply from a first-year injection that covered 7.2 per cent of costs to 29.5 per cent of costs being covered exactly a decade later, it then fell away steeply (in relative terms) to cover only around 12 per cent of these institutions' costs from the early 1990s onwards. Today this figure is around 10 per cent, which constitutes the second lowest proportion of government support for private higher education among the OECD countries (see Newby *et al.* 2008: 15).

5 There is also a small local government university sector known as 'public universities' in English. Whilst these do have some individual characteristics, for the most part they can be considered as an extension of the national universities in terms of academic culture and funding.

6 The recent growth of vocational schools (*senmon gakkō*) has taken educational commentators in Japan by surprise. The basic assumption had been that vocational schools (because of their relatively low status) would lose out to the junior colleges in the increasingly competitive higher education sector. The reality has been quite different. In 1992, with 541 institutions (88 per cent of them private), junior colleges in Japan enrolled over 44 per cent of all university students; by 2004, they catered to only 9.6 per cent of university students. Over almost exactly the same period, the proportion of high school graduates enrolling in vocational schools has grown by around 30 per cent to around 20 per cent in 2008 and the staff who teach in vocational schools have enjoyed, from the late 1990s, increasingly high status and often been headhunted to teach in universities. Vocational schools, which in the 1970s were dominated (80 per cent) by female students, are now roughly 50:50 in their gender ratios and, whilst the successful job placement rate dropped among university male graduates from around 80 per cent to 60 per cent during the 1990s, the rate for those from vocational schools remained consistently around 80 per cent, which largely explained their increased attractiveness. (For more detail on the changing status of vocational higher education in Japan, see Goodman, Hatakenaka and Kim, 2009).

7 See: http//www.timeshighereducation.co.uk (accessed 7 January 2009).

8 There are, of course, many problems with such league tables, especially in an international comparative context and in particular in the way they collect data from Japanese institutions. There is a growing literature which demonstrates why the league tables disfavour non-Anglophone institutions. Ishikawa (2008) talks about the way that 'vernacular language education and research may be marginalized' by such comparative exercises and Yonezawa and Horta (2009) point out that leading Japanese institutions actually score as well as their Western counterparts in the QS/THE survey on peer review, employer review, citations per staff and staff per student metrics but are severely, they suggest disproportionately, penalized on the two measures of international staff and student. The fact remains, however, that these league tables have engendered a sense of national crisis in Japan about the state of the country's higher education institutions.

9 The *teiin* determines not just funding, but also, among other things, the number of faculty which a university must have and the size of its physical plant. In the 'good' years of the 1990s, most colleges aimed to take in, on average, 130 percent of the *teiin* number of students, knowing that if they went over that figure the government would dock its subsidy. The fact that so many institutions now find themselves unable even to reach their *teiin* makes it even more difficult for them to deal with the new situation they find themselves in.

10 For more information on the demand for higher education in the UK over the next decade, see HEPI (2007), which also sets out some of the key differences in the composition of the UK student body from the Japanese system. In the UK, only 67 per cent of full-time higher education first-degree entrants are under 21 (as compared to around 95 per cent in Japan) and the Higher Education Initial Participation Rate is only around 43 per cent compared to the Japanese figure of closer to 75 per cent.

11 The actual number of students in higher education changed very little between 1990 and 2004 (from 1.08 million to 1.05 million) but since the 18-year-old population in this period changed from 2.01 million to 1.41 million, this meant that the participation rate increased dramatically from 54 per cent to 75 per cent (Ogata 2006: 89).

12 Of all tertiary students enrolled in Japan, 3.3 per cent are of international origins, which is 45 per cent of the OECD average of 7.3 per cent (Newby *et al.* 2008: 80). The danger in the Japanese situation lies in the fact that 65 per cent of the overseas students in Japan come from mainland China which is rapidly building its own tertiary education infrastructure that is liable to lead to a drop in demand for overseas higher education. (For a detailed account of the role of overseas students in the Japanese higher education system, see Goodman 2007).

13 In English, these new corporations are dubbed Independent Administrative Institutions (IAIs) (see Yonezawa 1998: 21–22) and a clear recognition is made of the debt for this model to the reforms which took place in the UK higher education sector in the 1980s under Prime Minister Margaret Thatcher. For an interesting overview of areas of convergence between Japanese and UK higher education, see Yokoyama (2006).

14 Indeed, the next round of COE awards was allocated even before the final review of the initial projects was carried out and those institutions which had received funds in the first round tended to receive funds also in the second round suggesting that the underlying motivation for the whole programme had been to focus and institutionalize government research funding in a small number of research intensive universities.

15 By way of comparison, in the UK the top 20 universities (out of 120) secure nearly two-thirds of all available government research funds (Corbyn 2008).

16 In leading UK research intensive universities, such as Oxford, over two-thirds of those on the academic payroll are contract research staff; in top US institutions, such as Massachusetts Institute of Technology (MIT), the proportion is even higher. Arimoto (2006b: 6), drawing on the Carnegie classification of institutions, estimates that around 35 of Japan's universities should be called 'research universities' and it is in these institutions that we will see the rapid growth in contract research staff.

17 In the 1950s, the number of professors in Japan who had earned their final degrees overseas (including foreign professors; there are no disaggregated figures) represented only 0.6 per cent of the total; by 2001, it had risen to 6.9 per cent, though this was still some way behind those who had received their highest degrees from the University of Tokyo (11.4 per cent) and Kyoto University (6.9 cent) (Yamanoi 2006b: 25).

18 In 2004, only 3.42 per cent of all full-time faculty in Japanese universities were non-Japanese nationals (Huang 2006: 206). As an indication of future plans, though, the president of the University of Tokyo announced as part of the university's strategic plan in that same year an intention to increase the number of foreign faculty five-fold to 1300 staff as well as increasing the proportion of female staff and students (*Asahi Shimbun*, 13 April 2007).

19 In July 2009, the Japanese Government announced the results of its so-called 'Global 30' initiative. Various qualities were sought from those seeking to be selected as a 'Global 30' institution, including: an environment that supports and facilitates international exchange students, provision for providing instruction in English, a system that facilitates the acceptance of international students, meaningful promotion of international cooperation, and working closely with international students in an environment supported by capable and active personnel, thereby being a worthy representative of the internationalization of Japan. Out of 22 Japanese universities that applied for recognition in the 'Global 30' group of 'bases' of internationalization, seven national universities (Tokyo, Osaka, Kyoto, Kyushu, Nagoya, Tohoku and Tsukuba) and six private universities (Ritsumeikan, Keiō, Waseda, Meiji, Sophia, Dōshisha) were selected.

References

Abe, Yoshiya (ed.) (1989) *Non-University Sector Higher Education in Japan*, Hiroshima: Research Institute for Higher Education.

Arimoto, Akira (2006a) 'The changing academic profession in Japan: its origins, heritage and current situation', *Reports of Changing Academic Profession Project Workshop on Quality, Relevance, and Governance in the Changing Academia: International Perspectives*, Research Institute for Higher Education, Hiroshima University (COE Publication Series 20), 183–94.

—— (2006b) 'Institutionalization of faculty development with a focus on Japan', *Reports of Changing Academic Profession Project Workshop on Quality, Relevance, and Governance in the Changing Academia: International Perspectives*, Research Institute for Higher Education, Hiroshima University (COE Publication Series 20), 3–19.

Corbyn, Zoe (2008) 'Top 20 secure nearly two-thirds of research funds while others are left with nothing', *Times Higher Education*, 21 August.

Cummings, William K. (2006) 'Globalization and knowledge production: an Asian tilt?' *Higher Education Forum*, No. 3, Research Institute for Higher Education, Hiroshima University.

Dearing Report (1997) *Higher Education in the Learning Society* (Appendix Five: Higher Education in Other Countries). London: National Committee of Inquiry into Higher Education.

Dugmore, Lucy (2008) 'The role of culture halls in contemporary Japanese society,' unpublished thesis, University of Oxford.

Eades, J.S. (2005) 'The Japanese 21st Center of Excellence program: internationalization in action?' in J.S. Eades, Roger Goodman and Yumiko Hada (eds), *The 'Big Bang' in Japanese Higher Education: the 2004 reforms and the dynamics of change*, Melbourne: Trans Pacific Press, pp. 295–323.

Fitzpatrick, Michael (2008) 'A closed book to outsiders', *Times Higher Education*, 13 November.

Goodman, Roger (2007) 'The concept of *kokusaika* and Japanese educational reform', in *Globalization, Societies and Education* (special issue edited by Ka-Ho Mok and Akiyoshi Yonezawa), 5, 1: 71–87.

Goodman, Roger, Hatakenaka, Sachi and Kim, Terri (2009) *The Changing Status of Vocational Higher Education in Contemporary Japan and the Republic of Korea: a discussion paper*, Bonn: UNESCO-UNEVOC International Centre for Technical and Vocational Education and Training.

Hall, Ivan P. (1998) *Cartels of The Mind: Japan's intellectual closed shop*, New York and London: W.W. Norton.

Hasumi, Shigehiko (2008) 'Hontō wa kyōiku ga kirai na Nihonjin e', *Chūō Kōron*, February: 26–35.

Hatakenaka, Sachi (2004) *University-Industry Partnerships in MIT, Cambridge, and Tokyo: storytelling across boundaries*, New York and London: RoutledgeFalmer.

Hawkins, John N. and Furuto, Linda (2008) 'Higher education reform in Japan: the tension between public good and commodification', *Journal of Asian Public Policy*, 2, 2: 164–73.

HEPI (Higher Education Policy Institute) (2007) *Demand for Higher Education to 2020 and Beyond*, HEPI Report Summary 31, Oxford: HEPI.

Huang, Futao (2006) 'The academic profession in Japan: major characteristics and new changes', *Reports of Changing Academic Profession Project Workshop on Quality,*

Relevance, and Governance in the Changing Academia: international perspectives, Research Institute for Higher Education, Hiroshima University (COE Publication Series 20), 195–208.

Ishikawa, Mayumi (2008) 'Emerging hegemony and the question of equity: a critical view from Japanese universities', paper presented at the 52nd Annual Conference of the Comparative and International Educational Society (CIES), Teachers' College, Columbia University, New York, March 18.

Kariya, Takehiko (2001) *Kaisōka Nihon to Kyōiku Kiki: fubyōdō saiseisan kara iyoku kakusa shakai (insentibu dibaido) e*, Tokyo: Yūshindō.

Kariya, Takehiko and James E. Rosenbaum (2003) 'Stratified incentives and life course behaviors', in J.T. Mortimor and M.J. Shanahan (eds), *Handbook of the Life Course*, New York: Kluwer Academic/Plenum Publishers, pp. 51–78.

Kinmonth, Earl (2005) 'From selection to seduction: the impact of demographic change on private higher education in Japan', in J.S. Eades, Roger Goodman and Yumiko Hada (eds), *The 'Big Bang' in Japanese Higher Education: the 2004 reforms and the dynamics of change*, Melbourne: Trans Pacific Press, pp. 106–35.

Kiyonari, Tadao (2001), *Shiritsu Daigaku no Chōsen*, Tokyo: Hōsei Daigaku Shuppankyoku.

Kobayashi, Tetsuo (2008) 'Henbō suru gakuchō wa kiki o sukuu', *Chūō Kōron*, February: 64–73.

LeTendre, Gerald (1995), 'The evolution of research on educational attainment and social status in Japan', *Research in Sociology of Education and Socialization*, 2: 205–34.

McVeigh, Brian J. (2002) *Japanese Higher Education as Myth*, Armonk, New York and London: M.E. Sharpe.

Nakai, Kōichi (2002) 'Kachigumi', *Daigaku Ranking*, Tokyo: Chūō Shinsho.

—— (2008) 'Konmei suru kokuritsu daigaku hōjinka', *Chūō Kōron*, February: 74–81.

Newby, Howard, Weko, Thomas, Breneman, David, Johanneson, Thomas and Maasen, David, (2008) *OECD Reviews of Tertiary Education: Japan*, Paris, OECD.

Nihon Shiritsu Daigaku Renmei (ed.) (1984) *Shiritsu Daigaku: kinō, kyō, ashita*, Tokyo: Nihon Shiritsu Daigaku Renmei.

Oba, Jun (2007) 'Incorporation of national universities in Japan and its impact upon institutional governance', *Changing Governance in Higher Education: incorporation, marketization, and other reforms – a comparative study*, Research Institute for Higher Education, Hiroshima University (COE Publication Series 29), 15–36.

OECD (Centre for Educational Research and Innovation) (2004) *Education at a Glance: OECD indicators*, Paris: OECD.

Ogata, Naoyuki (2006) 'Daigaku kyōiku to rōdō ichiba no kenkyū: kaiko to tenbō', *Daigaku Ronshū*, Research Institute for Higher Education, Hiroshima University, 36: 237–50.

Roesgaard, Marie Højlund (2006) *Japanese Education and the Cram School Business: functions, challenges and perspectives of the juku*, Copenhagen: NIAS Press.

Shepherd, Jessica (2008) 'Who will weather the financial storm?' *The Guardian*. Online. Available: http://www.guardian.co.uk/education/2008/feb/19/universityfunding.higher-education1 (accessed 19 February 2008).

Takeuchi, Jun (2005) 'Kankenhi Haibun no Genjō to Kadai: sekai issenkyū no kenkyū leberu o jitsugen suru tame ni', *Kenkyū to Kakenhi*, Tokyo: Nihon Shiritsu Daigaku Kyōkai Fuchi Shigaku Kōtō Kyōiku Kenkyūjo.

Takeuchi, Yō (2007) 'Tōdai, Kyōdai to no bundanka o ketteizukeru "kore de ii no da" bunka', *Chūō Kōron*, February: 41–49.

Trow, Martin (1973) *Problems in the Transition from Elite to Mass Higher Education*, New York: Carnegie Commission on Higher Education.

Tsuda, Takeyuki (1993) 'The psychological functions of liminality: the Japanese university experience', *The Journal of Psychohistory*, 20, 3: 305–30.

Willis, Paul (1977) *Learning to Labour: how working class kids get working class jobs*, Farnborough: Saxon House.

Wissema, J.G. (2009) *Towards the Third Generation University: managing the university in transition*, Cheltenham and Northampton, MA: Edward Elgar.

Yamamoto, Shinichi (1995) 'Traditionalism versus research and development at Japanese universities', in A.H. Yee (ed.) *East Asian Higher Education: traditions and transformations*, Oxford: Pergamon Press, pp. 25–35.

Yamanoi, Atsunori (2006a) 'The historical and political context of gender policy in Japanese higher education: from inter- and intra-national perspectives of the frameworks of gender policy', *Gender Inequity in Academic Profession and Higher Education Access: Japan, the United Kingdom, and the United States*, Research Institute for Higher Education, Hiroshima University (COE Publication Series 22), 69–84.

—— (2006b) 'The Japanese academic marketplace and academic productivity', *Reports of Changing Academic Profession Project Workshop on Quality, Relevance, and Governance in the Changing Academia: international perspectives*, Research Institute for Higher Education, Hiroshima University (COE Publication Series 20), 21–35.

Yokoyama, Keiko (2006) 'Entrepreneurialism in Japanese and UK universities: governance, management, leadership and funding', *Higher Education*, 52: 523–55.

Yomiuri Shimbun Ōsaka Honsha (2003) *Daigaku Dai Kyōsō*, Tokyo: Chūō Shinsho.

Yonezawa, Akiyoshi (1998) 'Further privatization in Japanese higher education?' *International Higher Education*, 13: 20–22.

Yonezawa, Akiyoshi and Horta, Hugo (2009) 'Reconsidering the realities of the international student market: a perspective from Japan and East Asia', unpublished paper presented at the CHER 22nd Conference.

Glossary of abbreviations

ARF	ASEAN Regional Forum
ASEAN	Association of Southeast Asian Nations
ASEM	Asia–Europe Meeting
ASG	Abu Sayyaf Group
CCP	Chinese Communist Party
CEFP	Council on Economic and Fiscal Policy
COE	Centres of Excellence
COL	Centres of Learning
DPJ	Democratic Party of Japan
DPRK	Democratic People's Republic of Korea (North Korea)
EAEC	East Asian Economic Caucus
EU	European Union
FDI	Foreign Direct Investment
FILP	Fiscal Investment and Loan Programme
FTA	Free Trade Agreement
G8	Group of Eight
GAM	Gerakan Aceh Merdaka (Free Aceh Movement)
GDP	Gross Domestic Product
GPS	Global Positioning Systems
GRU	Government Revitalization Unit
HMC	House Management Committee
IAEA	International Atomic Energy Agency
IAIs	Independent Administrative Institutions
ICC–CCS	International Chamber of Commerce–Commercial Crime Services
ILO	International Labour Organization
IMB	International Maritime Bureau
IMO	International Maritime Organization
Interpol	International Police Agency
IPRC	Interparty Relations Committees
IR	International Relations
ISAF	International Security Assistance Force
ISC	Information Sharing Centre
ISPS	International Ship and Port Security

JANU	Japan Association of National Universities
JCG	Japan Coast Guard
JCP	Japanese Communist Party
JCUF	Japan Community Union Federation
JDA	Japan Defence Agency (now Japan's Ministry of Defence)
JICA	Japan International Cooperation Agency
JIIA	Japan Institution of International Affairs
JSA	Japan Shipping Association
KCNA	Korean Central News Agency
KEDO	Korean Peninsula Energy Development Organization
KMT	*Kuomintang,* Chinese Nationalist Party
LDP	Liberal Democratic Party
MAC	Ministry of Agriculture and Commerce
METI	Ministry of Economy, Trade and Industry
MEXT	Ministry of Education, Culture, Sports, Science and Technology
MHLW	Ministry of Health, Labour and Welfare
MIAC	Ministry of Internal Affairs and Communications
MILF	Moro Islamic Liberation Front
MIT	Massachusetts Institute of Technology
MITI	Ministry of International Trade and Industry
MLIT	Ministry of Land Infrastructure and Transport
MMD	Multi-member District
MMEA	Malaysian Maritime Enforcement Agency
MOD	Ministry of Defence
MOF	Ministry of Finance
MOFA	Ministry of Foreign Affairs
MOT	Ministry of Transport
MSA	Maritime Safety Agency
MSDF	Maritime Self-Defence Force
MSIS	Maritime Safety Information System (Indonesia)
NAM	Non-Aligned Movement
NGA	National Governors' Association
NGO	Non-Governmental Organization
NHK	*Nippon Hōsō Kyōkai,* Japan's national public broadcaster
NIRA	National Institute of Research Advancement
NPM	New Public Management
NPO	Non-Profit Organization
NPT	Nuclear Non-Proliferation Treaty
NPU	National Policy Unit
ODA	Japan's Official Development Assistance
OECD	Organization for Economic Cooperation and Development
PARC	Policy Affairs Research Council
PFLP	Popular Front for the Liberation of Palestine
PISA	Programme for International Student Assessment
PR	Proportional Representation

PR	Public Relations
PRC	People's Republic of China
R&D	Research and Development
ReCAAP	Regional Cooperation Agreement on Combating Piracy and Armed Robbery against Ships in Asia
RMSI	Regional Maritime Security Initiative
ROK	Republic of Korea (South Korea)
SCAP	Supreme Commander of the Allied Powers
SDF	Self-Defence Forces
SDP	Social Democratic Party
SMD	Single Member District
SUA	1988 Convention for the Suppression of Unlawful Acts against the Safety of Maritime Navigation
UN	United Nations
UNCLOS	United Nations Convention on the Law of the Seas
US	United States
WTO	World Trade Organization

Glossary of non-English terms

All non-English terms are in Japanese unless otherwise indicated.

Ajia no daihyō	Representative of Asia
amakudari	'descent from heaven' term used especially regarding bureaucrats moving to positions in private corporations
amakudari gakuchō	'parachute president'
arbeit	part-time workers, casual or temporary workers, or employees taking on a second job
baishin	translated as 'jury', although it is not a jury
baishin-in	lay judge (system)
bukai	subcommittees
bunka kaikan	cultural centres
Chihō Seido Chōsakai	Committee to Investigate Local Government Systems
chii riyō	exploiting one's position, especially by ex-bureaucrats moving into political office
Chubu Keizai Rengōkai	Association of Business in central Japan
Chūgoku jin	term used for 'Chinese' people (more neutral than *shina jin*)
daigaku	academically oriented universities
daigaku kiki	university crisis
daisan sekuta	third-sector (organizations)
daiyō kangoku	police jail cells, or 'substitute prisons'
dankai hosei	grade adjustment (for tax purposes)
dogeza gaikō	kowtow diplomacy
dōgisei no kiwamete usui kuni	extremely unethical state
doken kokka	construction state
dokuritsu gyōsei hōjin	quasi-private corporations
dōro tokutei-zaigen	financial resources for road construction
Dō-Shū-sei	Regional system
Dō-Shū-sei Bijon Kondankai	Council for Creating a Vision for Regional Systems
Dō-Shū-sei Chōsakai	Investigative Committee on Regional Systems

Dō-Shū-sei ni Kansuru Kihonteki Kangaekata	'Basic Thinking Concerning a Regional System'
fukōfu dantai	allocation tax
fukuriji	associate managing directors
fukushi jimusho	welfare office
gakkō hōjin	educational corporation
Gappei Tokurei Hō	Special Law on the Merger of Municipalities
Gembatsuka	tougher punishment for offenders
Genjitsu Rosen-ha	Practical Faction
Giin Unei Iinkai	House Management Committee (HMC)
Gyōseitaisei Kentō Group	Review Group on Administrative Structures
gyōza	Chinese dumplings
habatsu	factions
haikin shugi	greedy
Haken Hō	Manpower Dispatch Business Law
haken shain	dispatch workers
han nichi teki nipponjin	anti-Japanese Japanese
Han-Shikkōbuha	Anti-Service Function Faction
Hanzai Higaisha nado Kihon Hō	2004 law establishing the rights of crime victims
Hanzai Higaisha no Kai (nicknamed *Asu no Kai*)	National Association of Crime Victims and Surviving Families (nicknamed Tomorrow Society), a victim's rights organization
hen ni joseika	become strangely feminized
hōjinka	incorporatization process
hoken-jo	health office
Hokyū-shien Tokubetu-sochi-hō	bill for a law focusing on fuel supply
Hone-buto no Hōshin	Basic Policies, or 'Robust Policies'
Honne	one's real opinion or intention, which is seldom openly expressed
Ishin Seitō Shinpū	Restoration Party – New Wind
jiaozi	Chinese word for Chinese dumplings
Jichirō	All-Japan Prefectural and Municipal Workers Union
jigo shorigata shakai	*ex post facto society*, after the fact society
jikochū	selfishness
jizen kiseigata shakai	*ex ante society*, before the event society
juku	cram school
jūsen	problem involving seven housing loan companies that had gone bankrupt in 1996
kachō hosa	deputy directors
kakemochi	the practice whereby full-time faculty in one institution earn a second income by teaching part-time in other institutions

kakusa shakai	gap-widening (disparity in) society
kanryō shudō	bureaucratic leadership
Kansai Keizai Rengōkai	Association of Business in the Kansai area
Kantei	prime minister and cabinet
kantei shudō	leadership from the prime minister (and his cabinet)
karōshi	death from overwork
Keidanren	see Nippon Keidanren
keiyaku shain	contract workers
Keizai Dōyūkai	Japan Association of Corporate Executives
Keizai Senryaku Kaigi	Economic Strategy Council
Keizai-zaisei Shimon-kaigi	Council on Economic and Fiscal Policy (CEFP)
kenchū kanjō	anti-Chinese sentiment
kengen	strengthening central 'authority'
kikan inin jimu	delegated function system
kokka kōmuin	national civil servants
Kokkai Taisaku Iinkai	Interparty Relations Committees (IPRCs)
Kokumin Seiji Kyōkai	People's Political Association
Kokumin Shintō	People's New Party
Kōmeitō	Clean Government Party
kōkyōteki dantai	public organizations
Kyōiku Kaihatsu Shien Senta	educational reform centre
kyōiku shuji	education advisers
kyōjukai	professorial faculty meeting
limen	Latin word for threshold
mukikei	unlimited imprisonment/sentences
mutōha-sō	'floating' voters
narazumono kokka	what America calls a 'rogue state'
Nihon Izokukai	Japan Association of War-Bereaved Families
Nikkeiren	Japan Federation of Employers' Association
Nippon Kaigi	largest of the conservative civil society organizations
Nippon Keidanren	Japan Business Federation
omoiyari no aru minzoku	a nation that cares so much about others
omote and *ura*	'formal and informal' or 'front and back'
Oriibu no Ki	The Olive Tree, a newsletter
otoko rashisa, otoko kusasa	manliness, like a man
oya hanare, kohanare	'separation of mother-and-child'
racchi jiken	the kidnappings of Japanese citizens by North Korean government agents throughout the 1970s and 1980s
Rengō	Japan Trade Union Confederation
Rengō-no-kai	political arm of Rengō (won seats in the upper house)
rieki sōhan	conflict of interests
riji	director

saishū iken benron	final statement of views
sangaku renkei	joint university-industry projects
sanmi ittai kaikaku	trinity reform
seikei bunri	separating politics from economics
seireishitei toshi	major city
seishō	politically well-connected businessmen
senmon gakkō	vocational colleges
shakaifukushi kyōgikai	the council of social welfare
Shigenobu Fusako-san o Sasaeru Kai	support organization for Shigenobu
shikaku	'assassins'
shina jin	term used for 'Chinese' people (widely considered derogatory)
shinryaku sensō	wars of aggression
shisei chōson sei	local government system
shitashimi o kanjinai	unfriendly feelings
shiteikanrisha seido	designated manager system
shokutaku	retired part-time workers
taihō oyobi kankin	hostage-taking and other forms of kidnapping and holding people
Takajin no Soko Made Itte Iinkai	Osaka-based television talk show
tanki daigaku	junior college
Tatemae	the position or opinion one expresses in public
teiin	government-regulated quota
teiin-ware	under-enrolled
teikō-seiryoku	the forces of resistance
Tero-taisaku Tokubetsu-sochi-hō	Anti-Terrorism Special Measures Law
tetori ashitori de oshieta	teach all there is to know
tokunin senmonin	specially appointed experts
tokurei-shi	special case cities
tokushū hōjin	special legal organization
Tokyo Saiban Shi Kan	Tokyo War Crimes Tribunal
ukezara-ron	'saucer' or receptacle for receiving
wataridori	'migratory bird', term describing retired bureaucrats who move on to several different positions
yobiko	pre-school
yokosuberi	'sidestep' or moving to an equivalent position, especially from a central ministry or agency to a public corporation
yoshin shūketsu ketteishō	preliminary trial investigation document
zainichi	literally, 'staying in Japan', refers to foreigners (often Koreans) living in Japan
Zaisei Shimon Kaigi	Council on Economic and Fiscal Policy

zantei-zeiritsu	provisional rates
zeigen ijō	tax transfer
Zenrōkyō	National Trade Union Council
Zenrōren	National Confederation of Trade Unions
zettai fukanyō	absolute intolerance (towards the dead)
zoku	policy tribes

Name indicators

kan	public servant in the central government, indicating a high social rank
kō	public servant in a local authority, indicating a mid-level social rank
min	former term for citizen, indicating the lowest social rank

Index

Page numbers in **bold** refer to figures and tables.

For Product Safety Concerns and Information please contact our EU
representative GPSR@taylorandfrancis.com
Taylor & Francis Verlag GmbH, Kaufingerstraße 24, 80331 München, Germany

For Product Safety Concerns and Information please contact our EU
representative GPSR@taylorandfrancis.com
Taylor & Francis Verlag GmbH, Kaufingerstraße 24, 80331 München, Germany